HSPT • TACHS
Catholic High School Entrance Exams

ARGO BROTHERS

Anayet Chowdhury • Fahim Rofique • Vladislav Suleyman
Rawan Shafi • Mohammed Siraj

Authors	**Anayet Chowdhury**
	Fahim Rofique
	Vladislav Suleyman
	Rawan Shafi
	Mohammed Siraj
Interior Design	**Vladislav Suleyman**
Cover Design	**Vladislav Suleyman**

ALL RIGHTS RESERVED
Copyright © 2016, by Argo Brothers Inc.

ISBN-13: 978-0692685280
Published by Argo Brothers Inc.

HSPT® is a registered trademark of Scholastic Testing Service, which is not affiliated with this book nor endorses this product.
Test for Admissions into Catholic High Schools (TACHS) is administered by the Archdiocese of New York, which is not affiliated with this book nor endorses this product.

All rights reserved, no part of this book may be reproduced or distributed in any form or by any means without the written permission of Argo Brothers Inc.

All the materials within are the exclusive property of Argo Brothers Inc.

TABLE OF CONTENTS

Introduction 5
English Overview 8
Arithmetic Overview 35
Algebra Fundamentals 41
Geometry 46
HSPT Practice Tests 55
   HSPT Exam 1 57
   HSPT Exam 1 Answer and Explanations 115
   HSPT Exam 2 139
   HSPT Exam 2 Answer and Explanations 197
   HSPT Exam 3 221
   HSPT Exam 3 Answer and Explanations 279
TACHS Practice Tests 303
   TACHS Exam 1 305
   TACHS Exam 1 Answer and Explanations 351
   TACHS Exam 2 365
   TACHS Exam 2 Answer and Explanations 411
   TACHS Exam 3 425
   TACHS Exam 3 Answer and Explanations 474
Vocabulary 487

INTRODUCTION

TACHS OVERVIEW

The Test for Admission into Catholic High Schools (TACHS) is an exam given to eighth graders to gain entrance into Catholic High Schools in New York City. In some instances, schools may use exam scores to determine which students get scholarships. The TACHS exam is given once each year in November. This exam measures aptitude in reading, language arts, mathematics, and general reasoning skills. The reading section tests vocabulary and reading comprehension. The language section tests spelling, capitalization, punctuation, and usage. The math section tests concepts, estimation, problem solving, and data interpretation. The abilities section tests abstract reasoning. The exam contains approximately 200 multiple-choice questions. The exam lasts 137 minutes.

There are a total of 200 questions to be done in 137 minutes

TEST CONTENT:
Reading: Vocabulary - 20 Questions

The vocabulary questions of the reading portion present a word in a short sentence and asks which of the given answer choices have the closest meaning.

Reading: Reading Comprehension - 30 Questions

The reading comprehension portion measures your ability to discern the main idea of a passage and recall key details. Most of the questions will require you to make conclusions or summarize what you have read.

TACHS Subject Area	Number of Questions	Time Limit (minutes)
Reading - Vocabulary	20	10
Reading - Comprehension	30	25
Language - Spelling, Capitalization, Punctuation, Usage	40	23
Language - Paragraphs	10	7
Math - Concepts, Data Interpretatio, Problem Solving	32	33
Math - Estimation	18	7
Ability - Similarities and Changes	40	25
Ability - Abstract Reasoning	10	7
Total	**200**	**137**

Language: Spelling, Punctuation, Usage, Capitalization - 40 Questions

This language section tests your knowledge of sentence structure and paragraphs. Language conventions such as spelling, punctuation, and capitalization will be presented by itself in separate groups.

Language: Paragraphs - 10 Questions

The usage questions may present a short paragraph that is followed by one or two questions about its organization of ideas, and clarity.

INTRODUCTION

Math: Concepts, Data Interpretation, Problem Solving - 32 Questions

This section tests your knowledge of understanding math concepts, problem solving, and data interpretation. This includes knowledge of number relations, and the ability to answer questions based on tables and graphs.

HSPT OVERVIEW

The High School Placement Test (HSPT) is an exam that is given nationwide to eighth grade students in order to gain admission to Catholic High Schools. The HSPT exam lasts 2 hours and 21 minutes. The exam is structured to test three key skillsets: Total Cognitive, Total Basic, and Composite skills. Total Cognitive skills deals with verbal and quantitative knowledge. Total Basic skills include reading, mathematics, and language. Lastly, Composite skills are measured in the Verbal, Quantitative, Language, Mathematics, and Reading subtests.

There are a total of 298 questions on the exam to be done in 141 minutes.

TEST CONTENT:
Mathematics Skills - 64 Questions

The mathematics section tests knowledge of problem solving, arithmetic, algebra, and geometry. These questions make up 21% of the test.

HSPT Subject Areas	Number of Questions	Time Limit (minutes)
Verbal	60	16
Quantitative	52	30
Reading	62	25
Mathematics	64	45
Language	60	25
Total	**298**	**141**

Language Skills - 60 Questions

The language portion of the exam tests knowledge of capitalization, spelling, composition, usage, and punctualization. This comprises 20% of the exam.

Verbal Skills - 60 Questions

The verbal skills section of the exams primarily tests knowledge of synonyms, antonyms, analogies, logic, and verbal classifications. It is important to be able to identify which type each question falls under when doing the exam. Verbal skills comprise of approximately 20% of this exam.

Quantitative Skills - 52 Questions

The quantitative portion of the exam tests knowledge of series, number manipulations, geometric comparisons, and non-geometric comparisons.

Reading Skills - 62 Questions

The reading skills section of the exam focuses on reading comprehension and vocabulary. In this section, you will be given a passage and asked to answer comprehension and vocabulary questions that relate to the passage.

How can I study for this exam?

The first thing you need to understand is to do well on this exam, you must put in the time and effort to study. This is a challenging exam, so here is a list of a few important tips.

- **Practice and PRACTICE!**
  Take as many practice exams as you can find. Taking simulated exams will give you a very good idea on the type of questions that will be asked during the exam and will make you more confident.

- **Read Books**
  The best way to raise your score in the Verbal Section of the exam is to read books, articles and newspapers. You will develop a better vocabulary list and find it easier to read the passages provided in the exam.

- **Learn from your mistakes**
  When you go over your practice exams, make sure you understand **why** you got the question wrong. Did you read the corrections correctly? Was it a simple calculation error? Try to understand why you got the answer wrong.

ENGLISH

LANGUAGE ARTS

The Language Arts section of the exam includes grammar, spelling, usage and composition. The primary objective of these questions is to identify the error in the sentence(s) provided. If there is in fact no mistakes to be found in the question, an option usually marked "No mistakes" will be provided.

There are two forms of Language Arts questions provided on the exams: sentences and passages. The first provides either one or multiple sentences that you must survey to decide whether or not any errors are present. The second form of question provides you with a reading passage similar to the ones provided for the Reading Comprehension section. However, your objective is to NOT read the passages and instead FOCUS ONLY ON THE QUESTIONS GIVEN. More context on this will be provided later in this chapter.

While there are two different forms of questions to be found in this section, the core concept remains the same. Determine the grammatical, spelling, usage and composition errors found in the sentences. Do not waste any time on the logic or hidden meaning of what is written as it does not matter.

GRAMMAR

What is a sentence?
In order to begin tackling the grammar portion of the Language Arts section, you must understand what a sentence is made up of.

A proper sentence has, at the very least, a *subject* and a *verb*.

The *subject* is the person, place or thing that is causing an action to occur.
The *verb* is the action that is taking place by the subject.

For example, let's say we have the very simple sentence:

The boy kicks.

The subject in this sentence would be "the boy", and the verb would be "kicks". Simple enough, right?

There is one more part that, while it is <u>not</u> necessary, is usually found in a sentence: the *object*.
The *object* of a sentence is the person, place or thing that the subject performs the action on.

Let's look at the previous sentence with an object added:

<u>The boy</u> <u>kicks</u> <u>the ball</u>.

In this sentence, the subject is again "the boy," the verb is "kicks," and finally, the object is "the ball."

The sentence can also be broken down more roughly to just the *subject* and *predicate*. The *predicate* can be made up of just the verb, or both a verb and an object.

ENGLISH

In the above sentence, "kicks the ball" would be the predicate.

Here are a few more examples of proper sentences:
- Henry loved to eat apples.
- Jenna and Margaret will get ready for the party.
- Moe needs a haircut.

Subject-Verb Agreement

As mentioned before, every subject must be connected to a verb. However, the conjugation (form of the verb) must also agree with the subject given.

The three friends <u>play</u> video games every Saturday and Sunday. (CORRECT)
The three friends <u>plays</u> video games every Saturday and Sunday. (INCORRECT)

The book on animals <u>provides</u> a good understanding on habitats. (CORRECT)
The book on animals <u>provide</u> a good understanding on habitats. (INCORRECT)

Depending on the sentence, this may or may not prove to be difficult. For all sentences, the subject of the sentence, whether it is a person, place or thing, can be changed to its appropriate *pronoun*.

A *pronoun* is a word that is used in place of a person, place or thing (noun).

Pronouns:

	Singular (ONE)	Plural (TWO OR GREATER)
1st Person	I	we
2nd Person	you	you
3rd Person	he, she, it	they

Example of Conjugated Verbs:

to eat	Singular (ONE)	Plural (TWO OR GREATER)
1st Person	I eat	we eat
2nd Person	you eat	you eat
3rd Person	he, she, it eats	they eat

ENGLISH

The core idea is to be able to identify the subject of the sentence and then determine whether the verb agrees with the pronoun.

Looking back at the two previous examples for sentences, the subjects can be changed as such:

The three friends play video games every Saturday and Sunday.
They play video games every Saturday and Sunday.

The book on animals provides a good understanding on habitats.
It provides a good understanding on habitats.

Understanding how to change a subject to its appropriate noun is crucial in being able to grasp subject-verb agreement. The focus is mainly on *3rd-Person Singular (he, she, it)* and *3rd-Person Plural (they)*

Here are some examples of each:

- He: the boy, the man, the male cat, Tom
- She: the girl, the woman, the female cat, Ashley
- They: the boys, the girls, the men, the women, the cats, Tom and Ashley

ENGLISH

Collective Nouns:

However, there are a few tricky subjects as well. *Collective nouns* are subjects that refer to *groups* of things. A collective noun can be a class of students, a team, or a committee. It can even be a collection of *ideas*.

Collective nouns can be both singular and plural.

It: singular collective nouns
They: plural collective nouns

Examples of singular collective nouns include:
- team
- squad
- audience
- analysis of reports
- interaction between two students

Note: For the last two examples, the grouping itself is the subject. The rest of the subject is a description of the group.

Example of plural collective nouns include:

- teams
- squads
- audiences
- analyses of reports
- interactions between two students

Individuals Among Groups

The opposite can be said for subjects that are considered to be individuals among collective nouns.

Such nouns are associated with the pronoun, *it*.

Examples of individual subjects include:

- each of the boys
- every teacher
- one of the women
- a member of the group

11

ENGLISH

Indefinite Pronouns (Singular or Plural)
Indefinite pronouns can be defined as words that replace nouns without specifying the noun being replaced. There are a few words that can be used as *either* singular or plural.

Singular or Plural Pronouns:

- all
- any
- some
- more
- most
- none

Pronoun-Antecedent Agreement

In some examples, the pronoun in the sentence will be used later to refer to the subject that has already been introduced. These questions are easily answered using the principles of Subject-Verb agreement to identify the associated pronoun.

Some examples include:

Students must provide *his or her* homework at the beginning of class. (INCORRECT)
Students must provide *their* homework at the beginning of class. (CORRECT)

In the example above, the subject of the sentence is "Students" and as such, the pronoun associated to it would be "they" or "their," not the singular pronouns "his or her."

The *person* can pick up *their* bag on the way out. (INCORRECT)
The *person* can pick up *his or her* bag on the way out. (CORRECT)

The opposite idea is provided in this example. The "person" is the subject of the sentence, and the associated pronoun would be the 3rd - Person singular "his or her" and not 3rd - Person plural "their."

ENGLISH

Subject vs. Object Pronouns

Since you can now identify and differentiate between subjects and objects, it is crucial to understand that there are significant differences in the pronouns used for both instances.

Subject Pronouns:

	Singular (ONE)	Plural (TWO OR GREATER)
1st Person	I	we
2nd Person	you	you
3rd Person	he, she, it	they

Object Pronouns:

	Singular (ONE)	Plural (TWO OR GREATER)
1st Person	mine, me, myself	mine, me, myself
2nd Person	your, yourself	your, yourself
3rd Person	his, her(s), its	his, her(s), its

> I vs. me
> One of the biggest mistakes that many test takers make is misusing "I" and "me." The first is used in the context of the subject of the sentence, and the second for the object of a sentence.
>
> **SUBJECT:** I
> **OBJECT:** me
>
> The following two examples provide context to the misuse of the subject pronoun.
>
> *John and me are both extremely hungry. (INCORRECT)*
> *John and I are both extremely hungry. (CORRECT)*
>
> The next two sentences provide examples of the misuse of the object pronoun.
>
> *Ms. Evergreen gave John and I failing grades this marking period. (INCORRECT)*
> *Ms. Evergreen gave John and me failing grades this marking period. (CORRECT)*

ENGLISH

Who vs. whom

The same context can be provided for who and whom:

SUBJECT: who
OBJECT: whom

Whom is going to open that door for me? (INCORRECT)
Who is going to open that door for me? (CORRECT)

Who are you going to the movies with? (INCORRECT)
Whom are you going to the movies with? (CORRECT)

Note that in the second pair of examples given, the subject of the sentence is "you." Thus, the object MUST be "whom." Another example of such has been provided below:

To whom is she writing that letter? (CORRECT)
Whom did he hire for the new position? (CORRECT)

Reflexive Pronouns

Reflexive pronouns are object pronouns that end in either "-self" or "-selves" and refer back to the subject of the sentence.

Object Pronouns:

	Singular (ONE)	Plural (TWO OR GREATER)
1st Person	myself	ourselves
2nd Person	yourself	yourself
3rd Person	himself, herself, itself	themselves

ENGLISH

Here are a number of examples of reflexive pronouns in use:

- *I gave me a note to read in the near future. (INCORRECT)*
- *I gave myself a note to read in the near future. (CORRECT)*

- *You must give yourself some time to rest from the injury. (CORRECT)*

- *He cannot help himself out of bed. You should go aid him. (CORRECT)*

Ambiguous Pronouns

The word ambiguous itself means unclear, and an ambiguous pronoun is found in situations when it is unclear which noun the pronoun refers to.

Between Ms. Jameson and Ms. Richard, she gives the harder exams. (INCORRECT)
Among Ms. Jameson and Ms. Richard, Ms. Richard gives the harder exams. (CORRECT)

In the first sentence, who is "she" referring to in this sentence? Both the subjects are female, making it hard to differentiate between who the pronoun is referring to.

Christie loves their artwork. (INCORRECT)
Christie loves the Metropolitan Art Students' artwork. (CORRECT)

In the first example, who is "their" referring to? There is no indication of who the artists are.

ENGLISH

PUNCTUATION

Commas

Notice how in a previous example, commas were used to separate the clauses and phrase in the previous example:

By the way, when John jumps very high, Alicia eats two pies.

A *comma* **separates segments of a sentence.**

The use of a comma includes:

1. Separate two **independent clauses** when they are separated by the following words:
   a. and, but, or, nor, so, yet, for

   Amy is very hungry today, ***but*** *she does not have any food at home.*

2. Separate **dependent clauses, phrases,** and **words** that come before the **main independent clause.**

   However, before his mother could answer the phone, ***John was out of the house.***

3. Separate three or more clauses, phrases or words that are written in a series.

   Jumping rope, climbing fences, and running on the track are all exercises.

   John likes to read comics written by Marvel, DC, and Image Comics.

Misuse of Commas
Unless in extreme cases, **commas are not needed for dependent clauses or phrases.**

I went to eat some apples, after swimming ten laps. (INCORRECT)
Tim does not want to see her, while he is eating. (INCORRECT)

ENGLISH

SENTENCE STRUCTURE

While a basic sentence can be broken down to just a subject and predicate, most sentences are much more complex and are made up of two components: clauses and phrases.

Clause vs. Phrase

A *clause* is a part of a sentence that **contains both a subject and predicate.** There are two types of clauses:

1. **Independent clause**: a clause that can stand on its own as a sentence
   Example: Alicia eats two pies.

2. **Dependent clause**: a clause that cannot stand on its own as a sentence
   Example: When John jumps very high...

> *The most basic sentence consists of just a clause:*
>
> - *Cats meow.*
> - *Girl runs.*
> - *Jack cooks.*

A phrase is a part of a sentence **that lacks either a subject, predicate or both.**

Example: By the way...
Example: Without Jimmy...

Sentences can be comprised of all three of these concepts:

<u>By the way,</u> <u>when John jumps very high,</u> <u>Alicia eats two pies.</u>
A. Phrase   B. Dependent clause   C. Independent clause

ENGLISH

Semicolons

A *semicolon* **separates major sentence elements or independent clauses.**

In other words, a semicolon is used to separate two stand-alone sentences that are not already joined by a period or conjunction.

Hint: Consider semicolons to be almost identical to periods. If a period cannot fit in the sentence provided, neither can a semicolon.

Look at the following few examples, and just replace the periods with semicolons.

John loves snowballs. He eats them whenever there is a blizzard. (CORRECT)
Without any money. Tara cannot go to Florida to search for her missing pants. (INCORRECT)

↓

John loves snowballs; he eats them whenever there is a blizzard. (CORRECT)
Without any money; Tara cannot go to Florida to search for her missing pants. (INCORRECT)

In the first example, both "John loves snowballs" and "He eats them whenever there is a blizzard" are considered to be independent clauses: they can be read as complete sentences. Therefore, either a period or semicolon can separate the clauses.

In the second example, "Without any money" is a **phrase**, *and "Tara cannot go to Florida to search for her missing pants" is an independent clause. As such, the two parts should be separated by a* **comma**, *as was discussed in the previous section.*

Without any money, Tara cannot go to Florida to search for her missing pants. (CORRECT)

ENGLISH

Colons

A *colon* **introduces quotations, examples or lists.**

A few examples of each are as follows:

Quotations:

- *I will recite the first sentence on the note: "Always remember to brush and floss."*
- *Never forget his final choice of words: "Live, laugh and love."*

Examples:

- *We all know who will win this fight: the dog.*
- *There are only two options right now: stand up or back down.*

Lists:

- *I want to visit a number of places while in Europe: London, Rome and Athens.*
- *Here is the full list of items needed from the store: eggs, milk, orange juice and double-stuffed chocolate cookies.*

Quotation Marks

Quotation marks are **used to indicate either dialogue or direct quotes.** While that is simple enough to understand, punctuation is a bit trickier to grasp.

The rules of punctuation in quotation marks are as follows:

1. If the quotation is at the start of the sentence and is followed by a clause, the first word is capitalized and ends in a comma inside the quotation marks. If the quote is a question, use a question mark in place of the comma.

- *"The door is open," said John.*
- *"One of these days, I will win," replied Ralph.*
- *"Where is the bathroom?" asked Brienne of Tarth.*

ENGLISH

2. If a clause precedes a quotation, the ending punctuation is placed within the quotation marks. The first word of the quote is capitalized.

   - Albert asked, "Are you hungry?"
   - She replied, "I will always love basketball."
   - Did he really ask, "Is that a tree?"

3. In some instances, the quotation may be separated with a clause in between. Separate such quotes with commas as such.

   - "When you were walking," Ralph asked, "did you see a black dog?"
   - "You can walk," Beth said uneasily, "if you are ready to walk."
   - "One day," Mufasa told Simba, "this entire valley will be yours."

Question Marks and Periods

A *question mark* is **used at the end of a direct question.** A *period* is **used at the end of a direct statement.** Understanding the difference between a statement and question is the key to avoiding mistakes between the two.

Here are a few examples of differentiating between statements and questions.

- *Will Timothy run ten laps today. (INCORRECT)*
- *Renee will never be a great martial artist? (INCORRECT)*
- *I must write a hundred page paper tomorrow? (INCORRECT)*
- *Did the chicken come before the egg. (INCORRECT)*

- *Will Timothy run ten laps today? (CORRECT)*
- *Renee will never be a great martial artist. (CORRECT)*
- *I must write a hundred page paper tomorrow. (CORRECT)*
- *Did the chicken come before the egg? (CORRECT)*

ENGLISH

Apostrophes

An *apostrophe* has two specific functions: **to indicate contractions and to show possessive form.**

Examples of contractions include:

- will not: won't
- cannot: can't
- I am: I'm
- he is: he's

Examples of possessive form include:

- Lisa's jacket
- Jeff's basketball
- The Yankees' field
- Ross' hat

> **Common Mistake: It's vs. Its**
> It is crucial to understand the difference between "it's" and "its"
>
> *Contraction*: It's (it is)
> - *It's* getting hot in here.
> - *It's* almost time for bed.
>
> *Possessive*: Its
> - *Its* tail is now blue!
> - *Can* you please give *its* hair back?

SENTENCE STRUCTURE ERRORS

Run-on Sentences
A run-on sentence is a combination of two or more independent clauses that are joined inappropriately.

Remember, there are four different ways to join or separate independent clauses. The following will be a review of the list, used to appropriately fix the given run-on sentences.

1. Combination of commas with the conjunctions: and, but, or, nor, so, yet, for

    John loves to go skiing he cannot due to Pasadena's warm weather. (INCORRECT)
    *John loves to go skiing, **but** he cannot due to Pasadena's warm weather. (CORRECT)*

ENGLISH

2. Semicolons

> *John loves to go skiing he cannot due to Pasadena's warm weather. (INCORRECT)*
> *John loves to go skiing; he cannot due to Pasadena's warm weather. (CORRECT)*

3. Subordinate conjunctions and commas (although, if, since, while, after)

> *John loves to go skiing he cannot due to Pasadena's warm weather. (INCORRECT)*
> ***Although*** *John loves to go skiing, he cannot due to Pasadena's warm weather. (CORRECT)*

4. Periods

> *John loves to go skiing he cannot due to Pasadena's warm weather. (INCORRECT)*
> *John loves to go skiing. He cannot due to Pasadena's warm weather. (CORRECT)*

Sentence Fragments

Sentence fragments are otherwise known an incomplete sentence. An incomplete sentence **lacks either a subject, predicate, both, or is not a complete thought.**

Remember, just because a sentence is long and connected with a number of phrases and clauses does not mean that it is a complete sentence.

Examples of sentence fragments include:

Incomplete Thoughts:

- *Because his mother told him to* ***(...what did he do?)***
- *After the snowstorm ends.* ***(...what after?)***
- *If you are willing to buy a ticket from Expedia for a one-way trip to Alaska.* ***(...what will happen?)***

VERB TENSES

Grammatical tenses are forms taken to show the time of action.

Simple Tense:

Present	I eat
Past	I ate
Future	I will eat

Perfect Tense

The perfect tense shows that the action has already been completed.

Perfect Present	I have eaten
Perfect Past	I had eaten
Perfect Future	I will have eaten

Example: *I had eaten by the time the news about Antonio reached me.*
Example: *Thank you, but I have eaten my share of food today.*

Progressive Tense

The progressive tense shows an action that is still continuing.

Present Progressive	I am eating
Past Progressive	I was eating
Future Progressive	I will be eating

Example: *I am eating right now.*
Example: *I was eating while they burned down my house.*

Perfect Progressive Tense

Perfect Present Progressive	I have been walking
Perfect Past Progressive	I had been eating
Perfect Future Progressive	I will have been eating

ENGLISH

ADJECTIVES VS. ADVERBS

Adjectives and adverbs are both used to describe words. It is essential to know the different uses of the two.

- Adjectives describe or modify pronouns and nouns.
  EXAMPLE: red ball, angry Jim, funny clown

- Adverbs describe or modify verbs, adjectives or other adverbs.
  EXAMPLE: hardly running, recklessly paint, drastically different

HINT: Most adverbs ends in "-ly".

Here are a few examples of the incorrect use of adverbs.

> *Driving <u>reckless</u> in the snow and ice is a very dangerous decision. (INCORRECT)*
> *Driving <u>recklessly</u> in the snow and ice is a very dangerous decision. (CORRECT)*

> *Amber finished her homework <u>quick</u>. (INCORRECT)*
> *Amber finished her homework <u>quickly</u>. (CORRECT)*

COMPARATIVES AND SUPERLATIVES

Comparatives and superlatives are adjectives used to compare different objects.

- Comparatives compare two objects.
  "-er" is added to the end of the adjective.
  If adding "-er" is inappropriate, the word "more" is added.

- Superlatives compare more than objects.
  "-est" is added to the end of the adjective
  If adding "-er" is inappropriate, the word "more" is added.

HINT: "More" and "most" is added to adjectives with three or more syllables (beautiful, important).

ENGLISH

COMPARATIVES AND SUPERLATIVES		
Adjective	**Comparative**	**Superlative**
fast	faster	fastest
big	bigger	biggest
rich	richer	richest
ridiculous	more ridiculous	most ridiculous

In some instances, the entire structure of the adjective changes to suit the comparative and superlative.

IRREGULAR COMPARATIVES AND SUPERLATIVES		
Adjective	**Comparative**	**Superlative**
good	better	best
bad	worse	worst
much	more	most
little	less	least
far	farther	farthest

Remember that comparatives are used when comparing two nouns or pronouns, and superlatives are used for three or more nouns or pronouns.

Between Jacob and Edward, Jacob is the <u>strongest.</u> (INCORRECT)
Between Jacob and Edward, Jacob is the <u>stronger.</u> (CORRECT)

Among Harry, Ron and Hermione, Hermione is the <u>smarter.</u> (INCORRECT)
Among Harry, Ron and Hermione, Hermione is the <u>smartest.</u> (CORRECT)

Illogical Comparisons

When comparing two or more objects, the nouns or pronouns must be of the same entity. For instance, one cannot compare a painter to a painting, or an author to a book. Painters are compared with other painters, and books are compare with other books.

Satoshi's <u>test scores</u> are higher than <u>John</u>. (INCORRECT)
Satoshi's <u>test scores</u> are higher than <u>John's</u>. (CORRECT)

ENGLISH

The <u>coffee from Starbucks</u> is much better than Dunkin Donuts. (INCORRECT)
The coffee from Starbucks is much better than <u>Dunkin Donuts coffee.</u> (CORRECT)

OTHER GRAMMATICAL TRAITS

Double Negatives

The use of two negative words can turn the sentence into a positive one, which may not be the intent of the writer. Double negatives are usually discouraged.

Don't say nothing. (INCORRECT)
Don't say anything. (CORRECT)

Redundancy

Unnecessary repetition makes writing more difficult to read and makes the sentence seem longer than it actually is. The objective is to remove any repeated information.

The meeting on Tuesday has been <u>postponed until later</u>. (INCORRECT)
The meeting on Tuesday has been <u>postponed</u>. (CORRECT)

The definition of "postpone" is to take place at a later time; "until later" is not needed.

The attack was an <u>unintentional mistake</u>. (INCORRECT)
The attack was a <u>mistake</u>. (CORRECT)

A "mistake" is something that is misguided and unintentional.

ENGLISH

LIST OF MOST COMMONLY MISUSED WORDS

A, an
The article a is used before a consonant sound, and an is used before a vowel sound.
a car, an apple

Accept, except
Accept is a verb meaning to receive, and except means to leave out.
I accepted the gift.
Everyone went to the party except me.

Affect, effect
Affect is a verb meaning to influence, and effect is a noun that means result.
The disaster affected everyone in town.
The effect of the disaster was saddening.

Already, all ready
Already means by a certain time, and *all already* means completely ready.
I have already completed my homework.
My homework is all ready to be submitted.

Altogether, all together
Altogether means entirely, and *all together* means as an entire group.
He is altogether a very capable individual.
All together, there is a total of twenty members.

Among, between
Among is used in groups of three or more, whereas *between* is used for two individuals.
Among the three friends, Henry is the coolest.
Between the two friends, Henry is the uglier.

Amount, number
Amount is a numberless bulk, and *number* refers to a specific count.
The amount of homework I have is ridiculous.
The number of homework packets I have is ridiculous.

As, like
not
As is a conjunction that is followed by a verb, while *like* is a preposition and is followed by a verb.
Please cook the recipe as I instructed.
This food looks like dung.

Beside, besides
Beside means next to, and *besides* means apart from.
The bird flew beside his fellow friends.
Besides watching birds fly, I enjoy eating pie.

Farther, further
Farther is used to compare distances that are measurable, and *further* is used to describe the advancement of an idea or object.
The boat is twenty miles farther than from here.
We must explore this experiment further

ENGLISH

Fewer, less
Fewer applies to objects that can be counted, and less is used for degrees that cannot be measured.
There are five <u>fewer</u> cupcakes than there was yesterday.
I am <u>less</u> happy today.

Its, it's
Its is possessive, and it's is a contraction for it is.
Its horns are enormous.
It's quite enormous.

Principal, principle
Principal refers to the head of something, and principle refers to a fundamental truth.
The principal of the school laid down the rules.
The principle behind survival is to lay low at all times.

Than, then
Than is used to compare things, whereas then is used in reference to time.
I am smarter than you.
I will study for the test and then get a higher score than you.

Their, there, they're
Their is the possessive form of they, there is an indication of place, and they're is the contraction of they are.
I can't wait to go to their party.
Over there, you will find a list of party foods.
They're 30 minnutes away from the party.

CAPITALIZATION

Here is a list of nouns, otherwise known as "proper nouns" that must be capitalized in any sentence.

- Proper first and last names, names of organizations
  - Amanda Greenberg, Yankees, Wall Street
- Titles that precede names
  - Doctor Johnson, Mister Freddy, Aunt Jemima
- Days of the week and months in a year
  - Monday, January, Thursday
- Holidays
  - Fourth of July, Thanksgiving, Halloween, Memorial Day

The first word of a sentence or quotation must also be capitalized.

My name is Diane Johnson.
John replied, "The dog is blue."

ENGLISH

VOCABULARY

The HSPT and TACHS exam all have a vocabulary portion in their exams, which tests your ability to identify synonyms, antonyms and the definition of words with the context provided.

Some questions will be easily answered through basic knowledge of vocabulary, but ultimately, you will see a number of questions that may prove difficult to answer. Building your vocabulary is the best way to answer such questions: the more words you know, the easier this portion of the exam will get. This book provides a list of the most frequently used words on the exams, which can be located in the back.

Roots, Prefixes and Suffixes

Also provided is a table of roots, prefixes and suffixes that may prove to be just as helpful as memorizing a long list of vocabulary. Many large and difficult words can often be broken down to a few core ideas, allowing that extra bit of boost needed to answer some of these questions.

Root or Prefix	Meaning	Root or Prefix	Meaning
a, an	not, without	inter, intro	between
ab	away from	intra	within, intro
ante	before	meta	change
anti, ant	against, opposite	micro	small
auto	self	non	not
chron	time	omni	all
circum	around	poly	many
con, com	with	re	back, again
de	from, down, away	retro	backwards
e, ex	out, away, from	semi	half
hyper	over, above	sub	under, below
hypo	below, less than	syn	together
in, im	not	vita	life

ENGLISH

ANALOGIES

Analogy questions ask to find similar relationships between two sets of words. On the HSPT exam, a pair of words is provided. After determining the relationship between the two words, you are asked to look for an answer choice that extends that same relationship.

An analogy question may look like this:

Scissors is to cut as car is to

a) mend
b) drive
c) walk
d) close

Approach to analogies
1. Create a "test sentence" between the first pair of words provided.
2. Use the first word of the second pair to guess the answer.
3. Compare the guess word to the answer choices provided.

The first pair of words, "scissors" and "cut", is given to interpret their association. A second, incomplete, pair is given. The first word provided is "car." Your objective is to find the word that best associates to car in a similar way that scissors relates to cut.

In this instance, scissors are used to cut. You can ask yourself, "What is a car used for?" And of course, the answer that should come to mind is "drive." Low and behold, the answer must then be choice b.

The test sentence is a simple, distinct sentence that defines the relationship between the two words. How are the two words relatable?

Let's take a look at another pair of words that can be turned into a test sentence.

Quart is to ounce as mile is to

The words quarts and ounces are both units of measurement for liquids. A test sentence for the pair could be:

A quart is made up of ounces.

In turn, a second test sentence can be made for the word "yard."

A mile is made up of...

A mile is a unit of measurement and the second word must be something it is made up of. Inches? Feet? Yards? Any one of these words can work.

30

ENGLISH

READING COMPREHENSION

READING PASSAGES ARE NOTHING TO BE WARY OF.

Whether you are planning on taking the HSPT or TACHS test, you will be presented with a broad variety of reading passages that discuss a multitude of different topics. The passages will range from one to four paragraphs regarding the sciences, history and even current events. It's true. Reading questions can be intimidating and even overwhelming at times. Nonetheless, they are a large part of the Catholic high school entrance exams and cannot afford to be ignored.

Fortunately, you most likely already have the skills required to successfully answer most if not all of the questions that may be present on any of the three tests. Most individuals feel this is true if you are an avid reader. However, that is not so. Reading and understanding even basic day-to-day instructions and summaries has placed you in a suitable position.

Take walking into a health clinic as an example. While passing by the main office desk, you happen to come across an Alzheimer's Association brochure labeled, "Basics of Alzheimer's Disease." Admittedly, you nor anyone you know is suffering from Alzheimer's, but the booklet catches your interest. Skimming through that pamphlet while waiting on your appointment, you gain a general understanding of what the disease concerns. If someone were to strike a conversation with you ten minutes later, you would very likely be able to summarize the gist of Alzheimer's: symptoms including memory problems from mild cognitive impairment usually first appear after the age of sixty-five, roughly five million Americans suffer from the disease, and so on.

Now, what does reading a brochure have anything to with the HSPT or TACHS test, you may ask? The knowledge that you can pick up from reading something as relatable as a leaflet is all the information that you will need to answer the passage-based questions found on the exams. The idea is to spend as little time as possible on the minor details of the passages and rather focus on the general understanding that the reading provides.

Common Reading Comprehension Mistakes

Remember, the Reading section is not quizzing you on how well you read and understand the passage; rather, it tests you on how easily and swiftly you recognize the author's intended answer. Increasing your score by earning points is only achieved by arriving to the correct answer choice. The main focus should always be placed on spending as much time as possible on the reading questions provided. The best way to do so is by avoiding a few common reading mistakes:

- Studying all of the questions before the passage
- Reading the passage too closely
- Nitpicking sentences you have difficulty understanding

ENGLISH

Notice how all of the main difficulties listed above center around one element: time management. The reading excerpts are relatively short, so there is no particular need to waste time trying to memorize the questions before even attempting to read the passage. Besides, you will never be able to simultaneously remember the questions, remember the answer choices and interpret the passage. Attempting to do so will only leave you flustered and out of time.

The last two mistakes go hand in hand. Recall that the primary purpose is to gain only a general understanding of the passage to tackle the questions. You will be required to reread certain parts of the passage when attempting to answer the questions anyway, so why waste additional time fussing over specific details?

Tackling Reading Comprehension Questions

Phase I: Read the Passage
As mentioned before, all of the reading passages are comprised of anywhere from one to four short paragraphs. The plan is to quickly skim through each of the paragraphs and look for the topic sentence of each paragraph and the main idea of the passage.

It is recommended that you also make a small note or comment on the major themes and concepts that are covered in each paragraph. Try to refrain from underlining and specific details as you do not yet know if you will be asked on it. **DO NOT READ THE PASSAGE TOO CLOSELY.**

Phase II: Identifying the Question Types
Now that you've gained a good understanding of how to approach the passage itself, you can finally start to look at the most important part of the section: the questions themselves. Determining the type of question being asked is the first step; doing so will allow you to effectively read parts of the passage to answer appropriately.

A. Main Idea Questions
The main idea question focuses on summarizing the most important idea of the passage. It is helpful to understand that the main idea ties all of the paragraphs together and is the overall central theme.

Common Traps in Main Idea Questions. The main idea should be neither too narrow nor too broad. Too narrow of an answer choice tends to cover some details in the passage, but not all that were discussed. Adversely, an answer choice may cover all of the ideas in the passage, but may include others that were not mentioned directly in the reading. Any answer covering unsupported or new information will be incorrect.

Examples of main idea questions can include:

- What is the main idea of this passage?
- What is the passage mainly about?
- A good title for this passage would be...?
- Which of the following most accurately describes the passage?
- What is the author's primary purpose in this passage?

ENGLISH

B. Detail Questions

Detail questions are the most common form of questions found in the Reading Comprehension section. Thankfully, they are very easy to master and answer correctly; just consider them to be a part of an open book test. Whatever the question is asking, the passage must provide the details. Depending on what you are asked, you just have to locate that information in the passage.

It is always important to read information outside of the reference provided in the question. The questions most likely require some amount of context clues to fully answer, so reading the sentence before and even the following sentence can help.

Identifying detail questions is simple enough. In some instances, a phrase in the question may refer to back to the passage: "According to the passage...".

Common Traps in Detail Questions. Detail questions involve looking for answers that are directly stated in the passage. Every once in a while, there will be an answer that seems as though it could be in the passage, but is not directly stated – this would clearly be wrong. *THE CORRECT ANSWER CHOICE WILL ALWAYS BE DECLARED IN THE PASSAGE.*

Examples of detail questions can include:

- According to the passage, which of the following is true?
- John was best known for his ability to do what?
- During its final trip to the Atlantic Ocean, what did the ship come across?

C. Inference Questions

Inference questions mainly ask you to draw conclusions based on information provided directly in the passage. Note that the inference is never directly stated in the reading.

For example, a passage can discuss the travels of a character. It may describe in great detail surroundings of the area that the character is set in, but may not explicitly state the location. Take a look at the passage below.

> "Hundreds of cars honked on the road as Jim walked down the littered streets. The view of the sky was completely blocked by the dozens of skyscrapers. The air was thick with smoke and smog. Jim felt sickened and disgusted; this was not what he had imagined at all."

From this excerpt, a number of details can be inferred. While it is not directly stated, it can be concluded that Jim is most likely visiting a city. It is most likely his first time stepping into the city as well, according to his negative reaction to his experience. All of this can easily be interpreted without having any direct details on Jim's whereabouts or past travels.

Common Traps in Inference Questions. Remember, the answer to inference questions are never directly stated in the passage – answers that discuss the exact details are to be avoided.

ENGLISH

Examples of inference questions can include:
- The character in this passage is most likely...
- This passage can most likely be found in a...

D. Vocabulary Questions

Vocabulary questions ask you to find synonyms of specific words that are to be found in the reading passage. The word provided may or not be a word that you recognize, but the key to answering such questions correctly lies in using context clues.

Answering vocabulary questions is very simple. Read the sentence that the word is located in, as well as the sentences that come both before and after for better reference. Once you have a general understanding of what the word is, replace the vocabulary word with each of the answer choices and select the word that best fits the definition of the word.

Examples of vocabulary questions can include:
- The word _____ most nearly means...
- According to the passage, which word most closely represents _____?

Summarizing the Reading Passage Strategies

1. Read the passage for the first time.
   a. Skim the reading passage, making sure to make notes or comments on the main topics of each paragraph.
   b. The leading sentence of each paragraph usually provides a good understanding of what the rest of the paragraph entails.
   c. Do not focus too much on the details on the first reading.

2. Identify the Questions
   a. Main Idea
   b. Detail
   c. Inference
   d. Vocabulary
   e. Refer back to the passage when needed.

ARITHMETIC REVIEW

BASIC MATH TERMS YOU MUST KNOW

There is no reference sheet provided during the exam, so you must know all the formulas and be familiar with the words and methods.

Please look at the following terms that we have provided you with. This is not a comprehensive list, however these are a few terms that you must understand.

INTEGERS	Whole numbers that are positive or negative, and include zero. Example: $-1, 0, 1, 4.0, \frac{-20}{2}$ are all integers.
CONSECUTIVE INTEGERS	1, 2, 3, 4 are consecutive integers. 4, 6, 8, 10 are consecutive even integers. 1, 3, 5, 7 are consecutive odd integers.
WHOLE NUMBERS	These are counting numbers, including 0. There are no negative numbers in whole numbers. Example: 0, 1, 2, 3, 4...
RATIONAL NUMBERS	All integers, fractions, decimals, repeating decimals and terminating decimals. Example: $1, 0.121212, \frac{1}{8}, 191.01$
IRRATIONAL NUMBERS	These numbers cannot be written as fractions. These are non-repeating decimals. Example: $0.162728..., \sqrt{2}, \pi$
SCIENTIFIC NOTATION	When you have a large number, it is easier to express it in scientific notation. You must know how to correctly convert numbers into scientific notation for the exam. Example: $281{,}000{,}000 = 2.81 \times 10^8$
PEMDAS	Parenthesis, Exponents, Multiplication, Addition, Subtraction This is the order of operations that must be followed to get the correct answer.
PRIME NUMBERS	A positive integer greater than 1, whose factors are 1 and the number itself. Example: 2, 3, 5, 7, 11 Note: 1 is not a prime number. Make sure you know that!

ARITHMETIC REVIEW

COMPOSITE NUMBERS A number that has more than two factors.
Example: 4, 10, 20, 55

GREATEST COMMON FACTOR It is the largest number that is a factor of two or more numbers. In order to find the GCF, list all the prime factors of each number and multiply the factors that both numbers have in common. Example: If we wanted to find the GCF of 12 and 15, you need to list the prime factors of both numbers.

Prime Factors of 12: 2 • 2 • 3
Prime Factors of 16: 2 • 2 • 2 • 2

The only numbers that are common in both sets is 2 and 2, so when you multiple 2 • 2 , you get 4. Therefore, 4 is the greatest common factor of 12 and 16.

LEAST COMMON MULTIPLE It is the lowest common multiple between two or more numbers. In order to find the LCM, list all the prime factors of each number and multiply the factors by the greatest number of times it appears. For example, if you are finding the LCM of 8, 10 and 25; first list their respective prime numbers.

Prime Factors of 8: 2 • 2 • 2
Prime Factors of 10: 2 • 5
Prime Factors of 25: 5 • 5

2 is a factor of both 8 and 10, however, the greatest number of times 2 appears in a set is three times. Therefore, we want to multiply 2 • 2 • 2 when finding the LCM. 5 is a factor of both 10 and 25, however, the greatest number of times 5 appears in a set is two times. Therefore, we want to multiply 5 • 5 when finding the LCM. Combining this, we get:

2 • 2 • 2 • 5 • 5 = 200
Therefore, 200 is the LCM of 8, 10 and 25.

RULE FOR EVEN AND ODD INTEGERS

Even + Even = Even
Even + Odd = Odd
Odd + Odd = Even

Even • Even = Even
Even • Odd = Even
Odd • Odd = Odd

PERCENTAGES Percent means "out of 100". There are a few key things you need to know for percent problems.
If you are given the question: 15 is what percent of 60?
You need to always remember that **"is"** means an equal sign and **"of"** means multiply. Now simply set up the equation.
15 = ? % • 60. The variable here is the percentage, so if you solve for that you get .25 or 25%

ARITHMETIC REVIEW

FORMULAS FOR AREA

Rectangle: $A = l \cdot w$ Square: $A = l \cdot w$
Triangle: $A = \frac{1}{2} b \cdot h$ Trapezoid: $A = \frac{1}{2}(b_1 + b_2) \cdot h$
Parallelogram: $A = b \cdot h$ Circle: $A = \pi r^2$

STATISTICS

If you want to find the average of a set of numbers, you must add them up and divide by the number of terms. Use the following formula: **Average = $\dfrac{\text{Sum of terms}}{\text{Number of terms}}$**

Here is a very important rule to remember:
In a **consecutive** series of numbers, the **mean is also equal to the median.** This rule will help you answers quicker to save time on the exam.

For example: If the sum of 5 consecutive even integers is 280, then what is the largest value of the 5 consecutive even integers?

The first thing you need to realize is that, 280 is the sum, and there are 5 number of terms. You can easily find the average, by simply dividing 280 by 5, which is 56. Now, using the rule we just learned, we know that 56 is the median value in this consecutive integer series. That means 56 is the third consecutive even integer, and we want to find the fifth even integer. Using simple math, the 5th even integer is 60. Therefore, 60 is the largest value of the 5 consecutive even integers. If you practice using this rule, you will be able to solve these problems in under 45 seconds.

Average Rate is a little different from the usual average formula.
If you want to find the average rate or speed, the formula you need to use is: **Average Speed = $\dfrac{\text{Total Distance}}{\text{Total Time}}$**

For example: If you are trying to find the average speed for 100 miles at 50 mph and 100 miles at 25 mph, you cannot just average the two speeds given. You must figure out the total distance and then divide it by the total time. The total distance is simply 100 miles + 100 miles = 200 miles. Don't get confused when finding out the total time. If you are going 50 mph and traveled 100 miles, that is 2 hours. If you are going 25 mph and traveled 100 miles, that is 4 hours. Therefore, a total of 6 hours. The average speed, then, is $\frac{200}{6} = 33.33$ mph.

The **Median** is a number that is in the middle of the set, and the set must be in sequential order.

For example: If we are given the numbers 5, 3, 1, 7, and 9 then what is the median value? First order them in sequential order and then find the middle value.
1, 3, 5, 7, 9 so the median is 5.

The **Mode** is a number that appears the most often in a set of numbers. You can have more then one Mode, if one or more number shows up the same number of times.

For example: 1, 1, 2, 5, 6, 7, 6
The Mode for this set of numbers is 1 and 6.

PROBABILITY

$$\text{Probability} = \frac{\text{Favorable Outcomes}}{\text{Total Possible Outcomes}}$$

EXPONENT RULES

If you are multiplying, and have the same base, you need to add the exponents and keep the same base.

Example: $y^2 \cdot y^3 = y^{2+3} = y^5$

If you are dividing, and have the same base, you need to subtract the exponents and keep the same base.

Example: $\frac{y^{10}}{y^5} = y^5$

If you are raising a power to a power, then you must multiply the exponents.

Example: $(y^2)^{(3)} = y^{2 \cdot 3} = y^6$

SLOPE

If you are given two points, you can find the slope by using the formula **Slope = $\frac{\text{Change in Y}}{\text{Change in X}}$**

If you want to write an equation in slope-intercept form, the formula you need to use is **y = mx + b**

ARITHMETIC REVIEW

UNIT CONVERSIONS

You are required to know basic units of measurements and how to convert from one unit to another to correctly solve a problem. Below is a list of units you should already know.

WEIGHT

16 ounces = 1 pound

DISTANCE

1 foot = 12 inches
1 yard = 3 feet = 36 inches
1 kilometer = 1,000 meters

VOLUME

8 ounces = 1 cup
2 cups = 1 pint
2 pints = 1 quart
4 cups = 1 quart
4 quarts = 1 gallon
1 meter = 100 centimeters
1 meter = 1,000 millimeters

PLACE VALUE

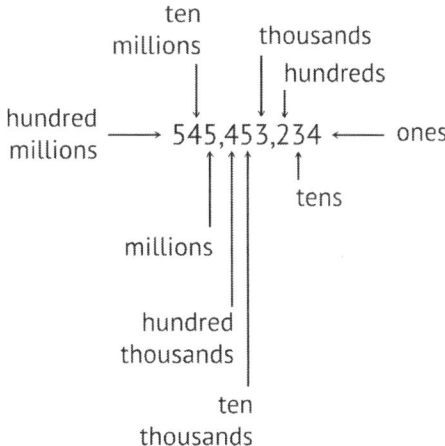

ARITHMETIC REVIEW

CONVERTING FRACTIONS TO DECIMALS TO PERCENTS

You are not required to memorize this entire chart. This chart is to help you become familiar with the relationships between percents, decimals and fractions. In order to convert a fraction or decimal to a percent, always multiply by 100%. Alternatively to convert a percent to a fraction or decimal divide by 100%.

FRACTION	DECIMAL	PERCENT
$\frac{1}{20}$	0.05	5%
$\frac{1}{10}$	0.10	10%
$\frac{1}{8}$	0.125	$12\frac{1}{2}$%
$\frac{1}{5}$	0.20	20%
$\frac{1}{4}$	0.25	25%
$\frac{1}{3}$	$0.33\overline{3}$	$33\frac{1}{3}$%
$\frac{3}{8}$	0.375	37.5%
$\frac{2}{5}$	0.40	40%
$\frac{1}{2}$	0.50	50%
$\frac{3}{5}$	0.60	60%
$\frac{2}{3}$	$0.66\overline{6}$	$66\frac{2}{3}$%
$\frac{3}{4}$	0.75	75%
$\frac{4}{5}$	0.80	80%

ALGEBRA FUNDAMENTALS

Algebra is a key concept on the HSPT/TACHS tests that will be tested. However, only the basics will be tested. This chapter will outline the key algebra fundamentals that are needed to ace the exam.

Algebra is an important mathematical concept that allows you to solve unique problems. In algebra, there is a use of letters, that is known as the **variable**. The variable is represented by a letter, and is an unknown value that needs to be determined. The same mathematical operations with arithmetic are applicable to these unknown variables. An example of a practical algebra application is shown below.

Sam buys three bicycles, one for himself, one for his sister, and one for his dad for a total of 400 dollars. If one bicycle was 100 dollars, and the other two were the same price, how much were the other two bicycles?

In order to solve this problem, an equation needs to be written to find how much the other bicycle was. In algebra, any letter can be used to represent an unknown value. In this question, the unknown value is the cost of the second bike. We can let the cost of the second bike be represented by the letter b.

The equation becomes:

$2b + 100 = 400$

In math, the most common variables used are *a, b, c, x, y,* and *z*. In many algebra problems, there is a constant that does not change. Specifically, the number in front of the variable, is a constant that stays the same, and is known as a **coefficient**.

To solve how much the two bicycles were, solve the equation.

$2b + 100 = 400$
$-100 -100$
$2b = 300$
$\dfrac{(2b)}{2} = \dfrac{(300)}{2}$
$b = 150$ dollars

Therefore, the price of each of the two bicycles was 150 dollars. Algebraic equations will be explained in a later section.

Algebraic Expressions

Many algebraic problems can be broken down into smaller components. They can be broken down into expressions and terms. A **term** is the product of a constant and a variable or variables. In the algebraic problem mentioned earlier, the term is $2b$. An expression is the combination of a term or multiple terms that are connected by operational symbols. The **expression** for the first problem would be $2b + 100$.

ALGEBRA FUNDAMENTALS

Let's look at the expression in the problem from above:

$2b + 100$

This expression is known as a **monomial** because there is only one term. If there were two terms such as the expression $3x + 2x$, this is known as a **binomial** because there are two terms. If there are two or more terms like $3x + 2x + y$, this is known as a **polynomial**.

Adding and Subtracting Expressions

It is crucial to note that like terms can be combined in expressions. In the binomial $3x + 2x$, the $3x$ and $2x$ can be added because they both have the same variable. The combined term becomes $5x$. The contrary is also important to note, in that different variables cannot be combined. If there are three different variables in the same problem, they cannot be combined as each variable represents something different. An example of an expression with like and unlike terms are shown below.

$4x - 2y + 3z - 2x + y + 4z$

This expression can be simplified by grouping The like terms together and performing the operation.

$(4x - 2x) - (2y + y) + (3z + 4z)$

This simplifies to

$2x - y + 7z$

Note: You cannot combine variables that are not raised to the same exponent. For example:

$5x + 5x^2$ cannot be combined because the exponents are not the same. However, $5x^2 + 5x^2$ can be combined to $10x^2$ because the exponents are the same.

Multiplying and Dividing Expressions

Multiplying and Dividing expressions on the other hand are a little different from adding and subtracting expressions. It is possible to multiply and divide terms that are different. In order to multiply monomials, multiply the coefficients and variables. If there are exponents, add them. An example is shown below.

$(10y)(3yz) = (10 \cdot 3)(y^{1+1} z) = 30y^2 z$

To multiply and divide binomials, use the FOIL method. **FOIL** is an acronym for "**F**irst **O**uter **I**nner **L**ast." This is the order that terms should be multiplied In order to use the FOIL method, arrange the binomials in a manner where each term that is multiplied is a like term. Look at the example shown below.

ALGEBRA FUNDAMENTALS

$(y + 5)(y + 7) = (y \cdot y) + (7 \cdot y) + (5 \cdot y) + (5 \cdot 7)$
$ \text{(First)} \quad \text{(Outer)} \quad \text{(Inner)} \quad \text{(Last)}$

$= y^2 + 7y + 5y + 35$
$= y^2 + 12y + 35$

Now, we will move on to algebraic equations.

Algebraic Equations

Algebraic equations are very important and will definitely be tested on the exam you are taking. Mastering algebraic equations is key to mastering the mathematical portions of the exams. In order to solve algebraic equations, do the same thing on both sides of the equation. Keep going back and forth doing this with the goal of isolating the variable on one side of the equation, and the numbers on the other side. An example is presented below.

$\frac{3}{4}x + 9 = 6x + 6$

Subtract 6 on both sides of the equation first.

$\frac{3}{4}x + 9 - 6 = 6x + 6 - 6$

Multiply both sides by $\frac{4}{3}$.

$\frac{4}{3}(\frac{3}{4}x + 3) = 6x(\frac{4}{3})$

Subtract x on both sides to isolate x.

$x + 4 - x = 8x - x$

Divide both sides of the equation by 7.

$\frac{4}{7} = \frac{(7x)}{7}$

$x = \frac{4}{7}$

Algebraic Inequalities

Algebraic **inequalities** are very similar to algebraic equations. The only difference is that there are the inequality symbols >, <, ≥, and ≤. Solve these problems as you would do with any algebraic equation, where you do onto one side, as you do onto the other in order to isolate the variable. The difference with inequalities is that you get a range of values for the variable instead of one exact answer. An example is given below.

ALGEBRA FUNDAMENTALS

$5x - 3 > 21 - 3x$

Add 3 on both sides.

$5x - 3 + 3 > 21 + 3 - 3x$
$5x > 24 - 3x$

Add $3x$ on both sides to isolate the terms with x in them.

$5x + 3x > 24 - 3x + 3x$
$8x > 24$

Divide by 8 on both sides.

$\dfrac{(8x)}{8} > \dfrac{24}{8}$
$x > 3$

Here, the answer to the problem can be any number that is greater than 3, not any number 3 or less than that.

It is critical to note that there is a key difference when solving inequalities. This difference is that when an inequality is multiplied or divided by a negative number the direction of the sign of the inequality changes. This is shown below.

$-3x > 9$
$\dfrac{(-3x)}{(-3)} > \dfrac{(9)}{(-3)}$
$x < -3$

Two Variables

There will be questions where two variables are given. In situations like these, the question will ask to solve for one variable in terms of the other. In this case, solve for the variable that the question is asking for, and isolate it on one side. The other side will have an expression with the other variable. In other cases, the two variables will already be present. However, only one variable may be able to be solved initially. Solve for the first variable, and plug in that known information to find the second variable.

Solve for x in terms of y

$3x + 6y - 3 = 2x - 3y + 12$

ALGEBRA FUNDAMENTALS

Subtract 6y on both sides because we want to isolate x on one side.

$3x + 6y - 6y - 3 = 2x - 3y - 6y + 12$
$3x - 3 = 2x - 9y + 12$

Add 3 on both sides to get all the numbers on the right side.

$3x - 3 + 3 = 2x - 9y + 12 + 3$
$3x = 2x - 9y + 15$

Subtract both sides by $2x$ to isolate x by itself.

$3x - 2x = 2x - 2x - 9y + 15$
$x = -9y + 15$

Algebraic Substitution

Many times a question will ask you to find the value of an expression with given values of variables. These problems are **substitution** problems. Simply plug in the numbers given with their respective variables and solve the equation. As always, follow PEMDAS during the operations. An example is given below.

If $x = 4$ and $y = 7$, what is the value of $x^2 + y^2 - (xy)$?

Insert 4 for x and 7 for y. The equation becomes

$4^2 + 7^2 - (4 \cdot 7)$
$16 + 49 - 28 = 37$

GEOMETRY

The HSPT exam will definitely incorporate basic geometry into its problems. In order to master the geometry problems on these tests, you will need to be proficient with your knowledge of lines, angles, quadrilaterals, and triangles.

This section will outline the key topics that should be known in order to do well on the test you are taking. Review and hone your geometry skills by taking time to understand the concepts and doing practice problems. It is crucial to note that the diagram given may not always be to scale, so it would be inappropriate to assume so and guess an answer just by looking at the diagram.

Lines

All **lines** are straight and extend in both directions indefinitely. There are 180 degrees in a line. If there are ends, it is not called a line, but a **line segment**. A line has no end, but a line segment does. A line segment has an exact length. In questions with line segments, one or two lengths of a line segment might be given, and the question may ask you to calculate what the missing lengths are.

This is a line.

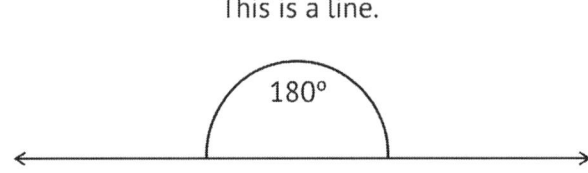

This is a line segment, where *x* is the value of line segment AB.

If DF = 9, and EF = 3, what is the value of DE?

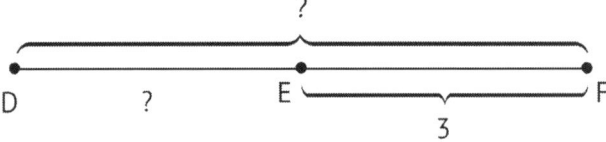

GEOMETRY

DF = 9, EF = 3
DF = DE + EF
DF - EF = DE
9 - 3 = DE
6 = DE

Again, note that in the line segment, it may seem like DE is half of the whole segment. However, when you solve the problem, this is not the case. Therefore, it is important to assume that figures are not drawn to scale. The point that is exactly in the middle of a line segment is called the **midpoint** of the line segment. The midpoint bisects the line segment into half.

Angles

There are multiple different kinds of angles that you will see on the test. Three that are important to know are the right angle, acute angle, and the obtuse angle. We will first talk about the right angle.

A right angle is an angle that measures 90°. Often times, this is shown in a diagram with a little box that is connected to both lines.

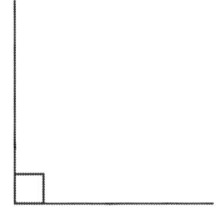

The two lines that intersect to create the right angle are known to be perpendicular to each other. When it is said that two lines are perpendicular to each other, this means that if they were to intersect, they would create a 90° angle.

As mentioned earlier, lines are made up of 180°. Many times, two angles add up to create a straight line, and add up to 180°. This is shown in the figure below.

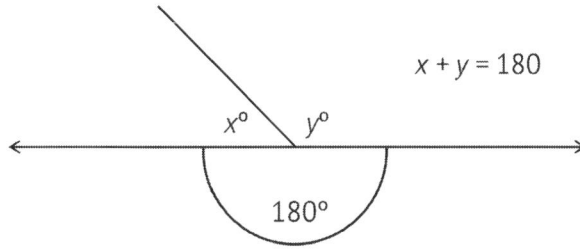

In this diagram, angle x is known as an acute angle because it measures less than 90°. Angle y is known as an obtuse angle because it measures greater than 90°.

In summary, a right angle is equal to 90°, an acute angle has less than 90°, and an obtuse angle measures greater than 90°.

Additionally, in the figure above, angles x and y are supplementary angles. This means that they add up to 180°. Supplementary angles are created when two lines intersect.

Along these lines, all angles around any specific point add up to 360°. In the diagram shown below, the sum of the angles w, x, y, and z is 360°.

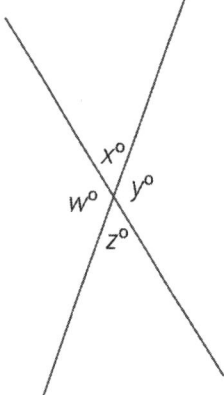

Furthermore, when lines intersect, angles that are opposite to each other across the vertex are vertical angles. Vertical angles are equal to each other, therefore, $w = y$ and $x = z$.

Triangles

In all triangles, the three interior angles add up to 180°. Interior angles are angles that are inside the shape, whereas exterior angles are angles outside the shape.

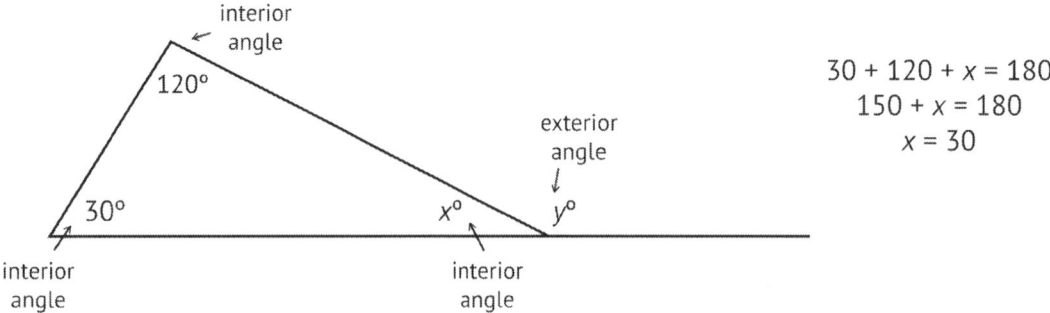

$30 + 120 + x = 180$
$150 + x = 180$
$x = 30$

GEOMETRY

An exterior angle in a triangle is equal to the addition of the remote interior angles. **Remote interior angles** are the two angles inside the triangle that are not adjacent to the exterior angle. In the example above, the remote interior angles are 30 and 120. 30 and 120 add up to 150, which is the measurement of angle *y*.

Another important rule about all triangles that you should know is that one side of a triangle has to be less than the sum and greater than the positive difference of the other two sides of the triangle. If one of the sides of the triangle is 5, and the other side is 7, the third sides has to be less than 12 which is the sum of the other two sides and greater than 2 which is the positive difference of the other two sides.

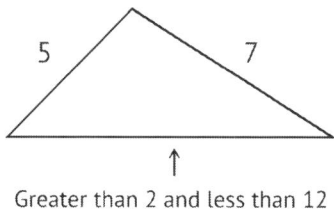

↑
Greater than 2 and less than 12

The **perimeter** of a triangle is equal to the sum of the lengths of all three sides.

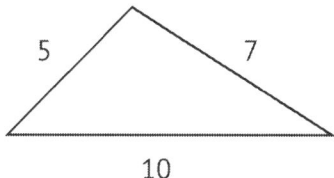

The perimeter of this triangle is equal to 5 + 7 + 10 = 22.

The **area** of a triangle can be found using the equation $A = \frac{1}{2}bh$ where b is equal to the length of the base and h is equal to the length of the height. The base can be chosen to be any side of the triangle, however, the longest side of the triangle is often chosen as the base. The height is the line from the opposite vertex to the base. The height must be perpendicular to the base.

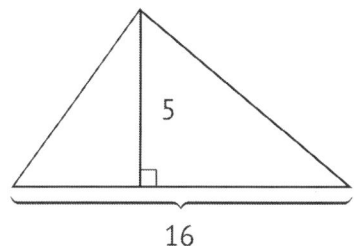

In the triangle, if the base is chosen to be 16, the height is 5.

Area = $\frac{1}{2}bh = \frac{1}{2}(16)(5) = 40$

GEOMETRY

Similar Triangles

If two triangles are said to be similar, their corresponding angles are equal, and their corresponding sides are proportional. If two triangles have three of the same angles, they are similar. Look at the two similar triangles below.

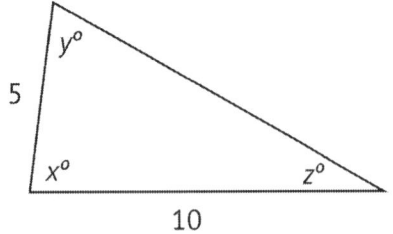 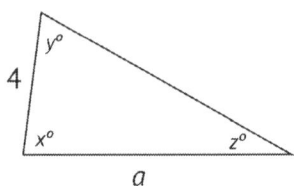

In the two triangles, the 5 corresponds to the 4 and the 10 corresponds to the *a*. In order to solve for *a*, we can set up a ratio.

$$\frac{5}{4} = \frac{10}{a}$$
$5a = 40$
$a = 8$

Special Triangles

There are three types of special triangles that you might see on the exam. They are the isosceles triangle, equilateral triangle, and the right triangle.

In an **isosceles triangle,** two sides are equal. Additionally, the angles opposite to the equal sides are equal.

In an **equilateral triangle**, all three sides are equal. All interior angles also have the same measurement. If all angles are equal, and a triangle has 180°, all equilateral triangles have angles that each measure at 60°.

In a right triangle, there is one angle that measures 90°. All right triangles have two acute angles and the right angle. The sides opposite to the acute angle are known as legs. The **hypotenuse** is the side opposite to the right angle.

GEOMETRY

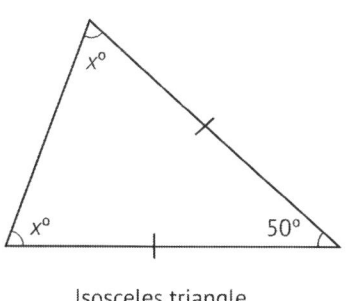
Isosceles triangle

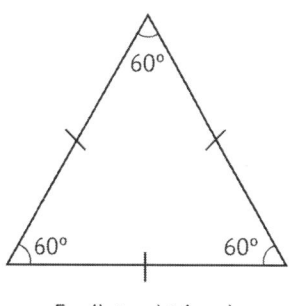
Equilateral triangle

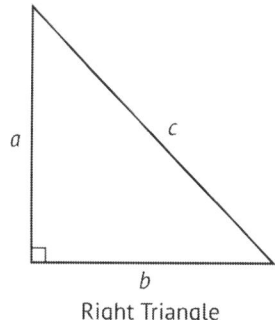
Right Triangle

The **Pythagorean Theorem** is a theorem that works only with right triangles. This rule states that the sum of the square of the legs is equal to the hypotenuse squared. This can be shown by the equation:

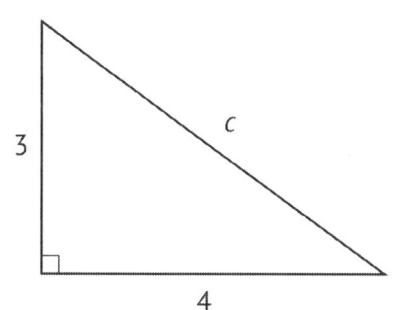

$$a^2 + b^2 = c^2$$

$$3^2 + 4^2 = c^2$$
$$9 + 16 = c^2$$
$$25 = c^2$$
$$c = 5$$

Quadrilaterals

A **quadrilateral** is any shape that has four sides. To find the perimeter of any quadrilateral, add up the lengths of the four sides.

A **rectangle** is a special form of quadrilateral where there are four right angles, and opposite sides are parallel to each other. A rectangle, is also a special type of parallelogram, which is a quadrilateral that has opposite sides that are parallel to each other. In a rectangle, opposite sides also have the same length.

The area of a rectangle is equal to the length times width, or $A = lw$. The perimeter is equal to $2(l + w)$.

GEOMETRY

A **square** is a special type of rectangle that has four equal side lengths. For a square, the area is equal to one side squared, or $A = s^2$ where s stands for the length of one side.

The perimeter of a square is simply equal to 4 times s, or $4s$ because all sides have the same length, and $s + s + s + s = 4s$.

Circles

A circle is a shape in which all points in a plane are of equal distance from a center. In the figure below, C represents the center of the circle.

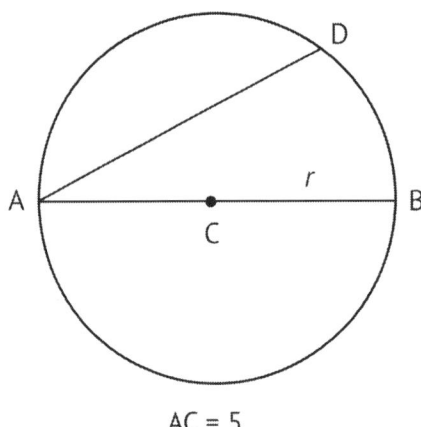

AC = 5

In the diagram, the **radius**, r, is the distance from the center to any point on the circle. Every radii in the circle has equal lengths. Think of it this way; let's say you had a rope of 5 feet tied to a pole. If you rotate the rope around the pole, you would outline a circle, with a radius of 5 feet. The length of the rope does not change, so all radii in a circle are equal. In the diagram above, CB, and AC, can both represent a radius.

GEOMETRY

A **diameter**, d, is the distance of a line that passes through the center. Any line that passes through the center is a diameter. All diameters have the same distance, and are equal to 2 times the radius. AB represents a diameter in the circle.

A **chord** is any line segment that attaches to two points on the circle. In the diagram, AD is a chord. The diameter is a special type of chord that passes through the center of the circle.

The **area** of a circle is equal to π multiplied by the square of the radius, r^2. This simplifies to $A = \pi r^2$. In the circle above, since AC is a radius and it equals 5, the area is $\pi(25)$ or 25π.

The **circumference** of a circle is the distance around the circle. The circumference is equal to πd, or 2πr since the diameter is equal to twice the radius.

HSPT
PRACTICE TESTS

ARGO BROTHERS

EXAM 1
HSPT

ARGO BROTHERS

To calculate your score and watch video tutorials, visit
our web site: www.einstein-academy.com/catholic

HSPT PRACTICE TEST 1
ANSWER SHEET

Verbal Skills (Part I)

1. Ⓐ Ⓑ Ⓒ Ⓓ
2. Ⓐ Ⓑ Ⓒ Ⓓ
3. Ⓐ Ⓑ Ⓒ Ⓓ
4. Ⓐ Ⓑ Ⓒ Ⓓ
5. Ⓐ Ⓑ Ⓒ Ⓓ
6. Ⓐ Ⓑ Ⓒ Ⓓ
7. Ⓐ Ⓑ Ⓒ Ⓓ
8. Ⓐ Ⓑ Ⓒ Ⓓ
9. Ⓐ Ⓑ Ⓒ Ⓓ
10. Ⓐ Ⓑ Ⓒ Ⓓ
11. Ⓐ Ⓑ Ⓒ Ⓓ
12. Ⓐ Ⓑ Ⓒ Ⓓ
13. Ⓐ Ⓑ Ⓒ Ⓓ
14. Ⓐ Ⓑ Ⓒ Ⓓ
15. Ⓐ Ⓑ Ⓒ Ⓓ
16. Ⓐ Ⓑ Ⓒ Ⓓ
17. Ⓐ Ⓑ Ⓒ Ⓓ
18. Ⓐ Ⓑ Ⓒ Ⓓ
19. Ⓐ Ⓑ Ⓒ Ⓓ
20. Ⓐ Ⓑ Ⓒ Ⓓ
21. Ⓐ Ⓑ Ⓒ Ⓓ
22. Ⓐ Ⓑ Ⓒ Ⓓ
23. Ⓐ Ⓑ Ⓒ Ⓓ
24. Ⓐ Ⓑ Ⓒ Ⓓ
25. Ⓐ Ⓑ Ⓒ Ⓓ
26. Ⓐ Ⓑ Ⓒ Ⓓ
27. Ⓐ Ⓑ Ⓒ Ⓓ
28. Ⓐ Ⓑ Ⓒ Ⓓ
29. Ⓐ Ⓑ Ⓒ Ⓓ
30. Ⓐ Ⓑ Ⓒ Ⓓ
31. Ⓐ Ⓑ Ⓒ Ⓓ
33. Ⓐ Ⓑ Ⓒ Ⓓ
33. Ⓐ Ⓑ Ⓒ Ⓓ
34. Ⓐ Ⓑ Ⓒ Ⓓ
35. Ⓐ Ⓑ Ⓒ Ⓓ
36. Ⓐ Ⓑ Ⓒ Ⓓ
37. Ⓐ Ⓑ Ⓒ Ⓓ
38. Ⓐ Ⓑ Ⓒ Ⓓ
39. Ⓐ Ⓑ Ⓒ Ⓓ
40. Ⓐ Ⓑ Ⓒ Ⓓ
41. Ⓐ Ⓑ Ⓒ Ⓓ
42. Ⓐ Ⓑ Ⓒ Ⓓ
43. Ⓐ Ⓑ Ⓒ Ⓓ
44. Ⓐ Ⓑ Ⓒ Ⓓ
45. Ⓐ Ⓑ Ⓒ Ⓓ
46. Ⓐ Ⓑ Ⓒ Ⓓ
47. Ⓐ Ⓑ Ⓒ Ⓓ
48. Ⓐ Ⓑ Ⓒ Ⓓ
49. Ⓐ Ⓑ Ⓒ Ⓓ
50. Ⓐ Ⓑ Ⓒ Ⓓ
51. Ⓐ Ⓑ Ⓒ Ⓓ
52. Ⓐ Ⓑ Ⓒ Ⓓ
53. Ⓐ Ⓑ Ⓒ Ⓓ
54. Ⓐ Ⓑ Ⓒ Ⓓ
55. Ⓐ Ⓑ Ⓒ Ⓓ
56. Ⓐ Ⓑ Ⓒ Ⓓ
57. Ⓐ Ⓑ Ⓒ Ⓓ
58. Ⓐ Ⓑ Ⓒ Ⓓ
59. Ⓐ Ⓑ Ⓒ Ⓓ
60. Ⓐ Ⓑ Ⓒ Ⓓ

Quantitative (Part II)

61. Ⓐ Ⓑ Ⓒ Ⓓ
62. Ⓐ Ⓑ Ⓒ Ⓓ
63. Ⓐ Ⓑ Ⓒ Ⓓ
64. Ⓐ Ⓑ Ⓒ Ⓓ
65. Ⓐ Ⓑ Ⓒ Ⓓ
66. Ⓐ Ⓑ Ⓒ Ⓓ
67. Ⓐ Ⓑ Ⓒ Ⓓ
68. Ⓐ Ⓑ Ⓒ Ⓓ
69. Ⓐ Ⓑ Ⓒ Ⓓ
70. Ⓐ Ⓑ Ⓒ Ⓓ
71. Ⓐ Ⓑ Ⓒ Ⓓ
72. Ⓐ Ⓑ Ⓒ Ⓓ
73. Ⓐ Ⓑ Ⓒ Ⓓ
74. Ⓐ Ⓑ Ⓒ Ⓓ
75. Ⓐ Ⓑ Ⓒ Ⓓ
76. Ⓐ Ⓑ Ⓒ Ⓓ
77. Ⓐ Ⓑ Ⓒ Ⓓ
78. Ⓐ Ⓑ Ⓒ Ⓓ
79. Ⓐ Ⓑ Ⓒ Ⓓ
80. Ⓐ Ⓑ Ⓒ Ⓓ
81. Ⓐ Ⓑ Ⓒ Ⓓ
82. Ⓐ Ⓑ Ⓒ Ⓓ
83. Ⓐ Ⓑ Ⓒ Ⓓ
84. Ⓐ Ⓑ Ⓒ Ⓓ
85. Ⓐ Ⓑ Ⓒ Ⓓ
86. Ⓐ Ⓑ Ⓒ Ⓓ
87. Ⓐ Ⓑ Ⓒ Ⓓ
88. Ⓐ Ⓑ Ⓒ Ⓓ
89. Ⓐ Ⓑ Ⓒ Ⓓ
90. Ⓐ Ⓑ Ⓒ Ⓓ
91. Ⓐ Ⓑ Ⓒ Ⓓ
92. Ⓐ Ⓑ Ⓒ Ⓓ
93. Ⓐ Ⓑ Ⓒ Ⓓ
94. Ⓐ Ⓑ Ⓒ Ⓓ
95. Ⓐ Ⓑ Ⓒ Ⓓ
96. Ⓐ Ⓑ Ⓒ Ⓓ
97. Ⓐ Ⓑ Ⓒ Ⓓ
98. Ⓐ Ⓑ Ⓒ Ⓓ
99. Ⓐ Ⓑ Ⓒ Ⓓ
100. Ⓐ Ⓑ Ⓒ Ⓓ
101. Ⓐ Ⓑ Ⓒ Ⓓ
102. Ⓐ Ⓑ Ⓒ Ⓓ
103. Ⓐ Ⓑ Ⓒ Ⓓ
104. Ⓐ Ⓑ Ⓒ Ⓓ
105. Ⓐ Ⓑ Ⓒ Ⓓ
106. Ⓐ Ⓑ Ⓒ Ⓓ
107. Ⓐ Ⓑ Ⓒ Ⓓ
108. Ⓐ Ⓑ Ⓒ Ⓓ
109. Ⓐ Ⓑ Ⓒ Ⓓ
110. Ⓐ Ⓑ Ⓒ Ⓓ
111. Ⓐ Ⓑ Ⓒ Ⓓ
112. Ⓐ Ⓑ Ⓒ Ⓓ

Reading (Part III)

113. Ⓐ Ⓑ Ⓒ Ⓓ
114. Ⓐ Ⓑ Ⓒ Ⓓ
115. Ⓐ Ⓑ Ⓒ Ⓓ
116. Ⓐ Ⓑ Ⓒ Ⓓ
117. Ⓐ Ⓑ Ⓒ Ⓓ
118. Ⓐ Ⓑ Ⓒ Ⓓ
119. Ⓐ Ⓑ Ⓒ Ⓓ
120. Ⓐ Ⓑ Ⓒ Ⓓ
121. Ⓐ Ⓑ Ⓒ Ⓓ
122. Ⓐ Ⓑ Ⓒ Ⓓ
123. Ⓐ Ⓑ Ⓒ Ⓓ
124. Ⓐ Ⓑ Ⓒ Ⓓ
125. Ⓐ Ⓑ Ⓒ Ⓓ
126. Ⓐ Ⓑ Ⓒ Ⓓ
127. Ⓐ Ⓑ Ⓒ Ⓓ
128. Ⓐ Ⓑ Ⓒ Ⓓ
129. Ⓐ Ⓑ Ⓒ Ⓓ
130. Ⓐ Ⓑ Ⓒ Ⓓ
131. Ⓐ Ⓑ Ⓒ Ⓓ
132. Ⓐ Ⓑ Ⓒ Ⓓ
133. Ⓐ Ⓑ Ⓒ Ⓓ
134. Ⓐ Ⓑ Ⓒ Ⓓ
135. Ⓐ Ⓑ Ⓒ Ⓓ
136. Ⓐ Ⓑ Ⓒ Ⓓ
137. Ⓐ Ⓑ Ⓒ Ⓓ
138. Ⓐ Ⓑ Ⓒ Ⓓ
139. Ⓐ Ⓑ Ⓒ Ⓓ
140. Ⓐ Ⓑ Ⓒ Ⓓ
141. Ⓐ Ⓑ Ⓒ Ⓓ
142. Ⓐ Ⓑ Ⓒ Ⓓ
143. Ⓐ Ⓑ Ⓒ Ⓓ
144. Ⓐ Ⓑ Ⓒ Ⓓ
145. Ⓐ Ⓑ Ⓒ Ⓓ
146. Ⓐ Ⓑ Ⓒ Ⓓ
147. Ⓐ Ⓑ Ⓒ Ⓓ
148. Ⓐ Ⓑ Ⓒ Ⓓ
149. Ⓐ Ⓑ Ⓒ Ⓓ
150. Ⓐ Ⓑ Ⓒ Ⓓ
151. Ⓐ Ⓑ Ⓒ Ⓓ
152. Ⓐ Ⓑ Ⓒ Ⓓ
153. Ⓐ Ⓑ Ⓒ Ⓓ
154. Ⓐ Ⓑ Ⓒ Ⓓ
155. Ⓐ Ⓑ Ⓒ Ⓓ
156. Ⓐ Ⓑ Ⓒ Ⓓ
157. Ⓐ Ⓑ Ⓒ Ⓓ
158. Ⓐ Ⓑ Ⓒ Ⓓ
159. Ⓐ Ⓑ Ⓒ Ⓓ
160. Ⓐ Ⓑ Ⓒ Ⓓ
161. Ⓐ Ⓑ Ⓒ Ⓓ
162. Ⓐ Ⓑ Ⓒ Ⓓ
163. Ⓐ Ⓑ Ⓒ Ⓓ
164. Ⓐ Ⓑ Ⓒ Ⓓ
165. Ⓐ Ⓑ Ⓒ Ⓓ
166. Ⓐ Ⓑ Ⓒ Ⓓ
167. Ⓐ Ⓑ Ⓒ Ⓓ
168. Ⓐ Ⓑ Ⓒ Ⓓ
169. Ⓐ Ⓑ Ⓒ Ⓓ
170. Ⓐ Ⓑ Ⓒ Ⓓ
171. Ⓐ Ⓑ Ⓒ Ⓓ
172. Ⓐ Ⓑ Ⓒ Ⓓ
173. Ⓐ Ⓑ Ⓒ Ⓓ
174. Ⓐ Ⓑ Ⓒ Ⓓ

ARGO BROTHERS

To calculate your score and watch
video tutorials, visit our web site:
www.einstein-academy.com/catholic

HSPT PRACTICE TEST 1
ANSWER SHEET

Mathematics (Part IV)

175. Ⓐ Ⓑ Ⓒ Ⓓ
176. Ⓐ Ⓑ Ⓒ Ⓓ
177. Ⓐ Ⓑ Ⓒ Ⓓ
178. Ⓐ Ⓑ Ⓒ Ⓓ
179. Ⓐ Ⓑ Ⓒ Ⓓ
180. Ⓐ Ⓑ Ⓒ Ⓓ
181. Ⓐ Ⓑ Ⓒ Ⓓ
182. Ⓐ Ⓑ Ⓒ Ⓓ
183. Ⓐ Ⓑ Ⓒ Ⓓ
184. Ⓐ Ⓑ Ⓒ Ⓓ
185. Ⓐ Ⓑ Ⓒ Ⓓ
186. Ⓐ Ⓑ Ⓒ Ⓓ
187. Ⓐ Ⓑ Ⓒ Ⓓ
188. Ⓐ Ⓑ Ⓒ Ⓓ
189. Ⓐ Ⓑ Ⓒ Ⓓ
190. Ⓐ Ⓑ Ⓒ Ⓓ
191. Ⓐ Ⓑ Ⓒ Ⓓ
192. Ⓐ Ⓑ Ⓒ Ⓓ
193. Ⓐ Ⓑ Ⓒ Ⓓ
194. Ⓐ Ⓑ Ⓒ Ⓓ
195. Ⓐ Ⓑ Ⓒ Ⓓ
196. Ⓐ Ⓑ Ⓒ Ⓓ
197. Ⓐ Ⓑ Ⓒ Ⓓ
198. Ⓐ Ⓑ Ⓒ Ⓓ
199. Ⓐ Ⓑ Ⓒ Ⓓ
200. Ⓐ Ⓑ Ⓒ Ⓓ
201. Ⓐ Ⓑ Ⓒ Ⓓ
202. Ⓐ Ⓑ Ⓒ Ⓓ
203. Ⓐ Ⓑ Ⓒ Ⓓ
204. Ⓐ Ⓑ Ⓒ Ⓓ
205. Ⓐ Ⓑ Ⓒ Ⓓ
206. Ⓐ Ⓑ Ⓒ Ⓓ
207. Ⓐ Ⓑ Ⓒ Ⓓ
208. Ⓐ Ⓑ Ⓒ Ⓓ
209. Ⓐ Ⓑ Ⓒ Ⓓ
210. Ⓐ Ⓑ Ⓒ Ⓓ
211. Ⓐ Ⓑ Ⓒ Ⓓ
212. Ⓐ Ⓑ Ⓒ Ⓓ
213. Ⓐ Ⓑ Ⓒ Ⓓ
214. Ⓐ Ⓑ Ⓒ Ⓓ
215. Ⓐ Ⓑ Ⓒ Ⓓ
216. Ⓐ Ⓑ Ⓒ Ⓓ
217. Ⓐ Ⓑ Ⓒ Ⓓ
218. Ⓐ Ⓑ Ⓒ Ⓓ
219. Ⓐ Ⓑ Ⓒ Ⓓ
220. Ⓐ Ⓑ Ⓒ Ⓓ
221. Ⓐ Ⓑ Ⓒ Ⓓ
222. Ⓐ Ⓑ Ⓒ Ⓓ
223. Ⓐ Ⓑ Ⓒ Ⓓ
224. Ⓐ Ⓑ Ⓒ Ⓓ
225. Ⓐ Ⓑ Ⓒ Ⓓ
226. Ⓐ Ⓑ Ⓒ Ⓓ
227. Ⓐ Ⓑ Ⓒ Ⓓ
228. Ⓐ Ⓑ Ⓒ Ⓓ
229. Ⓐ Ⓑ Ⓒ Ⓓ
230. Ⓐ Ⓑ Ⓒ Ⓓ
231. Ⓐ Ⓑ Ⓒ Ⓓ
232. Ⓐ Ⓑ Ⓒ Ⓓ
233. Ⓐ Ⓑ Ⓒ Ⓓ
234. Ⓐ Ⓑ Ⓒ Ⓓ
235. Ⓐ Ⓑ Ⓒ Ⓓ
236. Ⓐ Ⓑ Ⓒ Ⓓ
237. Ⓐ Ⓑ Ⓒ Ⓓ
238. Ⓐ Ⓑ Ⓒ Ⓓ

Language (Part V)

239. Ⓐ Ⓑ Ⓒ Ⓓ
240. Ⓐ Ⓑ Ⓒ Ⓓ
241. Ⓐ Ⓑ Ⓒ Ⓓ
242. Ⓐ Ⓑ Ⓒ Ⓓ
243. Ⓐ Ⓑ Ⓒ Ⓓ
244. Ⓐ Ⓑ Ⓒ Ⓓ
245. Ⓐ Ⓑ Ⓒ Ⓓ
246. Ⓐ Ⓑ Ⓒ Ⓓ
247. Ⓐ Ⓑ Ⓒ Ⓓ
248. Ⓐ Ⓑ Ⓒ Ⓓ
249. Ⓐ Ⓑ Ⓒ Ⓓ
250. Ⓐ Ⓑ Ⓒ Ⓓ
251. Ⓐ Ⓑ Ⓒ Ⓓ
252. Ⓐ Ⓑ Ⓒ Ⓓ
253. Ⓐ Ⓑ Ⓒ Ⓓ
254. Ⓐ Ⓑ Ⓒ Ⓓ
255. Ⓐ Ⓑ Ⓒ Ⓓ
256. Ⓐ Ⓑ Ⓒ Ⓓ
257. Ⓐ Ⓑ Ⓒ Ⓓ
258. Ⓐ Ⓑ Ⓒ Ⓓ
259. Ⓐ Ⓑ Ⓒ Ⓓ
260. Ⓐ Ⓑ Ⓒ Ⓓ
261. Ⓐ Ⓑ Ⓒ Ⓓ
262. Ⓐ Ⓑ Ⓒ Ⓓ
263. Ⓐ Ⓑ Ⓒ Ⓓ
264. Ⓐ Ⓑ Ⓒ Ⓓ
265. Ⓐ Ⓑ Ⓒ Ⓓ
266. Ⓐ Ⓑ Ⓒ Ⓓ
267. Ⓐ Ⓑ Ⓒ Ⓓ
268. Ⓐ Ⓑ Ⓒ Ⓓ
269. Ⓐ Ⓑ Ⓒ Ⓓ
270. Ⓐ Ⓑ Ⓒ Ⓓ
271. Ⓐ Ⓑ Ⓒ Ⓓ
272. Ⓐ Ⓑ Ⓒ Ⓓ
273. Ⓐ Ⓑ Ⓒ Ⓓ
274. Ⓐ Ⓑ Ⓒ Ⓓ
275. Ⓐ Ⓑ Ⓒ Ⓓ
276. Ⓐ Ⓑ Ⓒ Ⓓ
277. Ⓐ Ⓑ Ⓒ Ⓓ
278.. Ⓐ Ⓑ Ⓒ Ⓓ
279 Ⓐ Ⓑ Ⓒ Ⓓ
280. Ⓐ Ⓑ Ⓒ Ⓓ
281. Ⓐ Ⓑ Ⓒ Ⓓ
282. Ⓐ Ⓑ Ⓒ Ⓓ
283. Ⓐ Ⓑ Ⓒ Ⓓ
284. Ⓐ Ⓑ Ⓒ Ⓓ
285. Ⓐ Ⓑ Ⓒ Ⓓ
286. Ⓐ Ⓑ Ⓒ Ⓓ
287. Ⓐ Ⓑ Ⓒ Ⓓ
288. Ⓐ Ⓑ Ⓒ Ⓓ
289 Ⓐ Ⓑ Ⓒ Ⓓ
290. Ⓐ Ⓑ Ⓒ Ⓓ
291. Ⓐ Ⓑ Ⓒ Ⓓ
292. Ⓐ Ⓑ Ⓒ Ⓓ
293. Ⓐ Ⓑ Ⓒ Ⓓ
294. Ⓐ Ⓑ Ⓒ Ⓓ
295. Ⓐ Ⓑ Ⓒ Ⓓ
296. Ⓐ Ⓑ Ⓒ Ⓓ
297. Ⓐ Ⓑ Ⓒ Ⓓ
298. Ⓐ Ⓑ Ⓒ Ⓓ

ARGO BROTHERS

To calculate your score and watch
video tutorials, visit our web site:
www.einstein-academy.com/catholic

VERBAL SKILLS
PART I (16 MIN)

DIRECTIONS: For questions 1-60, follow the directions and choose the best answer.

1. Which word does *not* belong with the others?

   A. lilly
   B. rose
   C. orchid
   D. stem

2. Which word does *not* belong with the others?

   A. yard
   B. meter
   C. gram
   D. inch

3. Marker is to whiteboard as chalk is to

   A. paper
   B. blackboard
   C. clipboard
   D. glass

4. Harry runs faster than Marry. Barry runs slower than Harry. Barry runs faster than Marry. If the first two statements are true, the third is

   A. true
   B. false
   C. uncertain

5. A haughty person is

   A. humble
   B. easy-going
   C. friendly
   D. arrogant

6. Bookbag is to school as luggage is to

   A. museum
   B. aquarium
   C. airport
   D. supermarket

7. Which word does *not* belong with the others?

   A. distinct
   B. beautiful
   C. unique
   D. exceptional

8. Bricks are to house as pages are to

   A. book
   B. letters
   C. sentences
   D. words

CONTINUE ON TO THE NEXT PAGE ➡

61

VERBAL SKILLS
PART I

9. Which word does *not* belong with the others?

   A. USA
   B. South America
   C. Antarctica
   D. Australia

10. <u>Derogatory</u> most nearly means

    A. difficult
    B. offensive
    C. hinder
    D. elongate

11. <u>Candid</u> most nearly means

    A. straightforward
    B. deceitful
    C. patriotic
    D. nonchalant

12. Gym is to weights as aquatic center is to

    A. swimming
    B. pool
    C. diving board
    D. rescue tubes

13. Which word does *not* belong with the others?

    A. building
    B. corporation
    C. company
    D. business

14. Cub is to lion as tadpole is to

    A. amphibian
    B. reptile
    C. animal
    D. frog

15. Shark is to teeth as elephant is to

    A. trunk
    B. feet
    C. eyes
    D. tail

16. Chicken has more protein than turkey but less than egg whites. Turkey has more protein than fish. Egg whites have more protein than fish. If the first two statements are true, the third is

    A. true
    B. false
    C. uncertain

CONTINUE ON TO THE NEXT PAGE ➡

VERBAL SKILLS
PART I

17. To be <u>eloquent</u> is to be

    A. fatigued
    B. articulate
    C. petrified
    D. surprised

18. <u>Auspicious</u> most nearly means

    A. opportune
    B. brave
    C. fastidious
    D. worried

19. To be <u>meticulous</u> is to be

    A. sloppy
    B. carefree
    C. diligent
    D. healthy

20. Boat is to water as car is to

    A. exhaust pipe
    B. steering wheel
    C. road
    D. oil

21. Stroke is to painting as word is to

    A. sound
    B. essay
    C. apology
    D. movie

22. <u>Laborious</u> most closely means

    A. gigantic
    B. spoiled
    C. enhanced
    D. taxing

23. All bananas are fruits. No fruits are vegetables. Some bananas are vegetables. If the first two statements are true, the third is

    A. true
    B. false
    C. uncertain

24. Which word does not belong with the others?

    A. biology
    B. physics
    C. history
    D. chemistry

CONTINUE ON TO THE NEXT PAGE ➡

63

VERBAL SKILLS
PART I

25. To be <u>muffled</u> means to be

    A. quiet
    B. chatty
    C. congruent
    D. favorable

26. W is south of X. Y is north of X. Y is north of W. If the first two statements are true, the third is

    A. true
    B. false
    C. uncertain

27. To be <u>pompous</u> means to be

    A. loud
    B. condescending
    C. savvy
    D. untalkative

28. To be <u>ambiguous</u> means to be

    A. lucid
    B. clear
    C. obscure
    D. certain

29. Desert is to sand as rainforest is to

    A. insects
    B. precipitation
    C. trees
    D. animals

30. <u>Malevolent</u> most closely means

    A. evil
    B. vibrant
    C. dynamic
    D. volatile

31. Affluent means the *opposite* of

    A. prosperous
    B. weak
    C. poor
    D. react

32. Which word does *not* belong with the others?

    A. doctor
    B. nurse
    C. patient
    D. psychiatrist

CONTINUE ON TO THE NEXT PAGE ➡

VERBAL SKILLS
PART I

33. Which word does *not* belong with the others?

   A. anger
   B. hard-working
   C. love
   D. remorse

34. Benign means the *opposite* of

   A. reverse
   B. hostile
   C. calm
   D. uncertain

35. Lake A is larger than lake B. Lake C is larger than lake B. Lake C is larger than lake A. If the first two statements are true, the third is

   A. true
   B. false
   C. uncertain

36. Dexterous means the *opposite* of

   A. clumsy
   B. react
   C. gather
   D. talented

37. To be zealous means to be

   A. apathathetic
   B. unapologetic
   C. indifferent
   D. passionate

38. Abundant means the *opposite* of

   A. bulky
   B. sophisticated
   C. scarce
   D. limitless

39. Potent means the *opposite* of

   A. weak
   B. uncertain
   C. shallow
   D. change

40. Which word does *not* belong with the others?

   A. student
   B. teacher
   C. school
   D. principal

CONTINUE ON TO THE NEXT PAGE ➡

VERBAL SKILLS
PART I

41. Which word does *not* belong with the others?

   A. nose
   B. eyes
   C. leg
   D. mouth

42. Jenny finished the race before Jack but not before Jordy. Janice finished the race after Jordy but before Jenny. Janice finished the race before Jack. If the first two statements are true, the third is

   A. true
   B. false
   C. uncertain

43. Which word does *not* belong with the others?

   A. chalk
   B. pen
   C. paper
   D. marker

44. Narcissistic most closely means

   A. whimsical
   B. egotistical
   C. frugal
   D. basic

45. Immaculate means the *opposite* of

   A. flexible
   B. maintain
   C. dirty
   D. obey

46. A lump is more than a hunk. A hunk is less than a bunch but more than a piece. A piece is more than a lump. If the first two statements are true, the third is

   A. true
   B. false
   C. uncertain

47. Repugnant means the *opposite* of

   A. attractive
   B. insane
   C. horrendous
   D. decrease

48. Retain means the *opposite* of

   A. retrieve
   B. discard
   C. associate
   D. fond

CONTINUE ON TO THE NEXT PAGE ➡

VERBAL SKILLS
PART I

49. Joseph is taller than Mike. Candice is taller than Mike. Joseph is taller than Candice. If the first two statements are true, the third is

A. true
C. false
D. uncertain

50. Robert can spell better than Matt. Dylan can spell better than Jackie but not better than Robert. Robert can spell better than Jackie. If the first two statements are true, the third is

A. true
B. false
C. uncertain

51. Sensible means the *opposite* of

A. giving
B. well-thought-out
C. foolish
D. unbelievable

52. Which word does *not* belong with the others?

A. sun
B. lamp
C. candle
D. flashlight

53. Which word does *not* belong with the others?

A. car
B. boat
C. truck
D. motorcycle

54. To be impetuous means to be

A. cautious
B. callous
C. impulsive
D. pessimistic

55. Initiate means the *opposite* of

A. promote
B. careful
C. sense
D. cease

56. Nemesis means the *opposite* of

A. friend
B. boss
C. illusion
D. tough

CONTINUE ON TO THE NEXT PAGE ➡

VERBAL SKILLS
PART I

57. Couch is to living room as refrigerator is to

   A. dining room
   B. bedroom
   C. oyer
   D. kitchen

58. Frivolous most closely means

   A. silly
   B. active
   C. powerful
   D. vulgar

59. Which word does *not* belong with the others?

   A. fragile
   B. flimsy
   C. tenuous
   D. brawny

60. Which word does *not* belong with the others?

   A. guitar
   B. keyboard
   C. harp
   D. violin

CONTINUE ON TO THE NEXT PAGE ➡

QUANTITATIVE
PART II (45 MIN)

DIRECTIONS: For questions 61-112, choose the best answer that fits the problem.

---

61. What is 2 more than 20% of 80?

  A. 6
  B. 42
  C. 4
  D. 18

---

62. What number is 6 more than $\frac{2}{3}$ of 27?

  A. 22
  B. 19
  C. 15
  D. 24

---

63. 67, 63, 60, 56, __, 49...
What is the missing number in the series above?

  A. 53
  B. 52
  C. 50
  D. 55

---

64. Examine (A), (B), and (C) and find the best answer.

(A) 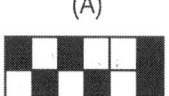 (B)   (C)

  A. A is more shaded than B.
  B. C is less shaded than A and B.
  C. All three are shaded equally.
  D. None of the above.

---

65. Examine (A), (B), and (C) and find the best answer.

(A) 0.375

(B) $\frac{5}{7}$

(C) 0.35 • 3.22

  A. B is greater than A but less than C.
  B. B is greater than A and C.
  C. C is greater than A but less than B.
  D. C is greater than A which is equal to B.

CONTINUE ON TO THE NEXT PAGE ➡

QUANTITATIVE
PART II

66. Examine (A), (B), and (C) and find the best answer.

(A) 3^3
(B) 4^2
(C) 2^5

A. B > A > C
B. C > A > B
C. A > B > C
D. C = A > B

67. Look at this series: 45, 55, 64, 72, 79... What number should come next?

A. 86
B. 80
C. 85
D. 83

68. Look at this series: 0.25, 0.50, 0.75 ... What number should come next?

A. 0.1
B. 0.90
C. 1.00
D. 1.001

69. What number divided by 5 is $\frac{1}{4}$ of 100 ?

A. 120
B. 25
C. 125
D. 625

70. Examine (A), (B), and (C) and find the best answer if a is less than b and both are greater than 0.

(A) $6(b - a)$
(B) $6a - 6b$
(C) $6(a - b)$

A. All three are equal.
B. A is smaller than B and C.
C. B and C are equal and smaller than A.
D. C is greater than A and B.

71. 125, 64, 27, __, 1...
What is the missing number in the series above?

A. 16
B. 8
C. 9
D. 25

CONTINUE ON TO THE NEXT PAGE ➡

QUANTITATIVE
PART II

72. Examine the triangle and find the best answer.

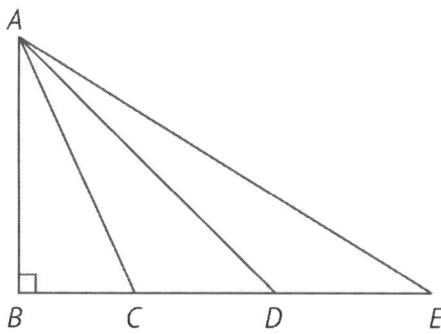

- **A.** $\overline{AC}$ is greater than $\overline{AD}$
- **B.** $\overline{BA}$ and $\overline{AE}$ are each less than $\overline{AD}$.
- **C.** $\overline{AE}$ is the greatest
- **D.** $\overline{AC}$ plus $\overline{AD}$ equals $\overline{AE}$.

---

73. Look at this series: N36, Q30, T24, W18... What comes next?

- **A.** X15
- **B.** Z12
- **C.** Z6
- **D.** Y12

---

74. Look at this series: 1, 3, 5, 8, 11, 15, 19, 24, 29... What number should come next?

- **A.** 35
- **B.** 34
- **C.** 33
- **D.** 30

---

75. Examine (A), (B), and (C) and choose the best answer

(A) 3(5 - 8)
(B) 6(5) - 36
(C) $3(1-2)^2$

- **A.** B is the largest.
- **B.** B > C > A
- **C.** |A| > C > B
- **D.** A > B > C

---

76. $\frac{5}{6}$ of what number is 2 less than 8 times 4?

- **A.** 36
- **B.** 30
- **C.** 20
- **D.** 24

---

77. Examine (A), (B), and (C) and find the best answer

(A) $\frac{1}{6}$ of 36

(B) $\frac{1}{9}$ of 63

(C) $\frac{1}{3}$ of 21

- **A.** A is the greatest.
- **B.** B = C > A
- **C.** B = C < A
- **D.** C > B > A

CONTINUE ON TO THE NEXT PAGE ➡

QUANTITATIVE
PART II

78. Examine (A), (B), and (C) and find the best answer.

(A) ▭

(B) ▭

(C) ▭

A. A is bigger than B and C.
B. C is the smallest.
C. C is bigger than A and B.
D. B is bigger than A and C.

79. 6, 18, 5, 15, 3, 9, __, 21, 8, 24...
What is the missing number in the series above?

A. 4
B. 63
C. 27
D. 7

80. 1, 4, 9, 16, __, 36, 49...
What is the missing number in the series above?

A. 23
B. 20
C. 25
D. 21

81. Examine the triangle and find the best answer.

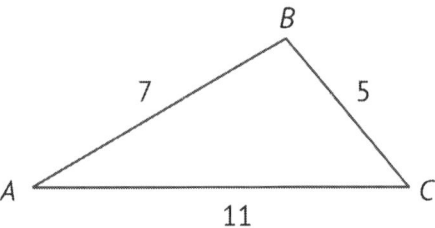

A. Angle C is the smallest.
B. Angle B > Angle C > Angle A
C. Angle C > Angle B > Angle A
D. Angle A = Angle C < Angle B

82. $\frac{1}{3}$ of what number is 7 times 2?

A. 21
B. 42
C. 63
D. 14

CONTINUE ON TO THE NEXT PAGE ➡

QUANTITATIVE
PART II

83. Examine (A), (B), and (C) and find the best answer.

(A) 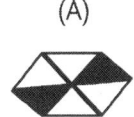   (B) 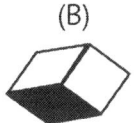   (C)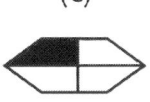

- **A.** C is more shaded than A and B.
- **B.** The three figures are shaded equally.
- **C.** C is less shaded than A and B.
- **D.** A is equally shaded as B and less than C.

84. What number divided by 6 leaves 2 more than 3?

- **A.** 30
- **B.** 36
- **C.** 12
- **D.** 6

85. Examine (A), (B), and (C) and find the best answer

(A) (4 • 6) - 7
(B) (5 • 9) + 2
(C) (5 • 10) - (5 • 2)

- **A.** C is the smallest.
- **B.** B is the largest.
- **C.** A is less than B, which is less than C.
- **D.** C is greater than B.

86. What number is 3 less than $\frac{2}{5}$ of 25?

- **A.** 12
- **B.** 9
- **C.** 13
- **D.** 7

87. What number subtracted from 20 leaves 2 more than $\frac{3}{4}$ of 16?

- **A.** 1
- **B.** 6
- **C.** 5
- **D.** 2

88. Examine (A), (B), and (C) and find the best answer

(A) 3^4
(B) 4^3
(C) (3 • 4)(4 • 3)

- **A.** A = B > C
- **B.** C > B = A
- **C.** C > B > A
- **D.** C > A > B

89. 43, 47, __, 55, 59 ...
What is the missing number in the series above?

- **A.** 51
- **B.** 53
- **C.** 57
- **D.** 52

CONTINUE ON TO THE NEXT PAGE ➡

QUANTITATIVE
PART II

90. Examine the pictograph and choose the answer choice that best fits.

(A) ☐ ☐ ☐ ▫
(B) ☐ ▫
(C) ☐ ☐ ☐ ☐
(D) ☐ ☐ ▫

☐ = 8 people
▫ = 4 people

A. A holds the most amount of people.
B. More people are in room C than in room B or D.
C. More people are in D than in A.
D. More people are in room D than either in C or A.

91. Look at this series: 2, 2, 4, 4, 8, 8, 16, 16, 32... What three numbers should come next?

A. 32, 64, 128
B. 32, 64, 64
C. 32, 32, 64
D. 32, 32, 128

92. The sum of 20% of a number and 70% of the same number is equal to 81. What is the number?

A. 99
B. 73
C. 90
D. 9

93. Examine (A), (B), (C), and (D) and find the best answer.

(A)   (B)   (C)   (D)
 +   ✱   ✶   ⚹

A. B has more spikes than combination of A and D.
B. Two times the spikes of D give the spikes of B.
C. The spikes of A and D add to B.
D. C has the most amount of spikes.

94. By how much does the average of 13, 88, 70, and 41 exceed the number 24?

A. 79
B. 54
C. 29
D. 24

95. What number subtracted from 80, leaves three more than $\frac{7}{8}$ of 64?

A. 56
B. 65
C. 22
D. 21

CONTINUE ON TO THE NEXT PAGE ➡

QUANTITATIVE
PART II

96. Examine (A), (B), and (C) and find the best answer

(A) 0.343
(B) .11 • 3.3
(C) $\frac{3}{9}$

A. A is greater than B.
B. C is greater than A
C. B > A > C
D. B = C

97. What number divided by 7 is $\frac{1}{4}$ of 36?

A. 81
B. 36
C. 9
D. 63

98. Examine (A), (B), and (C) and find the best answer

(A) $\frac{2}{5}$ of 40
(B) 60 %
(C) $\frac{3}{5}$ %

A. B = C
B. A is greater than B + C
C. A, B, are C are equal.
D. C is smaller than both A and B.

99. Examine (A), (B), and (C) and find the best answer.

(A) 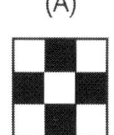 (B) 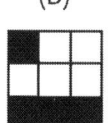 (C)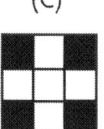

A. All are equally shaded.
B. B is more shaded than A or C.
C. C is equally shaded as A but more than B.
D. None of the above.

100. Look at this series: -7, -4, -2, -1...
What number should come next?

A. 2
B. 1
C. -1
D. 0

101. Look at this series:
98, 100, 96, 98, 94, 96, 92...
What number should come next?

A. 88
B. 96
C. 90
D. 94

CONTINUE ON TO THE NEXT PAGE ➡

QUANTITATIVE
PART II

102. Look at this series: 1, 0.3, 0.09, 0.027... What number should come next?

A. .081
B. .0081
C. 0.0027
D. 0.033

103. What number is 7 more than $\frac{5}{8}$ of 72?

A. 52
B. 38
C. 45
D. 104

104. What number divided by $\frac{2}{5}$ yields a quotient value of 10?

A. 25
B. 50
C. 4
D. 10

105. Look at this series: IV, IX, 14, XIX, XXIV, 29..... What should come next?

A. 39
B. XXXIX
C. XXXIV
D. 34

106. Look at this series:

$$\frac{5}{1}, \frac{5}{2}, \frac{5}{4}, \frac{5}{8}, \frac{5}{16} ....$$

What number should come next?

A. $\frac{5}{36}$
B. $\frac{5}{32}$
C. $\frac{10}{32}$
D. $\frac{5}{64}$

107. Examine the figure and find the best answer.

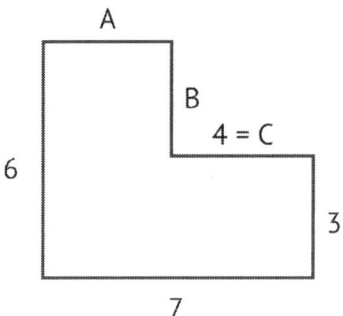

A. C < A = B
B. A = B = C
C. C = A > B
D. A = B < C

CONTINUE ON TO THE NEXT PAGE ➡

QUANTITATIVE
PART II

108. Look at this series: 11, 12, 14, 17, 21...
What number should come next?

- A. 25
- B. 26
- C. 32
- D. 24

109. If $\frac{3}{11}$ of a number is 9, then $33\frac{1}{3}\%$ of the number is

- A. 22
- B. 11
- C. 33
- D. 27

110. Look at this series:
22, 19, 21, 18, 20, 17, 19...
What three numbers should come next?

- A. 19, 18, 17
- B. 18, 16, 17
- C. 16, 18, 15
- D. 16, 19, 15

111. What number added to 10 is 4 times the product of 6 and 3?

- A. 28
- B. 72
- C. 62
- D. 82

112. What number increased by 20% of itself is 60?

- A. 30
- B. 40
- C. 70
- D. 50

CONTINUE ON TO THE NEXT PAGE ➡

READING
PART III (25 MIN)

DIRECTIONS: Read the passages below and pick the answer choices that fit accordingly. Fill in the appropriate letter on your answer sheet.

Questions 113-122 refer to the following passage.

Consider yourself in the following position: there is a railway trolley heading towards a group of five individuals who seemingly cannot get out of harm's way. The impact will most definitely lead to their imminent death, unless you decide to alter the direction of the trolley onto a different track with a switch. However, there is a single person tied to this set of tracks, and the trolley will end in his death. Most people would choose to flip the switch, as five lives have much greater weight than one. Now, think of the same scenario with a bit of a twist: there is no switch or other set of tracks, and in its place is a <u>morbidly</u> obese fat man on a cliff directly above the tracks. The bulk of the man would certainly stop the train, saving the five people from death, but would end in the <u>demise</u> of the fat man. If you were in that position, would you dare push the man, sacrificing one for five?

If you answered yes, congratulations; you may be a psychopath. The second part "trolley problem" described above is a psychological experiment that involves a much greater moral dilemma that affects the amygdala, the brain's "emotion center." As such, it's been found that most individuals would refuse to <u>heave</u> the man. Psychopaths, on the other hand, would be more than happy to push the hapless individual, without batting an eye. When analyzing the amygdala's processing of this situation, a normal person's would light up, whereas a psychopath's would remain in darkness.

This lack of emotion can actually at times be very beneficial in leadership positions, as it allows much more suitable and colder calculations. Famous psychopaths include King Henry VIII, Adolf Hitler, and even possibly former British Prime Minister Winston Churchill. In fact, many surgeons are considered to be psychopaths as well.

---

113. A good title for this passage would be

   A. The Trolley Incident
   B. Five or One?
   C. The Mind of a Psychopath
   D. The Amygdala

114. This passage can mostly likely be found in a

   A. science research paper
   B. psychology article
   C. history book
   D. fictional book

CONTINUE ON TO THE NEXT PAGE ➡

READING
PART III

115. The first paragraph of the passage discusses

   A. a moral scenario
   B. an outline of a trolley track
   C. psychopaths
   D. lever switches

116. The word <u>morbidly</u> most nearly means

   A. pleasantly
   B. healthily
   C. unusually
   D. unhealthily

117. The amygdala can control a person's

   A. decisions
   B. emotions
   C. sight
   D. brain

118. The word <u>heave</u> mostly nearly means

   A. lower
   B. run
   C. throw
   D. stop

119. It can be inferred that a psychopath's amygdala is

   A. superior
   B. flawed
   C. black
   D. emotional

120. The last paragraph describes

   A. famous individuals
   B. the usefulness of psychopathy
   C. surgeons
   D. calculations

121. The "moral dilemma" described in the passage is

   A. the graveness of killing someone
   B. flipping the switch
   C. being obese
   D. a dysfunctional amygdala

122. The word <u>demise</u> most nearly means

   A. death
   B. success
   C. rise
   D. failure

CONTINUE ON TO THE NEXT PAGE ➡

READING
PART III

Questions 123-132 refer to the following passage.

This passage is adapted from History of Phosphorus

It was a little late to search for the philosopher's' stone in 1669, yet it was in such a search that phosphorus was discovered. Wilhelm Homberg described it in the following manner: Brand, a man little known, of low birth, with a bizarre and mysterious nature in all he did, found this luminous matter while searching for something else. He was a glassmaker by profession, but he had abandoned it in order to be free for the pursuit of the philosophical stone with which he was <u>engrossed</u>. Having put it into his mind that the secret of the philosophical stone consisted in the preparation of urine, this man worked in all kinds of manners and for a very long time without finding anything. Finally, in the year 1669, after a strong distillation of urine, he found in the product a <u>luminous</u> matter that has since been called phosphorus."

Neither the name nor the phenomenon was really new. Organic phosphorescent materials were known to Aristotle, and a lithophosphorus was the subject of a book published in 1640, based on a discovery made by a shoemaker, Vicenzo Casciarolo on a mountain-side near Bologna in 1630. Johann Gottfried Leonhardi quotes a book of 1689 in which the author, Kletwich, claims that this phosphorus had already been known to Fernelius, the court physician of King Henri II of France.

To the same period belongs the "Ordinatio Alchid Bechil Saraceni philosophi," in which Ferdinand Hoefer found a distillation of urine with clay and carbonaceous material described, and the resulting product named escarbuncle. It would be worth looking for this source; although Bechil would still remain an entirely unsuccessful predecessor, it does seem strange that in all the distillations of <u>arbitrary</u> mixtures, the conditions should never before 1669 have been right for the formation and the observation of phosphorus.

---

123. According to the passage, who truly discovered phosphorous?

    A. Wilhelm Homberg
    B. Brand
    C. Fernelius
    D. Ferdinand

124. In the beginning of the second paragraph, what name is being referred?

    A. Aristotle
    B. Phosphorous
    C. Vicenzo Casciarolo
    D. Henri II

CONTINUE ON TO THE NEXT PAGE ➡

READING
PART III

125. The word <u>engrossed</u> most nearly means

- A. bored
- B. oblivious
- C. absorbed
- D. absent

126. The man Brand worked as a

- A. scientist
- B. glassmaker
- C. philosopher
- D. author

127. Which of the following is true?

- A. The discovery of phosphorus occurred through the distillation of urine.
- B. Phosphorous is considered to be a very dull material.
- C. It is certain that Fernelius discovered phosphorus in 1669.
- D. Phosphorous is in fact, the philosopher's stone.

128. The word <u>luminous</u> most nearly means

- A. glowing
- B. dull
- C. shiny
- D. mysterious

129. Lithophosphorous was discovered by

- A. Aristotle
- B. Brand
- C. a shoemaker
- D. Bechill

130. This passage can mostly likely be found in a

- A. science research paper
- B. personal journal
- C. philosophy book
- D. history book

131. According to the passage, the word <u>arbitrary</u> most nearly means

- A. same
- B. regular
- C. different
- D. logical

132. The man who discovered phosphorous was in fact looking to find

- A. lithophosphorous
- B. urine
- C. the philosopher's stone
- D. distillation

CONTINUE ON TO THE NEXT PAGE ➡

READING
PART III

Questions 133-142 refer to the following passage.

This passage is adapted from Forty-One Years in India

Forty years ago the departure of a cadet for India was a much more serious affair than it is at present. Under the regulation then, leave, except on medical certificate, could only be obtained once during the whole of an officer's service, and ten years had to be spent in India before that leave could be taken. Small wonder, then, that I felt as if I were bidding England farewell for ever when, on the 20th February, 1852, I set sail from Southampton with Calcutta for my destination. Steamers in those days ran to and from India but once a month, and the fleet employed was only capable of transporting some 2,400 passengers in the course of a year. This does not include the Cape route; but even taking that into consideration, I should doubt whether there were then as many travellers to India in a year as there are now in a fortnight at the busy season.

My ship was the Peninsular and Oriental Company's steamer *Ripon*, commanded by Captain Moresby, an ex-officer of the Indian Navy, in which he had earned distinction by his survey of the Red Sea. A few Addiscombe friends were on board, leaving England under the same depressing circumstances as myself, and what with wind and weather, and the thought that at the best we were bidding farewell to home and relations for ten long years, we were anything but a cheerful party for the first few days of the voyage. Youth and high spirits had, however, re-asserted themselves long before Alexandria, which place we reached without incident beyond the customary halts for coaling at Gibraltar and Malta. At Alexandria we bade <u>adieu</u> to Captain Moresby, who had been most kind and attentive, and whose graphic accounts of the difficulties he had had to overcome whilst mastering the navigation of the Red Sea served to while away many a <u>tedious</u> hour.

---

133. The author of the passage is most likely a

A. traveler
B. soldier
C. sailor
D. tradesman

134. The narrator of the story had to stay in India for a minimum of

A. forty-one years
B. ten years
C. one month
D. one year

CONTINUE ON TO THE NEXT PAGE ➡

READING
PART III

135. Every year, the maximum number of passengers the steamers could carry was

A. 2,000
B. 240
C. 2,400
D. 4,000

136. The name of the narrator's ship was the

A. Peninsular
B. Oriental Company
C. Southampton
D. Ripon

137. Captain Moresby was known for his work in

A. Calcutta
B. England
C. The Red Sea
D. Alexandria

138. In the passage, the word <u>adieu</u> most nearly means

A. farewell
B. removal
C. greeting
D. journey

139. A good title for this passage would be

A. Voyage to India
B. Homesick
C. New Friends in Calcutta
D. Captain Moresby's Ship

140. The word <u>tedious</u> most nearly means

A. tiring
B. easy
C. pleasant
D. exciting

141. The passengers aboard the Ripon at first were feeling

A. excited
B. homesick
C. afraid
D. adventurous

142. The narrator's final stop on the steamer was

A. Gibraltar
B. The Red Sea
C. Alexandria
D. Malta

CONTINUE ON TO THE NEXT PAGE ➡

READING
PART III

Questions 143-148 refer to the following passage.

This passage is adapted from The Conquest of Bread

One of the current objections to Communism, and Socialism altogether, is that the idea is so old, and yet it has never been realized. Schemes of ideal States haunted the thinkers of Ancient Greece; later on, the early Christians joined in communist groups; centuries later, large communist brotherhoods came into existence during the Reform movement. Then, the same ideals were revived during the great English and French Revolutions; and finally, quite lately, in 1848, a revolution, inspired to a great extent with Socialist ideals, took place in France. "And yet, you see," we are told, "how far away is still the realization of your schemes. Don't you think that there is some fundamental error in your understanding of human nature and its needs?"

At first sight this objection seems very serious. However, the moment we consider human history more attentively, it loses its strength. We see, first, that hundreds of millions of men have succeeded in maintaining amongst themselves, in their village communities, for many hundreds of years, one of the main elements of Socialism—the common ownership of the chief instrument of production, the land, and the apportionment of the same according to the labour capacities of the different families; and we learn that if the communal possession of the land has been destroyed in Western Europe, it was not from within, but from without, by the governments which created a land monopoly in favour of the nobility and the middle classes. We learn, moreover, that the medieval cities succeeded in maintaining in their midst, for several centuries in succession, a certain socialized organization of production and trade; that these centuries were periods of a rapid intellectual, industrial, and artistic progress; while the decay of these communal institutions came mainly from the incapacity of men of combining the village with the city, the peasant with the citizen, so as jointly to oppose the growth of the military states, which destroyed the free cities.

143. The idea of Communism and Socialism can date as far back as

   A. the early Christians
   B. Ancient Greece
   C. French Revolution
   D. Soviet Russia

144. The ideals that fueled the French Revolution were considered to be

   A. schemes
   B. Socialist
   C. Communism
   D. reformist

CONTINUE ON TO THE NEXT PAGE ➡

READING
PART III

145. One of the main elements of Socialism includes

   A. free trade
   B. death and destruction
   C. oppression
   D. common ownership

146. Communal possession in Western Europe was destroyed by the

   A. noble and middle class
   B. poor distribution
   C. labour
   D. industrial age

147. The word <u>monopoly</u> most nearly means

   A. distribution
   B. exclusive ownership
   C. possession
   D. market

148. The author of the passage is most likely a

   A. philosopher
   B. historian
   C. noble
   D. soldier

CONTINUE ON TO THE NEXT PAGE ➡

READING
PART III

Questions 149-152 refer to the following passage.

Bertie, the later King George VI, not only had issues with stammering while presenting speeches to a public audience, but also had problems with speaking clearly in even normal conversations with his wife and associates. After going through numerous different physicians to find some way to correct his dysfunction, the then prince - nicknamed Bertie - finally managed to meet therapist Lionel Logue, who eventually was able to have great success in helping the future king "find his voice".

One of the first therapeutical practices that Lionel tried in order to help the <u>faltering</u> prince was to read aloud a piece of text from a Shakespearean play. Although at first Bertie had issues with stuttering, he later was able to read the piece aloud fluently while Lionel played music so loudly that he could not hear his own voice. From there, Bertie was instructed to follow a number of physical practices that would help him speak more clearly. On a daily basis, he was told to roll on the ground, massage his diaphragm and strengthen his breathing and core to better his ability.

Such stunts and physical actions were not the only forms of therapy that Lionel used to help Bertie. The therapist believed that no stutterer is born with such an issue, and that the stammering usually appears due to troubling events of the past. When Lionel finally gained Bertie's trust, he was able to question the Duke of York's past, and it was revealed that his stuttering began around the age of four or five. From there, it was learned that he was continuously mistreated as a child.

149. The main idea of the passage discusses

   A. King George VI's problem and solution of stuttering
   B. therapist Lionel Logue's ideology
   C. the relationship between Bertie and Lionel
   D. explains why the king began stuttering

150. The passage can most likely be found in a

   A. philosophy book
   B. biography
   C. science paper
   D. journal

151. It was concluded that Bertie's stuttering originated from

   A. when he was mistreated as a child
   B. massaging his diagram
   C. rolling on the ground
   D. strengthening his breathing and core

152. The word <u>faltering</u> most nearly means

   A. calming
   B. holding
   C. stumbling
   D. maintaining

CONTINUE ON TO THE NEXT PAGE ➡

VOCABULARY
PART III (25 MIN)

VOCABULARY

DIRECTIONS: In this section, you will need to determine the choice that is closest in meaning to the underlined words provided below. Pick the answer choice that fits accordingly and fill in the appropriate letter on your answer sheet.

153. the innocuous reptile

A. poisonous
B. harmless
C. gigantic
D. aggressive

154. the girl's wan complexion

A. bright
B. spotless
C. pale
D. ugly

155. a pliable rope

A. broken
B. bendable
C. aged
D. firm

156. a jubilant occasion

A. crazy
B. joyful
C. stressful
D. unfortunate

157. Rob's disingenuous girlfriend

A. talkative
B. rude
C. loving
D. deceitful

158. a notorious villain

A. amusing
B. infamous
C. tactical
D. harsh

CONTINUE ON TO THE NEXT PAGE ➡

VOCABULARY
PART III

159. a dormant project

A. busy
B. complicated
C. unsuccessful
D. inactive

160. a heinous act

A. poor
B. calm
C. brutal
D. forgiving

161. a counterfeit document

A. fake
B. detailed
C. monetary
D. important

162. a garrulous student

A. talkative
B. intelligent
C. successful
D. failing

163. an acrid taste

A. delicious
B. bitter
C. bland
D. mild

164. a candid judge

A. dissatisfied
B. pleasant
C. frank
D. unfair

165. an incredulous article

A. informative
B. truthful
C. passionate
D. skeptical

166. the valorous warrior

A. courageous
B. injured
C. timid
D. bulky

CONTINUE ON TO THE NEXT PAGE ➡

VOCABULARY
PART III

167. a mundane task

    A. thrilling
    B. mandatory
    C. difficult
    D. ordinary

168. a shrewd lawyer

    A. lazy
    B. rude
    C. soporific
    D. clever

169. an esteemed surgeon

    A. know-it-all
    B. intrusive
    C. respected
    D. bright

170. a pugnacious individual

    A. strong
    B. intimidating
    C. diseased
    D. aggressive

171. a lax attitude

    A. negligent
    B. helpful
    C. positive
    D. boring

172. a stealthy operative

    A. terrifying
    B. bold
    C. dangerous
    D. sneaky

173. a copious feast

    A. scarce
    B. tasty
    C. abundant
    D. dreadful

174. being tenacious

    A. understanding
    B. adamant
    C. caring
    D. rude

CONTINUE ON TO THE NEXT PAGE ➡

MATHEMATICS
PART IV (45 MIN)

CONCEPTS (24 Questions)

DIRECTIONS: Choose the answer that best fits the problem. You may use scratch paper while working on these problems.

175. $9^4 \cdot 8^3$

    A. $9 \cdot 4 \cdot 8 \cdot 3$
    B. $9 \cdot 9 \cdot 9 \cdot 9 \cdot 8 \cdot 8 \cdot 8 \cdot 8$
    C. $9 \cdot 9 \cdot 9 \cdot 9 \cdot 8 \cdot 8 \cdot 8$
    D. $9 \cdot 9 \cdot 9 \cdot 8 \cdot 8 \cdot 8$

176. Which of the following has the same value as .25?

    A. $\frac{1}{5}\%$
    B. 25
    C. $\frac{1}{4}$
    D. .25%

177. Seven hundred thirty-three million seven hundred thousand three hundred and twenty is equal to

    A. 7,337,320
    B. 73,370,320
    C. 733,007,320
    D. 733,700,320

178. What number belongs in the triangle to make this equation true?
    +7 △ = -1

    A. -6
    B. +6
    C. -8
    D. +8

179. Set X = {2, 4, 6, 8} ; Set Y = {1, 2, 3, 4}. The intersection (∩) of the two sets is

    A. {2, 4, 8}
    B. {1, 2, 3, 4, 6, 8}
    C. {1, 2, 4, 6, 8}
    D. {2, 4}

180. The greatest common factor of 60 and 10 is

    A. 1
    B. 5
    C. 10
    D. 60

CONTINUE ON TO THE NEXT PAGE ➡

MATHEMATICS
PART IV

181. Which of the following statements is true?

A. 29.3 > 34 - 6
B. 11 x 3 = 29 + 3
C. 8 x 2 > 9 x 2
D. 100 ÷ 2 > 50

182. If Luis is m years old now and his best friend is 2 years older, which expression represents how old his best friend will be 8 years from now?

A. 6 years
B. $m + 6$ years
C. $m + 2$ years
D. $m + 10$ years

183. The area of the circle below is

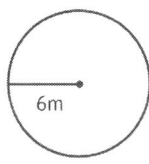

A. 6π meters
B. 12π sq. meters
C. 36π meters
D. 36π sq. meters

184. $\frac{2 \cdot 4}{3 \cdot 6} =$

A. $\frac{4}{9}$
B. $\frac{2}{18}$
C. $\frac{8}{9}$
D. $\frac{6}{9}$

185. The ratio of 4 yards to 24 inches is

A. 4 to 24
B. 1 to 6
C. 6 to 1
D. 4 to 8

186. $\{1, 2, 5\} \cap \{1, 2, 3, 4, 5\}$

A. $\{1, 2, 5\}$
B. $\{2, 5\}$
C. $\{1, 2, 3, 4, 5\}$
D. $\{3, 4\}$

187. 8,734.261 to the nearest tenth is

A. 8,734.26
B. 8,734.3
C. 8,730.0
D. 8,734.2

CONTINUE ON TO THE NEXT PAGE ➡

188. Which fraction has the greatest value?

A. $\frac{4}{5}$
B. $\frac{1}{4}$
C. $\frac{2}{3}$
D. $\frac{9}{20}$

189.

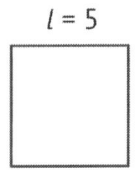

In the figure above, the length of the square is 5. What is the area of the square subtracted by the perimeter of the square?

A. 4
B. 5
C. 20
D. 25

190. What is the measure of angle A?

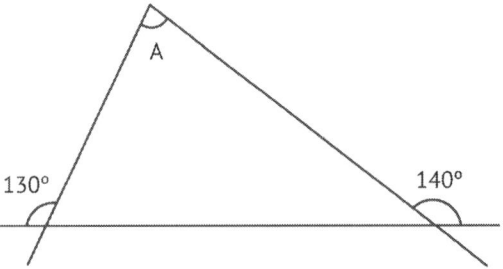

Note: Diagram is not drawn to scale.

A. 50°
B. 40°
C. 90°
D. 30°

191. The prime factorization of 50 is

A. 20 + 5
B. 25 • 5
C. 2 • 5 • 5
D. 10 • 5

192. How many integers are between $\frac{22}{5}$ and 15.8?

A. 9
B. 10
C. 11
D. 12

CONTINUE ON TO THE NEXT PAGE ➡

MATHEMATICS
PART IV

193. Simplify: $4(-4)^2$

A. -64
B. 64
C. -256
D. 256

194. The least common multiple of 5 and 6 is

A. 5
B. 5
C. 24
D. 30

195. Which of the following is *not* a type of triangle?

A. equilateral
B. scalene
C. trapezoid
D. acute

196. Which of the following is *not* a type of quadrilateral?

A. isosceles trapezoid
B. rhombus
C. parallelogram
D. hexagon

197. How many millimeters are in one meter?

A. .001 mm
B. 10 mm
C. 1000 mm
D. .01 mm

198. The square root of 172 is between

A. 12 and 13
B. 13 and 14
C. 14 and 15
D. 170 and 180

CONTINUE ON TO THE NEXT PAGE ➡

MATHEMATICS
PART IV

PROBLEM SOLVING QUESTIONS (40 Questions)

199. Solve: -5 - 6 + (-3) + (2) - (-1) =

A. -7
B. -13
C. -11
D. -6

200. If Mike spends $12,000 per year on utility bills, then how much did he spend approximately per month on his utility bills?

A. $100.00
B. $1,000
C. $1,200
D. $1,300

201. If $17 + 4x = -6x + 37$, then what is x?

A. 2
B. 20
C. -2
D. -20

202. Samantha purchases two shirts that cost $3.75 each and two hats that cost $1.25 each. Since Samantha is a student, she used her coupon that gave her 50% off all items she bought. Assuming there is no sales tax, how much did Samantha spend?

A. $4.50
B. $5.00
C. $10.00
D. $4.25

203. 121.3 • 0.81 =

A. 0.98253
B. 9.8253
C. 98.253
D. 982.53

204. 0.1 - (-0.903) + 1.202 =

A. 2.205
B. 3.105
C. 0.399
D. -2.005

CONTINUE ON TO THE NEXT PAGE ➡

MATHEMATICS
PART IV

205. Sally would like to purchase a couch and finds one for $1,000. She uses a 25% discount coupon that is applied to the original cost of the couch. If there is 8% tax on the couch, how much did Sally spend on her new couch?

A. $270.00
B. $810.00
C. $250.00
D. $1,080.00

206. What is the volume of this rectangular prism?

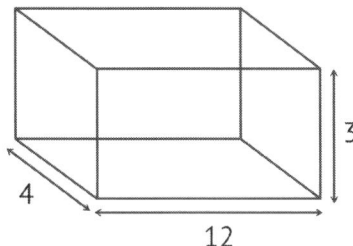

A. 48
B. 64
C. 144
D. 192

207. What number is a multiple of 40?

A. 220
B. 420
C. 320
D. 352

208. 78 is 50% of what number?

A. 39
B. 15.6
C. 156
D. 1,560

209. If $7x + 22 = 57$, then what is $x^2 - 1$?

A. 5
B. 25
C. 35
D. 24

CONTINUE ON TO THE NEXT PAGE ➡

MATHEMATICS
PART IV

210. Looking at the figure below, if you subtract the area from the perimeter, what is the value?

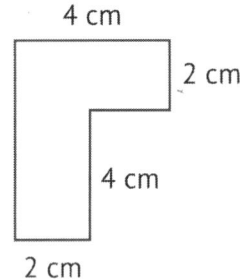

- A. 4
- B. 20
- C. 16
- D. 8

211. What is the length of *BD* of *BDC*?

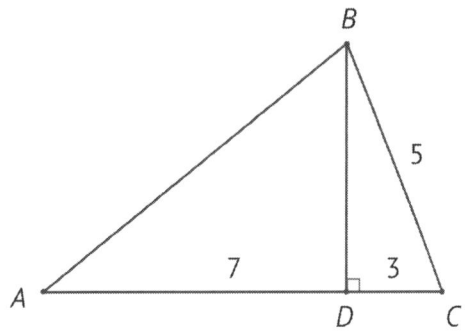

- A. 7.5
- B. 4
- C. 7
- D. 16

212. The product of 7 and 4 is 11 more than *y*. What is *y*?

- A. 16
- B. 17
- C. 39
- D. 37

213. Bob sells watches and makes a 3% commission on every watch he sells. If he sells five watches at $2,500 each, how much commission did Bob make?

- A. $75
- B. $300
- C. $2,425
- D. $375

214. $3.34\overline{)2.254}$ is approximately

- A. .77
- B. 77
- C. 67
- D. .67

CONTINUE ON TO THE NEXT PAGE ➡

MATHEMATICS
PART IV

215. What is the area of the figure shown in the diagram?

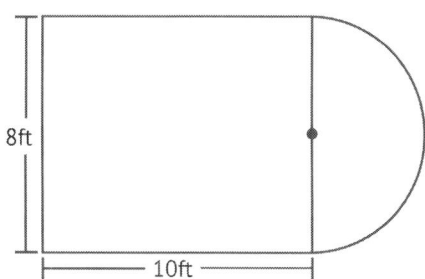

A. $(80 + 64\pi) ft^2$
B. $(80 + 16\pi) ft^2$
C. $(80 + 8\pi) ft^2$
D. $(80 + 4\pi) ft^2$

216. The formula for the circumference of a circle is

A. $C = (\pi r^2)$
B. $C = (\pi)(l)(r)$
C. $C = 2(\pi)(r)$
D. $C = \frac{1}{2}(\pi)(r)$

217. Which of the following is not equivalent to $30\frac{1}{4}\%$?

A. 0.3025
B. $\frac{30.25}{100}$
C. $\frac{60.5}{200}$
D. 30.25

218. What is the value of $2x^3 + 2.5y$, if $x = 1$ and $y = 4$?

A. 10
B. 12
C. 14
D. 16

219. Ms. Lane drove 12,000 miles for the entire year. If Ms. Lane drove everyday for the same distance, approximately how many miles on average did she drive per week?

A. 250 miles
B. 1,000 miles
C. 1,200 miles
D. 125 miles

220. If $\frac{1}{5} + \frac{2}{x} = \frac{1}{3}$, then what is x?

A. 15
B. $-2\frac{3}{4}$
C. -15
D. $2\frac{3}{4}$

221. If $25x - 100 < 250$, then what could be a possible value of x?

A. 16
B. 15
C. 14
D. 13

CONTINUE ON TO THE NEXT PAGE ➡

MATHEMATICS
PART IV

222. 21.02, 22.05, 23.08, 24.11, ...
What is the sixth term of this sequence above?

A. 25.14
B. 26.14
C. 25.17
D. 26.17

223. A container holds $5\frac{1}{2}$ gallons of water. How many ounces of water does this container hold?

Note: 1 cup = 16 ounces

A. 176 ounces
B. 704 ounces
C. 640 ounces
D. 44 ounces

224. A karaoke lounge has a daily fixed fee of $15 and charges $2 to sing each song. If Jonathan has $50.00 to spend at the karaoke lounge, what is the maximum number of songs she can sing?

A. 16 songs
B. 17 songs
C. 18 songs
D. 19 songs

225. What is the sum of $\frac{4}{3x}$ and $\frac{3}{2x}$?

A. $\frac{17}{6x}$
B. $\frac{7}{5x}$
C. $\frac{17}{12x}$
D. $\frac{12}{6x^2}$

226. If, $\sqrt{x+3} = 13$, then $x =$

A. 100
B. 160
C. 166
D. 172

227. A shirt has a starting value of 5 dollars and increases by 20 percent every year. What is the price of the shirt after 2 years?

A. $7.00
B. $6.00
C. $7.20
D. $6.20

CONTINUE ON TO THE NEXT PAGE ➡

MATHEMATICS
PART IV

228. The height of a tree on a blueprint is 4 inches. If the actual height of the tree is 30 feet, what is the ratio of the blueprint to the actual height of the tree?

- A. 30:4
- B. 1:90
- C. 4:30
- D. 1:80

229. If A = 5, B = 4, and C = 3, then $\frac{1}{2}$ ABC =

- A. 60
- B. 120
- C. 45
- D. 30

230. Lisa has $3 less than three times the amount Marty has. If Marty has $24 dollars, how much does Lisa have?

- A. $5
- B. $69
- C. $75
- D. $63

231. Chloe wants to purchase fifty-five notebooks. The store sells notebooks in packages, where each package has 5 notebooks. Each package costs $0.89. How much will Chloe spend at the store? (Assume there is no tax.)

- A. $4.45
- B. $8.90
- C. $9.79
- D. $48.95

232. It takes George 3 minutes to read 300 words. If each page in a book that he is reading has 750 words, how long will it take George to read 6 pages?

- A. 30 minutes
- B. 45 minutes
- C. 60 minutes
- D. 90 minutes

233. $(\sqrt{100})(\sqrt{64})$

- A. 8
- B. 10
- C. 18
- D. 80

234. John works 40 hours a week, and his monthly salary in June was $4,000. In the month of July, John got a 4% raise on his monthly salary. In the month of July, what was John's hourly rate? Assume there are 4 weeks in every month.

- A. $25
- B. $26
- C. $40
- D. $100

CONTINUE ON TO THE NEXT PAGE ➡

MATHEMATICS
PART IV

235. An adult male Diptera has a mass of 11.5 milligrams. What is the Diptera's mass in grams?

A. 0.0115 g
B. 0.115 g
C. 1.15 g
D. 11.5 g

236. $\left(\frac{2}{3} + \frac{1}{4}\right) \div 2 =$

A. $\frac{22}{12}$
B. $\frac{1}{12}$
C. $\frac{11}{24}$
D. $\frac{1}{3}$

237. If, $\frac{2000}{2x} = 10$, then what is $\sqrt{x}$?

A. $\sqrt{10}$
B. 10
C. $\sqrt{100}$
D. 100

238.

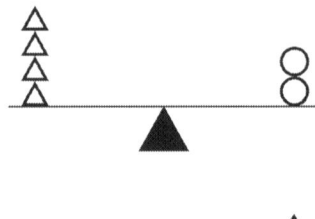

In the figure above, there are two balance beams that have triangles, circles and squares on them. Both beams are fully balanced. How many circles are needed to balance 70 squares?

A. 10
B. 12
C. 35
D. 70

CONTINUE ON TO THE NEXT PAGE ➡

LANGUAGE
PART V (25 MIN)

PUNCTUATION, CAPITALIZATION, & USAGE

DIRECTIONS: For Questions 239-278, choose the sentence that contains an error in punctuation, capitalization, or usage. If there is no error present, select answer choice D.

239. A. My doctor, doctor John, got his degree from Yale University.
    B. Sam asked, "Who left the task unfinished?"
    C. The annual marathon held in San Francisco is very competitive.
    D. No Mistakes

240. A. After being fired five different times, it was then that John realized he should be his own boss and started his own company.
    B. Even after the teacher continuously told Robert to keep quiet, Robert rebelled and yelled out, "You're not my mom."
    C. The Infinity-Chew is a gum that lasts such a long time; I have been chewing in my gum for about 4 hours now and it still has flavor.
    D. No Mistakes

241. A. Why should I paint over the art with white?
    B. "Have you received the homework posted today?" asked my teacher, Ms. Davis.
    C. Veteran's day is a holiday to celebrate those who have helped fight for our country.
    D. No Mistakes

242. A. John Wick was an extraordinary forensic scientist who applied his skills to the fullest extent.
    B. I will give this assignment to all who want it, but to whom I should give the extra credit is solely based on my judgement.
    C. The eminent danger was apparent since they had gone too close to the lions.
    D. No Mistakes

243. A. The American Psychological Association is a certain way to format when citing evidence when writing a bibliography.
    B. The diversity of the animals in the Amazonian Rainforest is much more than any other land biome.
    C. When the question was asked, Gabriela could not respond correctly.
    D. No Mistakes

CONTINUE ON TO THE NEXT PAGE ➡

LANGUAGE
PART V

244.
A. Given the harsh conditions, I was still able to push through the military training at West Point.
B. Aaron wanted assistance when he was lifting the heavy books, but no one wanted to help.
C. To enter the building, one needs to have correct id with the proper date of birth and residency.
D. No Mistakes

245.
A. By using the most effective plan, Martha was able to pass her test.
B. The Grand Canyon is a site for many tourists visiting America.
C. Neither was I allowed to play basketball or was I allowed to play soccer.
D. No Mistakes

246.
A. Is this textbook on the history of America mine or your's?
B. A light year is about 6 trillion miles and it refers to the distance a light photon can travel in a year.
C. The Big Dipper, a constellation filled with stars, are found in the Northern Hemisphere.
D. No Mistakes

247.
A. "Happy Birthday" is a song that actually comes from "Good Morning to All".
B. Will you be able to come with me to the event at City Hall?
C. Black coffee is too bitter for me and I would much rather prefer one with milk and sugar.
D. No Mistakes

248.
A. Raphael's teacher said, "Today we will cover a lot in class; I expect to get many questions."
B. Very large stars can become black holes which when they do, have high densities.
C. Basketball was invented as an alternative to football making the sport safer and less injury-prone.
D. No Mistakes

249.
A. Whoever completes the challenging course gets two things: a trophy and a trip to Hawaii.
B. A smart way to study is to incorporate as much of the five senses as possible; if you see and hear the material as you study, you will have better recollection than just by seeing the material.
C. The high specific heat of water makes it an excellent property by maintaining temperature in all organisms.
D. No Mistakes

CONTINUE ON TO THE NEXT PAGE ➡

LANGUAGE
PART V

250. A. The consistency of the salt was much more than the sugar.
     B. I was asked to do the following tasks: clean my room, throw out the trash, and mow the lawn.
     C. He was great rugby player being both agile and strong and was chosen as the most valuable player on the team.
     D. No Mistakes

251. A. Working hard to get good at a sport is a great way to be determined, but to be the very best requires the right body type; basketball is dominated by taller people.
     B. Whoever has found out about my secret has spread it among the whole school.
     C. We like to visit many places in America and last year we went to Albany, New York; Las Vegas, California; and Phoenix, Arizona.
     D. No Mistakes

252. A. Fortune cookies are often connect to Chinese culture; however, it is actually American.
     B. Chai is a Persian word for tea.
     C. The wisdom tooth is the set of teeth that appears around the age of twenty.
     D. No Mistakes

253. A. Theodore Roosevelt with few other presidents has won the Nobel Peace Prize.
     B. The National Cancer Institute was created by Congress in 1937 and they are established near my house.
     C. John Clayton is Tarzan's real name and Tarzan was his ape name.
     D. No Mistakes

254. A. Birds will often migrate from north to south before winter for more food sources.
     B. Deer is very docile creatures with a keen sense of hearing.
     C. We were working on our project for school as Ms. Robinson had told us to.
     D. No Mistakes

255. A. To whom should I give the letter with pink slips to?
     B. The commentator of the football game mentioned that the Eagles would verse the Hawks; the winner would go on to verse the patriots.
     C. The French-American War was surprisingly on the grand scale a conflict between Britain and France.
     D. No Mistakes

CONTINUE ON TO THE NEXT PAGE ➡

LANGUAGE
PART V

256.
- **A.** Samantha was given the hardest task, but she preferred it that way.
- **B.** Ruminants are animals that are able to process cellulose and therefore are able to eat grass.
- **C.** I had came like you told me to; I do not see what I did wrong.
- **D.** No Mistakes

257.
- **A.** Between Susan and David lies a table full of food.
- **B.** Among the three sisters, Julie is the taller one.
- **C.** The light shone brightly on front of the store.
- **D.** No Mistakes

258.
- **A.** The Russian cosmonaut, Yuri Gagarin, was the first to enter space.
- **B.** Who should go to the market to get me the essential ingredients for a Sundae- a banana, whip cream, and icecream?
- **C.** Unics tend to be taller than normal men since testosterone limits the growth of bones.
- **D.** No Mistakes

259.
- **A.** Ethylene gas is the chemical that helps ripen fruits and are used for making fruits ready for selling.
- **B.** The company Volvo is the first car company known for making seatbelts.
- **C.** Between you and me, I feel there is a strong bond developing.
- **D.** No Mistakes

260.
- **A.** The development of the Virginian opossum only takes 12 days in the mother's womb; and its gestation is the shortest currently recognized.
- **B.** Iodine is added to salt since it is an essential mineral for development and the mind.
- **C.** Dogs don't have sweat glands and instead sweat from their nose and feet.
- **D.** No Mistakes

261.
- **A.** A cow can produce around 200,000 glasses of milk in their lifetime- about 23 quarts a day.
- **B.** Tahmid was not sure about how he did on his test, but he felt that he studied well.
- **C.** A group of unicorns surprisingly has a name; it is called a blessing.
- **D.** No Mistakes

CONTINUE ON TO THE NEXT PAGE ➡

LANGUAGE
PART V

262.
A. Mark believed that he could complete his homework before class and so he started as soon as possible.
B. Vincent was able to play for his school concert.
C. The satellites (moons) of Saturn are higher in number than Earth.
D. No Mistakes

263.
A. The famous painter Pablo Picasso painted around 50,000 paintings in his lifetime.
B. Ninety percent of the population is right handed.
C. The moon does not have its own light like the sun; it provides light from the other.
D. No Mistakes

264.
A. Salt can be added to water to make it boil faster; it allows the water to have a lower specific heat.
B. Countries usually have real animals as their national animal, however, the Scottish have a unicorn.
C. After a lot of consistent results, the conclusion seems to be valid, unless the experiment is flawed in any way.
D. No Mistakes

265.
A. The human heart contains 4 chambers and 2 divisions which allow double circulation.
B. The Lamborghini and Ferrari which are considered luxurious cars by many, are actually priced much higher than the actual cost of making; it shows how the name sells rather than the actual car.
C. To be considered an organic molecule, at the bare minimum, it needs carbon and hydrogen.
D. No Mistakes

266.
A. The hot air balloon was invented in November 21, 1783.
B. In the first few months babies can only breath through their nose.
C. Albert Einstein married twice and his second wife was his cousin, Elsa Löwenthal.
D. No Mistakes

267.
A. Sea otters have no blubber and use their thick fur for warmth.
B. The Statue of Liberty is a classic figure of American freedom.
C. Colors can be used to manipulate and for this reason McDonald's has used red on it's logo, a color that stimulates hunger.
D. No Mistakes

CONTINUE ON TO THE NEXT PAGE ➡

LANGUAGE
PART V

268.
- A. Microsoft Word is a useful program for typing up documents.
- B. The speakers were loud and I am not able to hear what my friend has to say.
- C. We reserved seats for the restaurant called Famiglia, yet were disappointed when those same seats were occupied.
- D. No Mistakes

269.
- A. Bones stop growing after puberty, but cartilage continues to grow through a lifetime.
- B. Hanging still on trees, the claws of the sloth help it stay fixed and it sleeps for about 16 hours a day.
- C. Your jacket has a hole in the back if you didn't notice.
- D. No Mistakes

270.
- A. As they all got out of the store after shoplifting, the police approached, so they ran as fast as possible.
- B. Pennies are made out of copper, they were made out of steel during WWII due to the necessity of copper for war; those pennies have a higher value of 12 to 15 cents.
- C. UR stands for something that is unrated, which means it can be viewed by anyone over 6.
- D. No Mistakes

271.
- A. Australia and South American are the only continents without glaciers.
- B. In order to salute properly, it must be done with the right hand, the left hand is never used in military respect.
- C. Halley's comet orbits the sun around every 70 to 80 years and its first orbit was recorded in 1682.
- D. No Mistakes

272.
- A. The affect of placing plants in water with red dye alters the color of the plant itself.
- B. Hydrogen is the lightest element on the periodic table.
- C. My doctor prescribed me pain medication after I had an accident on my bike.
- D. No Mistakes

273.
- A. Braces are used to align teeth, but the practice of aligning has existed since the times of Ancient Egypt.
- B. Hippopotami are one of the most violent creatures often killing crocodiles and leaving them as display.
- C. The pyramid at Khufu at Egypt is the world's tallest and is made with small square bases on top of larger ones.
- D. No Mistakes

CONTINUE ON TO THE NEXT PAGE ➡

LANGUAGE
PART V

274.
- **A.** He wrongly assumed I was sad; I merely had tears from cutting onions.
- **B.** I did more better on my physics exam than on my Islamic history exam.
- **C.** Camels, though they are great travelers in the desert, cannot swim and only know how to float.
- **D.** No Mistakes

275.
- **A.** Michael Faraday invented the rubber balloon to assist him with his experiments involving hydrogen.
- **B.** Of all the presidents, president William Taft was the heaviest and once got stuck in his bathtub.
- **C.** Conspiracy theorists often take a look at big events such the assassination of Kennedy, the Nixon scandal, the bombing of the World Trade Center to draw conclusions.
- **D.** No Mistakes

276.
- **A.** Carrots were originally purple, but cultivators took the less common white and yellow ones which eventually turned out orange.
- **B.** A crocodile's tongue is different from an alligator, since the alligator can stick it out unlike the crocodile.
- **C.** The essential way to study is take breaks after some time so that your mind can recuperate.
- **D.** No Mistakes

277.
- **A.** The island of Manhattan was purchased for $24 from the Native Americans; this is approximately six hundred eighty dollars by today's standard.
- **B.** Teeth chattering in the cold is a form of shivering your body does in response to cold.
- **C.** Franklin Delano Roosevelt ran for president for more then 2 terms.
- **D.** No Mistakes

278.
- **A.** Most nuts grow on trees; therefore, peanuts grow under the ground.
- **B.** Giraffes are animals with the highest blood pressure and often use their necks as weapons when fighting for a mate.
- **C.** The Bermuda Triangle is a place where many ships and aircrafts have disappeared.
- **D.** No Mistakes

CONTINUE ON TO THE NEXT PAGE ➡

LANGUAGE
PART V

SPELLING

DIRECTIONS: For questions 279-288, find the sentence that contains a spelling error. If there is no error present, select answer choice D.

279. A. I believe I can see the Eiffel Tower from my hotel unless the window of my room is facing away.
B. The pshyscology of humans is much more complex that scientists can comprehend.
C. You do not have to be a genius to solve this problem; Mr. Halpern would be let down.
D. No mistakes

280. A. The North Atlantic Treaty Organization was made in 1949 as a secure measure against the Soviet Union.
B. Many believe that the hundred dollar bill is the bill with the highest value, but the Treasury also included bills that were worth 10,000 dollars.
C. My friend sincereley agreed to help Katy out.
D. No mistakes

281. A. The amature athlete tried his best to swim as many miles as his captain, but his muscles did not have the endurance.
B. Hydrofluoric acid cannot melt through plastic, yet it can melt many other compounds.
C. Thanksgiving is a holiday that originates from the Pilgrims celebrating from their harvest in autumn.
D. No mistakes

282. A. The calender behind the desk was made by Jacob.
B. An ostrich's eye is bigger than its brain.
C. Alpha and beta are the first two Greek letters in the Greek alphabet.
D. No mistakes

283. A. Chocolate is considered toxic for dogs and at large amounts can be fatal.
B. Among all the colors, violet has the highest frequency.
C. The ulnar nerve in your elbow is also known as the funny bone.
D. No mistakes

CONTINUE ON TO THE NEXT PAGE ➡

LANGUAGE
PART V

284. A. Benjamin Franklin did not want the bald eagle to be the national symbol of the US; he preferred the turkey.
B. He is definitley the most competent in terms of accomplishing the hard problem.
C. Among the five main oceans, the Arctic Ocean is the smallest.
D. No Mistakes

285. A. The flag of Switzerland is shaped like a square and the flag of Nepal is shaped with two triangles.
B. The existance of God is questioned by many atheists
C. Autumn leaves have many colors including red, orange, yellow, and brown.
D. No mistakes

286. A. As a foriegner, George was lost in the streets of India.
B. My friend was very hungry and so he asked me for food.
C. The car near my street was fancy and blue; I wonder who owns the car
D. No mistakes

287. A. Many people find clowns scary, but I find them hilarious.
B. If you devote extra time into your studies, you will hopefully do well on the test.
C. My teacher said, " Ignorance is bliss."
D. No mistakes

288. A. A day on Venus is longer than a year on Venus.
B. Everyone in the cafeteria eats hamburgers.
C. Though not noticable on the outside, the human DNA sequence is 50% similar to a banana.
D. No mistakes

CONTINUE ON TO THE NEXT PAGE ➡

109

LANGUAGE
PART V

COMPOSITION

DIRECTIONS: For questions 289-298, follow the directions for each question and select the best answer choice.

---

289. Choose the best word or words to join the thoughts together.

The end of the game gave results ____ showed who would continue to the next round.

A. that
B. who
C. so
D. None of these

290. Choose the best word or words to join the thoughts together.

_____ I was told that my methods of writing notes was horrendous, I am still able to pass the exams.

A. Because
B. Although
C. Since
D. None of these

291. Choose the best word or words to join the thoughts together.

Samantha was able to arrive at her test in time by_____

A. quickly running from her house.
B. running from her house quickly.
C. running quickly from her house.
D. running from quickly her house.

292. Which of these expresses the idea most clearly?

A. You can buy the delicious apples in the supermarket, the verdant vegetables, and many different types of meat.
B. Many different types of meat can be bought in the supermarket including delicious apples and divide and vegetables
C. In the supermarket, the verdant vegetables, delicious apples, and many different types of meat can be bought by you.
D. In the supermarket, you can buy many things including the delicious apples, the verdant vegetables, and many different types of meat.

CONTINUE ON TO THE NEXT PAGE ➡

LANGUAGE
PART V

293. Which of these expresses the idea most clearly?

    A. One can win a chess game by changing up the strategies since there are multiple possibilities even though the moves are simple for individual pieces.
    B. To win a game of chess, one must learn to change strategies since the moves in a chess game are simple for individual pieces with multiple possibilities.
    C. Even though the moves in a chess game are simple for individual pieces, one must learn to change up strategies since there are multiple possibilities.
    D. Chess is a game with multiple possibilities and simple moves for individual pieces, and one must learn to change up strategies in order to win the game.

294. Choose the pair of sentences that best develops this topic sentence.
    The evolution of technology is allowing tasks to be completed at a much faster rate.

    A. The computer is a device made up of complex parts and lights, but it is made from human parts.
    B. For example, phones are used today.
    C. Cities of replacing rural areas due to reliance of bigger buildings.
    D. Communication, medicine, agriculture have all been made to be more efficient in modern times.

295. Which of the following sentences offers least support to the topic "The Need to Preserve the Amazonian Rainforest"?

    A. The Amazonian rainforest has a diverse set of animals
    B. Many contractors are cutting down trees which are habitats too many of the endangered animals.
    C. Laws should be more strict because of the decline of animals.
    D. The animals in the Amazonian rainforest can sometimes be dangerous to approach.

296. Which of these best fits under the topic "Mathematics- The Underlying Truth of Chemistry, Physics, and Biology"?

    A. Mathematics is often hard for students.
    B. Math can be found within all major sciences and unifies many other subjects.
    C. Science relies a lot on math.
    D. Biology is the science of life, chemistry is the central science, and physics is the most mathematical science.

CONTINUE ON TO THE NEXT PAGE ➡

LANGUAGE
PART V

297. Which sentence does not belong in the paragraph?

(1) The Mongols were one of the fiercest societies in ancient times. (2) Many were able to conquer vast lands. (3) Mongols would make pyramids of the heads of their enemies. (4) The weapons used were deadly.

A. Sentence 1
B. Sentence 2
C. Sentence 3
D. Sentence 4

298. Where should the sentence "Practice makes perfect!" be placed in the paragraph below?

(1) Jeff did not do well on his algebra exam. (2) His teacher said that he would allow Jeff a retake of the test. (3) He studied extra hard and was able to get a 95 on the makeup exam.

A. Before sentence 1
B. Between sentence 1 & 2
C. Between sentence 2 & 3
D. After sentence 3

HSPT PRACTICE TEST 1
ANSWER KEY

ENGLISH

Verbal Skills (Part I)

1. D	11. A	21. B	31. C	41. C	51. C
2. C	12. B	22. D	32. C	42. A	52. A
3. B	13. A	23. B	33. B	43. C	53. B
4. C	14. D	24. C	34. B	44. B	54. C
5. D	15. A	25. A	35. C	45. C	55. D
6. C	16. C	26. A	36. A	46. B	56. A
7. B	17. B	27. B	37. D	47. A	57. D
8. A	18. A	28. C	38. C	48. B	58. A
9. A	19. C	29. C	39. A	49. C	59. D
10. B	20. C	30. A	40. C	50. A	60. B

Language (Part V)

239. A	249. D	259. A	269. B	279. B	289. A
240. A	250. A	260. A	270. B	280. C	290. B
241. C	251. D	261. A	271. A	281. A	291. A
242. C	252. D	262. C	272. A	282. A	292. A
243. B	253. A	263. C	273. A	283. D	293. C
244. C	254. B	264. B	274. B	284. B	294. D
245. C	255. B	265. B	275. C	285. B	295. D
246. C	256. C	266. B	276. B	286. A	296. B
247. A	257. B	267. C	277. C	287. D	297. D
248. C	258. B	268. B	278. A	288. C	298. D

Reading (Part III)

113. C	128. A	143. B	158. B
114. B	129. C	144. B	159. D
115. A	130. D	145. D	160. C
116. D	131. C	146. A	161. A
117. B	132. C	147. B	162. A
118. C	133. B	148. A	163. B
119. B	134. B	149. A	164. C
120. B	135. C	150. B	165. D
121. A	136. D	151. A	166. A
122. A	137. C	152. C	167. D
123. B	138. A	153. B	168. D
124. B	139. A	154. C	169. C
125. C	140. A	155. B	170. D
126. B	141. B	156. B	171. A
127. A	142. C	157. D	172. D
			173. C
			174. B

ARGO BROTHERS

To calculate your score and watch video tutorials, visit our web site:
www.einstein-academy.com/catholic

MATHEMATICS

Quantitative (Part II)

61. D	74. A	87. B	100. C
62. D	75. C	88. D	101. D
63. A	76. A	89. A	102. B
64. B	77. B	90. B	103. A
65. A	78. D	91. B	104. C
66. B	79. D	92. C	105. C
67. C	80. C	93. B	106. B
68. C	81. B	94. C	107. D
69. C	82. B	95. D	108. B
70. C	83. C	96. C	109. B
71. B	84. A	97. D	110. C
72. C	85. B	98. B	111. C
73. B	86. D	99. A	112. D

Mathematics (Part IV)

175. C	188. A	201. A	214. D	227. C
176. C	189. B	202. B	215. C	228. B
177. D	190. C	203. C	216. C	229. D
178. C	191. C	204. A	217. D	230. B
179. D	192. C	205. B	218. B	231. C
180. C	193. B	206. C	219. A	232. B
181. A	194. D	207. C	220. D	233. D
182. D	195. C	208. C	221. D	234. B
183. D	196. D	209. D	222. D	235. A
184. A	197. C	210. A	223. B	236. C
185. C	198. B	211. B	224. B	237. B
186. A	199. C	212. B	225. A	238. D
187. B	200. B	213. D	226. C	

ANSWER EXPLANATIONS

VERBAL SECTION

1. **The correct answer is D.**
   Lilly, rose, and orchid are all types of flowers. A stem is a part of a plant, not of a flower.

2. **The correct answer is C.**
   All of the measurements given measure length except for choice C, grams.

3. **The correct answer is B.**
   Identify the relationship between the two words in the question. A marker is used to write on a whiteboard whereas chalk is used to write on a blackboard.

4. **The correct answer is C.**
   Since Harry runs faster than Marry, and Barry runs slower than Harry, this says that both Barry and Marry run slower than Harry. However, it is not clear whether Barry runs faster than Marry.

5. **The correct answer is D.**
   Haughty means disdainful or arrogantly superior. Choice D, arrogant, best fits this.

6. **The correct answer is C.**
   A bookbag is used to take to school. The most common place luggage is taken to is the airport.

7. **The correct answer is B.**
   Distinct, unique and exceptional are all synonyms of one another, meaning "different." Beautiful is the only word that does not mean different.

8. **The correct answer is A.**
   A brick is used to build a house, while a page is used to make a book. Letters, words, and sentences are all words that make up a page.

9. **The correct answer is A.**
   South America, Antarctica and Australia are all continents. The USA is a country in the continent of North America.

10. **The correct answer is B.**
    Derogatory is an adjective that means disrespectful. Offensive is the option that has the closest meaning to derogatory.

11. **The correct answer is A.**
    Candid is an adjective that means truthful and honest. Straightforward is the option that has the closest meaning to candid.

12. **The correct answer is B.**
    A gym holds weights as its primary use. An aquatic center holds a pool as its primary use.

13. **The correct answer is A.**
    Corporation, company and business are all groups of people working together for a purpose. A building is a structure.

14. **The correct answer is D.**
    A cub is the adolescent version of a lion. A tadpole is the adolescent version of a frog.

15. **The correct answer is A.**
    The most distinct body part of a shark is its teeth. The most distinct body part of an elephant is its trunk.

ANSWER EXPLANATIONS

16. The correct answer is C.
Using the first two statements, it can be determined that as chicken has more protein than turkey and eggs have more more protein than chicken, egg whites have greater protein than both turkey and chicken.
C > T, E > C
E > C > T
However, this information does not give any validity to the protein content of fish. As such, it cannot be determined if egg whites have more protein than fish.

17. The correct answer is B.
To be eloquent means to be fluent or persuasive in speaking or writing. Articulate is a synonym for eloquent.

18. The correct answer is A.
To be auspicious means to be conducive to success, or opportune.

19. The correct answer is C.
To be meticulous means to pay attention to detail and be precise. The word closest to this would be diligent.

20. The correct answer is C.
A boat travels through the water while a car travels through the road.

21. The correct answer is B.
Many strokes make up a painting while many words make up an essay.

22. The correct answer is D.
Laborious is an adjective that describes something that requires considerable effort, or something that is taxing.

23. The correct answer is B.
If a banana is a fruit, and no fruits are vegetables, a banana can not be a vegetable.

24. The correct answer is C.
Biology, physics, and chemistry are all scientific subjects. History is not a science.

25. The correct answer is A.
Muffled is an adjective that means to be muted. Quiet is the option that has the closest meaning to muted.

26. The correct answer is A.
If Y is north of X, and W is south of X, this must mean that Y is north of W.

27. The correct answer is B.
Pompous is an adjective that means to be self-absorbed and haughty. Condescending is the option that has the closest meaning to haughty.

28. The correct answer is C.
To be ambiguous means to be open to more than one interpretation, or unclear. Obscure would be a synonym for ambiguous.

29. The correct answer is C.
A desert is primarily made up of sand whereas a rainforest is primarily made up of trees.

30. The correct answer is A.
Malevolent means having or showing a wish to do evil to others.

31. The correct answer is C.
Affluent means having a great deal of money; the opposite would be poor.

32. The correct answer is C.
A doctor, nurse, and psychiatrist are all professions that treat the ill. The ill would be the patient, and not the care provider.

ANSWER EXPLANATIONS

33. **The correct answer is B.**
Anger, remorse, and love are all emotions while hard-working is an adjective that describes something.

34. **The correct answer is B.**
Benign means kind or gentle; the opposite would be hostile or aggressive.

35. **The correct answer is C.**
Both lake A and lake C are larger than lake B. However, there is no direct relationship between lake C and A given, therefore it is uncertain whether lake C is larger than lake A.

36. **The correct answer is A.**
Dexterous means to be skillful in the use of hands or body; the opposite would be clumsy.

37. **The correct answer is D.**
Zealous means to be devoted and passionate.

38. **The correct answer is C.**
Abundant means existing in large quantities; the opposite would be scarce.

39. **The correct answer is A.**
Potent means to have great power or influence; the opposite would be weak.

40. **The correct answer is C.**
Student, teacher, and principal are all roles within a school, therefore school is the correct answer.

41. **The correct answer is C.**
The nose, eye, and mouth are all body parts on your face, while your leg is part of your lower body.

42. **The correct answer is A.**
Janice finished the race before Jenny and Jenny finished the race before Jack, therefore Janice finished the race before Jack.

43. **The correct answer is C.**
Chalk, pen, and marker are all writing utensils while paper is something that you write on.

44. **The correct answer is B.**
Narcissistic means having an excessive interest in oneself and physical appearance. Egotistical would be a synonym for narcissistic.

45. **The correct answer is C.**
Immaculate means perfectly neat and clean; the opposite would be dirty.

46. **The correct answer is B.**
If a lump is more than a hunk, and a hunk is more than a piece, this would imply that a lump is more than a piece. Therefore, the third statement is false.

47. **The correct answer is A.**
Repugnant means extremely distasteful and repulsive; the opposite would be attractive.

48. **The correct answer is B.**
Retain means to keep possession of something; the opposite would be discard.

49. **The correct answer is C.**
Both Joseph and Candice are taller than Mike. However, we do not know if Joseph or Candice is taller than the other. Therefore, the third statement is uncertain.

ANSWER EXPLANATIONS

50. **The correct answer is A.**
    Robert can spell better than Dylan and Dylan can spell better than Jackie. This implies that Robert can spell better than Jackie, therefore, the third statement is true.

51. **The correct answer is C.**
    Sensible is an adjective that means practical. Foolish is the option that has the closest meaning to the opposite of practical.

52. **The correct answer is A.**
    Although all four answer choices are sources of light, the sun is the only natural source of light of the four.

53. **The correct answer is B.**
    A car, boat, and motorcycle all run on land, while a boat runs on water.

54. **The correct answer is C.**
    To be impetuous means to be done quickly and impulsively.

55. **The correct answer is D.**
    Initiate means to begin; the opposite would be to stop or cease.

56. **The correct answer is A.**
    A nemesis is a long-standing rival; the opposite would be friend.

57. **The correct answer is D.**
    A couch resides in the living room while the refrigerator resides in the kitchen.

58. **The correct answer is A.**
    Frivolous means not having any serious purpose, or silly.

59. **The correct answer is D.**
    Fragile, flimsy, and tenuous are all synonyms of each other that means easily broken. Brawny is the only word that doesn't mean this.

60. **The correct answer is B.**
    While all answer choices are instruments, the guitar, harp, and violin are stringed instruments whereas the keyboard is not.

QUANTITATIVE SECTION

61. **The correct answer is D.**
    To find 2 more than 20% of 80, first find 20% of 80. Multiply 80 by the decimal version of 20%, .2. This gives 16. Add 2 to 16 to get 18.

62. **The correct answer is D.**
    Multiply 27 by the $\frac{2}{3}$. This gives a fraction of $\frac{54}{3}$. Simplified, this gives 18. Add 6 to 18 to receive 24.

63. **The correct answer is A.**
    The first four numbers are 67, 63, 60, and 56. The pattern here is subtract 4, then subtract 3, subtract 4 again, then subtract 3. According to this pattern, the next number should be 3 less than the previous, which is 53.

64. **The correct answer is B.**
    In figure A, 6 out of 12 blocks are shaded in, which means half the blocks are shaded in. In figure B, 3 out of 6 blocks are shaded in, which means half the blocks are shaded in as well. In figure C, 4 out of 9 blocks are shaded in which means less than half the blocks are shaded in. Therefore, C, is less shaded than A or B.

ANSWER EXPLANATIONS

65. The correct answer is A.
Convert each of the numbers to decimals. $\frac{5}{7}$ is approximately 0.7.
0.35 multiplied by 3.22 is 1.127. Looking at the following answer choices, only answer choice A is valid, where $\frac{5}{7}$ is greater than 0.375 but less than 1.127.

66. The correct answer is B.
Quantify each of the numbers given in each choice. A would equal 27. B would equal 16 and C would equal 32. Therefore, C is greater than A which is greater than B.

67. The correct answer is C.
The series goes 45, 55, 64, 72, 79. To get to each consecutive number, add one less than was done for the previous number. 10 is added first, then 9, then 8, then 7, and to get the answer, 6 needs to be added to get 85.

68. The correct answer is C.
The numbers in this series are increasing by 0.25. The third term in the sequence is 0.75, and adding 0.25 gives us 1.00. Therefore, the correct answer choice is C.

69. The correct answer is C.
First find $\frac{1}{4}$ of 100 which can be found by multiplying 100 by $\frac{1}{4}$. This gives 25. 25 multiplied by 5 gives 125 which is the answer.

70. The correct answer is C.
Statements B and C are equal to each other because when the distributive property is applied to statement C, we get statement B. B and C must be smaller than A because a is smaller than b.

71. The correct answer is B.
This number series is decreasing in cubes with each number. 125 is 5 cubed, 64 is 4 cubed, 27 is 3 cubed, 8 is 2 cubed and 1 is 1 cubed.

72. The correct answer is C.
Line segment AE must have the greatest length of all segments in the figure because it is the hypotenuse of the largest triangle in the figure.

73. The correct answer is B.
First look at the relationship between the letters. The difference between N and Q, Q and T, T and W is 2 letters. Therefore, the next letter should be Z. The numbers go from 36 to 30 to 24 to 18 which is subtracting 6 each time. The next number should be 12 which gives an answer of Z12, B.

74. The correct answer is A.
The series adds 2 for each of the first two numbers, then 3 for the next 2, then 4 for the next 2, and 5 for the next 2. The next number in the series should be 6 more than the previous.

75. The correct answer is C.
Quantify each of the three statements. Statement A comes out to -9. Statement B comes out to -6 and statement C comes out to 3. Given this, answer choice C is correct.

119

ANSWER EXPLANATIONS

76. The correct answer is A.
Simplify the latter portion of the question first. 8 times 4 is 32. 2 subtracted from 32 is 30. Then, since $\frac{5}{6}$ is a fraction, multiply 30 by the reciprocal of $\frac{5}{6}$, to get 36.

77. The correct answer is B.
Simplify each statement. Statement A gives 6. Statement B and C both give 7.
Therefore, B = C > A.

78. The correct answer is D.
Looking at the length of each figure, clearly B is the largest. Therefore the correct answer is D, B is greater than A and C.

79. The correct answer is D.
Each first number in a set of 2 is 3 times smaller than the second number directly following it. The blank is in an odd positioned spot, therefore the number following it must be 3 times greater. 21 divided by 3 gives 7.

80. The correct answer is C.
The numbers in this series are going according to the squares of consecutive numbers. 1 squared is 1, 2 squared is 4, 3 squared is 9, 4 squared is 16 and 5 squared is 25.

81. The correct answer is B.
The angle opposing the largest side is always the greatest. The angle opposing segment AC, the largest segment is B. According to this, the next largest angle is C, and A after that.

82. The correct answer is B.
First multiply 7 by 2 to get 14. Then multiply 14 by the reciprocal of $\frac{1}{3}$, which is 3 to get 42.

83. The correct answer is C.
In figure A, 2 out of 6 equal portions are shaded, which means a total of $\frac{1}{3}$ is shaded. In figure B, 1 out of 3 equal portions are shaded which again gives a total of $\frac{1}{3}$ that is shaded. In figure C, 1 out of 4 portions are shaded to give a total of $\frac{1}{4}$ that is shaded. Therefore, answer choice C is the correct answer.

84. The correct answer is A.
2 more than 3 is 5. 5 multiplied by 6 gives 30.

85. The correct answer is B.
Simply each of the statements given. Statement A gives 17. Statement B gives 47. Statement C gives 40. Therefore, statement B gives the largest value.

86. The correct answer is D.
$\frac{2}{5}$ of 25 gives 10. 3 subtracted from 10 gives 7.

87. The correct answer is B.
$\frac{3}{4}$ of 16 gives 12. 2 more than that is 14. 14 subtracted from 20 gives 6.

88. The correct answer is D.
Simply each of the statements given. Statement A gives a total of 81. Statement B gives a total of 64 and statement C gives a total of 144. Therefore, C > A > B.

120

ANSWER EXPLANATIONS

89. The correct answer is A.
The numbers are increasing consecutively. Each number is 4 units greater than the previous number. 4 units greater than 47 and 4 units less than 55 will both result in the number 51.

90. The correct answer is B.
From the figures, add up the total amount of people in each room. Figure A gives a total of 28 people, figure B gives a total of 12 people, figure C gives a total of 32 people, and figure D gives a total of 20 people. The only valid answer choice is B.

91. The correct answer is B.
This series goes times 2 then times 1 with each 2 consecutive numbers. From 16 to 32 it is times 2, then the next number should be times 1 followed by times 2 followed by times 1. Therefore B is the right answer.

92. The correct answer is C.
An equation can be set up in this problem. Set x to be the number. 20% as a decimal is .2 and 70% as a decimal is .7. The equation we have is $.2x + .7x = 81$. Simplified, this gives. $9x = 81$. Divide both sides by .9 to solve for x and get $x = 90$.

93. The correct answer is B.
Count the number of spikes each figure has. Figure A has a total of 4 spikes, figure B has a total of 6 spikes, figure C also has 6 spikes, and figure D has 3 spikes. The correct answer is that two times the spikes of D, 6, gives the amount of spikes on figure B.

94. The correct answer is C.
Find the average of the numbers given, 13, 88, 70 and 41. The average of these numbers gives 53. The difference between 53 and 24 is 29.

95. The correct answer is D.
To find $\frac{7}{8}$ of 64, multiply 64 by $\frac{7}{8}$. This yields 56. 3 added to 56 gives 59. Subtract 59 from 80 to receive an answer of 21.

96. The correct answer is C.
Simply each of the statements given. The second statement comes out to 0.363, and the third statement comes out to repeating .33. Therefore, answer choice C is correct.

97. The correct answer is D.
$\frac{1}{4}$ of 36 is found by multiplying 36 by $\frac{1}{4}$. This gives 9 and when multiplied by 7, gives 63.

98. The correct answer is B.
Convert each of the statements into decimals. The first statement simplifies to 16. The second simplifies to .60 and the third simplifies to 0.006. Therefore, choice B is correct.

99. The correct answer is A.
Look at each figure individually. In each figure, a total of 4 out of 9 boxes are shaded. This means that each figure is equally shaded.

100. The correct answer is C.
With each consecutive number, the series is subtracting one less than was done from the previous number. The series goes, subtract 3, subtract 2, subtract 1, then

121

ANSWER EXPLANATIONS

101. The correct answer is D.
The series goes add 2, subtract 4, add 2, subtract 4 and so on. The last two numbers are 96 and 92. The difference is 4 so the next number needs to be 2 more than the last. 2 more than 92 is 94.

102. The correct answer is B.
To get each successive number in the series, the number previous to it is multiplied by .3. To find the next number in the series, multiply 0.027 by .3 to get 0.0081.

103. The correct answer is A.
First find $\frac{5}{8}$ of 72 by multiplying the two numbers. This gives 45. Add 7 to this to get the final answer of 52.

104. The correct answer is C.

$x \div \frac{2}{5} = 10$

$x \cdot \frac{5}{2} = 10$

$5x = 20; x = 4$

Remember you are dividing a fraction, and in order to do that you must take the reciprocal of the fraction and change the division sign into multiplication. By doing this, you get the answer as 4. To double check if the answer works out, simply plug 4 back in the original question. 4 divided by $\frac{2}{5}$ does indeed give us 10. Tip: Always double check your answers by trying to plug it back into the question.

105. The correct answer is C.
With each consecutive number, there is a pattern of adding 5 to the previous number. There is also a second pattern that follows the format: two roman numeral numbers followed by an integer number. The next number should be in roman numerals and should be 5 greater than 29. 34 in roman numerals is XXXIV.

106. The correct answer is B.
The pattern in this series is that each consecutive number is being multiplied by $\frac{1}{2}$. The last number in the series given is $\frac{5}{16}$. This multiplied by $\frac{1}{2}$ is $\frac{5}{32}$.

107. The correct answer is D.
To find the missing values of A, set up the equation of A + C = 7 which can be seen from the figure. Since C is 4, that must mean A is 3. Similarly set up the equation 6 - 3 = B which gives B a value of 3. Therefore, A = B < C.

108. The correct answer is B.
The second term is increased by one from the first term. The third term is increased by two from the second term. The pattern here is +1, +2, +3, +4 and so on. Since the question asks to find the 6th term, we need to add +5 to the previous term which is 21. 21 + 5 = 26.

ANSWER EXPLANATIONS

109. The correct answer is B.
To find the number, multiply 9 by the reciprocal of $\frac{3}{11}$, which is $\frac{11}{3}$. This gives 33. 33 multiplied by $\frac{1}{3}$, or $33\frac{1}{3}$ % is 11.

110. The correct answer is C.
The pattern for this series goes subtract 3, add 2, subtract 3, add 2 and so on. The last two numbers were 17 and 19 and their difference is 2, so subtract 3, then add 2, and then subtract 3 again to get the answer C.

111. The correct answer is C.
The product of 3 and 6 yields 18. This multiplied by 4 gives 72. A number added to 10 needs to give 72. Set up the equation, $x + 10 = 72$. The missing variable is 62.

112. The correct answer is D.
Set up an equation to answer this problem. An increase of 20% would mean that the number is multiplied by 1.2 or $\frac{6}{5}$. Multiply 60 by the reciprocal of $\frac{6}{5}$, $\frac{5}{6}$ to get an answer of 50.

READING SECTION

113. The correct answer is C.
The passage discusses a specific trolley scenario and ties that with a discussion on the mindset of a psychopath.

114. The correct answer is B.
The main idea of the passage discusses how the mind of a psychopath works. The only two possible choices would be either science research paper or psychology article, but the latter is the more specific choice.

115. The correct answer is A.
The first paragraph discusses the choice of sacrificing one for the betterment of five individuals. Thus, it is a moral scenario.

116. The correct answer is D.
Looking at the context of the word, the word *morbidly* is describing an obese fat man. In this situation, if the word *morbidly* is replaced with any of the words provided in the answer choices, only *unhealthily* would make sense.

117. The correct answer is B.
In the second paragraph, it states that the amygdala is considered to be the brain's emotion center.

118. The correct answer is C.
Looking for context clues for the word, in the following sentence, the author refers to pushing the man. Of the answer choices, only *throw* seems to fit with the synonym for push.

119. The correct answer is B.
In the second paragraph, it is stated that a person with a normal amygdala would have trouble making the decision to push a man whereas a psychopath would not. Thus, it can be inferred that a psychopath's amygdala is flawed.

120. The correct answer is B.
The last paragraph discusses the role of psychopaths in leadership positions, which allows more calculated decisions. Thus, it can be said that psychopathy can be useful.

ANSWER EXPLANATIONS

121. The correct answer is A.
The moral dilemma speaks of the situation that is described in the introductory paragraph.

122. The correct answer is A.
Using the context of the word *demise*, it discusses the pushing and ultimate death of the man.

123. The correct answer is B.
In the first paragraph, it is stated that Brand mistakenly discovered phosphorous in his attempt to make a philosophical stone.

124. The correct answer is B.
The beginning of the second paragraph ties to the previous paragraph, which discusses the discovery of phosphorous.

125. The correct answer is C.
Looking for the context clues for *engrossed* in the first paragraph, the only word it can be replaced by is *absorbed*. The glassmaker was bent on creating the philosopher's stone.

126. The correct answer is B.
As it is discussed in the first paragraph, Brand was a glassmaker by profession.

127. The correct answer is A.
In the first paragraph, it is stated that the glassmaker Brand discovered phosphorus through the strong distillation of urine.

128. The correct answer is A.
Luminous can be defined as bright. Only *glowing* fits the category as a replacement for the word.

129. The correct answer is C.
As stated in the beginning of the second paragraph, lithophosphorus was discovered by the shoemaker Vicenzo Casciarolo.

130. The correct answer is D.
The passage discusses the history of the discovery of phosphorus. Thus, the only possible answer choice would be a history book. It cannot be found in a science research paper as there is not enough scientific information provided.

131. The correct answer is C.
The word *arbitrary* can best be described as random choices. Thus, the word that best fits the description would be *different*.

132. The correct answer is C.
In the first paragraph, it was stated that the shoemaker Brand who discovered phosphorus was looking to find a philosophical stone.

133. The correct answer is B.
In the first sentence of the passage, it is stated that the narrator of the passage was sent to India as a cadet, which is a ranking in the military. Thus, it can be inferred that the narrator is a soldier.

134. The correct answer is B.
In the first paragraph, the author mentions that leave could only be used as an option after ten years of stay in India.

135. The correct answer is C.
It is stated in the first paragraph that the fleet was only capable of transporting 2,400 passengers in the period of a year.

ANSWER EXPLANATIONS

136. The correct answer is D.
In the beginning of the second paragraph, it is stated that the steamer is named Ripon, and is commanded by Captain Moresby.

137. The correct answer is C.
It is stated in the second paragraph that Captain Moresby was an ex-officer of the Indian Navy, known for his distinction in the Red Sea.

138. The correct answer is A.
From the context of the word, it can be inferred that the passengers were bidding the captain goodbye. *Farewell* would be the most appropriate word to replace *adieu*.

139. The correct answer is A.
The main idea of the passage discusses the narrator's departure and crossing of India. Thus, "Voyage to India" would be the most appropriate title for the passage.

140. The correct answer is A.
The context of the word *tedious* provides that it would be synonymous to the difficulties discussed earlier in the sentence. Tiring would be the best fit to replace the word.

141. The correct answer is B.
As discussed in the second paragraph, it is stated by the author that "leaving England under the same depressing circumstances…we were bidding farewell to home." As such, homesick would be an accurate description of the passengers' feelings.

142. The correct answer is C.
In the final moments of the passage, it is stated that the passengers bade the captain farewell at Alexandria.

143. The correct answer is B.
In the first paragraph, it is mentioned that the ideals of sociology and communism were discussed as early as Ancient Greece.

144. The correct answer is B.
It is stated in the first paragraph that the French Revolution was inspired by Socialist ideals.

145. The correct answer is D.
In the second paragraph, it is stated that the main elements of Socialism includes common ownership of production and land.

146. The correct answer is A.
In the second paragraph, it is mentioned that communal possession was destroyed in Western Europe by the nobility and middle classes.

147. The correct answer is B.
Using the context of the word *monopoly*, it discusses the seizing of land and resources by the nobility and middle class. Thus, B would be the best choice. While possession is a possible choice, *exclusive ownership* describes control.

148. The correct answer is A.
The primary idea of the passage discusses the ideology of Socialism and Communism. While the author could be a historian, philosopher would be the best choice as it discusses philosophies.

149. The correct answer is A.
The passage discusses the problem of King George's stuttering issues and his use of Lionel to find a solution through numerous different methods.

ANSWER EXPLANATIONS

150. The correct answer is B.
The passage discusses the life of King George IV, and so can be found in either a history book or a biography.

151. The correct answer is A.
In the second paragraph, it is discovered that the stammering usually occurs due to troubling events of the past. From there, it was found that he had issues from mistreatment as a child.

152. The correct answer is C.
The first paragraph discusses the future King's problems with stuttering. Thus, it can be inferred that faltering must have something to do with stumbling and stalling. As such, C is the best choice.

153. The correct answer is B.
Innocuous means harmless or safe.

154. The correct answer is C.
The word wan means pale or weak.

155. The correct answer is B.
Something that is pliable is flexible or bendable.

156. The correct answer is B.
The word jubilant refers to the feeling of happiness or being joyful.

157. The correct answer is D.
To be disingenuous is to be dishonest or deceitful.

158. The correct answer is B.
The word notorious means to be infamous or getting fame for a wrongful deed.

159. The correct answer is D.
The word dormant refers to sleeping or being inactive.

160. The correct answer is C.
To be heinous is to be wicked or evil. Brutal is closest in meaning to either definition.

161. The correct answer is A.
To be counterfeit is to be forged or phony.

162. The correct answer is A.
The adjective garrulous refers to someone who talks excessively.

163. The correct answer is B.
Something that is acrid is bitter and unpleasant.

164. The correct answer is C.
To be candid is to be open or honest. The best answer choice that fits this definition is answer choice C, to be frank.

165. The correct answer is D.
To be incredulous is to be unable to believe something, to be a skeptic or to be find mistrustful.

166. The correct answer is A.
To be valorous is to be courageous.

167. The correct answer is D.
If something is mundane, then it is dull, tedious and tiresome. The best answer choice that fits is answer choice D, ordinary.

168. The correct answer is D.
Shrewd means to be sharp, intelligent and clever.

ANSWER EXPLANATIONS

169. The correct answer is C.
The word esteemed means to have respect and admiration.

170. The correct answer is D.
Someone or something pugnacious is usually quick to fight or become aggressive.

171. The correct answer is A.
Lax means to lack in firmness or rigor. The best answer choice that fits is answer choice D, negligent.

172. The correct answer is D.
To be stealthy is to be secretive.

173. The correct answer is C.
Copious means abundant and plentiful.

174. The correct answer is B.
Tenacious means to be persistent. The best answer choice that fits is answer choice B, adamant.

MATH SECTION

175. The correct answer is C.
A number raised to an exponent is equal to that number multiplied by itself by the amount of the exponent. The first number is 9 to the fourth power so this equals 9 times 9 times 9 times 9. Apply this to the second number and you get answer choice C.

176. The correct answer is C.
The last number in the decimal is in the hundredths position so divide 25 by 100. This gives the fraction $\frac{25}{100}$ which can be simplified to $\frac{1}{4}$.

177. The correct answer is D.
There should be a total of 9 numbers in the correct answer choice because the number is in the hundreds of millions. This leaves choices C and D. Choice C cannot be the answer because there is seven hundred thousand. Choice C only has 7 thousand.

178. The correct answer is C.
Solve for the triangle by subtracting 7 from both sides. This leaves the triangle to equal -8.

179. The correct answer is D.
The intersection of the two sets is asking for the numbers that belong to both sets. Only numbers 2 and 4 belong to both sets of numbers.

180. The correct answer is C.
List the factors of 60 and 10. The factors of 60 are 1, 2, 3, 4, 5, 6, 10, 12, 15, 20, 30, and 60. The factors of 10 are 1, 2, 5, and 10. The greatest factor in both sets is 10.

181. The correct answer is A.
Evaluate each of the answer choices given. Answer choice A comes out to 29.3 > 28 when you work out 34 - 6. This is the correct answer.

182. The correct answer is D.
Set up an expression for both Luis and his friends age. If Luis is m years old, his friend is $m + 2$ years old. If we add 8 years, he will be $m + 10$ years old. It is crucial to note that m is Luis's current age, and will not be his age in 8 years.

ANSWER EXPLANATIONS

183. The correct answer is D.
The equation for the area of a circle is A = (π)r . The radius in the circle is 6*m*. 6*m* squared is 36 square meters. Multiply this by π to get an answer of 36π square meters.

184. The correct answer is A.
Multiply across for the denominator and numerator. This leaves $\frac{8}{18}$. This can be simplified to $\frac{4}{9}$.

185. The correct answer is C.
There are 36 inches in a yard. If there are 4 yards, this equals 144 inches. The ratio can be converted to 144 inches to 24 inches. 144 is 6 times bigger than 24, therefore, the ratio is 6 to 1.

186. The correct answer is A.
The symbol is asking for the intersection of both sets. The intersection of both sets is represented by the numbers that are common in both sets. The number common between both sets are 1, 2 and 5.

187. The correct answer is B.
The hundredths place of the number is 6, which is greater than 5, so the number must be rounded up. 8,734.261 rounded to the nearest tenth place is 8734.3.

188. The correct answer is A.
Convert each fraction into decimal values. To do this, multiply the numerator and denominator by a number that would increase the denominator to 100. For choice A, multiply the top and bottom by 20 to get a fraction of $\frac{80}{100}$. For choice B, multiply both the numerator and denominator by 25 to get $\frac{25}{100}$. Multiply choice C by 33.33 for both the numerator and denominator to get $\frac{66.66}{100}$. Multiply choice D by 5 on the numerator and denominator to get $\frac{45}{100}$. Choice A has the highest value.

189. The correct answer is B.
Find both the perimeter and the area of the square. The perimeter is four times the length of the square, which gives us 5 • 4 = 20. To find the area of a square, simply take the length value and square it. 5^2 = 25. Since the question asks to subtract area by perimeter, 25 - 20 = 5.

190. The correct answer is C.
The angles already given in the problem are supplements to angles that are in the triangle. Supplementary angles add up to 180°. The supplement to the 130° angle is 50°. The supplement to the 140° angle is 40°. So far, 50° and 40° add up to 90°. A triangle must have 180°, therefore, the last angle must be equal to 90°.

191. The correct answer is C.
Answer choice A can be ruled out because prime factorization only contains multiplication. Answer choices B and D can also be ruled out because 25 and 10 are not prime numbers.

192. The correct answer is C.
Convert $\frac{22}{5}$ to decimal form. This gives 4.4. From 4.4 to 15.8, there are a total of 11

ANSWER EXPLANATIONS

integers in between. They are: 5, 6, 7, 8, 9, 10, 11, 12, 13, 14, and 15.

193. The correct answer is B.
Any number squared is always a positive value. Therefore, -4 squared is 16. 16 multiplied by 4 is 64.

194. The correct answer is D.
List out the multiples of 5 and 6 until there is a common multiple. Consecutive multiples of 5 are 5, 10, 15, 20, 25, and 30. Some consecutive multiples of 6 are 6, 12, 18, 24 and 30. 30 is the least common multiple.

195. The correct answer is C.
An equilateral triangle is a type of triangle that has equal side lengths and angle values. A scalene triangle is a triangle that has all unequal length values. An acute triangle is a triangle that has all angles less than 90°. A trapezoid is a quadrilateral.

196. The correct answer is D.
An isosceles trapezoid is a trapezoid that has a line of symmetry bisecting opposite sides. A rhombus is a parallelogram with 4 sides. A parallelogram is a quadrilateral in which opposite sides are parallel to each other. A hexagon is a six sided figure.

197. The correct answer is C.
The prefix milli represents the number 1,000 such as the word millennium represents 1,000 years. Therefore, 1,000 mm are needed in one meter.

198. The correct answer is B.
The square root of 169 is 13. The square root of 196 is 14. Therefore, the square root of 172 lies between 13 and 14.

Problem Solving Questions

199. The correct answer is C.
Perform the operations across as shown.
-5 - 6 = -11
-11 + (-3) = -14
-14 + 2 = -12
-12 - (-1) = -11

200. The correct answer is B.
There are 12 months in a year. If Mike spends $12,000 on utility bills, each month, he spends $\frac{\$12,000}{12}$. This comes out to $1,000 a month.

201. The correct answer is A.
Solve for x. Add $6x$ on both sides. This gives $17 + 10x = 37$. Subtract 17 on both sides to get $10x = 20$. Divide by 10 to get $x = 2$.

202. The correct answer is B.
2 shirts at $3.75 each come out to $7.50. Two hats at $1.25 each come out to $2.50. Add both of these to get $10.00 total. With a 50% discount applied, the total becomes $5.00.

203. The correct answer is C.
Approximate the answer just by looking at the numbers in the question. 0.81 is close to one. 121.3 times 1 is equal to 121.3. The number closest to 121.3 is answer choice C, 98.253.

204. The correct answer is A.
Perform the operations across as shown.
0.1 - (-0.903) = 1.103
1.003 + 1.202 = 2.205

205. The correct answer is B.
25% of $1,000 can be found by multiplying 1,000 by .25 which is 250. 250 off the couch

ANSWER EXPLANATIONS

is 750. Multiply 750 by 0.08, which is the tax, to get 60 additional dollars. 750 + 60 is 810. The cost of the couch is $810.

206. The correct answer is C.
The volume of a rectangular prism can be found by the equation V = l • w • h. This comes out to 4 • 12 • 3 in this problem. This is equal to 144.

207. The correct answer is C.
Any multiple of 40 must be divisible by the number. Only 320 evenly divides by 40.

208. The correct answer is C.
If 78 is 50% of a number, multiply 78 by 2 to get 100% of the number. 78 x 2 = 156.

209. The correct answer is D.
Solve for x first. Subtract 22 on both sides of the first equation. This leaves $7x = 35$. Divide by 7 on both sides to find $x = 5$. Plug $x = 5$ into the second equation.
$x^2 = 25$
25 - 1 = 24.

210. The correct answer is A.
The length of the missing vertical side can be found by adding the 2 lengths given that are parallel to the missing side. These lengths add up to 6. The length of the missing horizontal sde can be found by subtracting 2 from 4. The perimeter is then equal to 4 + 2 + 2 + 4 + 2 + 6. This gives 20. The area can be found by breaking the figure into two rectangles. The first rectangle has dimensions of 2 cm and 6 cm. The second rectangle has dimensions of 2 cm and 2 cm. Simply add the area of both rectangles to get the area of the figure.
12 + 4 = 16.
Since the question to subtract the area from the perimeter, we get 20 - 16 = 4.

211. The correct answer is B.
Notice that triangle BDC is a 3-4-5 triangle. One side has a length of 3, and the hypotenuse has a length of 5. Therefore, the last side must have a length of 4.

212. The correct answer is B.
The product of 7 and 4 is 28. If 28 is 11 more than y, then $y = 28 - 11$ which is 17.

213. The correct answer is D.
If Bob sells a total of five watches at $2,500 each then he sells 5 • 2,500 dollars worth of watches which is $12,500. This multiplied by his commision, .03 is equal to $375.
$12,500 • 0.3 = $375.

214. The correct answer is D.
Answer choices B and C can be eliminated since 3.34 is larger than 2.254. Multiply 3.34 by both .6 and .7 to see which is under the amount of 2.254. If multiplied by 0.7, the number is 2.338 and too great. Therefore, the answer choice is D.

215. The correct answer is C.
Break the figure up into two shapes, a rectangle and a semicircle. The area of the rectangle is 8 times 10, which is 80. The area of a circle is represented by $A = \pi(r)^2$. Since the figure has a semicircle, divide the area equation by 2. It then becomes
$A = (\frac{1}{2})\pi(r)^2$. The radius of the semicircle is 4.
$4^2 = 16$.
Half of 16 is 8.
Therefore, the answer is $(80 + 8\pi)$ square feet.

ANSWER EXPLANATIONS

216. The correct answer is C.
The circumference of a circle is $C = \pi d$. The diameter, d, is equal to $2r$. Therefore, the circumference is $2\pi r$.

217. The correct answer is D.
30.25 converted into a decimal is 3025%, and is not the same as the percentage in question.

218. The correct answer is B.
Plug in the values of x and y into the equation. $2(1)^3 + 2.5(4) = 2 + 10 = 12$.

219. The correct answer is A.
If Ms. Lane drove 12,000 miles for the entire year, and there are 52 weeks in a year divide 12,000 by 52 to find how many miles Ms. Lane drove on average each week. 52 can be approximated to 50. Doing so gives an amount of 240 miles per week. The closest answer choice is A.

220. The correct answer is D.
Find the least common multiple of 5 and 3. The least common multiple is 15. Multiply the top and bottom of the first fraction $\frac{1}{5}$ by $\frac{3}{3}$. This gives $\frac{3}{15}$. Multiply the top and bottom of the last fraction $\frac{1}{3}$ by $\frac{5}{5}$ which gives $\frac{5}{15}$. Subtract $\frac{3}{15}$ on both sides to get $x = 15$.

221. The correct answer is D.
Solve the inequality. Add 100 to both sides. The equation becomes $25x < 350$. Divide by 25 to get $x < 14$. The only number less than 14 in the answer choices is 13.

222. The correct answer is D.
Each consecutive number in this series is 1.03 greater than the previous number, therefore, in order to get to the sixth term, 1.03 added once to 24.11 gives 25.14 as the fifth term and when added to 1.03 again, gives 26.17 as the sixth term.

223. The correct answer is B.
There are 16 cups in one gallon. If there are 5 and a half gallons, to find the total amount of cups, multiply $5\frac{1}{2}$ by 16. This gives 88. Multiply 88 by 16 to get 704 ounces.

224. The correct answer is B.
Subtract the fixed fee from the amount Jonathan has. This leaves $35 left to sing songs. If each song is $2, divide 35 by 2 to see how many songs he can sing. This comes out to 17 and a half. Therefore, he can sing 17 full songs.

225. The correct answer is A.
Find the least common denominator between 3 and 2. The LCD is 6. Multiply the top and bottom of the first fraction by $\frac{2}{2}$ which converts the fraction to $\frac{8}{6x}$. Multiply the second fraction by $\frac{3}{3}$ which converts this fraction to $\frac{9}{6x}$. Since we have common denominators, we can add them to get $\frac{17}{6x}$.

226. The correct answer is C.
Solve for x. First square both sides of the equation. This leaves $x + 3 = 169$. Subtract 3 from both sides to get $x = 166$.

ANSWER EXPLANATIONS

227. The correct answer is C.
20% • 5 = 1. After the first year, the price of the shirt raises to 6 dollars. Do this once more, and multiply 6 by 0.2 which is 1.2. After the second year, the price raises to 7.20 dollars.

228. The correct answer is B.
There are 12 inches in a feet. If the height of the tree is actually 30 feet, multiply 30 by 12, which is 360. The ratio then becomes 4:360 but can be simplified to 1:90. Remember, for these types of problem you must always have the same units. You can not have a ratio of feet to inches.

229. The correct answer is D.
Plug in the necessary variables into the equation. The equation becomes $\frac{1}{2}(5)(4)(3)$ which is 30.

230. The correct answer is B.
Set up an equation to represent the problem. Lisa has 3 less than 3 times the amount of Marty. This can be represented by the equation $3x - 3 = l$ where x represents the amount Marty has and l represents the amount Lisa has. Substitute 24 for x as Marty has 24 dollars and solve for x. $3(24) - 3 = 69$.

231. The correct answer is C.
If Chloe wants to purchase 55 notebooks, and packages are sold in 5, she would need $\frac{55}{5}$ = 11 packages. 11 packages multiplied by $0.89 per package equals $9.79 for 11 packages and 55 notebooks.

232. The correct answer is B.
If there are 750 words per page, in 6 pages, there would be 6 times 750 words which is 4,500 words. 4,500 divided by 300 is 15. 15 times 3 minutes is 45 minutes.

233. The correct answer is D.
Simplify each number in the parenthesis first. The square root of 100 is 10, and the square root of 64 is 8. 10 times 8 is 80.

234. The correct answer is B.
If John got a 4% increase for July, multiply 4,000 by 0.04. This gives 160, so in July, John makes 4,160. If there are 4 weeks in a month, John would work 160 hours a month. Divide 4,160 by 160 to get $26 per hour.

235. The correct answer is A.
To convert milligrams to grams, move the decimal point over 3 units to the left. This leaves 0.0115g.

236. The correct answer is C.
Perform the operations across as shown. Find the least common denominator for the first two fractions, which is 12. The fractions become $\frac{8}{12}$ and $\frac{3}{12}$. When added they become $\frac{11}{12}$. Divide by 2, or multiply by $\frac{1}{2}$ to find the answer of $\frac{11}{24}$.

ANSWER EXPLANATIONS

237. The correct answer is B.
Solve for x. Multiply both sides by $2x$, $2000 = 20x$. Divide both sides by 20 to get $x = 100$. The square root of 100 is 10.

238. The correct answer is D.
If two circles can balance 4 triangles, then 2 triangles can balance 1 circle. If 2 triangles balance 1 square, then 1 square balances 1 circle. Therefore, to balance 70 squares, 70 circles are needed.

LANGUAGE SECTION

239. The correct answer is A.
An official title before a name should be capitalized and in this case since John is a doctor. The word "doctor" in front of John should be capitalized.

240. The correct answer is A.
The error is due to the dangling modifier. Here, the subject or the person doing the action in the sentence is John and so John should come after the comma because he is the one was being fired five different times.

241. The correct answer is C.
The word "day" should be capitalized since it is part of a holiday.

242. The correct answer is C.
Here, the word eminent is incorrectly used. Eminent means famous and in this case it should be imminent which means something that is about to happen.

243. The correct answer is B.
Here, the error is with the comparison of animals of the Amazonian rainforest compared to other land biomes. It should have mentioned "the animals of other land biomes" as a correct comparison.

244. The correct answer is C.
The word "id" should be capitalized to "I.D" since it is an acronym standing for identification.

245. The correct answer is C.
Anytime a sentence starts with neither, nor should usually follow along. The word "or" is incorrectly used.

246. The correct answer is C.
This is an error in subject verb agreement. The Big Dipper is a single constellation and therefore the verb should be is instead of are.

247. The correct answer is A.
Periods and commas should be placed within quotations at the end of sentences.

248. The correct answer is C.
Here, the error is with the comparison of the players to the sport of basketball. Basketball as a sport cannot be injury-prone because the basketball doesn't get hurt. It is the players that are less injury-prone.

249. The correct answer is D.
No mistakes.

250. The correct answer is A.
Here, the error is with the comparison of consistency of the salt compared to sugar. It should have mentioned "the consistency of sugar" as a correct comparison.

251. The correct answer is D.
No mistakes.

252. The correct answer is D.
No mistakes.

ANSWER EXPLANATIONS

253. The correct answer is A.
The pronoun they is incorrect because it is a single institution and so it should be replaced with it. This is an error in pronoun antecedent.

254. The correct answer is B.
There is no English word "deers." The plural of deer is still deer.

255. The correct answer is B.
The word Patriots should be capitalized since it is the name of a team.

256. The correct answer is C.
Here, the word "came" should be "come" since it follows the word had, which is part of the perfect tense. A past participle should come after the perfect tense. Here, there is an error with the verb tense.

257. The correct answer is B.
There is an error with comparison since there are 3 people within the sentence. Here taller is incorrectly used because it refers to a comparison between two people. The correct word should have been tallest.

258. The correct answer is B.
The word "Sundae" should be lowercase.

259. The correct answer is A.
This is an error in subject verb agreement. Ethylene gas is a singular and therefore the verb should be "is used" instead of "are used."

260. The correct answer is A.
A semicolon separates two independent clauses and therefore "and" should not belong in the sentence. The semicolon can be replaced by a comma to make the sentence correct since it is the comma that separates two independent clauses with a conjunction.

261. The correct answer is A.
The pronoun their is incorrect because it is a singular subject (one cow) and so it should be replaced with its. This is an error in pronoun antecedent.

262. The correct answer is C.
Here, the error is with the comparison of satellites of Saturn compared to Earth. It should have mentioned "the satellite(moon) of Earth" as a correct comparison.

263. The correct answer is C.
Here there is an error in pronoun vagueness. One cannot tell what provides light from the other; is it the moon that provides light to the Sun with the Sun that provides light to the moon?

264. The correct answer is B.
This is an error in subject verb agreement. The Scottish is singular and therefore the verb should be "has" instead of "have."

265. The correct answer is B.
There should be a comma between Ferrari and which.

266. The correct answer is B.
There should be a comma between months and babies.

ANSWER EXPLANATIONS

267. **The correct answer is C.**
"It's" should be "Its" since the contraction can be replaced with "it is", but "Its" shows possession. The possession of logo must be shown through the word its.

268. **The correct answer is B.**
There is an error with verb tense since part of the sentence is in the past tense and part of it is in the present tense.

269. **The correct answer is B.**
The error is due to the dangling modifier. Here, the subject or the person doing the action in the sentence is the sloth and so it should come after the comma because the sloth is the one hanging still on trees.

270. **The correct answer is B.**
A comma separates two independent clauses but it needs a conjunction such as "and". The comma can be replaced by a semicolon to make the sentence correct since it is the semicolon that separates two independent clauses without a conjunction.

271. **The correct answer is A.**
A comma separates two independent clauses but it needs a conjunction such as "and". The comma can be replaced by a semicolon between "right hand" and "the left hand" to make the sentence correct since it is the semicolon that separates two independent clauses without a conjunction.

272. **The correct answer is A.**
The incorrect word "affect" is used. "Affect" is used as a verb, but here it should be the word "effect" since it is a noun.

273. **The correct answer is A.**
The word ancient does not need to be capitalized.

274. **The correct answer is B.**
Here there is an error of double positives. The word "more" is unnecessary since one can just say I did better on my physics exam. This is an error in comparison.

275. **The correct answer is C.**
The words "The" before "Nixon scandal" should not be capitalized.

276. **The correct answer is B.**
Here, the error is with the comparison of tongue of crocodiles compared to alligators. It should have mentioned "different from an alligator's tongue" as a correct comparison.

277. **The correct answer is C.**
The incorrect word "then" is used. "Then" is used to describe a following event, but here it should be the word "than" since it is being used as a comparison.

278. **The correct answer is A.**
The transition word therefore is incorrect since the two independent clauses are opposing sentences. It should be replaced with the word however.

279. **The correct answer is B.**
The correct spelling is psychology.

280. **The correct answer is C.**
The correct spelling is sincerely.

281. **The correct answer is A.**
The correct spelling is amateur.

ANSWER EXPLANATIONS

282. The correct answer is A.
The correct spelling is calendar.

283. The correct answer is D.
No mistakes.

284. The correct answer is B.
The correct spelling is definitely.

285. The correct answer is B.
The correct spelling is existence.

286. The correct answer is A.
The correct spelling is foreigner.

287. The correct answer is D.
No mistakes.

288. The correct answer is C.
The correct spelling is noticeable.

289. The correct answer is A.
The word of "that" makes the sentence sound correct. Who is only used as a pronoun is the noun is a living being and so is used usually as a cause and effect situation.

290. The correct answer is B.
The correct transition word should allow the two sentences to be opposing and the only word that does that is although from the choices is given.

291. The correct answer is A.
Quickly should come before the verb since it is an adverb.

292. The correct answer is A.
This sentence should be placed in active voice and this means placing the subject usually at the beginning of a sentence. The subject here is you and the sentence that correctly uses the correct modifier between choice A and D is choice D. For these kind of questions, try to have a dependent clause followed by an independent clause.

293. The correct answer is C.
For these kind of questions, again try to have a dependent clause followed by an independent clause. The only choices that follow this rule are B & C. However, C. is a simpler sentence then B.

294. The correct answer is D.
The essential idea here is that tasks are completed at a much faster rate and this correlates with the word efficient in choice D.

295. The correct answer is D.
The animals being dangerous has nothing to do with the preservation of the Amazonian rainforest.

296. The correct answer is B.
Choice B best connects with the principle that mathematics is the underlying truth of all the other sciences.

297. The correct answer is D.
The short paragraph is mainly concerned with the fierceness of the Mongols and does not really talk about how the weapons were used.

ANSWER EXPLANATIONS

298. The correct answer is D.
Only after practicing for the second time was Jeff able to do well on his exam. The moral of the story should go at the end of all three sentences.

EXAM 2
HSPT

ARGO BROTHERS

To calculate your score and watch video tutorials, visit
our web site: www.einstein-academy.com/catholic

HSPT PRACTICE TEST 2
ANSWER SHEET

Verbal Skills (Part I)

1. Ⓐ Ⓑ Ⓒ Ⓓ
2. Ⓐ Ⓑ Ⓒ Ⓓ
3. Ⓐ Ⓑ Ⓒ Ⓓ
4. Ⓐ Ⓑ Ⓒ Ⓓ
5. Ⓐ Ⓑ Ⓒ Ⓓ
6. Ⓐ Ⓑ Ⓒ Ⓓ
7. Ⓐ Ⓑ Ⓒ Ⓓ
8. Ⓐ Ⓑ Ⓒ Ⓓ
9. Ⓐ Ⓑ Ⓒ Ⓓ
10. Ⓐ Ⓑ Ⓒ Ⓓ
11. Ⓐ Ⓑ Ⓒ Ⓓ
12. Ⓐ Ⓑ Ⓒ Ⓓ
13. Ⓐ Ⓑ Ⓒ Ⓓ
14. Ⓐ Ⓑ Ⓒ Ⓓ
15. Ⓐ Ⓑ Ⓒ Ⓓ
16. Ⓐ Ⓑ Ⓒ Ⓓ
17. Ⓐ Ⓑ Ⓒ Ⓓ
18. Ⓐ Ⓑ Ⓒ Ⓓ
19. Ⓐ Ⓑ Ⓒ Ⓓ
20. Ⓐ Ⓑ Ⓒ Ⓓ
21. Ⓐ Ⓑ Ⓒ Ⓓ
22. Ⓐ Ⓑ Ⓒ Ⓓ
23. Ⓐ Ⓑ Ⓒ Ⓓ
24. Ⓐ Ⓑ Ⓒ Ⓓ
25. Ⓐ Ⓑ Ⓒ Ⓓ
26. Ⓐ Ⓑ Ⓒ Ⓓ
27. Ⓐ Ⓑ Ⓒ Ⓓ
28. Ⓐ Ⓑ Ⓒ Ⓓ
29. Ⓐ Ⓑ Ⓒ Ⓓ
30. Ⓐ Ⓑ Ⓒ Ⓓ
31. Ⓐ Ⓑ Ⓒ Ⓓ
33. Ⓐ Ⓑ Ⓒ Ⓓ
33. Ⓐ Ⓑ Ⓒ Ⓓ
34. Ⓐ Ⓑ Ⓒ Ⓓ
35. Ⓐ Ⓑ Ⓒ Ⓓ
36. Ⓐ Ⓑ Ⓒ Ⓓ
37. Ⓐ Ⓑ Ⓒ Ⓓ
38. Ⓐ Ⓑ Ⓒ Ⓓ
39. Ⓐ Ⓑ Ⓒ Ⓓ
40. Ⓐ Ⓑ Ⓒ Ⓓ
41. Ⓐ Ⓑ Ⓒ Ⓓ
42. Ⓐ Ⓑ Ⓒ Ⓓ
43. Ⓐ Ⓑ Ⓒ Ⓓ
44. Ⓐ Ⓑ Ⓒ Ⓓ
45. Ⓐ Ⓑ Ⓒ Ⓓ
46. Ⓐ Ⓑ Ⓒ Ⓓ
47. Ⓐ Ⓑ Ⓒ Ⓓ
48. Ⓐ Ⓑ Ⓒ Ⓓ
49. Ⓐ Ⓑ Ⓒ Ⓓ
50. Ⓐ Ⓑ Ⓒ Ⓓ
51. Ⓐ Ⓑ Ⓒ Ⓓ
52. Ⓐ Ⓑ Ⓒ Ⓓ
53. Ⓐ Ⓑ Ⓒ Ⓓ
54. Ⓐ Ⓑ Ⓒ Ⓓ
55. Ⓐ Ⓑ Ⓒ Ⓓ
56. Ⓐ Ⓑ Ⓒ Ⓓ
57. Ⓐ Ⓑ Ⓒ Ⓓ
58. Ⓐ Ⓑ Ⓒ Ⓓ
59. Ⓐ Ⓑ Ⓒ Ⓓ
60. Ⓐ Ⓑ Ⓒ Ⓓ

Quantitative (Part II)

61. Ⓐ Ⓑ Ⓒ Ⓓ
62. Ⓐ Ⓑ Ⓒ Ⓓ
63. Ⓐ Ⓑ Ⓒ Ⓓ
64. Ⓐ Ⓑ Ⓒ Ⓓ
65. Ⓐ Ⓑ Ⓒ Ⓓ
66. Ⓐ Ⓑ Ⓒ Ⓓ
67. Ⓐ Ⓑ Ⓒ Ⓓ
68. Ⓐ Ⓑ Ⓒ Ⓓ
69. Ⓐ Ⓑ Ⓒ Ⓓ
70. Ⓐ Ⓑ Ⓒ Ⓓ
71. Ⓐ Ⓑ Ⓒ Ⓓ
72. Ⓐ Ⓑ Ⓒ Ⓓ
73. Ⓐ Ⓑ Ⓒ Ⓓ
74. Ⓐ Ⓑ Ⓒ Ⓓ
75. Ⓐ Ⓑ Ⓒ Ⓓ
76. Ⓐ Ⓑ Ⓒ Ⓓ
77. Ⓐ Ⓑ Ⓒ Ⓓ
78. Ⓐ Ⓑ Ⓒ Ⓓ
79. Ⓐ Ⓑ Ⓒ Ⓓ
80. Ⓐ Ⓑ Ⓒ Ⓓ
81. Ⓐ Ⓑ Ⓒ Ⓓ
82. Ⓐ Ⓑ Ⓒ Ⓓ
83. Ⓐ Ⓑ Ⓒ Ⓓ
84. Ⓐ Ⓑ Ⓒ Ⓓ
85. Ⓐ Ⓑ Ⓒ Ⓓ
86. Ⓐ Ⓑ Ⓒ Ⓓ
87. Ⓐ Ⓑ Ⓒ Ⓓ
88. Ⓐ Ⓑ Ⓒ Ⓓ
89. Ⓐ Ⓑ Ⓒ Ⓓ
90. Ⓐ Ⓑ Ⓒ Ⓓ
91. Ⓐ Ⓑ Ⓒ Ⓓ
92. Ⓐ Ⓑ Ⓒ Ⓓ
93. Ⓐ Ⓑ Ⓒ Ⓓ
94. Ⓐ Ⓑ Ⓒ Ⓓ
95. Ⓐ Ⓑ Ⓒ Ⓓ
96. Ⓐ Ⓑ Ⓒ Ⓓ
97. Ⓐ Ⓑ Ⓒ Ⓓ
98. Ⓐ Ⓑ Ⓒ Ⓓ
99. Ⓐ Ⓑ Ⓒ Ⓓ
100. Ⓐ Ⓑ Ⓒ Ⓓ
101. Ⓐ Ⓑ Ⓒ Ⓓ
102. Ⓐ Ⓑ Ⓒ Ⓓ
103. Ⓐ Ⓑ Ⓒ Ⓓ
104. Ⓐ Ⓑ Ⓒ Ⓓ
105. Ⓐ Ⓑ Ⓒ Ⓓ
106. Ⓐ Ⓑ Ⓒ Ⓓ
107. Ⓐ Ⓑ Ⓒ Ⓓ
108. Ⓐ Ⓑ Ⓒ Ⓓ
109. Ⓐ Ⓑ Ⓒ Ⓓ
110. Ⓐ Ⓑ Ⓒ Ⓓ
111. Ⓐ Ⓑ Ⓒ Ⓓ
112. Ⓐ Ⓑ Ⓒ Ⓓ

Reading (Part III)

113. Ⓐ Ⓑ Ⓒ Ⓓ
114. Ⓐ Ⓑ Ⓒ Ⓓ
115. Ⓐ Ⓑ Ⓒ Ⓓ
116. Ⓐ Ⓑ Ⓒ Ⓓ
117. Ⓐ Ⓑ Ⓒ Ⓓ
118. Ⓐ Ⓑ Ⓒ Ⓓ
119. Ⓐ Ⓑ Ⓒ Ⓓ
120. Ⓐ Ⓑ Ⓒ Ⓓ
121. Ⓐ Ⓑ Ⓒ Ⓓ
122. Ⓐ Ⓑ Ⓒ Ⓓ
123. Ⓐ Ⓑ Ⓒ Ⓓ
124. Ⓐ Ⓑ Ⓒ Ⓓ
125. Ⓐ Ⓑ Ⓒ Ⓓ
126. Ⓐ Ⓑ Ⓒ Ⓓ
127. Ⓐ Ⓑ Ⓒ Ⓓ
128. Ⓐ Ⓑ Ⓒ Ⓓ
129. Ⓐ Ⓑ Ⓒ Ⓓ
130. Ⓐ Ⓑ Ⓒ Ⓓ
131. Ⓐ Ⓑ Ⓒ Ⓓ
132. Ⓐ Ⓑ Ⓒ Ⓓ
133. Ⓐ Ⓑ Ⓒ Ⓓ
134. Ⓐ Ⓑ Ⓒ Ⓓ
135. Ⓐ Ⓑ Ⓒ Ⓓ
136. Ⓐ Ⓑ Ⓒ Ⓓ
137. Ⓐ Ⓑ Ⓒ Ⓓ
138. Ⓐ Ⓑ Ⓒ Ⓓ
139. Ⓐ Ⓑ Ⓒ Ⓓ
140. Ⓐ Ⓑ Ⓒ Ⓓ
141. Ⓐ Ⓑ Ⓒ Ⓓ
142. Ⓐ Ⓑ Ⓒ Ⓓ
143. Ⓐ Ⓑ Ⓒ Ⓓ
144. Ⓐ Ⓑ Ⓒ Ⓓ
145. Ⓐ Ⓑ Ⓒ Ⓓ
146. Ⓐ Ⓑ Ⓒ Ⓓ
147. Ⓐ Ⓑ Ⓒ Ⓓ
148. Ⓐ Ⓑ Ⓒ Ⓓ
149. Ⓐ Ⓑ Ⓒ Ⓓ
150. Ⓐ Ⓑ Ⓒ Ⓓ
151. Ⓐ Ⓑ Ⓒ Ⓓ
152. Ⓐ Ⓑ Ⓒ Ⓓ
153. Ⓐ Ⓑ Ⓒ Ⓓ
154. Ⓐ Ⓑ Ⓒ Ⓓ
155. Ⓐ Ⓑ Ⓒ Ⓓ
156. Ⓐ Ⓑ Ⓒ Ⓓ
157. Ⓐ Ⓑ Ⓒ Ⓓ
158. Ⓐ Ⓑ Ⓒ Ⓓ
159. Ⓐ Ⓑ Ⓒ Ⓓ
160. Ⓐ Ⓑ Ⓒ Ⓓ
161. Ⓐ Ⓑ Ⓒ Ⓓ
162. Ⓐ Ⓑ Ⓒ Ⓓ
163. Ⓐ Ⓑ Ⓒ Ⓓ
164. Ⓐ Ⓑ Ⓒ Ⓓ
165. Ⓐ Ⓑ Ⓒ Ⓓ
166. Ⓐ Ⓑ Ⓒ Ⓓ
167. Ⓐ Ⓑ Ⓒ Ⓓ
168. Ⓐ Ⓑ Ⓒ Ⓓ
169. Ⓐ Ⓑ Ⓒ Ⓓ
170. Ⓐ Ⓑ Ⓒ Ⓓ
171. Ⓐ Ⓑ Ⓒ Ⓓ
172. Ⓐ Ⓑ Ⓒ Ⓓ
173. Ⓐ Ⓑ Ⓒ Ⓓ
174. Ⓐ Ⓑ Ⓒ Ⓓ

ARGO BROTHERS

To calculate your score and watch
video tutorials, visit our web site:
www.einstein-academy.com/catholic

HSPT PRACTICE TEST 2
ANSWER SHEET

Mathematics (Part IV)

175. Ⓐ Ⓑ Ⓒ Ⓓ
176. Ⓐ Ⓑ Ⓒ Ⓓ
177. Ⓐ Ⓑ Ⓒ Ⓓ
178. Ⓐ Ⓑ Ⓒ Ⓓ
179. Ⓐ Ⓑ Ⓒ Ⓓ
180. Ⓐ Ⓑ Ⓒ Ⓓ
181. Ⓐ Ⓑ Ⓒ Ⓓ
182. Ⓐ Ⓑ Ⓒ Ⓓ
183. Ⓐ Ⓑ Ⓒ Ⓓ
184. Ⓐ Ⓑ Ⓒ Ⓓ
185. Ⓐ Ⓑ Ⓒ Ⓓ
186. Ⓐ Ⓑ Ⓒ Ⓓ
187. Ⓐ Ⓑ Ⓒ Ⓓ
188. Ⓐ Ⓑ Ⓒ Ⓓ
189. Ⓐ Ⓑ Ⓒ Ⓓ
190. Ⓐ Ⓑ Ⓒ Ⓓ
191. Ⓐ Ⓑ Ⓒ Ⓓ
192. Ⓐ Ⓑ Ⓒ Ⓓ
193. Ⓐ Ⓑ Ⓒ Ⓓ
194. Ⓐ Ⓑ Ⓒ Ⓓ
195. Ⓐ Ⓑ Ⓒ Ⓓ
196. Ⓐ Ⓑ Ⓒ Ⓓ
197. Ⓐ Ⓑ Ⓒ Ⓓ
198. Ⓐ Ⓑ Ⓒ Ⓓ
199. Ⓐ Ⓑ Ⓒ Ⓓ
200. Ⓐ Ⓑ Ⓒ Ⓓ
201. Ⓐ Ⓑ Ⓒ Ⓓ
202. Ⓐ Ⓑ Ⓒ Ⓓ
203. Ⓐ Ⓑ Ⓒ Ⓓ
204. Ⓐ Ⓑ Ⓒ Ⓓ
205. Ⓐ Ⓑ Ⓒ Ⓓ
206. Ⓐ Ⓑ Ⓒ Ⓓ
207. Ⓐ Ⓑ Ⓒ Ⓓ
208. Ⓐ Ⓑ Ⓒ Ⓓ
209. Ⓐ Ⓑ Ⓒ Ⓓ
210. Ⓐ Ⓑ Ⓒ Ⓓ
211. Ⓐ Ⓑ Ⓒ Ⓓ
212. Ⓐ Ⓑ Ⓒ Ⓓ
213. Ⓐ Ⓑ Ⓒ Ⓓ
214. Ⓐ Ⓑ Ⓒ Ⓓ
215. Ⓐ Ⓑ Ⓒ Ⓓ
216. Ⓐ Ⓑ Ⓒ Ⓓ
217. Ⓐ Ⓑ Ⓒ Ⓓ
218. Ⓐ Ⓑ Ⓒ Ⓓ
219. Ⓐ Ⓑ Ⓒ Ⓓ
220. Ⓐ Ⓑ Ⓒ Ⓓ
221. Ⓐ Ⓑ Ⓒ Ⓓ
222. Ⓐ Ⓑ Ⓒ Ⓓ
223. Ⓐ Ⓑ Ⓒ Ⓓ
224. Ⓐ Ⓑ Ⓒ Ⓓ
225. Ⓐ Ⓑ Ⓒ Ⓓ
226. Ⓐ Ⓑ Ⓒ Ⓓ
227. Ⓐ Ⓑ Ⓒ Ⓓ
228. Ⓐ Ⓑ Ⓒ Ⓓ
229. Ⓐ Ⓑ Ⓒ Ⓓ
230. Ⓐ Ⓑ Ⓒ Ⓓ
231. Ⓐ Ⓑ Ⓒ Ⓓ
232. Ⓐ Ⓑ Ⓒ Ⓓ
233. Ⓐ Ⓑ Ⓒ Ⓓ
234. Ⓐ Ⓑ Ⓒ Ⓓ
235. Ⓐ Ⓑ Ⓒ Ⓓ
236. Ⓐ Ⓑ Ⓒ Ⓓ
237. Ⓐ Ⓑ Ⓒ Ⓓ
238. Ⓐ Ⓑ Ⓒ Ⓓ

Language (Part V)

239. Ⓐ Ⓑ Ⓒ Ⓓ
240. Ⓐ Ⓑ Ⓒ Ⓓ
241. Ⓐ Ⓑ Ⓒ Ⓓ
242. Ⓐ Ⓑ Ⓒ Ⓓ
243. Ⓐ Ⓑ Ⓒ Ⓓ
244. Ⓐ Ⓑ Ⓒ Ⓓ
245. Ⓐ Ⓑ Ⓒ Ⓓ
246. Ⓐ Ⓑ Ⓒ Ⓓ
247. Ⓐ Ⓑ Ⓒ Ⓓ
248. Ⓐ Ⓑ Ⓒ Ⓓ
249. Ⓐ Ⓑ Ⓒ Ⓓ
250. Ⓐ Ⓑ Ⓒ Ⓓ
251. Ⓐ Ⓑ Ⓒ Ⓓ
252. Ⓐ Ⓑ Ⓒ Ⓓ
253. Ⓐ Ⓑ Ⓒ Ⓓ
254. Ⓐ Ⓑ Ⓒ Ⓓ
255. Ⓐ Ⓑ Ⓒ Ⓓ
256. Ⓐ Ⓑ Ⓒ Ⓓ
257. Ⓐ Ⓑ Ⓒ Ⓓ
258. Ⓐ Ⓑ Ⓒ Ⓓ
259. Ⓐ Ⓑ Ⓒ Ⓓ
260. Ⓐ Ⓑ Ⓒ Ⓓ
261. Ⓐ Ⓑ Ⓒ Ⓓ
262. Ⓐ Ⓑ Ⓒ Ⓓ
263. Ⓐ Ⓑ Ⓒ Ⓓ
264. Ⓐ Ⓑ Ⓒ Ⓓ
265. Ⓐ Ⓑ Ⓒ Ⓓ
266. Ⓐ Ⓑ Ⓒ Ⓓ
267. Ⓐ Ⓑ Ⓒ Ⓓ
268. Ⓐ Ⓑ Ⓒ Ⓓ
269. Ⓐ Ⓑ Ⓒ Ⓓ
270. Ⓐ Ⓑ Ⓒ Ⓓ
271. Ⓐ Ⓑ Ⓒ Ⓓ
272. Ⓐ Ⓑ Ⓒ Ⓓ
273. Ⓐ Ⓑ Ⓒ Ⓓ
274. Ⓐ Ⓑ Ⓒ Ⓓ
275. Ⓐ Ⓑ Ⓒ Ⓓ
276. Ⓐ Ⓑ Ⓒ Ⓓ
277. Ⓐ Ⓑ Ⓒ Ⓓ
278. Ⓐ Ⓑ Ⓒ Ⓓ
279. Ⓐ Ⓑ Ⓒ Ⓓ
280. Ⓐ Ⓑ Ⓒ Ⓓ
281. Ⓐ Ⓑ Ⓒ Ⓓ
282. Ⓐ Ⓑ Ⓒ Ⓓ
283. Ⓐ Ⓑ Ⓒ Ⓓ
284. Ⓐ Ⓑ Ⓒ Ⓓ
285. Ⓐ Ⓑ Ⓒ Ⓓ
286. Ⓐ Ⓑ Ⓒ Ⓓ
287. Ⓐ Ⓑ Ⓒ Ⓓ
288. Ⓐ Ⓑ Ⓒ Ⓓ
289. Ⓐ Ⓑ Ⓒ Ⓓ
290. Ⓐ Ⓑ Ⓒ Ⓓ
291. Ⓐ Ⓑ Ⓒ Ⓓ
292. Ⓐ Ⓑ Ⓒ Ⓓ
293. Ⓐ Ⓑ Ⓒ Ⓓ
294. Ⓐ Ⓑ Ⓒ Ⓓ
295. Ⓐ Ⓑ Ⓒ Ⓓ
296. Ⓐ Ⓑ Ⓒ Ⓓ
297. Ⓐ Ⓑ Ⓒ Ⓓ
298. Ⓐ Ⓑ Ⓒ Ⓓ

ARGO BROTHERS

To calculate your score and watch
video tutorials, visit our web site:
www.einstein-academy.com/catholic

VERBAL SKILLS
PART I (16 MIN)

DIRECTIONS: For questions 1-60, follow the directions and choose the best answer.

1. Which word does *not* belong with the others?

   A. stove
   B. microwave
   C. sofa
   D. sink

2. Which word does *not* belong with the others?

   A. finger
   B. nail
   C. palm
   D. elbow

3. Paint is to painter as wood is to

   A. engineer
   B. doctor
   C. carpenter
   D. construction worker

4. Larry can swim faster than Sue. Bob can not swim faster than Sue. Bob can swim faster than Larry. If the first two statements are true, the third is

   A. true
   B. false
   C. uncertain

5. <u>Intricate</u> most nearly means

   A. simple
   B. complicated
   C. short
   D. perplexing

6. Hair is to skin as plant is to

   A. soil
   B. leave
   C. flower
   D. water

7. Which word does not belong with the others?

   A. lobster
   B. shrimp
   C. whale
   D. seagull

8. Oil is to a car as charcoal is to

   A. black
   B. grill
   C. barbecue
   D. fire

CONTINUE ON TO THE NEXT PAGE ➡

VERBAL SKILLS
PART I

9. Which word does *not* belong with the others?

   A. positive
   B. optimistic
   C. hopeful
   D. successful

10. <u>Gratuitous</u> most closely means

    A. disdainful
    B. appreciative
    C. intelligent
    D. plentiful

11. To be <u>decorous</u> means to be

    A. proper
    B. joyous
    C. furious
    D. lively

12. Player is to coach as employee is to

    A. co-worker
    B. customer
    C. company
    D. manager

13. Which word does *not* belong with the others?

    A. leaves
    B. stem
    C. roots
    D. trunk

14. Rabbi is to synagogue as reverend is to

    A. mosque
    B. temple
    C. church
    D. gurdwara

15. Battery is to flashlight as gas is to

    A. a solar cell
    B. a windmill
    C. a water turbine
    D. car

16. Jesse is older than Jacob. James is older than Jesse. Jacob is older than James. If the first two statements are true, the third is

    A. true
    B. false
    C. uncertain

CONTINUE ON TO THE NEXT PAGE ➡

VERBAL SKILLS
PART I

17. Aloof most nearly means

    A. close
    B. amiable
    C. loveable
    D. distant

18. Assail most nearly means

    A. endearing
    B. attack
    C. lure
    D. sneaky

19. Hesitant most nearly means

    A. impulsive
    B. thoughtful
    C. carefree
    D. doubtful

20. Vacuum is to dirt as eraser is to

    A. blackboard
    B. pencil marks
    C. paper
    D. clean

21. Frame is to photo as screen protector is to

    A. headphones
    B. glass
    C. vase
    D. cellphone

22. Dependent most nearly means

    A. energetic
    B. helpless
    C. rich
    D. instructional

23. A cart can hold more than a bag. A bag can hold less than a box but more than a gallon. A box can hold more than a cart. If the first two statements are true, the third is

    A. true
    B. false
    C. uncertain

24. Which word does *not* belong with the others?

    A. morgue
    B. grave
    C. coffin
    D. tombstone

CONTINUE ON TO THE NEXT PAGE ➡

VERBAL SKILLS
PART I

25. <u>Conspicuous</u> most nearly means

    A. powerful
    B. noticeable
    C. fast
    D. honest

26. A civic is faster than a prius but not a station wagon. A prius is slower than a ferrari but faster than a lamborghini. A lamborghini is faster than a civic. If the first two statements are true, the third is

    A. true
    B. false
    C. uncertain

27. <u>Lucrative</u> most nearly means

    A. poor
    B. inferior
    C. profitable
    D. futile

28. <u>Berate</u> most nearly means

    A. applaud
    B. scold
    C. smother
    D. protect

29. Snow is to arctic as sand is to

    A. water
    B. beach
    C. shells
    D. waves

30. <u>Glorify</u> most nearly means

    A. sensible
    B. irrefutable
    C. praise
    D. visible

31. Alleviate means the *opposite* of

    A. reduce
    B. relieve
    C. aggravate
    D. weaken

32. Which word does not belong with the others?

    A. heart
    B. hair
    C. lungs
    D. liver

CONTINUE ON TO THE NEXT PAGE →

VERBAL SKILLS
PART I

33. Which word does *not* belong with the others?

- A. crazy
- B. lunatic
- C. bonkers
- D. sane

34. Benign means the *opposite* of

- A. malicious
- B. loyal
- C. plentiful
- D. heavy

35. Orange is to fruit as carrot is to

- A. greens
- B. vegetable
- C. grains
- D. meat

36. Diminish means the *opposite* of

- A. increase
- B. economical
- C. lavish
- D. worsen

37. <u>Scrutinize</u> most nearly means

- A. examine
- B. reward
- C. competent
- D. retaliate

38. Pretentious means the *opposite* of

- A. mild
- B. rich
- C. genuine
- D. frequent

39. Modest means the *opposite* of

- A. shorten
- B. extend
- C. shameless
- D. cowardly

40. Which word does *not* belong with the others?

- A. bicycle
- B. tricycle
- C. motorbike
- D. an airplane

CONTINUE ON TO THE NEXT PAGE ➡

VERBAL SKILLS
PART I

41. Which word does *not* belong with the others?

    A. door
    B. cave
    C. book
    D. refrigerator

42. Josh can jump higher than Jack but not higher than Joseph. Joseph can jump higher than Jimmy but not higher than Jeff. Jack can jump higher than Jeff. If the first two statements are true, the third is

    A. true
    B. false
    C. uncertain

43. Which word does *not* belong with the others?

    A. exemplary
    B. disreputable
    C. infamous
    D. dishonest

44. <u>Pompous</u> most nearly means

    A. agreeable
    B. overbearing
    C. civil
    D. barbaric

45. Impractical means the *opposite* of

    A. feasible
    B. punish
    C. annoy
    D. content

46. Goku is stronger than Vegeta. Gohan is stronger than Vegeta but not Krillin. Krillin is stronger than Goku. If the first two statements are true, the third is

    A. true
    B. false
    C. uncertain

47. Docile means the *opposite* of

    A. submissive
    B. disobedient
    C. unknown
    D. polished

48. Monumental means the *opposite* of

    A. tiny
    B. hostile
    C. colossal
    D. command

CONTINUE ON TO THE NEXT PAGE ➡

VERBAL SKILLS
PART I

49. Picasso is smarter than Michelangelo. Michelangelo is smarter than da Vinci. Da Vinci is smarter than Picasso. If the first two statements are true, the third is

    A. true
    C. false
    D. uncertain

50. Saitama is shorter than Paul but not shorter than Penny. Penny is taller than Tyler. Saitama is taller than Tyler. If the first two statements are true, the third is

    A. true
    B. false
    C. uncertain

51. Copious means the *opposite* of

    A. abundant
    B. dangerous
    C. sparse
    D. quick

52. Which word does *not* belong with the others?

    A. chaotic
    B. disorderly
    C. turmoil
    D. tidy

53. Which word does *not* belong with the others?

    A. park
    B. trailer
    C. home
    D. mansion

54. Refurbish most nearly means

    A. deplete
    B. restless
    C. renovate
    D. expensive

55. Intolerant means the *opposite* of

    A. fleeting
    B. unprejudiced
    C. permanent
    D. masculine

56. Lucrative means the *opposite* of

    A. neglect
    B. stimulate
    C. graceful
    D. unprofitable

CONTINUE ON TO THE NEXT PAGE ➡

VERBAL SKILLS
PART I

57. Librarian is to library as doctor is to

- **A.** patient
- **B.** healthcare
- **C.** hospital
- **D.** medicine

58. <u>Pugnacious</u> most nearly means

- **A.** aggressive
- **B.** summarize
- **C.** rare
- **D.** lenient

59. Which word does *not* belong with the others?

- **A.** ruby
- **B.** diamond
- **C.** emerald
- **D.** sapphire

60. Which word does *not* belong with the others?

- **A.** jacket
- **B.** hoodie
- **C.** mittens
- **D.** tanktop

CONTINUE ON TO THE NEXT PAGE ➡

QUANTITATIVE
PART II

65. Examine (A), (B), and (C) and find the best answer

    (A) 5(7 + 6)
    (B) (5 + 7)(5 + 7)
    (C) 5(7) + 6

    A. A is greater than C and B.
    B. C is greater than A.
    C. B is the greatest.
    D. B = C + A

66. Examine (A), (B), and (C) and find the best answer

    (A) 100% of 56
    (B) 56% of 100%
    (C) 56% of 100

    A. B is greater than A.
    B. C is greater than the combination of A and B.
    C. C = B < A
    D. A = C > B

67. Look at this series: 5, 10, 14, 17, 19, 20, 20 ... What number should come next?

    A. 21
    B. 17
    C. 20
    D. 19

68. Look at this series: 31, 25, 33, 27, __, 29, 37 ... What is the missing number in the series above?

    A. 33
    B. 21
    C. 35
    D. 19

69. What number is 3 times the average of the numbers 5, 11, 5, 40, and 9?

    A. 4
    B. 36
    C. 42
    D. 14

70. Examine (A), (B), and (C) and find the best answer

    (A) $\frac{1}{9}$ of 3^5
    (B) $\frac{1}{2}$ of 4^3
    (C) 2^2 times 7.5

    A. A is equal to B, which is greater than C.
    B. B > C > A
    C. A is the average of B and C.
    D. A is less than C but greater than B.

CONTINUE ON TO THE NEXT PAGE ➡

QUANTITATIVE
PART II (45 MIN)

DIRECTIONS: For questions 61-112, choose the best answer that fits the problem.

61. The number that is 9 less than 100 is the product of 7 and what other number?

- A. 8
- B. 14
- C. 12
- D. 13

62. What number is 2 less than the cube of 3 divided by 9?

- A. 3
- B. 5
- C. -1
- D. 1

63. Look at this series: 1, 2, 3, 6, 7, __, 15 ... What is the missing number in the series above?

- A. 12
- B. 11
- C. 8
- D. 14

64. Examine (A), (B), and (C) and find the best answer.

(A)

(B)

(C)

- A. A has more value than B and C.
- B. C has more value than A and B.
- C. All three are equal.
- D. A has the most value.

1 CONTINUE ON TO THE NEXT PAGE ➡

QUANTITATIVE
PART II

71. Look at this series: 78, 75, 76, 73, __, 71, 72 ...
What is the missing number in the series above?

   A. 74
   B. 70
   C. 76
   D. 72

72. Examine (A), (B), and (C) and find the best answer.

(A) 9 circles in a 3x3 grid
(B) 9 circles scattered
(C) 6 circles

   A. A has more circles than B and C combined.
   B. B has more circles than A and C.
   C. A has the most circles.
   D. B has the least amount of circles.

73. Look at this series: 5, 13, 22, 32, 43, 55...
What three number should come next?

   A. 68, 82, 97
   B. 68, 81, 94
   C. 67, 79, 91
   D. 67, 81, 96

74. Look at this series: 0, 1, 1, 2, 3, 5, __, 13, 21...
What is the missing number in the series above?

   A. 9
   B. 7
   C. 8
   D. 10

75. Examine (A), (B), and (C) and find the best answer

(A) (7 • 4) - 2
(B) (5 • 3) + 7
(C) (3 • 3 • 3) - 1

   A. A = C > B
   B. A > C > B
   C. (B + 6) is smaller than A.
   D. None of the above

76. What number is 12 less than 30% of 30?

   A. -3
   B. 3
   C. 9
   D. -9

CONTINUE ON TO THE NEXT PAGE ➡

QUANTITATIVE
PART II

77. Examine (A), (B), and (C) and find the best answer

(A) $(\frac{25}{5}) \cdot 3$

(B) $(\frac{39}{3}) \cdot 2$

(C) $(\frac{6}{2}) \cdot 8$

A. C is the largest.
B. 2A is smaller than B.
C. B > C > A
D. B + 2 = C

78. Examine (A), (B), and (C) and find the best answer.

(A) (B) (C)

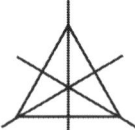 

A. B has fewer lines of symmetry than C but more than A.
B. B has the most number of lines of symmetry.
C. A has the most number of lines of symmetry.
D. None of the above

79. Look at this series: 595, 589, 584, 580, 577, 575...
What number should come next?

A. 577
B. 575
C. 574
D. 580

80. Look at this series: 44, 48, __, 56, 60
What is the missing number in the series above?

A. 52
B. 53
C. 56
D. 54

81. Examine (A), (B), and (C) and find the best answer.

(A) (B) (C)

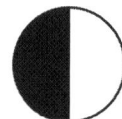  

A. B is more shaded than A but less shaded than C.
B. A is more shaded than B and C.
C. C is more shaded than B.
D. All three are shaded equally.

CONTINUE ON TO THE NEXT PAGE ➡

QUANTITATIVE
PART II

82. $\frac{5}{7}$ of what number is 15 times 3?

A. 72
B. 63
C. 42
D. 60

83. Examine the pyramid and find the best answer.

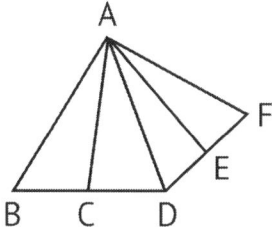

A. DF is equal to AD.
B. AC = AE
C. AC is the biggest.
D. BD is bigger than AB.

84. What number multiplied by 8 is 5 more than 59?

A. 8
B. 6
C. 12
D. 7

85. Examine (A), (B), and (C) and find the best answer

(A) 0.625

(B) $\frac{52}{91}$

(C) $\frac{2}{3}$

A. A is greater than B.
B. C is greater than 1.
C. B > A > C
D. B = C

86. $\frac{1}{5}$ of what number is 5 times 5?

A. 50
B. 625
C. 25
D. 125

87. What number added to 9 is 7 times the product 2 and 3?

A. 57
B. 33
C. 51
D. 48

CONTINUE ON TO THE NEXT PAGE ➡

QUANTITATIVE
PART II

88. Examine (A), (B), and (C) and find the best answer

(A) $5\frac{1}{2}$

(B) $4\frac{3}{2}$

(C) $5\frac{7}{9}$

A. A is the largest
B. A is bigger than B.
C. A = B < C
D. B is the smallest.

---

89. Look at this series: X, 13, XVI, 19, XXII, 25... What number should come next?

A. XXVIII
B. 28
C. XXIX
D. 32

---

90. Examine the graph and find the best answer.

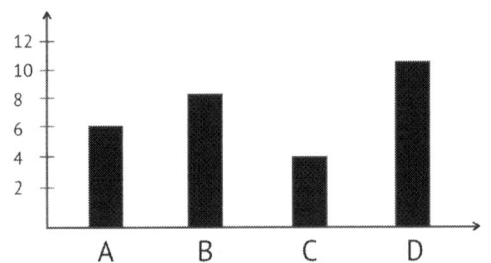

A. B is greater than D.
B. C + B = D
C. A + C = B
D. D - A = C

---

91. Look at this series: 1, 3, 4, 12, _, 39, 40, 120 ... What is the missing number in the series above?

A. 13
B. 36
C. 20
D. 21

---

92. What number divided by 3 is $\frac{1}{4}$ of 100?

A. 65
B. 50
C. 25
D. 75

---

93. Examine the parallelogram and find the best answer.

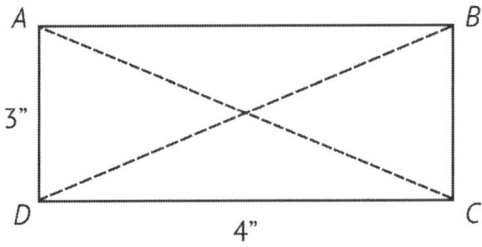

A. Triangle ABC has a bigger area than triangle ADC.
B. The area of triangle ADC is 12.
C. The perimeter of ABCD is 14.
D. The area of ABCD is 6.

CONTINUE ON TO THE NEXT PAGE ➡

QUANTITATIVE
PART II

94. What number subtracted from 32 leaves $\frac{1}{8}$ of 16?

A. 24
B. 28
C. 4
D. 30

95. What number divided by 5 is $\frac{1}{4}$ of 100?

A. 120
B. 25
C. 125
D. 625

96. Examine (A), (B), and (C) and find the best answer

(A) 0.755

(B) $\frac{4}{5}$

(C) $\frac{7}{8}$

A. A is the largest
B. C > B > A
C. All are equal.
D. B is less than A but greater than C.

97. $\frac{2}{3}$ of what number is 11 times 6?

A. 99
B. 66
C. 33
D. 11

98. Examine (A), (B), and (C) and find the best answer

(A) $\frac{2}{5}$ of 40

(B) $\frac{6}{7}$ of 42

(C) $\frac{1}{2}$ of 36

A. $\frac{2}{5}$
B. C = A + B
C. A + B < C
D. B > C > A

99. Examine the circle graph and find the best answer.

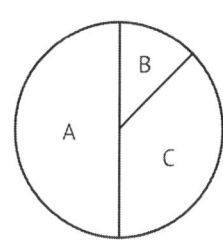

A. A has the biggest region.
B. B > C
C. 2C = A
D. B + C > A

CONTINUE ON TO THE NEXT PAGE →

QUANTITATIVE
PART II

100. Look at this series: 59, 89, 90, 120, 121, 151 ...
What number should come next?

- A. 131
- B. 180
- C. 152
- D. 181

101. Look at this series: 88, 90, 91, 93, 94...
What number should come next?

- A. 88
- B. 96
- C. 90
- D. 94

102. Look at this series:
100, 107, 105, 112, 110, 117 ...
What number should come next?

- A. 124
- B. 115
- C. 119
- D. 110

103. What is 4 times $\frac{1}{3}$ of 12?

- A. 20
- B. 16
- C. 9
- D. 1

104. What number is 7 less than $\frac{3}{7}$ of 49?

- A. 14
- B. 28
- C. 21
- D. 3

105. Look at this series: 2, 8, 4, 16, __, 36, 7, 28 ...
What is the missing number in the series above?

- A. 16
- B. 20
- C. 9
- D. 10

106. Look at this series: 11, 17, 20, 26, 29, __, 38 ...
What is the missing number in the series above?

- A. 35
- B. 36
- C. 32
- D. 30

CONTINUE ON TO THE NEXT PAGE ➡

QUANTITATIVE
PART II

107. Examine (A), (B), and (C) and find the best answer.

(A)  (B) 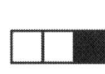 (C)

- **A.** The fraction shaded for B is equal to C.
- **B.** The fraction shaded for A = B but is bigger than C.
- **C.** The fraction shaded for B is bigger than A.
- **D.** None of the above.

108. Look at this series: B5, F7, J4, N6, R3,... What should come next?

- **A.** U5
- **B.** U0
- **C.** V0
- **D.** V5

109. $\frac{1}{5}$ of what number added to 7 is 6 times 2?

- **A.** 12
- **B.** 42
- **C.** 5
- **D.** 25

110. Look at this series: 72, 73, 69, 70, 66, 67 ... What three numbers should come next?

- **A.** 67, 63, 64
- **B.** 68, 64, 65
- **C.** 63, 64, 65
- **D.** 63, 64, 60

111. What number is 14 more than $\frac{7}{8}$ of 72?

- **A.** 81
- **B.** 77
- **C.** 59
- **D.** 63

112. What number when multiplied by 9 is 3 to the 4th power?

- **A.** 1
- **B.** 9
- **C.** 3
- **D.** 27

CONTINUE ON TO THE NEXT PAGE ➡

READING
PART III (25 MIN)

DIRECTIONS: Read the passages below and pick the answer choices that fit accordingly. Fill in the appropriate letter on your answer sheet.

Questions 113-122 refer to the following passage.

Dreams vary in nature, and are since the dawn of history, mankind has been absorbed with dreaming and the analysis of this phenomenon. During the time of ancient civilizations, wise men were chosen at courts to hold the title of interpreter of dreams, and successfully doing so would lead to the highest favor; failing to analyze correctly would mean an otherwise nasty end. However, the true question that comes to mind is: what exactly are dreams? As French philosopher Henri Bergson remarks, "A dream is this. I perceive objects and there is nothing there. I see men; I seem to speak to them and I hear what they answer; there is no one there and I have not spoken. It is all as if real things and real persons were there, then on waking all has disappeared, both persons and things." How does this happen?

Dreams are better defined as a series of images, ideas and sensations that occur involuntarily during a primary state of sleep called rapid-eye movement (otherwise called REM). During this stage of sleep, the brain activity is still relatively high, resembling similar activities to wakeful states. During this time, there are continuing random movement of the eyes and low muscle tone throughout the body. While dreams can and may occur during other stages of sleep, such occurrences are less memorable or lucid; when woken during REM sleep, a person is more likely to remember the details of the experience. In fact, while most people may have from four up to seven dreams per night, most dreams are forgotten immediately.

Believed to be connected to the unconscious mind, ranging from normal and ordinary images of everyday life to much more mysterious and frightening nightmares; some can even be outright bizarre. As such, many viewed dreaming as a form of communication during ancient times. The Egyptians and Babylonians believed that they could be used as a method to foretell the future and even speak to the divine. As such, only those with supernatural powers would be able to interpret such dreams. Those who failed to do so while claiming such powers faced either banishment or certain death.

---

113. This passage can most likely be found in a

    A. history book
    B. science article
    C. fantasy novel
    D. traveler's guide

114. The second paragraph of the passage mostly discusses

    A. dream interpretation
    B. the science of dreaming
    C. nightmares
    D. REM sleep

CONTINUE ON TO THE NEXT PAGE ➡

READING
PART III

115. A good title for this passage would be

   A. Dreaming in Ancient Egypt
   B. Rapid-Eye Movement Sleep
   C. Understanding Dreams
   D. Dream Interpretation in Ancient Times

116. Henri Bergson is mentioned in the first paragraph to

   A. bring reference from a credible source
   B. add a comical reference
   C. explain nightmares
   D. understand the philosophy of dreaming

117. The word <u>phenomenon</u> most nearly means

   A. regularity
   B. understanding
   C. experience
   D. sleep

118. A person is most likely to remember his or her dream if wakened during the stage

   A. non-REM
   B. awakening
   C. NREM 2
   D. REM

119. In ancient times, failing to interpret dreams correctly would lead to

   A. banishment
   B. death
   C. both a and b
   D. neither a nor b

120. The word <u>lucid</u> most nearly means

   A. vivid
   B. boring
   C. weak
   D. dar

121. In the passage the number of times a person can dream per night can number to

   A. 4
   B. 6
   C. 3
   D. 7

122. The Egyptians believed that dreams were connected to

   A. riches
   B. sleeping well
   C. happiness
   D. the future

CONTINUE ON TO THE NEXT PAGE ➡

READING
PART III

Questions 123-132 refer to the following passage.

For almost two decades the Fallout videogame series has been an excellent satire of society's paranoia during the Cold War and is a comprehensive depiction of what could happen if the world were to break out in nuclear warfare. One of the focuses of the series is the use of bomb shelters for human experimentation. While the knee jerk response would be to reject such a notion as implausible, further analyses of past experiments and war crimes reveal a parallel to what Fallout suggests. The lore of the vaults in this post-apocalyptic world is horrid; however, what is even more terrifying is its implication of how twisted human curiosity truly is.

The story follows history for a short period and then diverges after the conclusion of World War II. Soon after its victory, the United States devolves from its original fifty states to thirteen commonwealths in order to better fight the rise of communism; the commonwealths are made to be different enough to "quell internal political divisions." However, the newly divided America withers as a first world power, leading to a century long Cold War. By 2050, numerous European countries collapse due to extremely high oil prices and plagues devastate the United States. Through an act of desperation, China invades Alaska to seize more oil resources, and the US annexes Canada to engage the threat; war escalates, and nuclear weaponry is fired across nations, destroying the world.

While the fear of all-out nuclear war ravages the United States, a private corporation called Vault-Tec takes advantage of the situation and offers a "solution to the frightened American public" by building hundreds of elaborate underground fallout shelters across the country; codenamed "Project Safehouse", it presents a means for salvation. Labeled Vaults, these subterranean shelters were powered by geothermal and nuclear power generators, built to last for over two centuries without any outside interference. The Vaults were fully equipped with any and all facilities and resources – food, water and even entertainment in some situations – required for survival and had a maximum occupancy of a thousand residents. However, unbeknownst to the population – hereby called "vault dwellers" –Vault-Tec had ulterior motives. Having many ties to top-secret US military research and technology, Project Safehouse's true intentions included conducting secret studies of the vault dwellers during their time in the shelters.

---

123. The word implausible most nearly means

A. credible
B. possible
C. unbelievable
D. realistic

124. According to the passage, people thought the Vaults were created

A. to stop nuclear war
B. for luxury purposes
C. to store food
D. as a safehouse

CONTINUE ON TO THE NEXT PAGE ➡

162

READING
PART III

125. Project Safehouse was created by

  A. the United States
  B. China
  C. Vault-Tec
  D. the Cold War

126. According to the Fallout series, the United States was later divided into

  A. fifty states
  B. thirteen commonwealths
  C. thirteen colonies
  D. twenty-five states

127. The European countries collapsed due to

  A. China's attack
  B. high oil prices
  C. nuclear warfare
  D. the Soviet Union

128. According to the passage, annex most nearly means

  A. remove
  B. take over
  C. leave out
  D. ruin

129. The third paragraph of the passage discusses

  A. the aftermath of the war
  B. World War II
  C. Project Safehouse
  D. the Cold War

130. The true intentions of the Vaults were for the purpose of

  A. saving the civilians
  B. human experimentation
  C. survival
  D. to stockpile resources

131. The people who lived in the Vaults were named

  A. safe houses
  B. subway citizens
  C. raiders
  D. vault dwellers

132. The word subterranean most nearly means

  A. city
  B. underground
  C. under water
  D. bomb shelter

CONTINUE ON TO THE NEXT PAGE ➡

READING
PART III

Questions 133-142 refer to the following passage.

Evolution, by definition, is the process by which a certain something gradually develops and changes into something more different and complex. For eons, through natural selection and evolution, organisms have shed the <u>husks</u> of their former selves in order to change and better suit themselves in their present times. Remix culture, the concept that strengthens the idea to combine and edit original material to create a new entity, follows an extremely similar notion. Throughout present culture, this inclination of "remixing" is nothing out of the ordinary. In fact, remix culture is as old as culture itself. This idea plays a major factor in the progression of present culture and can be found in a variety of forms, from the music and movie industries to even technological innovations. Almost all new successful materials are built from previously conceived ideas.

Since the beginning of the film industry, remix culture has been quite prominently used to achieve success. One of the most famous trilogies of all time, George Lucas' *Star Wars*, is in fact a conglomeration of multiple different movies and ideas that came before it. The series, which debuted in 1977, was made up of various elements that are recognized from other works. For example, its widely appreciated opening title scene in which the text "crawls" up the screen to introduce the story is in fact taken from the *Flash Gordon* film serial from the 1930s. The outline of the plot itself follows the outlined plan of "the hero's journey" from Joseph Cambell's *The Hero with a Thousand Faces*. George Lucas himself claims to have used numerous elements from this <u>archetype</u>, which includes stages such as "The Call to Adventure," "The Belly of the Whale," and "The Road of Trials." All in all, the use of remixing created an extremely popular series of cult movies.

The music industry is widely known for its use and reuse of previously released materials, ranging from borrowing lyrics and rhythmic beats to entire songs. A great example of this would be the original bass line background beat that was created by the group The Sugarhill Gang for its song, "Rapper's Delight." Because of its upbeat and extremely rhythmic pattern, the beat was used multiple times throughout history. Popular songs that used the bass line include Chic's "Good Times" and Daft Punk's "Around the World." This practice of reusing and adopting certain significant parts of songs has been applied to lyrics as well. When a certain piece of music is successful, it is almost a shame not to remix it into other tunes for more appeal.

---

133. The example of evolution provided in the first paragraph serves to

   A. give real life context
   B. explain why natural selection is important
   C. introduce remix culture
   D. confuse the reader

134. A good title for the passage would be

   A. The Making of Star Wars
   B. Remix Culture: The Flowering of Ideas
   C. Stealing Ideas for Success
   D. The Evolution of Movies and Music

CONTINUE ON TO THE NEXT PAGE ➡

READING
PART III

135. This passage can most likely be found in a

A. history book
B. sociology article
C. survey
D. informative pamphlet

136. The word <u>husks</u> most nearly means

A. center
B. bark
C. covering
D. outside

137. George Lucas mimicked "Star Wars" text crawl from the show

A. The Road of Trials
B. The Belly of the Whale
C. The Hero with a Thousand Faces
D. Flash Gordon

138. The second paragraph of the passage discusses

A. the role of Star Wars in pop culture
B. the Flash Gordon serial
C. the use of remix culture in films
D. reusing beats in music

139. The word <u>archetype</u> most nearly means

A. ideal example
B. error
C. imperfection
D. pattern

140. The use of remix culture in music includes

A. outlining similar plots
B. borrowing rhythms
C. writing identical lyrics
D. all of the above

141. An example of a song's beat that was reused continuously was

A. "Rapper's Delight"
B. "The Sugarhill Gang"
C. "Star Wars"
D. "Good Times"

142. According to the passage, what is remix culture?

A. the stealing of ideas for economic benefits
B. adopting ideas to create more cultural works
C. copyright laws to stop the sharing of ideas
D. the boom of pop culture

CONTINUE ON TO THE NEXT PAGE ➡

READING
PART III

Questions 143-148 refer to the following passage.

The idea of body modification - the deliberate altering of the human body - has been a significant constituent in a vast number of different cultures since the dawn of man. The concept of marking the body with designs, whether permanent or temporary, has had an exceptional impact on a multitude of different cultures. However, body tattooing is not a practice that has been accepted universally. While it is found to be conventional and even customary in religions such as Hinduism, other systems of beliefs - a number of Abrahamic religions such as Judaism and Islam, for example - prohibit such acts entirely. Although tattooing and other forms of body modification have largely impacted many customs, they have not been always been received in a positive light.

In the Hindu religion, receiving specific tattoos is considered to be a show of devotion and adherence to one's spiritual-mindedness. The ordeal of receiving the tattoo through the excruciatingly painful process of implanting a color into the body alone is acknowledged as a zealous act. The different forms of colors and symbols also show reverence for the many individual deities in Hinduism. A prime example of the varying deference in the religion would be the different sects and subcultures found in Hinduism. In some areas of India the Untouchables, a caste that is considered to belong to those who are impurely reincarnated, have tattooed the name of Lord Rama onto every inch of their skin for centuries. Called the Ramnaamis, they have prevented persecution and abuse from higher castes by demonstrating their devotion to the main god. Others show their devotion to religion by depicting famous and popular gods such as Ganesh and Shiva. As it is a religion that derives its beliefs from the idea of reincarnation and the importance of souls, many individuals consider tattoos to be the only real form of identity, as the body is only a shell for the spirit.

---

143. Which of the following religions discussed in the passage promote tattoos?

A. Islam
B. Hinduism
C. Judaism
D. all of the above

144. The word conventional most nearly means

A. traditional
B. abnormal
C. original
D. exotic

CONTINUE ON TO THE NEXT PAGE ➡

READING
PART III

145. According to the passage, a person practicing Judaism would find body modification

A. acceptable
B. mandatory
C. forbidden
D. attractive

146. Another name for those considered to be the Untouchables is

A. Ganesh
B. Shiva
C. Lord Ram
D. Ramnaami

147. Tattoos are used in Hinduism to show devotion in various forms of

A. colors
B. symbols
C. both a and b
D. neither a nor b

148. According to the passage, tattoos are ideally considered to be used to

A. show devotion to their gods
B. identify oneself
C. prevent persecution
D. all of the above

CONTINUE ON TO THE NEXT PAGE ➡

READING
PART III

Questions 149-152 refer to the following passage.

This passage is adapted from The Life, Crime, and Capture of John Wilkes Booth

The box in which the President sat consisted of two boxes turned into one, the middle <u>partition</u> being removed, as on all occasions when a state party visited the theater. The box was on a level with the dress circle; about twelve feet above the stage. There were two entrances—the door nearest to the wall having been closed and locked; the door nearest the balustrades of the dress circle, and at right angles with it, being open and left open, after the visitors had entered. The interior was carpeted, lined with crimson paper, and furnished with a sofa covered with crimson velvet, three arm chairs similarly covered, and six cane-bottomed chairs. Festoons of flags hung before the front of the box against a background of lace.

President Lincoln took one of the arm-chairs and seated himself in the front of the box, in the angle nearest to the audience, where, partially screened from observation, he had the best view of what was transpiring on the stage. Mrs. Lincoln sat next to him, and Miss Harris in the opposite angle nearest the stage. Major Rathbone sat just behind Mrs. Lincoln and Miss Harris. These four were the only persons in the box.

The play proceeded, although "Our American Cousin," without Mr. Sothern, has, since that gentleman's departure from this country, been justly esteemed a very dull affair. The audience at Ford's, including Mrs. Lincoln, seemed to enjoy it very much. The worthy wife of the President leaned forward, her hand upon her husband's knee, watching every scene in the drama with amused attention. Even across the President's face at intervals swept a smile, robbing it of its habitual sadness.

149. The first paragraph discussed the

   A. seating of President Lincoln
   B. assassination attempt
   C. John Wilkes Booth's home
   D. entire theater

150. This passage can mostly likely be found in a

   A. science paper
   B. philosophy book
   C. personal journal
   D. history book

151. The number of people in the box was

   A. four
   B. five
   C. three
   D. ten

152. The word <u>partition</u> most nearly means

   A. enclosement
   B. division
   C. openness
   D. aid

CONTINUE ON TO THE NEXT PAGE ➡

168

VOCABULARY
PART III (25 MIN)

VOCABULARY

DIRECTIONS: In this section, you will need to determine the choice that is closest in meaning to the underlined words provided below. Pick the answer choice that fits accordingly and fill in the appropriate letter on your answer sheet.

153. a refurbished house

    A. run down
    B. new
    C. renovated
    D. historic

154. a lucrative business

    A. profitable
    B. failing
    C. well-known
    D. powerful

155. she was enamored by him

    A. entertained
    B. disenchanted
    C. disgusted
    D. captivated

156. a diminutive amount

    A. large
    B. horrifying
    C. tiny
    D. laughable

157. his energy was depleted

    A. renewed
    B. heated
    C. held in
    D. consumed

158. to be adamant

    A. stubborn
    B. giving
    C. caring
    D. quiet

CONTINUE ON TO THE NEXT PAGE ➡

VOCABULARY
PART III

159. they laughed at the inane response

- A. absurd
- B. thoughtful
- C. witty
- D. gratifying

160. the quirky boy

- A. intelligent
- B. peculiar
- C. boring
- D. talkative

161. my pompous boss

- A. modest
- B. amiable
- C. stern
- D. pretentious

162. the man was infatuated

- A. mesmerized
- B. annoyed
- C. repulsed
- D. concerned

163. an elated woman

- A. depressed
- B. quick
- C. rude
- D. joyful

164. my amiable neighbor

- A. unsociable
- B. friendly
- C. gloomy
- D. secretive

165. resilient material

- A. delicate
- B. soft
- C. rigid
- D. strong

166. an eccentric personality

- A. bizarre
- B. conventional
- C. dull
- D. kind

CONTINUE ON TO THE NEXT PAGE ➡

VOCABULARY
PART III

167. to squelch emotion

    A. encourage
    B. feel
    C. suppress
    D. release

168. to commence the race

    A. alter
    B. cease
    C. redo
    D. begin

169. to be malcontent

    A. relieved
    B. happy
    C. unsure
    D. dissatisfied

170. wanting to console

    A. play with
    B. comfort
    C. berate
    D. discipline

171. imminent danger

    A. immediate
    B. avoidable
    C. predictable
    D. unlikely

172. to berate

    A. criticize
    B. flatter
    C. compromise
    D. help

173. wanting to impede progress

    A. support
    B. nurture
    C. hinder
    D. take credit for

174. to mimic

    A. persuade
    B. mock
    C. assist
    D. harm

CONTINUE ON TO THE NEXT PAGE →

MATHEMATICS
PART IV (45 MIN)

CONCEPTS (24 Questions)

DIRECTIONS: Choose the answer that best fits the problem. You may use scratch paper while working on these problems.

---

175. The circumference of the circle is

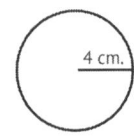

- A. 16π sq. cm.
- B. 8π sq. cm.
- C. 24π sq. cm.
- D. 4π sq. cm.

---

176. $2^3 \cdot 4^5$

- A. $2 \cdot 2 \cdot 2 \cdot 4 \cdot 4 \cdot 4 \cdot 4 \cdot 4$
- B. $3 \cdot 3 \cdot 3 \cdot 5 \cdot 5 \cdot 5 \cdot 5$
- C. $2 \cdot 3 \cdot 4 \cdot 5$
- D. $2 \cdot 2 \cdot 2 \cdot 2 \cdot 2 \cdot 4 \cdot 4 \cdot 4 \cdot 4$

---

177. A number is changed if

- A. 0 is subtracted from it
- B. the number is subtracted from 0
- C. the number is multiplied by 1
- D. the number is multiplied by -1 twice

---

178. $(4 \cdot 5) \div (3 \cdot 5) =$

- A. $\dfrac{5}{4}$
- B. 2.8
- C. $\dfrac{4}{5}$
- D. $\dfrac{4}{3}$

---

179. What number belongs in the triangle?
$-5 - \triangle = 5$

- A. 0
- B. 10
- C. 5
- D. -10

---

180. A number that is divisible by both 6 and 10 is also divisible by

- A. 70
- B. 15
- C. 30
- D. 45

CONTINUE ON TO THE NEXT PAGE ➡

MATHEMATICS
PART IV

181. Which of the following statements is true?

- A. 4 x 11 > 45
- B. 7 + 8 < 15.5
- C. -8 + 2 = -7 - 1
- D. $\frac{14}{2} < 5$

---

182. Nine hundred twenty-three million six hundred thousand three hundred and twenty is equal to

- A. 9,236,320
- B. 923,600,320
- C. 923,006,320
- D. 92,360,320

---

183. The least common multiple of 24 and 36 is

- A. 12
- B. 36
- C. 72
- D. 6

---

184. Which symbol belongs in the circle?
0.079 ◯ 0.00935

- A. =
- B. <
- C. ≤
- D. ≥

---

185. What is the value of x in the given triangle?

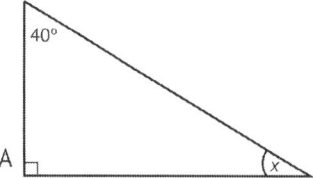

- A. 40°
- B. 50°
- C. 70°
- D. Cannot be determined

---

186. If $y - 5 > 18$, y is

- A. less than 13
- B. greater than 23
- C. equal to 23
- D. greater than 13

---

187. Set A = { 5, 6, 7, 8 }; Set B = { 5, 9, 10 }. The union (∪) of the two sets is

- A. { 5, 6, 7, 8, 9, 10 }
- B. { 5 }
- C. {10, 15, 17, 8 }
- D. {5, 5 }

CONTINUE ON TO THE NEXT PAGE ➡

MATHEMATICS
PART IV

188. What line segment represents the intersection of $\overline{JL}$ and $\overline{KM}$?

A. $\overline{KL}$
B. $\overline{JM}$
C. $\overline{JK}$
D. $\overline{LM}$

189. Which of the following does not have the same value as 6.25%

A. $\dfrac{1}{16}$
B. $\dfrac{100}{16}$ %
C. 6.25
D. 0.0625

190. Which of these numbers might be the value of a in the following inequality?
$7a - 3 < 9$

A. 4
B. 1
C. 2
D. 3

191. In the number 2,220,202 there are

A. 2 millions and 2 tens
B. 2 billion and 200 thousands
C. 2 millions and 2 thousands
D. 2 millions and 20 thousands

192. Write 521 in expanded form, using exponents.

A. $(5 \cdot 10^2) + (2 \cdot 10^1) + (1 \cdot 10^0)$
B. $(5 \cdot 10^2) + (20 \cdot 10^1) + (1 \cdot 10^0)$
C. $(500 \cdot 10^2) + (20 \cdot 10^1) + (1 \cdot 10^0)$
D. None of the above

193. How many fourths are there in $\dfrac{4}{9}$?

A. $\dfrac{7}{36}$
B. $\dfrac{1}{9}$
C. $\dfrac{16}{9}$
D. $\dfrac{23}{36}$

CONTINUE ON TO THE NEXT PAGE ➡

MATHEMATICS
PART IV

194. If $x < 3$, and the value of x is a positive integer, then which of the following is true?

   A. $x^2 > 8$
   B. $15 > x^2 + 5$
   C. $x^2 = 9$
   D. $x^2 - 5 = 4$

195. Which is the shortest distance?

   A. 0.5 meters
   B. 500 centimeters
   C. 50,000 millimeters
   D. 500 decimeters

196. Which pair of the following values for e and △ will make the following statement true? 3e △ 12

   A. (4, <)
   B. (6, <)
   C. (2, <)
   D. (0, >)

197. The ratio of 16 pints to 8 gallons is

   A. 2:1
   B. 1:2
   C. 1:1
   D. 1:4

198. If Charles is w years old and his brother is 4 years older, then 3 years ago, what was his brother's age?

   A. w - 1
   B. w - 12
   C. w + 1
   D. w + 7

CONTINUE ON TO THE NEXT PAGE ➡

MATHEMATICS
PART IV

PROBLEM SOLVING QUESTIONS (40 Questions)

199. Solve for x: $3.2x + 16 = 38.4$

   A. 7
   B. 9
   C. 17
   D. 70

200. The formula $C = \frac{5}{9}(F - 32) = C$ changes the temperature from Fahrenheit to Celsius. What is the Celsius temperature for 185° Fahrenheit?

   A. 68°
   B. 333°
   C. 275°
   D. 85°

201. If the tax rate is $8.09 for every $100, how much tax must be paid for a car that costs $18,000?

   A. $ 2,224.97
   B. $ 1,456.20
   C. $ 1,880.90
   D. $ 809.00

202. The ratio of staff to children in a certain school is 1:12. If there are 24 staff members in the school, how many students are there?

   A. 24
   B. 144
   C. 288
   D. 12

203. On a blueprint, 7 inches represents 21 feet. How long must the line be to represent 51 feet?

   A. 17 inches
   B. 153 inches
   C. 2.88 inches
   D. 2.42 inches

204. A certain clothing store charges 80% more than what they bought the item for. If it sells a shirt for $21.78 to customers, how much did the store pay for the shirt?

   A. $25.62
   B. $17.42
   C. $18.51
   D. $12.10

CONTINUE ON TO THE NEXT PAGE ➡

MATHEMATICS
PART IV

205. If the same store has a 30% discount on the shirt, then what is the new selling price to the nearest cent?

A. $3.63
B. $8.47
C. $15.25
D. $ 18.73

206. The area of the figure below is

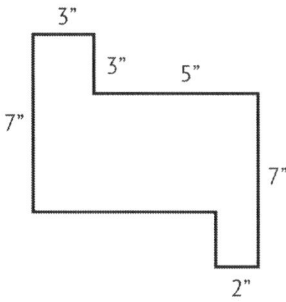

Note: In the figure above, assume that any angle which appears to be a right angle is right.

A. 36 square inches
B. 47 square inches
C. 33 square inches
D. 46 square inches

207. The perimeter of the figure above is

A. 47 inches
B. 46 inches
C. 33 inches
D. 36 inches

208. The charge for a particular taxi was $5.46 for the first 3 miles and $7 for each additional mile. What was the total charge for a 5 mile taxi ride?

A. $ 19.46
B. $ 9.10
C. $ 40.46
D. $ 26.46

209. The winner of a scholarship received one fourth of the total value of the prize. The second place finisher received $\frac{1}{3}$ of the winner's share. If the winner's share was $3,300, what was the total value of the prize?

A. $1,100
B. $9,900
C. $13,200
D. $825

CONTINUE ON TO THE NEXT PAGE ➡

MATHEMATICS
PART IV

210. As a bus leaves from station X, it has 16 empty seats, 12 seated passengers, and 8 standing passengers. At the next stop, 10 people get off, two passengers get on, and everyone takes a seat. How many empty seats are there?

A. 2
B. 16
C. 28
D. 4

211.

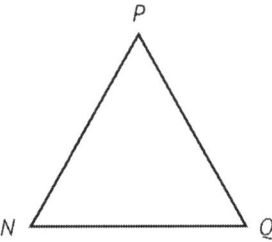

Triangle NPQ is an equilateral triangle. If its perimeter is 27, what is the length of $\overline{NP} + \overline{NQ}$?

A. 16
B. 18
C. 4
D. 32

212. Solve: 4.06 ÷ 1.45 =

A. 2.8
B. 5.887
C. 5.7
D. 3.17

213. Solve: -4 - [(7 + (-3)) - -(5 - 8)]

A. -11
B. 3
C. -5
D. -3

214. 170% of 62 is

A. 10.54
B. 105.40
C. 206.66
D. 36.47

215. 6 gallons 2 quarts 5 pints
         - 4 gallons 3 quarts 6 pints

A. 1 gallon 2 quarts 1 pint
B. 1 gallon 1 quart 1 pint
C. 1 gallon 3 quarts 2 pints
D. 2 gallons 2 quarts 1 pint

CONTINUE ON TO THE NEXT PAGE ➡

MATHEMATICS
PART IV

216. Solve: $8 \div \frac{1}{4} + \frac{1}{2} \cdot 12$

   A. 56
   B. 128
   C. 8
   D. 38

217. If $x = 4$, $y = 11$, and $c = 3$, the value of $\sqrt{x + 6y + 10c}$

   A. 8
   B. 4
   C. 10
   D. 18

218. 3 is to 24 as $\frac{5}{8}$ is to

   A. $\frac{5}{64}$
   B. 8
   C. 5
   D. $\frac{13}{8}$

219. The average of 5, -4, 8, 9, and -3 is

   A. 3
   B. 15
   C. -15
   D. -5

220. The number of cars in Brazil is 498,996. If this represents 249 cars for every 1000 people, the population of Brazil to the nearest million is

   A. 1,000,000
   B. 2,000,000
   C. 3,000,000
   D. 4,000,000

221. A plumber needs 5 pipes, each 1 foot and 7 inches long. If pipes are sold only by the foot, how many feet must he buy?

   A. 10
   B. 9
   C. 7
   D. 8

222. The difference between $(6 \cdot 10^3) + (3 \cdot 10^2) + (1 \cdot 10^0)$ and $(2 \cdot 10^3) + (5 \cdot 10^2) + (1 \cdot 10^1)$ is

   A. 1,091
   B. 3,791
   C. 5,780
   D. 3,800

CONTINUE ON TO THE NEXT PAGE ➡

MATHEMATICS
PART IV

223. A square has an area of 36 square inches. An equilateral triangle with the same side measurements has a perimeter of

  A. 18
  B. 24
  C. 15
  D. 12

224. If $g = 43 - (8 + 1)(-h)$ and $h = 7$, then what is the value of g?

  A. 20
  B. -20
  C. 106
  D. -238

225. $(1 + 5)^3$

  A. 16
  B. 127
  C. 125
  D. 216

226. A room has a male to female ratio of 3:2. If there are 40 people in the room, how many more males are there than females?

  A. 16
  B. 8
  C. 24
  D. 12

227. Solve for x: $x^2 + 37 = 118$

  A. 7
  B. 8
  C. 9
  D. 10

228. If 7 pints of water are needed to water a square foot garden, the minimum number of gallons of water needed to water a 9 feet • 14 feet garden is

  A. 110 gallons
  B. 111 gallons
  C. 112 gallons
  D. 113 gallons

229. Solve for x: $\frac{x}{4} + 5.5 = 11.75$

  A. 25
  B. 15.625
  C. 43.125
  D. 69

CONTINUE ON TO THE NEXT PAGE ➡

230. What is the length of $\overline{BD}$ of △ BDC?

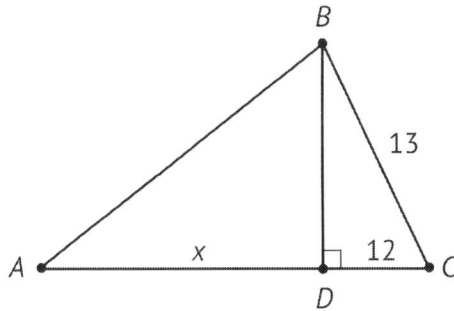

Note: Figure is not drawn to scale.

A. 12
B. 6
C. 5
D. 25

231. A hotel was valued at $494,000 and insured for 70% of that amount. Find the yearly premium if it is figured out $0.30 per $100 of value.

A. $444.60
B. $4,446
C. $103,740
D. $1,037.40

232. 150% of 56 is

A. 84
B. 28
C. 112
D. 70

233. Martha left the train station at 8:45 a.m. and arrived to her new location at 1:20 p.m. How long did the trip take in hours and minutes?

A. 4 hours 45 minutes
B. 4 hours 35 minutes
C. 3 hours 35 minutes
D. 3 hours 45 minutes

234. An object has a mass of 10.5 milligrams. What is the object's mass in grams?

A. 0.0105 g
B. 0.105 g
C. 1.05 g
D. 10.5 g

235.

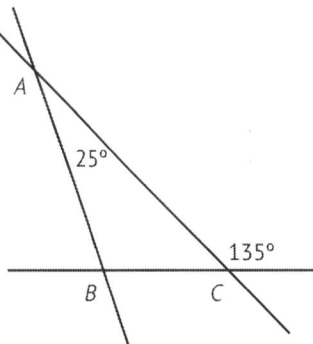

What is the degree measure of ∡ ABC?

A. 45°
B. 100°
C. 110°
D. 135°

CONTINUE ON TO THE NEXT PAGE ➡

236.

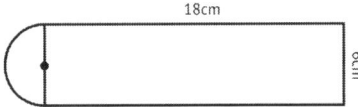

What is the area of the figure shown in the diagram?

A. $(108 + 35\pi)\,cm^2$
B. $(108 + 6\pi)\,cm^2$
C. $(108 + 12\pi)\,cm^2$
D. $(108 + \frac{9}{2}\pi)\,cm^2$

237.

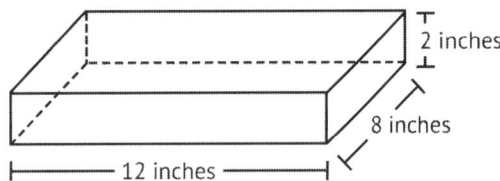

What is the volume, in cubic inches, of the rectangular prism?

A. 22 cubic inches
B. 192 cubic inches
C. 98 cubic inches
D. 196 cubic inches

238. In order to increase profits, a municipality is planning to raise its sales tax from 8% to 10%. How much more will it cost to buy a $300 computer desk if the sales tax is increased?

A. $3
B. $18
C. $54
D. $6

LANGUAGE
PART V (25 MIN)

USAGE

DIRECTIONS: For Questions 239-278, choose the sentence that contains an error in punctuation, capitalization, or usage. If there is no error present, select answer choice D.

239. A. The president holds much power but it is balanced by the legislative and judicial branch.
   B. Dylan asked, "Who had eaten my sandwich from Quiznos?"
   C. The yearly income of those in Manhattan is considerably higher than those who live in Queens.
   D. No Mistakes

240. A. After typing an essay for 5 hours, the essay was finally submitted by Joanna.
   B. The number 57 on the Heinz ketchup bottle represent the different pickles the company used to have.
   C. After going to the Smith gym for 2 months, I have gained much strength.
   D. No Mistakes

241. A. Why should I get the lowest grade when I have put the most effort out of my group?
   B. "Have you eaten breakfast today?" asked my teacher, Ms. Jones; she seemed to know I was tired since I not eaten.
   C. I am lucky that my girlfriend's birthday is on Valentine's day; I do not have to get her presents on two separate occasions.
   D. No Mistakes

242. A. Stuart O'Brien was a dedicated writer and eventually became famous from nothing much to start with.
   B. The most common first name in the world is Mohammed and the most common last name in the world is Lee or Li.
   C. Don't loose at the game tomorrow night as it gives us a chance to the final round.
   D. No Mistakes

CONTINUE ON TO THE NEXT PAGE ➡

LANGUAGE
PART V

243.
- **A.** Phobia is a term that is used for irrational fear of something.
- **B.** My dad would not let me use his car, but mom will.
- **C.** South Asia and Southeast Asia experience a season unlike other known as monsoon, which is filled with heavy rain.
- **D.** No Mistakes

244.
- **A.** Social anxiety disorder is something my friend faces everyday.
- **B.** My grandfather suffers from alzheimer's, a disease that attacks the memory.
- **C.** When the baby saw the chicken lay an egg for the first time, he let out a burst of joy.
- **D.** No Mistakes

245.
- **A.** Between Bobby and Martha is a cat that is terrified.
- **B.** Among the three animals, the Royal Bengal tiger is the stronger one
- **C.** The star could be seen from the Cornell observatory.
- **D.** No Mistakes

246.
- **A.** The pair of pants was filled with designs I have never seen before.
- **B.** After climbing the rock, the ropes were pulled up by Anastasia.
- **C.** Your shoe has a hole in the front; you should consider buying new ones.
- **D.** No Mistakes

247.
- **A.** We had called the taxi 20 minutes ago, but it has yet to come.
- **B.** World Tourism Day is a day that is recognized for travelers and was established on September 27.
- **C.** Since plants are green, they reflect green light and if that is the only source of light available they would die.
- **D.** No Mistakes

248.
- **A.** Agar.io is a game with the sole purpose of making a cell big and eating other cells.
- **B.** I have been doing this project for quite a while and I had very little time left to submit it.
- **C.** The cafe said that it would be open today after 5 p.m., but it was not and so I was disappointed.
- **D.** No Mistakes

249.
- **A.** Failure discouraged Roberto from going to college, but he took a gap year and was able to finally get his degree.
- **B.** Professor Rosen gave a lecture on the paradoxes of Newtonian principles.
- **C.** Alexander the great was a military leader who wanted the unity of lands all under one rule.
- **D.** No Mistakes

CONTINUE ON TO THE NEXT PAGE ➡

LANGUAGE
PART V

250.
A. The consistency of the crumbs in Gaby's bread was much more than Sheylla's ' bread.
B. President John F. Kennedy was a great man with personable qualities: both charming and conversational.
C. He was great wrestler being both swift on his feet and strong with his grip.
D. No Mistakes

251.
A. My parents asked, "Where were you last night"?
B. Suzanne asked, "Will you go to prom with me?"
C. For some reason, I avoid any food with cilantro in it.
D. No Mistakes

252.
A. Martha was known to have asthma and during the race, she became congested and needed to be quickly sent to the hospital.
B. The Gulf of Mexico at its deepest point is about the size of 11 Empire State buildings.
C. It was the first day of school and I knew people avoided associating to me since I forgot to take off my pajamas.
D. No Mistakes

253.
A. Chewing gum can help one concentrate for any particular task.
B. I had to run quick to reach the bus in time.
C. Most animals are instinctual swimmers, but humans have to learn how to do this.
D. No Mistakes

254.
A. The male peacock is alluring to look at and it uses its feathers as a way of mating.
B. The process of passing a bill through Congress is complicated, but they try their best to finish the task whether it is accepted or rejected.
C. I always get bubble tea from the nearest Chinese cafe.
D. No Mistakes

255.
A. The two terms associated with smartness and introversion are actually different; a nerd is not a geek.
B. My school supply consists of the following: pencils, folders, and a notebook.
C. The ongoing tension between Palestine and Israel is not just a modern phenomena.
D. No Mistakes

CONTINUE ON TO THE NEXT PAGE →

LANGUAGE
PART V

256.
  A. You should highlight the important notes from the past readings on Schroeder.
  B. When doing an essay, you should consider putting the thesis at the end of the introduction.
  C. John and Jim played basketball with each other; yesterday, he won.
  D. No Mistakes

257.
  A. My pet bird was much more bigger than Raphael's.
  B. Uranium is used to make a nuclear bomb explode because it is a starter for a chain reaction.
  C. My coach told my brother that he would have to take a break due to the injury.
  D. No Mistakes

258.
  A. Exercising daily is a great way to keep a healthy body; however, moderation is key so that the body is not too tired.
  B. The firefighter was able to rescue the cat near Ms. Smith's backyard.
  C. I had a dream where I met the scientist, Einstein; the philosopher, Socrates; and the mathematician, Archimedes.
  D. No Mistakes

259.
  A. I like the sweets from Dunkin Donuts, but I prefer coffee from Starbucks.
  B. Procrastination is the reason why I cannot seem to get an A in any one of my classes.
  C. The electric eels, each carrying currents within internal glands, has the ability to stun its prey.
  D. No Mistakes

260.
  A. My brothers' cats are unusually annoying; why did each one want 3 cats for Christmas?
  B. The Patriot act is a controversial act passed by Congress to stop terrorism.
  C. The five rings in the Olympics stand for the five areas: North and South America are considered one area, along with Africa, Australia, Asia and Europe.
  D. No Mistakes

261.
  A. Melanie's teacher said, "I hope you have all studied for this quiz."
  B. The very opposite of a black hole is in fact a white hole, which can connect to the Big Bang Theory.
  C. I am more quick than either of my friends.
  D. No Mistakes

CONTINUE ON TO THE NEXT PAGE ➡

LANGUAGE
PART V

262.
- A. His incite showed how brilliant of a scientist he really was.
- B. Mineral oil is a great lubricant for the intestines.
- C. The Life of Pi is a book and a movie which depicts a boy trying to survive with animals on a boat.
- D. No Mistakes

263.
- A. The city of Toledo in Spain is known for its vast array of swords.
- B. Albuterol is a medicine that can enlarge the pathways to the lungs, making it easier to breathe.
- C. Between whales and sharks, the whales are the biggest creatures.
- D. No Mistakes

264.
- A. The division between the two nostrils is called a septum and this term is also associated with the division between the two chambers of the heart.
- B. The wolverine which is a very ferocious creature is capable of killing prey much bigger than its own size.
- C. To be considered an ionic compound, the matter has to have an anion and a cation (negative and positive charges respectively).
- D. No Mistakes

265.
- A. Alexander Graham Bell was given credit in 1876 for inventing the telephone.
- B. All of my friends' bed sheets were missing; I wonder what she did with them.
- C. A flock of crows is called a murder.
- D. No Mistakes

266.
- A. Cats have a very keen sense of hearing and can hear ultrasound.
- B. There are about 4 million kangaroos in Australia: that is twice the number of people living there.
- C. The only mammal that can't jump is the elephant and it is also the only animal has four knees.
- D. No Mistakes

267.
- A. Karaoke is a Japanese term and it means "empty orchestra."
- B. A Neanderthal is a prehistoric human often regarded dimwitted in comparison to modern humans; however, its brain is bigger.
- C. An Italian coffee-flavored dessert, tiramisu, is the most delicious thing you can find here.
- D. No Mistakes

CONTINUE ON TO THE NEXT PAGE ➡

LANGUAGE
PART V

268. A. President Obama is the first African American president.
   B. Joseph was not ready for the test even after studying days beforehand.
   C. The stars of the galaxy of Andromeda seem harder to see than the Milky Way galaxy.
   D. No Mistakes

269. A. Sam took the responsibility of the entire group project.
   B. Cancer is the increased cellular division that a body undergoes through mutation.
   C. I had ran 2 miles every day to prep for the annual marathon held in Paris.
   D. No Mistakes

270. A. Fernando gave me the scissor and said, "be careful. This is my sharpest one."
   B. All radii of a circle are equivalent.
   C. I was invited to the school dinner and the chicken was the most delicious thing I have ever tasted.
   D. No Mistakes

271. A. Since I forgot to staple my homework, my teacher, Mr. Williams took off points.
   B. Surprisingly the king of hearts is the only king that does not have a mustache.
   C. In ancient Rome, a crooked nose was a sign of leadership.
   D. No Mistakes

272. A. Mike did not notice the skunk nearby so when he took a step back, he was sprayed.
   B. Goose are easily angered and will fight back when it feels danger is nearby.
   C. Albany is the capital of New York, not New York City.
   D. No Mistakes

273. A. Spain during the Middle Ages was the center of cultural diffusion; the three religions, Islam, Christianity, and Judaism, existed in harmony.
   B. The pancreas produces insulin, this hormone lowers blood sugar levels.
   C. That the fact that I was seventeen was probably the reason why the cop did not arrest me.
   D. No Mistakes

CONTINUE ON TO THE NEXT PAGE ➡

LANGUAGE
PART V

274. A. For Satanists, Satan is a symbol of free will.
   B. Achilles' heel is a term used for one's major weakness.
   C. My strongest grades are those in the humanities and my weakest ones are in the mathematics and the sciences.
   D. No Mistakes

275. A. The concept of time travel is puzzling to many because of its contradictions; but its confusion makes it a popular subject.
   B. Rhode Island is the smallest state in the United States of America.
   C. As expected, Monday is the day of the week that has the most heart attacks and suicides.
   D. No Mistakes

276. A. Neither was I allowed to enter the building nor was I allowed near its proximity.
   B. All of the individual were intact after the accident.
   C. The International Date Line is the line that separates today from tomorrow as the world spins.
   D. No Mistakes

277. A. Daily consider practicing a task everyday so that you can improve your hobby.
   B. Hitler is associated with the Volkswagen Beetle since he ordered for its creation.
   C. Please put away your phones for the remaining time of this lecture.
   D. No Mistakes

278. A. The temperature of negative 40 degrees Celsius is just as cold like the temperature of negative 40 degrees Fahrenheit.
   B. Ali hoped to get a bike for his birthday.
   C. Wrigley's gum was the first product to have a barcode.
   D. No Mistakes

CONTINUE ON TO THE NEXT PAGE ➡

LANGUAGE
PART V

SPELLING

DIRECTIONS: For questions 279-288, find the sentence that contains a spelling error. If there is no error present, select answer choice D.

279. A. It is a myth that one can see the Great Wall of China from space.
   B. He was a conoisseur of music and loved to listen to Beethoven.
   C. One of my mom's miscellaneous leisurely activities include eating sunflower seeds while sitting on the couch.
   D. No mistakes

280. A. I would like ketchup along with mustard on my sandwich.
   B. Those of us who have insecurities should learn to accept flaws and regard them as benefits.
   C. An entrepraneur is someone holds responsibility for a business or enterprise.
   D. No mistakes

281. A. When he tripped and fell, he became unconsious.
   B. Chlorine gas is a very toxic material; please avoid going near the laboratory for that reason.
   C. My face too much embarrassment after I passed gas in the library.
   D. No mistakes

282. A. The rooms in this building are small so your head so that they don't hit the cieling.
   B. Fluorescent light bulbs are much more efficient than regular light bulbs.
   C. His absence was unaccounted for since the teacher forgot to mark him yesterday.
   D. No mistakes

283. A. The miniature model of the Leaning Tower of Pisa was inaccurate.
   B. It is important that you notice the separate rhythms of the musical notes in an orchestra.
   C. The aftermath of of the nuclear bomb in Hiroshima and Nagasaki shows the mysterious consequences of total annihilation.
   D. No mistakes

CONTINUE ON TO THE NEXT PAGE ➡

LANGUAGE
PART V

284. A. Occasionally, the pigeon would come nearby and eat from her hand.
B. Johnny kept indulging in bad behavior.
C. It is a privilegde to receive knowledge from a great professor like him.
D. No mistakes

285. A. The movie was mediocre in comparison to the actual book.
B. It is neccesary to place a piece of paper near my desk with your name on it?
C. A sacrilegious figure found in monotheistic religions is Satan.
D. No mistakes

286. A. Shakespeare was a playwrite and famous to this day for many of his works.
B. She is truly special to me; I do not know what to get her for Mother's Day.
C. Whenever we turn on the vacuum, the dog immediately runs to the garage.
D. No mistakes

287. A. Mosquitoes are known to carry malaria so be careful when going camping.
B. He could guarantee that the village would be unkempt.
C. The official documentation of the accident was missing.
D. No mistakes

288. A. Every February, I go to the library to prepare for my March midterms.
B. The maintenance of good grades require a scheduled plan beforehand.
C. Please be as through as possible when you are checking your first draft.
D. No mistakes

CONTINUE ON TO THE NEXT PAGE ➡

LANGUAGE
PART V

COMPOSITION

DIRECTIONS: For questions 289-298, follow the directions for each question and select the best answer choice.

---

289. Choose the best word or words to join the thoughts together.

____ Kasparov was a chess champion, he lost to a machine.

A. Consequently
B. Because
C. Although
D. None of these

---

290. Choose the best word or words to join the thoughts together.

_____ I was told that my notes were all over the place, I tried to write in a more organized fashion.

A. Because
B. Although
C. Since
D. None of these

291. Choose the best word or words to join the thoughts together.

Maria was able to win first place in her science research by_____

A. attentively analyzing her design of the project.
B. analyzing her design of the project attentively.
C. analyzing attentively our design of the project.
D. attentively analyze her project design.

CONTINUE ON TO THE NEXT PAGE ➡

LANGUAGE
PART V

292. Which of these expresses the idea most clearly?

   A. After studying several days, the test was very easy for John and he was proud that case hard work paid off.
   B. Since he studied beforehand, the test was easy to John and he was proud of that.
   C. After studying several days, John. The test was easy and was proud that his hard work paid off.
   D. Since he studied beforehand, John thought the test was easy and was proud that his hard work paid off.

293. Which of these expresses the idea most clearly?

   A. By building new factories, stores, and farms, products can expand into further territories and generate business among cities.
   B. By building new factories, stores, and farms, territories can expanded further with products and business can be generated among cities.
   C. Building new factories, stores, and farms expand products into farther territories and generate business among cities.
   D. Building new factories, stores, and farms can expand products into farther territories and business can be generated among cities.

294. Choose the pair of sentences that best develops this topic sentence.

   The invention of the wheel was one of the most significant discovery made by mankind.

   A. Round objects can resist friction making things easier to carry.
   B. The wheel and axle is one of the simple machines.
   C. Wheels are associated with ramps.
   D. The wheels allowed transportation and movement of heavy objects from one place to another.

295. Which of the following sentences offers least support to the topic "Vaccines were a breakthrough in medicine"?

   A. It provides resistance too many viruses that pose a huge threat.
   B. Vaccines are made out of weak microbes which the body can fight easily.
   C. Louis Pasteur was able to cure rabies through his very own vaccine.
   D. Antibiotics can help fight off bacterial infections.

CONTINUE ON TO THE NEXT PAGE ➡

LANGUAGE
PART V

296. Which of these best fits under the topic "Patience is the key to success"?

A. Study hard to prepare well enough for a test.
B. Kahn held his hand out and waited until a bird finally landed to eat the bread.
C. However much I try, I cannot seem to get the task done.
D. Mike Tyson was a champion boxer due to his tremendous skills.

297. Which sentence does not belong in the paragraph?

(1) Wearing a suit shows formality. (2) What one wears can often depict the mood of the person. (3) For example, people who dress up fancy care about their self-image. (4) On the other hand, those who don't, usually don't really care about how they are perceived in society.

A. Sentence 1
B. Sentence 2
C. Sentence 3
D. Sentence 4

298. Where should the sentence "Religion is evolving" be placed in the paragraph below?

(1) Animism is the belief that inanimate objects can have a soul. (2) It is probably the oldest form of religion.(3) However, this can tie to non-physical aspects such as imaginative and abstract beings.

A. Before sentence 1
B. Between sentence 1 & 2
C. Between sentence 2 & 3
D. None of the above

CONTINUE ON TO THE NEXT PAGE ➡

HSPT PRACTICE TEST 2
ANSWER KEY

Verbal Skills (Part I)

1. C	11. A	21. D	31. C	41. B	51. C
2. D	12. D	22. B	32. B	42. B	52. D
3. C	13. D	23. C	33. D	43. A	53. A
4. B	14. C	24. D	34. A	44. B	54. C
5. B	15. D	25. B	35. B	45. A	55. B
6. A	16. B	26. B	36. A	46. C	56. D
7. D	17. D	27. C	37. A	47. B	57. C
8. D	18. B	28. B	38. C	48. A	58. A
9. D	19. D	29. B	39. C	49. B	59. B
10. B	20. D	30. C	40. D	50. A	60. D

Language (Part V)

239. A	249. B	259. C	269. C	279. B	289. C
240. A	250. A	260. B	270. A	280. C	290. A
241. C	251. A	261. C	271. B	281. A	291. A
242. C	252. C	262. A	272. B	282. A	292. D
243. B	253. B	263. C	273. A	283. D	293. C
244. B	254. B	264. B	274. D	284. B	294. D
245. B	255. D	265. B	275. A	285. B	295. D
246. B	256. C	266. B	276. B	286. A	296. B
247. C	257. A	267. C	277. A	287. D	297. A
248. B	258. D	268. C	278. A	288. C	298. D

Reading (Part III)

113. A	128. B	143. B	158. A
114. B	129. C	144. A	159. A
115. C	130. B	145. C	160. B
116. A	131. D	146. D	161. D
117. C	132. B	147. C	162. A
118. D	133. C	148. D	163. D
119. C	134. B	149. A	164. B
120. A	135. B	150. D	165. D
121. D	136. C	151. A	166. A
122. D	137. D	152. B	167. C
123. C	138. C	153. C	168. D
124. D	139. A	154. A	169. D
125. C	140. B	155. D	170. B
126. B	141. A	156. C	171. A
127. B	142. B	157. D	172. A
			173. C
			174. B

ARGO BROTHERS

To calculate your score and watch video tutorials, visit our web site:
www.einstein-academy.com/catholic

MATHEMATICS

Quantitative (Part II)

61. D	74. C	87. B	100. C
62. D	75. A	88. C	101. B
63. D	76. A	89. A	102. B
64. B	77. C	90. D	103. B
65. C	78. A	91. A	104. A
66. D	79. C	92. D	105. C
67. D	80. A	93. C	106. A
68. C	81. D	94. D	107. D
69. C	82. B	95. C	108. D
70. B	83. B	96. B	109. D
71. A	84. A	97. A	110. D
72. C	85. A	98. D	111. B
73. A	86. D	99. A	112. B

Mathematics (Part IV)

175. B	188. A	201. B	214. B	227. C
176. A	189. C	202. C	215. A	228. B
177. B	190. B	203. A	216. D	229. A
178. D	191. D	204. D	217. C	230. C
179. B	192. A	205. C	218. C	231. D
180. C	193. C	206. B	219. A	232. A
181. B	194. B	207. D	220. B	233. B
182. B	195. A	208. A	221. D	234. A
183. C	196. C	209. C	222. B	235. C
184. D	197. D	210. B	223. A	236. D
185. B	198. C	211. B	224. C	237. B
186. B	199. A	212. A	225. D	238. D
187. A	200. D	213. C	226. B	

ANSWER EXPLANATIONS

VERBAL SECTION

1. **The correct answer is C.**
   Stove, microwave and sink are all appliances that can be found in the kitchen. A sofa cannot be found in the kitchen.

2. **The correct answer is D.**
   Finger, nail and palm are all parts of your hand, while your elbow is not.

3. **The correct answer is C.**
   Paint is the primary medium that a painter works with, while wood is the primary medium that carpenters work with.

4. **The correct answer is B.**
   If Bob is slower than Sue, and Larry is faster than Sue at swimming, this must mean that Larry is a faster swimmer than Bob. Therefore, the third statement is false.

5. **The correct answer is B.**
   Intricate is an adjective that describes something that is very detailed or complicated.

6. **The correct answer is A.**
   Hair grows on skin, while plants grow on soil.

7. **The correct answer is D.**
   Lobster, shrimp, and whale are all sea creatures that live in the water. Seagulls, however, do not live in the water.

8. **The correct answer is D.**
   Oil is used to fuel a car, while charcoal is used to fuel a fire.

9. **The correct answer is D.**
   Positive, optimistic and hopeful are all synonyms of each other. Successful has a different meaning than the other three words.

10. **The correct answer is B.**
    Gratuitous means to be given or done free of charge. Appreciative would be a synonym for this.

11. **The correct answer is A.**
    Decorous is an adjective that means to be with good taste and propriety.

12. **The correct answer is D.**
    A player's boss is the coach, while an employee's boss is the manager.

13. **The correct answer is D.**
    Leaves, stem, and roots are all parts of a plant. A trunk is not part of a plant and is part of a tree.

14. **The correct answer is C.**
    A Rabbi preaches in a synagogue while a Reverend preaches in a church.

15. **The correct answer is D.**
    A battery powers a flashlight whereas gas powers a car.

ANSWER EXPLANATIONS

16. The correct answer is B.
If Jesse is older than Jacob, and James is older than Jesse, this must mean that James is older than Jacob. Therefore, the third statement is false.

17. The correct answer is D.
Aloof means not friendly or forthcoming. Distant would be a synonym for aloof.

18. The correct answer is B.
Assail means to make a concerted violent attack.

19. The correct answer is D.
Hesitant means tentative or doubtful.

20. The correct answer is B.
A vacuum is used to clean dirt, while an eraser is used to clean pencil marks.

21. The correct answer is D.
A frame is used to shield a photo, while a screen protector is used to shield a cellphone.

22. The correct answer is B.
Dependent means to require someone or something for some kind of support. Helpless most nearly means this.

23. The correct answer is C.
Both a cart, and box can hold more than a bag. However, it is uncertain which can hold more as there is no direct correlation between the two.

24. The correct answer is D.
A morgue, grave, and coffin are all places where dead bodies are kept. A tombstone is not a place where dead bodies are kept.

25. The correct answer is B.
Conspicuous means standing out so as to be clearly visible or noticeable.

26. The correct answer is B.
A prius is faster than a lamborghini. A civic is faster than a prius. This implies that a civic is faster than a lamborghini. Therefore, the third statement is false.

27. The correct answer is C.
Lucrative is an adjective that describes some thing that produces a great deal of profit

28. The correct answer is B.
Berate means to criticize or scold.

29. The correct answer is B.
The arctic is made up of snow while the beach is made up of sand.

30. The correct answer is C.
Glorify means to describe or represent as admirable. Praise would be a synonym for glorify.

31. The correct answer is C.
Alleviate means to make less severe; the opposite of this would be to aggravate.

32. The correct answer is B.
The heart, lungs, and liver are all internal body parts, while hair is an external body organ.

33. The correct answer is D.
Crazy, lunatic, and bonkers are all synonyms of each other. Sane would mean the opposite of those three words.

ANSWER EXPLANATIONS

ARGO BROTHERS

34. The correct answer is A.
Benign means gentle and kind; the opposite would be malicious.

35. The correct answer is B.
An orange is a fruit whereas a carrot is a vegetable.

36. The correct answer is A.
Diminish means to make or become less; the opposite would be to increase.

37. The correct answer is A.
Scrutinize means to inspect closely or examine.

38. The correct answer is C.
Pretentious is an adjective characterized by an assumption of dignity and importance that is often undeserved; the opposite would be genuine.

39. The correct answer is C.
Modest means unassuming or moderate in the estimation of one's abilities or achievements; the opposite would be shameless.

40. The correct answer is D.
A bicycle, tricycle, and motorcycle all run on land while an airplane flies through the air.

41. The correct answer is B.
A door, book, and a refrigerator can all be opened, whereas a cave cannot.

42. The correct answer is B.
Jack cannot jump higher than Joseph. Jeff can jump higher than Joseph. Therefore Jeff can jump higher than Jack. The third statement must be false.

43. The correct answer is A.
Disreputable, dishonest, and infamous are all negative characteristics while exemplary is a positive characteristic.

44. The correct answer is B.
Pompous means to be self-aggrandizing or overbearing.

45. The correct answer is A.
To be impractical refers to a course of action that is not adapted for use; the opposite would be feasible.

46. The correct answer is C.
Both Krillin and Goku are stronger than Vegeta. However, there is no discernible direct connection between Krillin and Goku. Therefore, the third statement is uncertain.

47. The correct answer is B.
Docile means to be ready to accept control or instruction; the opposite would be disobedient.

48. The correct answer is A.
Monumental refers to something of great importance or grand in size; the opposite would be tiny.

49. The correct answer is B.
Michelangelo is smarter than da Vinci, and Picasso is smarter than Michelangelo. This must imply that Picasso is smarter than da Vinci, therefore, the third statement is false.

50. The correct answer is A.
Saitama is taller than Penny, and Penny is taller than Tyler. This implies that Saitama is taller than Tyler. The third statement is true.

ANSWER EXPLANATIONS

51. **The correct answer is C.**
Copious means abundant in supply or quantity; the opposite would be sparse.

52. **The correct answer is D.**
Chaotic, disorderly, and turmoil are all synonyms of each other. Tidy is the only outlier that means neatly kept.

53. **The correct answer is A.**
Trailer, mansion, and home are all places where people live. People do not live in the park.

54. **The correct answer is C.**
Refurbish means to redecorate or renovate.

55. **The correct answer is B.**
Intolerant means to not allow or be able to endure specific views or beliefs; the the closest opposite answer choice would be unprejudiced.

56. **The correct answer is D.**
Lucrative means profitable or gainful; the opposite would be unprofitable.

57. **The correct answer is C.**
A librarian works in the library while a doctor works in the hospital.

58. **The correct answer is A.**
Pugnacious means eager or quick to argue; aggressive would be a synonym.

59. **The correct answer is B.**
A ruby, emerald, and sapphire are all gems that have color. A diamond does not.

60. **The correct answer is D.**
A jacket, hoodie, and mittens, are all winter garments whereas a tanktop is not.

QUANTITATIVE SECTION

61. **The correct answer is D.**
9 less than 100 would equal to 91. Divide 91 by 7 to get an answer of 13.

62. **The correct answer is D.**
The $3^3 = 27$.
27 divided by 9 equals 3.
2 less than 3 would give 1.

63. **The correct answer is D.**
The numbers in the series follow the pattern; multiply by 2, add 1, multiply by 2, and add 1. To go from 6 to 7, 1 is added, so to go from 7 to the next number, 7 needs to be multiplied by 2 which gives 14.

64. **The correct answer is B.**
Evaluate the total amount of money in each answer choice. Statement A has a total value of 30 cents. Statement B has a total value of 27 cents, and statement C has a total value of 35 cents. Therefore, C has more value than A and B.

65. **The correct answer is C.**
Evaluate all of the statements given to find their value. Statement A has a value of 65. Statement B has a value of 144. Statement C has a value of 41. Therefore, the value of statement B is the greatest.

ANSWER EXPLANATIONS

66. **The correct answer is D.**
    Simplify all of the statements. Statement A gives a value of 56. Statement B gives a value of 1 • .56 = .56. Statement C gives a value of 56 as well. Therefore statements A and C are equal to each other and both of them are greater than statement B.

67. **The correct answer is D.**
    Each consecutive number in this series is adding one less than was added to get the previous number. The numbers in the series progresses by adding 5, then 4, then 3, then 2, then 1, then 0, and to get the last number, adding -1.

68. **The correct answer is C.**
    Each consecutive number in this series goes according to the pattern; subtract 6, add 8, subtract 6, add 8 and so forth. To go from 33 to 27, 6 is subtracted so to find the next number, 8 needs to be added to 27 which gives 35.

69. **The correct answer is C.**
    Find the average of the numbers by adding up all the numbers and dividing by the total amount of numbers. Adding up all the numbers gives 70. There are a total of 5 numbers so dividing 70 by 5 gives 14. 3 times 14 is 42.

70. **The correct answer is B.**
    Evaluate all of the statements given. Statement A gives a value of 27. Statement B gives a value of 32. Statement C gives a value of 30. Therefore, B > C > A.

71. **The correct answer is A.**
    The numbers in this series go according to the pattern; subtract 3, add 1, subtract 3, add 1 and so on. To go from 76 to 73, 3 is subtracted so to go from 73 to the next number, add 1. Therefore the answer is 74.

72. **The correct answer is C.**
    Count the total amount of circles in each statement. Statement A has a total of 9 circles. Statement B has a total of 6 circles and statement C has a total of 6 circles. Only statement C is true.

73. **The correct answer is A.**
    The pattern in this problem can be seen by looking at the difference between each consecutive number. The difference between the consecutive numbers are 8, 9, 10, 11, and 12. Therefore, the difference between the next 3 numbers should be 13, 14, and 15. To find the next 3 numbers then, add 13, then 14, and then 15.

74. **The correct answer is C.**
    To find the next number in this series, add the two numbers previous to it. The two numbers previous to the missing number is 3, and 5, so the missing number is 8. This series is a special series know as the "Fibonacci Sequence." This sequence is very important in mathematics and its implications can be seen everywhere in nature.

75. **The correct answer is A.**
    Evaluate each of the statements given. The value of the first statement is 26. The value of the second statement is 22. The value of the third statement is 26. Therefore, statement A = C which is greater than B.

ANSWER EXPLANATIONS

76. The correct answer is A.
To find 30% of 30, multiply 30 by .3. This gives 9. 12 less than 9 is -3.

77. The correct answer is C.
Evaluate each of the statements given. The value of the first statement is 15. The value of the second statement is 26. The value of the third statement is 24. Therefore, B > C > A.

78. The correct answer is A.
Find the amount of lines of symmetry in each of the figures given. Figure A has 3 lines of symmetry. Figure B has 4 lines of symmetry and figure C has 5 lines of symmetry. Therefore, figure B has fewer lines of symmetry than C, but more than A.

79. The correct answer is C.
The numbers in this series go according to the pattern; subtract 6, subtract 5, subtract 4, subtract 3, and so on. From 577 to 575, 2 is subtracted so to go from 575 to the next number, 1 needs to be subtracted which gives 574.

80. The correct answer is A.
Each consecutive number in this series is four more than the number previous to it, so to get to each consecutive number, add four. 4 added to 48 is 52.

81. The correct answer is D.
Find the amount of shaded area in each circle. In figure A, exactly half is shaded. In figure B, 2 out of 4 equal parts are shaded in which is half that is shaded in. In figure C, 3 out of 6 equal parts are shaded in which is also half that is shaded in. Therefore, all three are shaded equally.

82. The correct answer is B.
15 times 3 is 45. Multiply 45 by the reciprocal of $\frac{5}{7}$, which is $\frac{7}{5}$, to get 63.

83. The correct answer is B.
In the pyramid given, side AC and AE are known as slant heights. All slant heights in a pyramid are equivalent to each other.

84. The correct answer is A.
5 more than 59 is 64. 64 divided by 8 is 8.

85. The correct answer is A.
Evaluate each of the answer choices given. Statement A is already simplified. Statement B simplifies to approximately 0.57 and statement C simplifies to repeating decimal .6666. The only choice that is true is A, A is greater than B.

86. The correct answer is D.
5 times 5 is 25. To find a number that if divided by 5, gives 25, multiply 25 by 5. This gives 125.

87. The correct answer is B.
The product of 2 and 3 is 6. 7 times 6 is 42. 9 subtracted from 42 is 33.

88. The correct answer is C.
Convert each of the statements into decimal form. Statement A converts to 5.5. Statement B converts to decimal 5.5. Statement C converts to repeating decimal 5.77. Therefore, A = B < C.

ANSWER EXPLANATIONS

89. The correct answer is A.
The numbers in the series are being increased by three and the numbers alternate from roman numerals to integers. The next number in the series should be a roman numeral and since the last number in the series is 25, simply add three to get 28. 28 in roman numeral form is XXVIII.

90. The correct answer is D.
Find the values of each of the bars. Bar A has a value of 6. Bar B has a value of 8. Bar C has a value of 4 and Bar D has a value of 10. Only choice D makes sense, where 10 - 6 = 4.

91. The correct answer is A.
This series of numbers has to be looked at in sets of twos. The relationship between each two numbers is that the first number is 3 times smaller than the second number. The first number is the smaller number and the next is 3 times larger. The blank is in a position where the number following it is 3 times larger than it. 39 divided by 3 is 13.

92. The correct answer is D.
A quarter of 100 is 25. 3 times 25 is 75.

93. The correct answer is C.
Side AD is equal to 3 and side DC is equal to 4. To find the perimeter of ABCD, add 3 and 4 and multiply by 2. This gives 14.

94. The correct answer is D.
One eighth of 16 is 2. 2 subtracted from 32 gives 30.

95. The correct answer is C.
One quarter of 100 is 25. 5 times 25 is 125.

96. The correct answer is B.
Simplify fractions B and C into decimal form. Fraction B simplifies to 0.8, and fraction C simplifies to 0.875. Therefore, C > B > A.

97. The correct answer is A.
11 times 6 is 66. 66 multiplied by the reciprocal of $\frac{2}{3}$, $\frac{3}{2}$, is 99.

98. The correct answer is D.
Evaluate each of the statements given. The first statement simplifies to 16. The second statement simplifies to 36. The third statement simplifies to 18. Therefore, B > C > A.

99. The correct answer is A.
From the picture, region A makes up exactly half of the circle. Both portions B and C make up less than half of the circle, therefore, region A has the biggest area.

100. The correct answer is C.
The numbers in this series go according to the pattern; add 30, add 1, add 30, add 1 and so on. To go from 121 to 151, 30 is added so to go to 151 to the next number, one needs to be added. This gives an answer of 152.

101. The correct answer is B.
The numbers in this series go according to the pattern; add 2, add 1, add 2, add 1 and so on. To go from 93 to 94, 1 is added so to go from 94 to the next number, 2 needs to be added. This gives an answer of 96.

ANSWER EXPLANATIONS

102. The correct answer is B.
The numbers in this series go according to the pattern; add 7, subtract 2, add 7, subtract 2 and so on. To go from 110 to 117, 7 is added so to go from 117 to the next number, 2 needs to be subtracted. This gives an answer of 115.

103. The correct answer is B.
12 divided by 3 is 4. 4 times 4 is 16.

104. The correct answer is A.
$\frac{3}{7}$ of 49 can be found by dividing 49 by 7 and then multiplying by 3. This equates to 21. 21 - 7 = 14.

105. The correct answer is C.
The numbers in this series should be looked at as sets of twos. Each consecutive odd and even positioned number is considered a pair. Each odd positioned number is four times less than the even positioned number following it. To go from 2 to 8, 4 is multiplied and to get from 4 to 16, 4 is also multiplied. To find the missing number, divide 36 by 4, which gives 9.

106. The correct answer is A.
The numbers in this series go according to the pattern; add 6, add 3, add 6, add 3 and so on. To go from 26 to 29, 3 is added so to go from 29 to the next number, 6 needs to be added. This gives 35.

107. The correct answer is D.
None of the answer choices given are true. The fraction shaded for C has to be greater than the fraction shaded for B because in C, one third is shaded and in B, less than one third is shaded. The fraction shaded for A is one fifth while the fraction shaded for B is less than one fifth. Therefore, none of the

108. The correct answer is D.
Look at the letters first and determine a relationship between the letters. Each consecutive letter is three letters ahead of the previous letter. This means that the missing letter should be a "V." Look at the numbers next. The numbers go according to the pattern; add 2, subtract 3, add 2, subtract 3 and so on. There is a difference of 3 between the last two numbers so the next number must be 2 more than the previous so the next number should be a "5."

109. The correct answer is D.
6 times 2 is 12. 7 subtracted from 12 is 5. 5 times 5 is 25.

110. The correct answer is D.
The numbers in this series go according to the pattern; add 1, subtract 4, add 1, subtract 4 and so on. The last two numbers have a difference of 1 in the question, so the next three numbers should subtract 4, add 1, and then subtract 4 respectively. Therefore, the answer is D.

111. The correct answer is B.
To find $\frac{7}{8}$ of 72, multiply $\frac{7}{8}$ by 72 which gives 63. 14 added to 63 is 77.

112. The correct answer is B.
3 to the fourth power is equal to 81. 81 divided by 9 is 9. The answer is 9.

ANSWER EXPLANATIONS

READING SECTION

113. The correct answer is A.
The passage discusses the history of dreams, and their significance in different cultures. A history book would be the best choice to find such information.

114. The correct answer is B.
The second paragraph discusses brain activity during the stages of dreaming and the REM state. Thus, it is describing the science of dreaming.

115. The correct answer is C.
The passage encompasses the history of dreams, its significance in multiple different parts of the world as well as the science that is behind it. The only answer choice that is general enough to include all of the information is C.

116. The correct answer is A.
In the first paragraph, the French Philosopher Henri Bergson discusses his experience with dreams. As he is a philosopher, he is considered to be a credible source.

117. The correct answer is C.
The word *phenomenon* is used to describe dreams. The only answer choice that can replace the word would be C, experience.

118. The correct answer is D.
In the second paragraph, it is stated that a person is likely to remember details of a dream if woken during REM sleep.

119. The correct answer is C.
In the first paragraph, it is stated that failing to analyze dreams correctly could be very unfavorable for the interpreter. It can be inferred that both A and B and possible.

120. The correct answer is A.
Using context clues, it can be seen that *lucid* would be synonymous to the word memorable. The only answer choice that has a similar meaning is *vivid*.

121. The correct answer is D.
In the end of the second paragraph, it is stated that a person can dream anywhere from four to seven times per night.

122. The correct answer is D.
In the third paragraph, it is stated that the Egyptians and Babylonians believed that dreams could be used to foretell the future.

123. The correct answer is C.
Using context clues, it can be inferred that the word *implausible* most nearly means unlikely. Out of the answer choices, *unbelievable* is the closest in meaning.

124. The correct answer is D.
In the third paragraph, it is stated that the civilians believed that the Vaults were to be used as bomb shelters against the ongoing war.

125. The correct answer is C.
It is stated in the third paragraph that Vault-Tec created Project Safehouse, which followed the idea of creating Vaults across the nation.

ANSWER EXPLANATIONS

126. The correct answer is B.
It is stated in the second paragraph that the United States devolved from fifty states to thirteen commonwealths to fight Communism.

127. The correct answer is B.
In the second paragraph, it was discussed that Europe fell due to the high oil prices.

128. The correct answer is B
Based on the context of the sentence, it can be understood that *annex* means something similar to overtaking Canada. B would be the best answer choice.

129. The correct answer is C.
The third paragraph introduces Vault Tec, which creates Project Safehouse to insure the survival of United States citizens.

130. The correct answer is B.
As stated in the final portion of the third paragraph, Project Safehouse's true intentions were to use the citizens as test subjects.

131. The correct answer is D.
In the end of the passage, it states that the citizens living in the Vaults were called vault-dwellers.

132. The correct answer is B.
The word *subterranean* can be understood to be underground, as it is described earlier in the passage.

133. The correct answer is C.
After the definition and brief background on evolution, the first topic that is introduced is remix culture. Understanding transitioning, evolution is used to introduce remix culture.

134. The correct answer is B.
The main idea of the passage discusses how remix culture is used in all aspects of art and society; remix culture is the idea of rehashing and developing new ideas from the old. Answer choice B best describes this idea.

135. The correct answer is B.
The passage discusses a great deal about the media, and thus would most likely be found in sociology texts.

136. The correct answer is C.
The word *husk* is synonymous to a shell, or in this case, covering.

137. The correct answer is D.
In the passage, it is stated that George Lucas uses multiple ideas from different movies and series' including the text crawl introductio that was taken from *Flash Gordon*.

138. The correct answer is C.
In the second paragraph, a few examples of remix culture used in films is introduced and described.

139. The correct answer is A.
Using context clues, it can be inferred that *archetype* refers to the outlined plan that George Lucas believed was used in most hero stories. Thus, an archetype would be considered an ideal example.

140. The correct answer is B.
In the third paragraph, it is mentioned that in music, remix culture includes using certain beats and even lyrics from other songs.

ANSWER EXPLANATIONS

141. The correct answer is A.
In the passage, it is stated that "Rapper's Delight" had an upbeat and rhythmic pattern that was reused in multiple different songs throughout history.

142. The correct answer is B.
From the first paragraph, it states that remix culture is the idea to combine and edit original material to create a new entity.

143. The correct answer is B.
It is stated in the first paragraph that body tattooing is found to be customary in Hinduism, but is forbidden in Judaism and Islam.

144. The correct answer is A.
Using context clues, it can be inferred that *conventional* is similar in meaning to the word customary. Traditional also has a synonymous definition to customary.

145. The correct answer is C.
In the first paragraph, it is stated that religions including Judaism and Islam forbid body modification.

146. The correct answer is D.
In the second paragraph, the Untouchables are described to also be known as Ramnaamis due to their devotion to the Lord Rama.

147. The correct answer is C.
In the second paragraph, the author discusses the use of different forms, colors and symbols to show reverence for the Gods.

148. The correct answer is D.
In the second paragraph, it is stated that tattoos are used in all the cases provided. As such, the answer must be choice D.

149. The correct answer is A.
The first paragraph fully describes the seating arrangement for President Lincoln at the theater box.

150. The correct answer is D.
The passage describes a historical event. Thus, the writing will most likely be found in a history book.

151. The correct answer is A.
In the second paragraph, it is stated that alongside President Lincoln sat Mrs. Lincoln, Major Rathbone and Miss. Harris. This adds up to four people.

152. The correct answer is B.
The word partition is a noun that refers to something that separates and divides. Thus, division would be the best choice as a synonym.

153. The correct answer is C.
Refurbished means to redecorate or renovate.

154. The correct answer is A.
To be lucrative means to be able to produce a great deal of profit, or something that is profitable.

ANSWER EXPLANATIONS

155. The correct answer is D.
Enamored means to be filled with a feeling of love for. Captivated best fits this.

156. The correct answer is C.
Diminutive means extremely or unusually small. Tiny best fits this.

157. The correct answer is D.
To be depleted means to have used up the supply or resource. Consumed would be a synonym.

158. The correct answer is A.
To be adamant means to refuse to be persuaded or to change one's mind. Stubborn means the same thing.

159. The correct answer is A.
Inane means to be silly or stupid. Absurd means the same thing.

160. The correct answer is B.
To be quirky means to be characterized by peculiar or unexpected traits.

161. The correct answer is D.
Pompous means to be affectedly and irritatingly grand and solemn. Pretentious is a synonym.

162. The correct answer is A.
To be infatuated means to be inspired with an intense but short-lived passion. Mesmerized is a synonym for this.

163. The correct answer is D.
Elated is an adjective that means to be ecstatically happy or joyful.

164. The correct answer is B.
Amiable means to have or display a friendly and pleasant manner.

165. The correct answer is D.
To be resilient means to be able to withstand or recover quickly from difficult situations. Strong is a synonym.

166. The correct answer is A.
Eccentric means to have an unconventional or slightly strange behavior. Bizarre is a synonym.

167. The correct answer is C.
To squelch means to forcefully silence or suppress.

168. The correct answer is D.
To commence means to start or begin.

169. The correct answer is D.
To be malcontent means to be rebellious or dissatisfied.

170. The correct answer is B.
Console means to comfort at a time of grief or disappointment.

171. The correct answer is A.
To be imminent means to be immediate or about to happen.

172. The correct answer is A.
To berate means to scold or criticize angrily.

173. The correct answer is C.
Impede means to delay or prevent by obstructing, or hinder.

ANSWER EXPLANATIONS

174. The correct answer is B.
To mimic means to imitate, typically in order to entertain or ridicule. Mock is a synonym.

MATH SECTION

175. The correct answer is B.
The circumference of a circle is, $C = 2\pi r$. The radius of the circle is 4 cm. Therefore, the circumference is 8π square centimeters.

176. The correct answer is A.
2 raised to the 3rd power is equal to 2 • 2 • 2. Apply the same method to 4 raised to the 5th power and multiply the two parts together. The correct answer choice is A.

177. The correct answer is B.
If a number is subtracted from 0, the number is undoubtedly changed because in this case, the sign of the number is changing. Let x represent the number. $0 - x = -x$. The number becomes negative, therefore changing the number.

178. The correct answer is D.
Multiply 4 by 5 to get 20. Multiply 3 by 5 to get 15. Divide 20 by 15 to get $\frac{20}{15}$ which can be simplified to $\frac{4}{3}$.

179. The correct answer is B.
Solve for the triangle by adding 5 to both sides. This gives the value of negative triangle to be 10, so triangle is equal to 10.

180. The correct answer is C.
The question is asking for a number that is both a multiple of 10 and 6. The only number on the list is 30.

181. The correct answer is B.
Evaluate each statement given. 7 + 8 is 15 which is less than 15.5. Therefore, statement B is true.

182. The correct answer is B.
Since the number is in the hundreds of millions, there must be a total of 9 digits in the number, so choices A and D can be eliminated. The number in the question has 600 thousand, therefore choice C can also be eliminated, leaving only answer choice B.

183. The correct answer is C.
Choice A is not a multiple of 24 or 36. Choice B is only a multiple of 36, but not 24. Choice D is a divisor of 24 and 36 but not a multiple. Only choice C is a multiple of both 24 and 36.

184. The correct answer is D.
0.079 is not equal to or less than 0.00935. It is greater than 0.00935 so the only choice that would make sense is D.

185. The correct answer is B.
A triangle has 180°. A right angle has a measure of 90°.
90° + 40° = 130°
180° - 130° = 50°

186. The correct answer is B.
Solve the inequality by adding 5 to both sides. This gives $y > 23$. Choice B represents this.

187. The correct answer is A.
The union of two sets asks for the numbers in both sets. Every number shown in set A and set B should be represented in the answer. Only choice A does this.

ANSWER EXPLANATIONS

188. The correct answer is A.
The intersection of $\overline{JL}$ and $\overline{KM}$ is represented by $\overline{KL}$ because segment $\overline{KL}$ is in both regions.

189. The correct answer is C.
$\frac{1}{16}$ in decimal form is equal to 0.0625 which is 6.25%. $\frac{100}{16}$% is equal to 6.25%. 6.25 is equal to 625%, not 6.25%, therefore the correct answer choice is C.

190. The correct answer is B.
Solve the inequality by first adding 3 on both sides, then dividing by 7. This gives the inequality $a < \frac{12}{7}$. Answer choice B, 1, is less than $\frac{12}{7}$.

191. The correct answer is D.
There are a total of 7 digits and there is a 2 in the millions place so there are 2 millions. There is a 2 in the ten thousands place so there are 20 thousands.

192. The correct answer is A.
Since there are a total of 3 digits, the first number 5, needs to be multiplied by 100, the second number, 2, by 10 and the third, 1, by 1. Choice A is the only one that includes this.

193. The correct answer is C.
Divide $\frac{4}{9}$ by $\frac{1}{4}$, or multiply $\frac{4}{9}$ by 4. This gives $\frac{16}{9}$.

194. The correct answer is B.
If x is a positive integer that is less than 3, choice A, C and D cannot be correct. Choices C and D are essentially the same answer when simplified. If you start to plug in values for x for answer choice B, the inequality holds true.

195. The correct answer is A.
Convert each answer to meters. Choice B converts to 5 meters. Choice C converts to 50 meters. Choice D converts to 50 meters also, therefore choice A is the answer.

196. The correct answer is C.
For this question, start to plug in the answer choices and see which answer choice makes the following statement true. Plugging in answer choice A gives us $12 < 12$, which is false. Plugging in answer choice B gives us $18 < 12$, which is false. Plugging in answer choice C gives us $6 < 12$, which is true, therefore the correct answer choice is C.

197. The correct answer is D.
There are 8 pints in a gallon. Therefore, the ratio can be converted to 2 gallons to 8 gallons. This is a 1:4 ratio.

198. The correct answer is C.
If Charles is w years old and his brother is 4 years older, $w + 4$ represents his brothers current age. 3 years ago, his brothers age would be $w + 4 - 3$ which simplifies to $w + 1$ years old.

Problem Solving Questions

199. The correct answer is A.
Subtract 16 on both sides to get $3.2x = 22.4$. Divide by 3.2 on both sides to get $x = 7$.

ANSWER EXPLANATIONS

200. The correct answer is D.
185 - 32 = 153.
$(153)(\frac{5}{9}) = 85$.

201. The correct answer is B.
Divide 18,000 by 100 to see how many times the tax rate needs to be paid. This comes out to 180. Multiply 180 by 8.09 to get $1,456.20.

202. The correct answer is C.
If the ratio is 1:12, there are 12 times as many children as staff. Therefore, multiply 12 by 24 to find the amount of children, which is 288.

203. The correct answer is A.
If 7 inches represents 21 feet, each inch represents 3 feet. Divide 51 by 3 which gives 17. Therefore, the line must be 17 inches long.

204. The correct answer is D.
The clothing store sells the shirt for 80% more than they paid for it. Set up an equation. The equation is 21.78 = x(1.8). 1.8 is obtained by understanding that the 21.78 is 80% greater than what they had paid for it. gives x to equal $12.10.

205. The correct answer is C.
Multiply 21.78 by 70% which is the adjusted price. The new price is 70% of the old price since there is a 30% discount. This comes to $15.25.

206. The correct answer is B.
Break the figure into 3 shapes as shown.

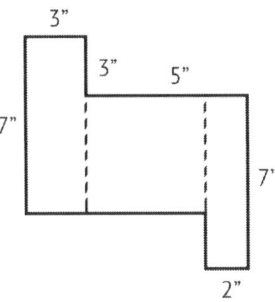

The first rectangle has an area of 21 because 3 times 7 is 21. The third rectangle has an area of 14 because 7 times 2 is 14. To find the dimensions of the second rectangle, first subtract 3 from 7 to find the vertical distance of the rectangle. This gives 4. To find the horizontal distance, add the total horizontal distance of the topside of the figure, which is 5 + 3 = 8. From 8, subtract 2 and then 3 which are the dimensions of the known lengths for the bottom side of the figure. This gives the length of the missing side to be 3. Multiply 3 by 4 to get 12. Add all three areas, 21 + 14 + 12 to get 47 square inches.

207. The correct answer is D.
With the missing dimensions mentioned in the previous question, add them up to get the perimeter. Adding the dimensions clockwise, we get 3 + 3 + 5 + 7 + 2 + 3 + 6 + 7 = 36 inches.

208. The correct answer is A.
For 5 miles, the first 3 miles was $5.46. For 2 more miles $14 is needed so add this to $5.46 to get $19.46, answer choice A.

ANSWER EXPLANATIONS

209. The correct answer is C.
The total value earned by the winner is one fourth of the total prize. If the winner's share was $3,300, multiply this by 4 to get the total prize value which is answer choice C.

210. The correct answer is B.
If 10 passengers get off and 2 get on, there is a net of 8 people that get off. There are a total of 20 people initially on the bus because there are 12 seated and 8 standing. If 8 get off, there is a total of 12 people on the bus. There are still 16 empty seats.

211. The correct answer is B.
If the equilateral triangle has a perimeter of 27, each side must be $\frac{1}{3}$ of that which is 9. The addition of 2 sides would be 9 + 9 = 18.

212. The correct answer is A.
Divide 4.06 by 1.45. Plug in each of the answer choices to see if they work. Answer choices B, C, and D can be eliminated just by seeing that multiplying 1.45 by 3= 4.35 which is too great. The answer has to be less than three. The only choice left is A.

213. The correct answer is C.
Perform the operations as shown across following PEMDAS. Perform the parenthesis first.
7 + -3 = 4
5 - 8 = -3
4 - (-(-3)) = 1
-4 - 1 = -5

214. The correct answer is B.
Multiply 62 by 1.7 which gives answer choice B.

215. The correct answer is A.
Simplify the problem by only dealing with the smallest unit, pints. 1 gallon is equal to 8 pints and one quart is equal to 2 pints. The first number has a total of 57 pints. The second number has a total of 44 pints.
57 pints - 44 pints = 13 pints.
See which answer choice has a total of 13 pints. Only answer choice A matches.

216. The correct answer is D.
Follow PEMDAS. Dividing by $\frac{1}{4}$ is the same as multiplying by 4. Multiply 8 by 4 to get 32. Multiply $\frac{1}{2}$ by 12 to get 6. Add 32 and 6 to get 38.

217. The correct answer is C.
Plug in the given values. The number under the square root becomes 4 + 6(11) + 10(3) which gives 100. The square root of 100 is 10.

218. The correct answer is C.
24 is 8 times bigger than 3. Multiply $\frac{5}{8}$ by 8 to get 5.

219. The correct answer is A.
Add the numbers 5, -4, 8, 9, and -3 to get 15. Divide by the amount of numbers, 5 to get 3.

220. The correct answer is B.
Round 498,996 to 500,000 and round 249 to 250. If there are 1,000 people for 250 cars, that is 4 people per car. Multiply 500,000 by 4 to get approximately 2 million.

ANSWER EXPLANATIONS

221. The correct answer is D.
The plumber needs 5 pipes and each pipe is 1 foot and 7 inches. Convert this into inches to make this problem a little easier. Each pipe is then 19 inches long. If the plumber needs 5 pipes, that is 19 inches • 5 = 95 inches. Convert that back into feet which is 7 feet and 11 inches. Since the pipes are only sold by the foot, the plumber must buy a minimum of 8 foot pipe to have 5 pipes.

222. The correct answer is B.
The first number comes out to 6,301. The second number comes out to 2,510. Subtract the two numbers to get 3,791.

223. The correct answer is A.
The area of a square is side squared. The square root of 36 is 6, so each side is 6 inches. If an equilateral triangle has a length of 6 inches, the total perimeter would be 3 times this which is 18.

224. The correct answer is C.
Plug in $h = 7$ into the equation. The equation becomes $g = 43 - (9)(-7)$. This simplifies to $43 - (-63) = 106$.

225. The correct answer is D.
$1 + 5 = 6$
$6 \times 6 \times 6 = 216$

226. The correct answer is B.
Set up an equation to represent the ratio. The equation is $3x + 2x = 40$. This simplifies to $5x = 40$ where $x = 8$. The $3x$ represents the amount of males and $2x$ represents the amount of females. If there are 16 girls, there would be 24 males. The difference is 8.

227. The correct answer is C.
Subtract 37 from both sides to get $x^2 = 81$. The square root of 81 is 9.

228. The correct answer is B.
Find the total square footage of the garden by multiplying 9 feet by 14 to get 126 square feet. Multiply this by $\frac{7}{8}$ to find the amount of gallons needed since there are 8 pints in a gallon. This gives 110.25. Since the question asks for the minimum number of gallons needed, one would need 111 gallons of water to water this garden. Therefore, the answer choice is B.

229. The correct answer is A.
Multiply both sides by 4. This gives $x + 22 = 47$. Subtract 22 on both sides to get $x = 25$.

230. The correct answer is C.
Use the pythagorean theorem to find BD in triangle BDC. The pythagorean theorem is $a^2 + b^2 = c^2$. The hypotenuse is 13 and 13 squared is 169. 12 squared is 144. 169 - 144 is 25. The square root of 25 is 5. Therefore, the missing side is C, 5. You could also recognize that this is a 5-12-13 triangle, one that is seen often.

231. The correct answer is D.
The hotel is insured 70% of the total value which is $494,000 • 0.7 = $345,800. For every $100 the insurance is covering, the individual must pay $0.30. In order to find out how much the individual is paying for the insurance for the hotel, divide $345,800 by a 100 to get $3,458 and then multiply by $0.30. The yearly premium payment on this hotel is $1,037.40, answer choice D.

ANSWER EXPLANATIONS

232. The correct answer is A.
Convert 150% to decimal which is 1.5.
1.5 • 56 = 84.

233. The correct answer is B.
If Martha left at 8:45 a.m and arrived at 1:20 p.m. there are 4 hours in between which takes us to 12:45 pm. From 12:45 p.m to 1:20 p.m. there are 35 minutes. Martha's trip took 4 hours and 35 minutes long.

234. The correct answer is A.
To convert milligrams to grams, move the decimal point 3 places to the left. This brings us to 0.0105 g.

235. The correct answer is C.
First find out what the degree measure of angle C's supplement is. Do this by subtracting 135 from 180 which is 45. To find the missing angle, add the two other angles measurements of the triangle which is 45 and 25. They add up to 70. In a triangle, there are 180° and 180 - 70 is 110.

236. The correct answer is D.
Break the figure up into two shapes, a rectangle and a semicircle. The area of the rectangle is 6 times 18, which is 108. The area of a circle is represented by $A = \pi(r)^2$. Since the figure has a semicircle, divide the area equation by 2. It then becomes $A = (\frac{1}{2})\pi(r)^2$. The radius of the semicircle is 3, which is half one of the sides of the rectangle. 3 squared is 9. Half of 9 is $\frac{9}{2}$.
Therefore, the answer is:
$(108 + \frac{9}{2}\pi)$ square cm.

237. The correct answer is B.
The volume of a rectangular prism can be found by the equation V = l • w • h. This comes out to 2 • 8 • 12 in this problem. This is equal to 192.

238. The correct answer is D.
Originally if the tax is 8%, the original price would be 300 • 1.08 which is $324. After the increase to 10 percent, the new price would be 300 • 1.10 which is $330. The difference is $6.

LANGUAGE SECTION

239. The correct answer is A.
There should be a comma between power and but.

240. The correct answer is A.
The error is due to the dangling modifier. Here, the subject or the person doing the action in the sentence is Joanna and so she should come after the comma because she is the one typing the essay.

241. The correct answer is C.
The word "day" should be capitalized since it is part of a holiday.

242. The correct answer is C.
The incorrect word "loose" is used. "Loose" is used as an adjective, but here it should be the word "lose" since it is a verb.

243. The correct answer is B.
The word mom should be lower cased if "my" precedes it. If there is no personal possessive such as "my," then it is usually capital.

ANSWER EXPLANATIONS

244. The correct answer is B.
The word "alzheimer's" should be capitalized to "Alzheimer's" since it is the name of a disease.

245. The correct answer is B.
There is an error with comparison since there are 3 animals within the sentence. Here stronger is incorrectly used because it refers to a comparison between two things. The correct word should have been strongest.

246. The correct answer is B.
The error is due to the dangling modifier. Here, the subject or the person doing the action in the sentence is Anastasia and so she should come after the comma because she is the one climbing the rocks, not the ropes.

247. The correct answer is C.
There should be a comma between available and they since a separation is necessary between an independent and dependent clause.

248. The correct answer is B.
There is an error with verb tense since part of the sentence is in the past tense and part of it is in the present tense.

249. The correct answer is B.
Great should be capitalized since it is part of the title of Alexander's name.

250. The correct answer is A.
Here, the error is with the comparison of consistency of Gaby's bread compared to Sheylla's bread. It should have mentioned "the consistency of Sheylla's bread" as a correct comparison.

251. The correct answer is A.
Question marks should be placed within quotations at the end of sentences.

252. The correct answer is C.
Here, there is an error with appropriate preposition. Instead of "associating to" it should be "associating with."

253. The correct answer is B.
There is an error with adjective over adverb or vice versa. The word "quick" is an adjective but in this sentence it has to describe the verb run. It should therefore be replaced with the word "quickly."

254. The correct answer is B.
Here there is an error in pronoun vagueness. One cannot tell who "they" refers to.

255. The correct answer is D.
No mistakes.

256. The correct answer is C.
Here there is an error in pronoun vagueness. One cannot tell who won the game.

257. The correct answer is A.
Here, the error is with the comparison of my bird compared to Raphael. It should have mentioned "Raphael's bird" as a correct comparison.

258. The correct answer is D.
No mistakes.

259. The correct answer is C.
This is an error in subject verb agreement. Electric eels is plural and therefore the verb should be "have" instead of "has."

ANSWER EXPLANATIONS

260. The correct answer is B.
Act should be capitalized since it is part of the title of Patriot Act.

261. The correct answer is C.
The correct comparative form of quick is quicker, not "more quick." This goes under the comparative and superlative category.

262. The correct answer is A.
Here, the word incite is incorrectly used. Incite means to provoke and in this case it should be insight which means perception.

263. The correct answer is C.
The correct comparative form of big is bigger, not "biggest." This goes under the comparative and superlative category and here it is comparing two things. This is why "er" should come after the adjective rather than "est."

264. The correct answer is B.
There should be a comma between wolverine and which and another comma between creature and is. This will allow a separation of the phrase from the main sentence.

265. The correct answer is B.
Since the narrator has one friend, the contraction should go between the "d" and the "s" in the word "friends."

266. The correct answer is B.
A colon is used usually when a writer is introducing a list of items or used to separate one idea from the one which follows. Clearly the colon does not belong in this sentence and is used incorrectly.

267. The correct answer is C.
Tiramisu should be capitalized since it is a name.

268. The correct answer is C.
Here, the error is with the comparison of stars of the galaxy of Andromeda to the Milky Way galaxy. It should have mentioned "than those of the Milky Way" as a correct comparison.

269. The correct answer is C.
Here, the word "ran" should be "run" since it follows the word had, which is part of the perfect tense. A past participle should come after the perfect tense. Here, there is an error with the verb tense.

270. The correct answer is A.
The first word after the quotation in a dialogue should be capitalized.

271. The correct answer is B.
There should be a comma after surprisingly.

272. The correct answer is B.
There are a couple of things incorrect within this sentence. Subject verb agreement is one error and here it should be "a goose is." The other error is the word "it" if "goose" is changed to "geese" as a correction.

273. The correct answer is A.
A comma separates two independent clauses but it needs a conjunction such as "and". The comma can be replaced by a semicolon to make the sentence correct since it is the semicolon (or colon) that separates two independent clauses without a conjunction.

ANSWER EXPLANATIONS

274. The correct answer is D.
No mistakes.

275. The correct answer is A.
A semicolon separates two independent clauses and therefore "but" should not belong in the sentence. The semicolon can be replaced by a comma to make the sentence correct since it is the comma that separates two independent clauses with a conjunction.

276. The correct answer is B.
All can either be singular or plural depending on the reference. Here it is one individual and so the verb should be was. This is an error in subject verb agreement.

277. The correct answer is A.
There is an error in redundancy since daily is mentioned: every day is not needed.

278. The correct answer is A.
Here, there is an error with appropriate preposition. Instead of "as cold like," it should be "as cold as."

279. The correct answer is B.
The correct spelling is connoisseur.

280. The correct answer is C.
The correct spelling is entrepreneur.

281. The correct answer is A.
The correct spelling is unconscious.

282. The correct answer is A.
The correct spelling is ceiling.

283. The correct answer is D.
No mistakes.

284. The correct answer is B.
The correct spelling is privilege.

285. The correct answer is B.
The correct spelling is necessary.

286. The correct answer is A.
The correct spelling is playwright.

287. The correct answer is D.
No mistakes.

288. The correct answer is C.
The correct spelling is thorough.

289. The correct answer is C.
The correct transition word should allow the two sentences to be opposing and the only word that does that is "although" from the choices given.

290. The correct answer is A.
The correct transition word should allow the two sentences to be agreeing and the only word that does that is "because" from the choices given.

291. The correct answer is A.
Attentively should come before the verb since it is an adverb.

292. The correct answer is D.
This sentence should be placed in active voice with no dangling modifiers. For these kind of questions, try to have a dependent clause followed by an independent clause.

293. The correct answer is C.
For these kind of questions, follow the correct parallelism and look for answers that are simple and correct.

ANSWER EXPLANATIONS

294. The correct answer is D.
The essential idea here is how the wheel was an important discovery and choice D shows that.

295. The correct answer is D.
Antibiotics are not vaccines since vaccines fend off viruses and antibiotics fight bacteria. D is therefore the least relevant.

296. The correct answer is B.
Choice B best shows how when someone waits, there is success at the end.

297. The correct answer is A.
Suits is too specific of an example of a clothing. The paragraph gives a general aspect of clothing. This sentence should either be removed or come much later in the paragraph.

298. The correct answer is D.
The sentence does not belong here since the paragraph talks about a specific religion.

EXAM 3
HSPT

ARGO BROTHERS

To calculate your score and watch video tutorials, visit
our web site: www.einstein-academy.com/catholic

HSPT PRACTICE TEST 3
ANSWER SHEET

Verbal Skills (Part I)

1. Ⓐ Ⓑ Ⓒ Ⓓ
2. Ⓐ Ⓑ Ⓒ Ⓓ
3. Ⓐ Ⓑ Ⓒ Ⓓ
4. Ⓐ Ⓑ Ⓒ Ⓓ
5. Ⓐ Ⓑ Ⓒ Ⓓ
6. Ⓐ Ⓑ Ⓒ Ⓓ
7. Ⓐ Ⓑ Ⓒ Ⓓ
8. Ⓐ Ⓑ Ⓒ Ⓓ
9. Ⓐ Ⓑ Ⓒ Ⓓ
10. Ⓐ Ⓑ Ⓒ Ⓓ
11. Ⓐ Ⓑ Ⓒ Ⓓ
12. Ⓐ Ⓑ Ⓒ Ⓓ
13. Ⓐ Ⓑ Ⓒ Ⓓ
14. Ⓐ Ⓑ Ⓒ Ⓓ
15. Ⓐ Ⓑ Ⓒ Ⓓ
16. Ⓐ Ⓑ Ⓒ Ⓓ
17. Ⓐ Ⓑ Ⓒ Ⓓ
18. Ⓐ Ⓑ Ⓒ Ⓓ
19. Ⓐ Ⓑ Ⓒ Ⓓ
20. Ⓐ Ⓑ Ⓒ Ⓓ
21. Ⓐ Ⓑ Ⓒ Ⓓ
22. Ⓐ Ⓑ Ⓒ Ⓓ
23. Ⓐ Ⓑ Ⓒ Ⓓ
24. Ⓐ Ⓑ Ⓒ Ⓓ
25. Ⓐ Ⓑ Ⓒ Ⓓ
26. Ⓐ Ⓑ Ⓒ Ⓓ
27. Ⓐ Ⓑ Ⓒ Ⓓ
28. Ⓐ Ⓑ Ⓒ Ⓓ
29. Ⓐ Ⓑ Ⓒ Ⓓ
30. Ⓐ Ⓑ Ⓒ Ⓓ
31. Ⓐ Ⓑ Ⓒ Ⓓ
33. Ⓐ Ⓑ Ⓒ Ⓓ
33. Ⓐ Ⓑ Ⓒ Ⓓ
34. Ⓐ Ⓑ Ⓒ Ⓓ
35. Ⓐ Ⓑ Ⓒ Ⓓ
36. Ⓐ Ⓑ Ⓒ Ⓓ
37. Ⓐ Ⓑ Ⓒ Ⓓ
38. Ⓐ Ⓑ Ⓒ Ⓓ
39. Ⓐ Ⓑ Ⓒ Ⓓ
40. Ⓐ Ⓑ Ⓒ Ⓓ
41. Ⓐ Ⓑ Ⓒ Ⓓ
42. Ⓐ Ⓑ Ⓒ Ⓓ
43. Ⓐ Ⓑ Ⓒ Ⓓ
44. Ⓐ Ⓑ Ⓒ Ⓓ
45. Ⓐ Ⓑ Ⓒ Ⓓ
46. Ⓐ Ⓑ Ⓒ Ⓓ
47. Ⓐ Ⓑ Ⓒ Ⓓ
48. Ⓐ Ⓑ Ⓒ Ⓓ
49. Ⓐ Ⓑ Ⓒ Ⓓ
50. Ⓐ Ⓑ Ⓒ Ⓓ
51. Ⓐ Ⓑ Ⓒ Ⓓ
52. Ⓐ Ⓑ Ⓒ Ⓓ
53. Ⓐ Ⓑ Ⓒ Ⓓ
54. Ⓐ Ⓑ Ⓒ Ⓓ
55. Ⓐ Ⓑ Ⓒ Ⓓ
56. Ⓐ Ⓑ Ⓒ Ⓓ
57. Ⓐ Ⓑ Ⓒ Ⓓ
58. Ⓐ Ⓑ Ⓒ Ⓓ
59. Ⓐ Ⓑ Ⓒ Ⓓ
60. Ⓐ Ⓑ Ⓒ Ⓓ

Quantitative (Part II)

61. Ⓐ Ⓑ Ⓒ Ⓓ
62. Ⓐ Ⓑ Ⓒ Ⓓ
63. Ⓐ Ⓑ Ⓒ Ⓓ
64. Ⓐ Ⓑ Ⓒ Ⓓ
65. Ⓐ Ⓑ Ⓒ Ⓓ
66. Ⓐ Ⓑ Ⓒ Ⓓ
67. Ⓐ Ⓑ Ⓒ Ⓓ
68. Ⓐ Ⓑ Ⓒ Ⓓ
69. Ⓐ Ⓑ Ⓒ Ⓓ
70. Ⓐ Ⓑ Ⓒ Ⓓ
71. Ⓐ Ⓑ Ⓒ Ⓓ
72. Ⓐ Ⓑ Ⓒ Ⓓ
73. Ⓐ Ⓑ Ⓒ Ⓓ
74. Ⓐ Ⓑ Ⓒ Ⓓ
75. Ⓐ Ⓑ Ⓒ Ⓓ
76. Ⓐ Ⓑ Ⓒ Ⓓ
77. Ⓐ Ⓑ Ⓒ Ⓓ
78. Ⓐ Ⓑ Ⓒ Ⓓ
79. Ⓐ Ⓑ Ⓒ Ⓓ
80. Ⓐ Ⓑ Ⓒ Ⓓ
81. Ⓐ Ⓑ Ⓒ Ⓓ
82. Ⓐ Ⓑ Ⓒ Ⓓ
83. Ⓐ Ⓑ Ⓒ Ⓓ
84. Ⓐ Ⓑ Ⓒ Ⓓ
85. Ⓐ Ⓑ Ⓒ Ⓓ
86. Ⓐ Ⓑ Ⓒ Ⓓ
87. Ⓐ Ⓑ Ⓒ Ⓓ
88. Ⓐ Ⓑ Ⓒ Ⓓ
89. Ⓐ Ⓑ Ⓒ Ⓓ
90. Ⓐ Ⓑ Ⓒ Ⓓ
91. Ⓐ Ⓑ Ⓒ Ⓓ
92. Ⓐ Ⓑ Ⓒ Ⓓ
93. Ⓐ Ⓑ Ⓒ Ⓓ
94. Ⓐ Ⓑ Ⓒ Ⓓ
95. Ⓐ Ⓑ Ⓒ Ⓓ
96. Ⓐ Ⓑ Ⓒ Ⓓ
97. Ⓐ Ⓑ Ⓒ Ⓓ
98. Ⓐ Ⓑ Ⓒ Ⓓ
99. Ⓐ Ⓑ Ⓒ Ⓓ
100. Ⓐ Ⓑ Ⓒ Ⓓ
101. Ⓐ Ⓑ Ⓒ Ⓓ
102. Ⓐ Ⓑ Ⓒ Ⓓ
103. Ⓐ Ⓑ Ⓒ Ⓓ
104. Ⓐ Ⓑ Ⓒ Ⓓ
105. Ⓐ Ⓑ Ⓒ Ⓓ
106. Ⓐ Ⓑ Ⓒ Ⓓ
107. Ⓐ Ⓑ Ⓒ Ⓓ
108. Ⓐ Ⓑ Ⓒ Ⓓ
109. Ⓐ Ⓑ Ⓒ Ⓓ
110. Ⓐ Ⓑ Ⓒ Ⓓ
111. Ⓐ Ⓑ Ⓒ Ⓓ
112. Ⓐ Ⓑ Ⓒ Ⓓ

Reading (Part III)

113. Ⓐ Ⓑ Ⓒ Ⓓ
114. Ⓐ Ⓑ Ⓒ Ⓓ
115. Ⓐ Ⓑ Ⓒ Ⓓ
116. Ⓐ Ⓑ Ⓒ Ⓓ
117. Ⓐ Ⓑ Ⓒ Ⓓ
118. Ⓐ Ⓑ Ⓒ Ⓓ
119. Ⓐ Ⓑ Ⓒ Ⓓ
120. Ⓐ Ⓑ Ⓒ Ⓓ
121. Ⓐ Ⓑ Ⓒ Ⓓ
122. Ⓐ Ⓑ Ⓒ Ⓓ
123. Ⓐ Ⓑ Ⓒ Ⓓ
124. Ⓐ Ⓑ Ⓒ Ⓓ
125. Ⓐ Ⓑ Ⓒ Ⓓ
126. Ⓐ Ⓑ Ⓒ Ⓓ
127. Ⓐ Ⓑ Ⓒ Ⓓ
128. Ⓐ Ⓑ Ⓒ Ⓓ
129. Ⓐ Ⓑ Ⓒ Ⓓ
130. Ⓐ Ⓑ Ⓒ Ⓓ
131. Ⓐ Ⓑ Ⓒ Ⓓ
132. Ⓐ Ⓑ Ⓒ Ⓓ
133. Ⓐ Ⓑ Ⓒ Ⓓ
134. Ⓐ Ⓑ Ⓒ Ⓓ
135. Ⓐ Ⓑ Ⓒ Ⓓ
136. Ⓐ Ⓑ Ⓒ Ⓓ
137. Ⓐ Ⓑ Ⓒ Ⓓ
138. Ⓐ Ⓑ Ⓒ Ⓓ
139. Ⓐ Ⓑ Ⓒ Ⓓ
140. Ⓐ Ⓑ Ⓒ Ⓓ
141. Ⓐ Ⓑ Ⓒ Ⓓ
142. Ⓐ Ⓑ Ⓒ Ⓓ
143. Ⓐ Ⓑ Ⓒ Ⓓ
144. Ⓐ Ⓑ Ⓒ Ⓓ
145. Ⓐ Ⓑ Ⓒ Ⓓ
146. Ⓐ Ⓑ Ⓒ Ⓓ
147. Ⓐ Ⓑ Ⓒ Ⓓ
148. Ⓐ Ⓑ Ⓒ Ⓓ
149. Ⓐ Ⓑ Ⓒ Ⓓ
150. Ⓐ Ⓑ Ⓒ Ⓓ
151. Ⓐ Ⓑ Ⓒ Ⓓ
152. Ⓐ Ⓑ Ⓒ Ⓓ
153. Ⓐ Ⓑ Ⓒ Ⓓ
154. Ⓐ Ⓑ Ⓒ Ⓓ
155. Ⓐ Ⓑ Ⓒ Ⓓ
156. Ⓐ Ⓑ Ⓒ Ⓓ
157. Ⓐ Ⓑ Ⓒ Ⓓ
158. Ⓐ Ⓑ Ⓒ Ⓓ
159. Ⓐ Ⓑ Ⓒ Ⓓ
160. Ⓐ Ⓑ Ⓒ Ⓓ
161. Ⓐ Ⓑ Ⓒ Ⓓ
162. Ⓐ Ⓑ Ⓒ Ⓓ
163. Ⓐ Ⓑ Ⓒ Ⓓ
164. Ⓐ Ⓑ Ⓒ Ⓓ
165. Ⓐ Ⓑ Ⓒ Ⓓ
166. Ⓐ Ⓑ Ⓒ Ⓓ
167. Ⓐ Ⓑ Ⓒ Ⓓ
168. Ⓐ Ⓑ Ⓒ Ⓓ
169. Ⓐ Ⓑ Ⓒ Ⓓ
170. Ⓐ Ⓑ Ⓒ Ⓓ
171. Ⓐ Ⓑ Ⓒ Ⓓ
172. Ⓐ Ⓑ Ⓒ Ⓓ
173. Ⓐ Ⓑ Ⓒ Ⓓ
174. Ⓐ Ⓑ Ⓒ Ⓓ

ARGO BROTHERS

To calculate your score and watch
video tutorials, visit our web site:
www.einstein-academy.com/catholic

HSPT PRACTICE TEST 3
ANSWER SHEET

Mathematics (Part IV)

175. Ⓐ Ⓑ Ⓒ Ⓓ
176. Ⓐ Ⓑ Ⓒ Ⓓ
177. Ⓐ Ⓑ Ⓒ Ⓓ
178. Ⓐ Ⓑ Ⓒ Ⓓ
179. Ⓐ Ⓑ Ⓒ Ⓓ
180. Ⓐ Ⓑ Ⓒ Ⓓ
181. Ⓐ Ⓑ Ⓒ Ⓓ
182. Ⓐ Ⓑ Ⓒ Ⓓ
183. Ⓐ Ⓑ Ⓒ Ⓓ
184. Ⓐ Ⓑ Ⓒ Ⓓ
185. Ⓐ Ⓑ Ⓒ Ⓓ
186. Ⓐ Ⓑ Ⓒ Ⓓ
187. Ⓐ Ⓑ Ⓒ Ⓓ
188. Ⓐ Ⓑ Ⓒ Ⓓ
189. Ⓐ Ⓑ Ⓒ Ⓓ
190. Ⓐ Ⓑ Ⓒ Ⓓ
191. Ⓐ Ⓑ Ⓒ Ⓓ
192. Ⓐ Ⓑ Ⓒ Ⓓ
193. Ⓐ Ⓑ Ⓒ Ⓓ
194. Ⓐ Ⓑ Ⓒ Ⓓ
195. Ⓐ Ⓑ Ⓒ Ⓓ
196. Ⓐ Ⓑ Ⓒ Ⓓ
197. Ⓐ Ⓑ Ⓒ Ⓓ
198. Ⓐ Ⓑ Ⓒ Ⓓ
199. Ⓐ Ⓑ Ⓒ Ⓓ
200. Ⓐ Ⓑ Ⓒ Ⓓ
201. Ⓐ Ⓑ Ⓒ Ⓓ
202. Ⓐ Ⓑ Ⓒ Ⓓ
203. Ⓐ Ⓑ Ⓒ Ⓓ
204. Ⓐ Ⓑ Ⓒ Ⓓ
205. Ⓐ Ⓑ Ⓒ Ⓓ
206. Ⓐ Ⓑ Ⓒ Ⓓ
207. Ⓐ Ⓑ Ⓒ Ⓓ
208. Ⓐ Ⓑ Ⓒ Ⓓ
209. Ⓐ Ⓑ Ⓒ Ⓓ
210. Ⓐ Ⓑ Ⓒ Ⓓ
211. Ⓐ Ⓑ Ⓒ Ⓓ
212. Ⓐ Ⓑ Ⓒ Ⓓ
213. Ⓐ Ⓑ Ⓒ Ⓓ
214. Ⓐ Ⓑ Ⓒ Ⓓ
215. Ⓐ Ⓑ Ⓒ Ⓓ
216. Ⓐ Ⓑ Ⓒ Ⓓ
217. Ⓐ Ⓑ Ⓒ Ⓓ
218. Ⓐ Ⓑ Ⓒ Ⓓ
219. Ⓐ Ⓑ Ⓒ Ⓓ
220. Ⓐ Ⓑ Ⓒ Ⓓ
221. Ⓐ Ⓑ Ⓒ Ⓓ
222. Ⓐ Ⓑ Ⓒ Ⓓ
223. Ⓐ Ⓑ Ⓒ Ⓓ
224. Ⓐ Ⓑ Ⓒ Ⓓ
225. Ⓐ Ⓑ Ⓒ Ⓓ
226. Ⓐ Ⓑ Ⓒ Ⓓ
227. Ⓐ Ⓑ Ⓒ Ⓓ
228. Ⓐ Ⓑ Ⓒ Ⓓ
229. Ⓐ Ⓑ Ⓒ Ⓓ
230. Ⓐ Ⓑ Ⓒ Ⓓ
231. Ⓐ Ⓑ Ⓒ Ⓓ
232. Ⓐ Ⓑ Ⓒ Ⓓ
233. Ⓐ Ⓑ Ⓒ Ⓓ
234. Ⓐ Ⓑ Ⓒ Ⓓ
235. Ⓐ Ⓑ Ⓒ Ⓓ
236. Ⓐ Ⓑ Ⓒ Ⓓ
237. Ⓐ Ⓑ Ⓒ Ⓓ
238. Ⓐ Ⓑ Ⓒ Ⓓ

Language (Part V)

239. Ⓐ Ⓑ Ⓒ Ⓓ
240. Ⓐ Ⓑ Ⓒ Ⓓ
241. Ⓐ Ⓑ Ⓒ Ⓓ
242. Ⓐ Ⓑ Ⓒ Ⓓ
243. Ⓐ Ⓑ Ⓒ Ⓓ
244. Ⓐ Ⓑ Ⓒ Ⓓ
245. Ⓐ Ⓑ Ⓒ Ⓓ
246. Ⓐ Ⓑ Ⓒ Ⓓ
247. Ⓐ Ⓑ Ⓒ Ⓓ
248. Ⓐ Ⓑ Ⓒ Ⓓ
249. Ⓐ Ⓑ Ⓒ Ⓓ
250. Ⓐ Ⓑ Ⓒ Ⓓ
251. Ⓐ Ⓑ Ⓒ Ⓓ
252. Ⓐ Ⓑ Ⓒ Ⓓ
253. Ⓐ Ⓑ Ⓒ Ⓓ
254. Ⓐ Ⓑ Ⓒ Ⓓ
255. Ⓐ Ⓑ Ⓒ Ⓓ
256. Ⓐ Ⓑ Ⓒ Ⓓ
257. Ⓐ Ⓑ Ⓒ Ⓓ
258. Ⓐ Ⓑ Ⓒ Ⓓ
259. Ⓐ Ⓑ Ⓒ Ⓓ
260. Ⓐ Ⓑ Ⓒ Ⓓ
261. Ⓐ Ⓑ Ⓒ Ⓓ
262. Ⓐ Ⓑ Ⓒ Ⓓ
263. Ⓐ Ⓑ Ⓒ Ⓓ
264. Ⓐ Ⓑ Ⓒ Ⓓ
265. Ⓐ Ⓑ Ⓒ Ⓓ
266. Ⓐ Ⓑ Ⓒ Ⓓ
267. Ⓐ Ⓑ Ⓒ Ⓓ
268. Ⓐ Ⓑ Ⓒ Ⓓ
269. Ⓐ Ⓑ Ⓒ Ⓓ
270. Ⓐ Ⓑ Ⓒ Ⓓ
271. Ⓐ Ⓑ Ⓒ Ⓓ
272. Ⓐ Ⓑ Ⓒ Ⓓ
273. Ⓐ Ⓑ Ⓒ Ⓓ
274. Ⓐ Ⓑ Ⓒ Ⓓ
275. Ⓐ Ⓑ Ⓒ Ⓓ
276. Ⓐ Ⓑ Ⓒ Ⓓ
277. Ⓐ Ⓑ Ⓒ Ⓓ
278.. Ⓐ Ⓑ Ⓒ Ⓓ
279 Ⓐ Ⓑ Ⓒ Ⓓ
280. Ⓐ Ⓑ Ⓒ Ⓓ
281. Ⓐ Ⓑ Ⓒ Ⓓ
282. Ⓐ Ⓑ Ⓒ Ⓓ
283. Ⓐ Ⓑ Ⓒ Ⓓ
284. Ⓐ Ⓑ Ⓒ Ⓓ
285. Ⓐ Ⓑ Ⓒ Ⓓ
286. Ⓐ Ⓑ Ⓒ Ⓓ
287. Ⓐ Ⓑ Ⓒ Ⓓ
288. Ⓐ Ⓑ Ⓒ Ⓓ
289 Ⓐ Ⓑ Ⓒ Ⓓ
290. Ⓐ Ⓑ Ⓒ Ⓓ
291. Ⓐ Ⓑ Ⓒ Ⓓ
292. Ⓐ Ⓑ Ⓒ Ⓓ
293. Ⓐ Ⓑ Ⓒ Ⓓ
294. Ⓐ Ⓑ Ⓒ Ⓓ
295. Ⓐ Ⓑ Ⓒ Ⓓ
296. Ⓐ Ⓑ Ⓒ Ⓓ
297. Ⓐ Ⓑ Ⓒ Ⓓ
298. Ⓐ Ⓑ Ⓒ Ⓓ

ARGO BROTHERS

To calculate your score and watch
video tutorials, visit our web site:
www.einstein-academy.com/catholic

VERBAL SKILLS
PART I (16 MIN)

DIRECTIONS: For questions 1-60, follow the directions and choose the best answer.

1. Which word does *not* belong with the others?

   A. loathing
   B. hate
   C. animosity
   D. lovely

2. Which word does *not* belong with the others?

   A. enlarge
   B. strengthen
   C. minimize
   D. decrease

3. Play is to script as movie is to

   A. actor
   B. screenplay
   C. setting
   D. director

4. All farsighted people wear glasses. Gavin is farsighted. Gavin wears glasses. If the first two statements are true, the third is

   A. true
   B. false
   C. uncertain

5. <u>Congruent</u> most nearly means

   A. identical
   B. different
   C. small
   D. increasing

6. Grocery store is to clerk as office is to

   A. secretary
   B. company
   C. building
   D. money

7. Which word does *not* belong with the others?

   A. haughty
   B. humble
   C. snobbish
   D. condescending

8. Speech is to hearing as picture is to

   A. enunciate
   B. feel
   C. talk
   D. see

CONTINUE ON TO THE NEXT PAGE ➡

VERBAL SKILLS
PART I

9. Which word does *not* belong with the others?

   A. penny
   B. nickel
   C. dollar
   D. quarter

10. <u>Abrupt</u> most nearly means

    A. hesitant
    B. cautious
    C. cagy
    D. sudden

11. <u>Fortuitous</u> most nearly means

    A. large
    B. lucky
    C. playful
    D. hardworking

12. Teacher is to classroom as researcher is to

    A. research article
    B. lab
    C. experiment
    D. question

13. Which word does *not* belong with the others?

    A. severe
    B. mild
    C. amazing
    D. slight

14. Drug is to pharmacy as bread is to

    A. dough
    B. yeast
    C. bakery
    D. newsstand

15. Piano is to finger as flute is to

    A. key
    B. tune
    C. mouth
    D. hand

16. Jack can ride a bike faster than Jill. Josh can ride a bike faster than Jack. Jill can ride faster than Josh. If the first two statements are true, the third is

    A. true
    B. false
    C. uncertain

CONTINUE ON TO THE NEXT PAGE ➡

VERBAL SKILLS
PART I

17. <u>Astute</u> most nearly means

    A. futile
    B. useless
    C. clever
    D. favorable

18. <u>Innovative</u> most nearly means

    A. repetition
    B. original
    C. excellent
    D. interesting

19. <u>Wane</u> most nearly means

    A. strengthen
    B. weaken
    C. quiet
    D. loud

20. Notebook is to school bag as clothes is to

    A. luggage
    B. briefcase
    C. a purse
    D. a room

21. Sky is to ground as ceiling is to

    A. roof
    B. pavement
    C. floor
    D. house

22. <u>Abominable</u> most nearly means

    A. hateful
    B. enchanting
    C. appealing
    D. irresistible

23. Point A is south of point B. Point C is south of point D, but north of point B. Point D is north of point A. If the first two statements are true, the third is

    A. true
    B. false
    C. uncertain

24. Which word does *not* belong with the others?

    A. alleviate
    B. aggravate
    C. mitigate
    D. dampen

CONTINUE ON TO THE NEXT PAGE ➡

VERBAL SKILLS
PART I

25. Lucid most nearly means

    A. unclear
    B. muddled
    C. fearful
    D. coherent

26. River A is longer than river B. River B is shorter than river C, but longer than river D. River C is longer than river A. If the first two statements are true, the third is

    A. true
    B. false
    C. uncertain

27. Ostracize most nearly means

    A. shun
    B. polish
    C. friendly
    D. serious

28. Alleviate most nearly means

    A. relieve
    B. excruciating
    C. condone
    D. healthy

29. Red is to anger as green is to

    A. jealousy
    B. furious
    C. plants
    D. sympathy

30. Empathy most nearly means

    A. responsible
    B. emphasize
    C. understanding
    D. fatigued

31. Hostile means the *opposite* of

    A. peaceful
    B. thunderous
    C. optimistic
    D. frightful

32. Which word does *not* belong with the others?

    A. homework
    B. test
    C. classwork
    D. teacher

CONTINUE ON TO THE NEXT PAGE ➡

VERBAL SKILLS
PART I

33. Which word does *not* belong with the others?

  A. recording
  B. textbook
  C. autobiography
  D. document

34. Amiable means the *opposite* of

  A. friendly
  B. loveable
  C. disagreeable
  D. scary

35. Rafael has scored more points than Jeff. Jeff scored more points than Rachel. Rachel scored more points than Rafael. If the first two statements are true, the third is

  A. true
  B. false
  C. uncertain

36. Appalled means the *opposite* of

  A. outraged
  B. excited
  C. forgive
  D. encouraged

37. <u>Miscellaneous</u> most nearly means

  A. varied
  B. sneaky
  C. familiar
  D. complex

38. Annihilate means the *opposite* of

  A. risky
  B. create
  C. chaos
  D. generous

39. Gullible means the *opposite* of

  A. naive
  B. suspicious
  C. emotional
  D. certain

40. Which word does *not* belong with the others?

  A. shampoo
  B. detergent
  C. conditioner
  D. soap

CONTINUE ON TO THE NEXT PAGE ➡

VERBAL SKILLS
PART I

41. Which word does *not* belong with the others?

- A. book
- B. character
- C. setting
- D. plot

42. A fireplace is brighter than a lamp. A torch is brighter than a lighter but not more than a fireplace. A lighter is brighter than a lamp. If the first two statements are true, the third is

- A. true
- B. false
- C. uncertain

43. Which word does *not* belong with the others?

- A. painting
- B. sculpture
- C. artist
- D. photograph

44. <u>Timid</u> most nearly means

- A. talkative
- B. shy
- C. lucrative
- D. imaginary

45. Tranquil means the *opposite* of

- A. disturbed
- B. hazardous
- C. malicious
- D. kind

46. Kingsley reads more than Pamela. Pamela reads more than Casey but not more than Candy. Kingsley reads more than Casey. If the first two statements are true, the third is

- A. true
- B. false
- C. uncertain

47. Opaque means the *opposite* of

- A. transparent
- B. sturdy
- C. blurry
- D. imaginative

48. Malice means the *opposite* of

- A. active
- B. fake
- C. benevolence
- D. knowledge

CONTINUE ON TO THE NEXT PAGE ➡

VERBAL SKILLS
PART I

49. A hole is deeper than an opening. An opening is deeper than a gap but not deeper than a indentation. An hole is deeper than a gap. If the first two statements are true, the third is

A. true
B. false
C. uncertain

50. Abigail scored higher than Jill. Betty scored higher than Jen, but less than Jill. Jen scored higher than Abigail. If the first two statements are true, the third is

A. true
B. false
C. uncertain

51. Consensus means the *opposite* of

A. rage
B. harmony
C. disagreement
D. safe

52. Which word does *not* belong with the others?

A. shoes
B. pants
C. shirt
D. jewelry

53. Which word does *not* belong with the others?

A. clown
B. liontamer
C. mime
D. circus

54. <u>Dexterous</u> most nearly means

A. optimistic
B. soft
C. noisy
D. skillful

55. Decisive means the *opposite* of

A. determined
B. halfhearted
C. calm
D. lucky

56. Exhilarate means the *opposite* of

A. intoxicate
B. delight
C. disgust
D. deplorable

CONTINUE ON TO THE NEXT PAGE ➡

VERBAL SKILLS
PART I

57. Glasses is to vision as hearing aid is to

　A. sight
　B. touch
　C. sound
　D. smell

58. Established most nearly means

　A. linger
　B. deprived
　C. recognized
　D. obscure

59. Which word does *not* belong with the others?

　A. garage
　B. bedroom
　C. living room
　D. backyard

60. Which word does *not* belong with the others?

　A. harmless
　B. dangerous
　C. vicious
　D. savage

CONTINUE ON TO THE NEXT PAGE ➡

QUANTITATIVE
PART II

65. Examine (A), (B), and (C) and find the best answer.

(A) $\frac{9}{10}$

(B) 93%

(C) 0.30 × π

A. B is greater than A but less than C.
B. B is greater than A and C.
C. C is greater than A but less than C.
D. C is greater than A which is equal to B.

66. Examine (A), (B), and (C) and find the best answer.

(A) 5% of 50
(B) 100% of 2.5
(C) 25% of 100

A. B > A > C
B. C > A = B
C. A > B > C
D. C = A > B

67. Look at this series: 35, 39, 37, 41, 39...
What number should come next?

A. 41
B. 35
C. 43
D. 37

68. 1, __, 27, 64, 125...
What is the missing number in the series above?

A. 16
B. 4
C. 8
D. 9

69. What number divided by 4 is $\frac{2}{5}$ of 65?

A. 40
B. 35
C. 104
D. 65

70. Examine (A), (B), and (C) and find the best answer

(A) 0.65
(B) 66%
(C) 13/20 %

A. A is greater than B or C.
B. A is greater than B + C.
C. A, B, are C are equal.
D. C is smaller than both A and B.

CONTINUE ON TO THE NEXT PAGE ➡

QUANTITATIVE
PART II (45 MIN)

DIRECTIONS: For questions 61-112, choose the best answer that fits the problem.

61. What is 5 more than 30% of 60?

    A. 61.5
    B. 58.5
    C. 13
    D. 23

62. What number is 7 more than $\frac{5}{6}$ of 30?

    A. 65
    B. 37
    C. 18
    D. 32

63. 72, 65, 68, 61, 64, __, 60...
    What is the missing number in the series above?

    A. 71
    B. 57
    C. 61
    D. 67

64. Examine (A), (B), and (C) and find the best answer.

    (A)    (B)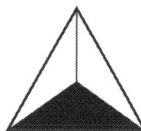

    (C)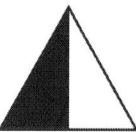

    A. A is more shaded than B.
    B. C is more shaded than A and B.
    C. All three are shaded equally.
    D. None of the above.

CONTINUE ON TO THE NEXT PAGE ➡

QUANTITATIVE
PART II

71. Look at this series:
0.875, 0.750, 0.625, 0.500, 0.375...
What number should come next?

- A. 0.1875
- B. 0.250
- C. 0.125
- D. 0.00

72. Examine (A), (B), and (C) and find the best answer.

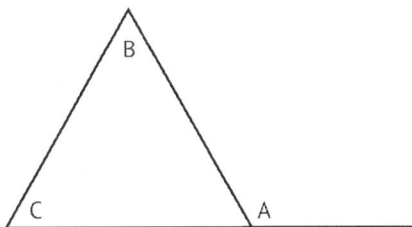

- A. A > B + C
- B. B is bigger than C
- C. A is bigger than B or C
- D. C = A + B

73. Look at this series: F92, I89, L86, O83...
What comes next?

- A. S80
- B. R80
- C. R86
- D. S86

74. Look at this series:
2, 4, 6, 10, 14, 20, 26, 34, 42...
What number should come next?

- A. 52
- B. 50
- C. 48
- D. 54

75. Examine (A), (B), and (C) and find the best answer if x is less than y and both are less than 0.

(A) $5(y - x)$
(B) $7x - 7y$
(C) $7(x - y)$

- A. All three are equal.
- B. A is smaller than B and C.
- C. B and C are equal and smaller than A.
- D. C is greater than A and B.

76. What number decreased by 9% of itself is 182?

- A. 191
- B. 210
- C. 202
- D. 200

CONTINUE ON TO THE NEXT PAGE ➡

QUANTITATIVE
PART II

77. Examine (A), (B), and (C) and find the best answer

(A) 3.23

(B) $\frac{10}{3}$

(C) $3.\overline{33}$

A. A is greater than B.
B. C is greater than A and less than B.
C. B > A > C
D. B = C

78. Examine (A), (B), and (C) and find the best answer.

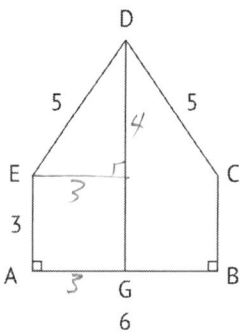

A. AD > AE + ED
B. DE < AG
C. DG > AB
D. DG = AB

79. Look at this series:
5, 20, 3, 12, 7, 28, 14, __, 9, 27...
What is the missing number in the series above?

A. 7
B. 27
C. 3
D. 42

80. Look at this series: 7, 21, 21, 63, 63...
What three numbers should come next?

A. 63, 189, 189
B. 189, 189, 567
C. 189, 567, 567
D. 189, 189, 189

81. Examine the triangle and find the best answer.

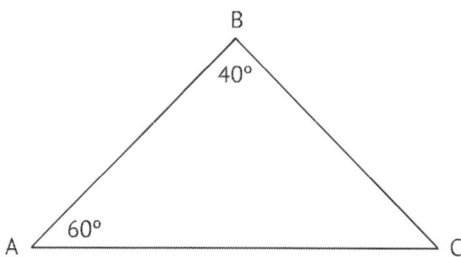

A. AB > BC + CA
B. AB > BC > AC
C. CA > BC > AB
D. AB = CB < CA

CONTINUE ON TO THE NEXT PAGE ➡

QUANTITATIVE
PART II

82. $\frac{3}{7}$ of what number is 4 less than 5 times 5?

   A. 49
   B. 35
   C. 20
   D. 21

83. Examine (A), (B), (C), and (D) and find the best answer.

   (A)   (B)   (C)   (D)

   A. B has more acute angles than combination of A and D.
   B. Two times the number of acute angles of D give the number of acute angles of B.
   C. The number of acute angles of A and D add to the number of acute angles of B.
   D. C has the most amount of acute angles.

84. $\frac{5}{4}$ of what number is 5 times 2?

   A. 12.5
   B. 10
   C. 20
   D. 8

85. Examine (A), (B), and (C) and find the best answer

   (A) 36 • 5
   (B) (5 • 6)(5 + 6)
   (C) (5 • 6)(6 • 5)

   A. A = B > C
   B. C > B = A
   C. C > B > A
   D. C > A > B

86. What number divided by 4 leaves 8 more than 5?

   A. 52
   B. 36
   C. 12
   D. 6

87. By how much does the average 12, 90, 69, and 41 exceed the number 22?

   A. 47
   B. 53
   C. 31
   D. 75

CONTINUE ON TO THE NEXT PAGE →

QUANTITATIVE
PART II

88. Examine (A), (B), and (C) and find the best answer

(A) (4 • 6) - (-8)
(B) (6 • 9) + 12
(C) (6 • 12) - (6 • 4)

A. C is the smallest.
B. B is the largest.
C. A is less than B, which is less than C.
D. C is greater than B.

89. Look at this series: 2, 4, 8, 16, __, 64, 128...
What is the missing number in the series above?

A. 40
B. 24
C. 32
D. 45

90. Examine (A), (B), and (C) and find the best answer.

(A)　　　(B)　　　(C)

A. C is more shaded than A and B.
B. The three figures are shaded equally.
C. C is less shaded than A and B.
D. A is equally shaded as B and less than C.

91. Look at this series: 51, 58, __, 72, 79...
What is the missing number in the series above?

A. 65
B. 60
C. 66
D. 64

92. What number is 9 less than $\frac{1}{4}$ of 36?

A. 12
B. 5
C. 81
D. 0

93. Examine (A), (B), and (C) and find the best answer.

(A)　　　(B)　　　(C)

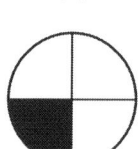  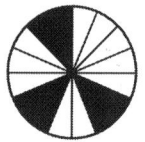

A. All are equally shaded.
B. B is more shaded than A or C.
C. C is equally shaded as A but more than B.
D. None of the above.

CONTINUE ON TO THE NEXT PAGE ➡

QUANTITATIVE
PART II

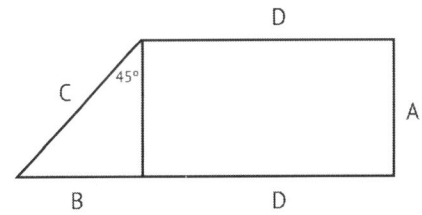

94. What number subtracted from 19 leaves 6 more than $\frac{5}{9}$ of 81?

- A. 45
- B. 70
- C. 51
- D. 32

95. The difference of 35% of a number and 105% of the same number is equal to 35. What is the number?

- A. 100
- B. 24.5
- C. 50
- D. 25

96. Examine (A), (B), and (C) and choose the best answer.

(A) 4(7 - 9)
(B) 4(5) - 36
(C) (-2)(-2)(-2)(-2)

- A. B is the largest.
- B. B > C > A
- C. |C| > A > B
- D. A > B > C

97. What number added to -7 is 5 times the product of 4 and 9?

- A. 159
- B. 173
- C. 187
- D. -11

98. Examine (A), (B), and (C) and find the best answer.

(A) $\frac{6}{5}$ of 36

(B) $\frac{3}{10}$ of 100

(C) $\frac{5}{6}$ of 36

- A. A is the greatest.
- B. B = C > A
- C. B = C < A
- D. C > B > A

99. Examine the figure and find the best answer.

- A. C < A = B
- B. A = B = C
- C. C = A > B
- D. A = B < C

CONTINUE ON TO THE NEXT PAGE ➡

239

QUANTITATIVE
PART II

100. Look at this series: -8, -5, -3, -2, -2...
What number should come next?

A. -2
B. -1
C. -3
D. 0

101. Look at this series:
103, 106, 104, 107, 105, 108...
What number should come next?

A. 105
B. 111
C. 110
D. 106

102. Look at this series:
0.6, 0.36, 0.216, 0.1296...
What number should come next?

A. .081
B. 0.07776
C. 0.216
D. 0.093

103. Solve: $\frac{5}{8}$ of 32

A. 20
B. 51.2
C. 256
D. 160

104. What number divided by 5 is $\frac{1}{3}$ of 36?

A. 48
B. 30
C. 180
D. 60

105. Look at this series: V, IX, 13, 17, XXI...
What should come next?

A. 20
B. XVII
C. 24
D. XXV

106. Look at this series: 4, $\frac{4}{5}$, $\frac{4}{25}$, $\frac{4}{125}$ ...
What number should come next?

A. $\frac{4}{625}$
B. 4
C. $\frac{4}{2125}$
D. $\frac{5}{124}$

CONTINUE ON TO THE NEXT PAGE ➡

107. Examine the cone and find the best answer.

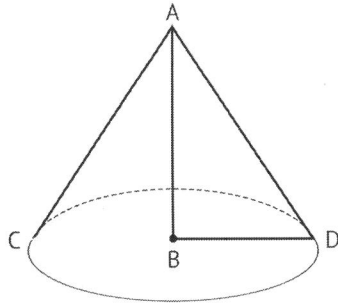

- A. BD > AB
- B. AD < BD + AB
- C. CB = AB
- D. None of the above

108. Look at this series: 33, 27, 31, 25, 29... What number should come next?

- A. 23
- B. 33
- C. 35
- D. 25

109. What number is 4 less than $\frac{1}{6}$ of 84?

- A. 10
- B. 18
- C. 56
- D. 48

110. Look at this series: 1, 2, 2, 3, 3, 3, 4, 4, 4,... What three number should come next?

- A. 4, 4, 5
- B. 4, 4, 4
- C. 4, 5, 5
- D. 5, 5, 5

111. What number multiplied by $\frac{3}{7}$ yields its reciprocal?

- A. $\frac{9}{49}$
- B. $\frac{2}{4}$
- C. $\frac{7}{3}$
- D. 1

112. If $\frac{3}{8}$ of a number is 6, then 25 % of the number is

- A. 8
- B. 4
- C. 16
- D. 12

CONTINUE ON TO THE NEXT PAGE ➡

READING
PART III (25 MIN)

DIRECTIONS: Read the passages below and pick the answer choices that fit accordingly. Fill in the appropriate letter on your answer sheet.

Questions 113-122 refer to the following passage.

This passage is adapted from Animals of the Past

Fossils are the remains, or even the indications, of animals and plants that have, through natural agencies, been buried in the earth and preserved for long periods of time. This may seem a rather meager definition, but it is a difficult matter to frame one that will be at once brief, exact, and comprehensive; fossils are not necessarily the remains of extinct animals or plants, neither are they, of necessity, objects that have become petrified or turned into stone.

Bones of the Great Auk and Rytina, which are quite extinct, would hardly be considered as fossils; while the bones of many species of animals, still living, would properly come in that category, having long ago been buried by natural causes and often been changed into stone. And yet it is not essential for a specimen to have had its animal matter replaced by some mineral in order that it may be classed as a fossil, for the Siberian Mammoths, found entombed in ice, are very properly spoken of as fossils, although the flesh of at least one of these animals was so fresh that it was eaten. Likewise the mammoth tusks brought to market are termed fossil-ivory, although differing but little from the tusks of modern elephants.

Many fossils indeed merit their popular appellation of petrifactions, because they have been changed into stone by the slow removal of the animal or vegetable matter present and its replacement by some mineral, usually silica or some form of lime. But it is necessary to include 'indications of plants or animals' in the above definition because some of the best fossils may be merely impressions of plants or animals and no portion of the objects themselves, and yet, as we shall see, some of our most important information has been gathered from these same imprints.

---

113. The main idea of the passage is the

    A. formation and usefulness of fossils
    B. bones of extinct animals
    C. process of fossilization
    D. use of fossils to understand the past

114. The word meager most nearly means

    A. descriptive
    B. lazy
    C. insignificant
    D. wealthy

CONTINUE ON TO THE NEXT PAGE ➡

READING
PART III

115. A good title for this passage would be

    A. Fossils and How They Are Formed
    B. The Earliest Known Animals
    C. Impressions of the Past
    D. The Riddles in the Rocks

116. Fossils can be best described as

    A. extremely old stones
    B. minerals found in silica and lime
    C. imprints of plants
    D. remains of prehistoric living organisms

117. The example the author provided of mistaken fossils

    A. Siberian Mammoths found in ice
    B. Bones of the Rytina
    C. plants found in silica
    D. mosquitos trapped in amber

118. The word <u>petrification</u> most nearly means

    A. crystallization
    B. pleasant
    C. boiling
    D. raw

119. The author states that most knowledge of ancient plants

    A. is lost in the fossils
    B. tells us that life was wiped out during the Ice Age
    C. is gained through fossils in sand and stone
    D. has yet to be understood

120. Imprints are useful in that they

    A. petrify animals and plants
    B. contain lost information of past living things
    C. can be found everywhere
    D. replace animal matter with minerals

121. Siberian mammoths are mentioned in the passage to

    A. provide an example of a non-petrified fossil
    B. show that any bones are considered fossils
    C. explain the market for fossil mammoth tusks
    D. understand impressions

122. This passage can most likely be found in a

    A. history book
    B. science article
    C. fantasy novel
    D. traveler's guide

CONTINUE ON TO THE NEXT PAGE ➡

READING
PART III

Questions 123-132 refer to the following passage.

This passage is adapted from Project Trinity

The development of a nuclear weapon was a low priority for the United States before the outbreak of World War II. However, scientists exiled from Germany had expressed concern that the Germans were developing a nuclear weapon. Confirming these fears, in 1939 the Germans stopped all sales of uranium ore from the mines of occupied Czechoslovakia. In a letter sponsored by group of concerned scientists, Albert Einstein informed President Roosevelt that German experiments had shown that an induced nuclear chain reaction was possible and could be used to construct extremely cataclysmic bombs.

In response to the potential threat of a German nuclear weapon, the United States sought a source of uranium to use in determining the feasibility of a nuclear chain reaction. After Germany occupied Belgium in May 1940, the Belgians turned over uranium ore from their holdings in the Belgian Congo to the United States. Then, in March 1941, the element plutonium was isolated, and the plutonium-239 isotope was found to fission as readily as the scarce uranium isotope, uranium-235. The plutonium, produced in a uranium-fueled nuclear reactor, provided the United States with an additional source of material for nuclear weapons.

In the summer of 1941, the British Government published a report written by the Committee for Military Application of Uranium Detonation (MAUD). This report stated that a nuclear weapon was possible and concluded that its construction should begin immediately. The MAUD report, and to a lesser degree the discovery of plutonium, encouraged American leaders to think more seriously about developing a nuclear weapon. On 6 December 1941, President Roosevelt appointed the S-1 Committee to determine if the United States could constitute a nuclear weapon. Six months later, the S-1 Committee gave the President its report, recommending a fast-paced program that would cost up to $100 million and that might produce the weapon by July 1944.

---

123. A good title for this passage would be

A. Project Trinity
B. Preparing for Nuclear War
C. Attacking Germany
D. Understanding Uranium and Plutonium

124. At the start of World War II, the United States

A. prepared nuclear weapons
B. began research on plutonium
C. formed the S-1 Committee
D. were informed of Germany's nuclear plans

CONTINUE ON TO THE NEXT PAGE ➡

READING
PART III

125. Germany's development of nuclear weapons was confirmed by

A. exiled German scientists
B. American spies in Germany
C. Germany's halt in its sale of uranium
D. British intelligence

126. It is implied in the passage that uranium could potentially

A. lower America's economic growth
B. be used to create powerful bombs
C. destroy the entire world
D. take over Czechoslovakia

127. The word cataclysmic most nearly means

A. deadly
B. strong
C. harmless
D. productive

128. The S-1 Committee was employed by the US to

A. determine if creating nuclear weapons was possible
B. help Britain with its research
C. gather funds for the war
D. ruin Germany's plans

129. President's final choice to create nuclear weapons was encouraged by

A. Germany's reservation of uranium
B. intel from German scientists
C. Britain's report on nuclear weaponry
D. Albert Einstein

130. The additional source for nuclear weapons that was discovered was

A. S-1
B. plutonium-239
C. MAUD
D. uranium-235

131. The word constitute most nearly means

A. disorganize
B. neglect
C. lessen
D. create

132. According to the passage, how did the US found its additional source of uranium?

A. It took over Czechoslovakia after defeating the Germans in combat.
B. The United States, along with its ally Great Britain, created uranium using a plutonium reactor.
C. The Belgians provided their uranium after being occupied by Germany.
D. Albert Einstein created a better alternative to uranium.

CONTINUE ON TO THE NEXT PAGE ➡

READING
PART III

Questions 133-142 refer to the following passage.

This passage is adapted from The Nervous Child

There is an old fairy story concerning a pea which a princess once slept upon—a little offending pea, a minute disturbance, a trifling departure from the normal which grew to the proportions of intolerable suffering because of the too sensitive and undisciplined nervous system of Her Royal Highness. The story, I think, does not tell us much else concerning the princess. It does not tell us, for instance, if she was an only child, the sole preoccupation of her parents and nurses, surrounded by the most anxious care, reared with some difficulty because of her extraordinary "daintiness," suffering from a variety of illnesses which somehow always seemed to puzzle the doctors, though some of the symptoms—the vomiting, for example, and the high temperature—were very severe and persistent. Nor does it tell us if later in life, but before the suffering from the pea arose, she had been taken to consult two famous doctors, who had removed the appendix. At any rate, the story with these later additions, which are at least in keeping with what we know of her history, would serve to indicate the importance which attaches to the early training of childhood. Among the children even of the well-to-do often enough the hygiene of the mind is overlooked, and faulty management produces restlessness, instability, and hyper-sensitiveness, which pass insensibly into adult life.

To prevent so distressing a result is our aim in the training of children. No doubt the matter concerns in the first place parents and nurses, school masters and mistresses, as well as medical men. Yet because of the certainty that physical disturbances of one sort or another will follow upon nervous unrest, it will seldom happen that medical advice will not be sought sooner or later; and if the physician is to intervene with success, he must be prepared with knowledge of many sorts. He must be prepared to make a thorough and complete physical examination, sufficient to exclude the presence of organic disease.

---

133. The fairy tale in the first paragraph describes

A. a sleeping princess
B. a princess's difficulty sleeping under a pea
C. the nervous system
D. intolerable suffering

134. The author uses the story of the princess to

A. create an interesting introduction to psychology
B. explain the emotional issues of the princess
C. make fun of royalty
D. understand the issues of sleep

CONTINUE ON TO THE NEXT PAGE ➡

READING
PART III

135. The details left out by the story of the princess include her

    A. suffering from multiple illnesses
    B. being brought up as an only child
    C. consultation by doctors
    D. all of the above

136. The word daintiness most nearly means

    A. delicacy
    B. advantage
    C. health
    D. perfection

137. The author elaborated on the details of the princess' childhood to

    A. give interesting background information
    B. make a point on the importance of early childhood training
    C. explain why the princess could not sleep
    D. argue that peas are actually comfortable

138. At the end of the first paragraph, it is implied that

    A. childhood issues can lead to adult problems
    B. instability can easily be corrected
    C. the princess needed sleeping pills
    D. anxiety is the ultimate childhood precaution

139. The word insensibly can be replaced by

    A. gradually
    B. caringly
    C. coldly
    D. mindfully

140. Training children from an early age is mainly to

    A. allow restlessness
    B. aggressively treat mental issues
    C. prevent childhood distresses
    D. none of the above

141. It is implied in the passage that

    A. physical and mental trauma are related
    B. mental problems can never truly be cured
    C. the princess lived a far too luxurious life
    D. taking a child to any doctor can lead to success

142. When examining a child, the doctor must first

    A. determine if the issue is due to a problematic upbringing
    B. follow through with a thorough physical examination
    C. examine if the issue is a disease
    D. understand the child's background

CONTINUE ON TO THE NEXT PAGE ➡

READING
PART III

Questions 143-148 refer to the following passage.

This passage is adapted from The Witch-cult in Western Europe

It is impossible to understand the witch-cult without first understanding the position of the chief personage of that cult. He was known to the <u>contemporary</u> Christian judges and recorders as the Devil, and was called by them Satan, Lucifer, Beelzebub, the Foul Fiend, the Enemy of <u>Salvation</u>, and similar names appropriate to the Principle of Evil, the Devil of the Scriptures, with whom they identified him. This was far from the view of the witches themselves. To them this so-called Devil was God, manifest and incarnate; they adored him on their knees, they addressed their prayers to him, they offered thanks to him as the giver of food and the necessities of life, they dedicated their children to him, and there are indications that, like many another god, he was sacrificed for the good of his people.

Among the believers in witchcraft everything which could not be explained by the knowledge at their disposal was laid to the credit of supernatural powers and as everything incomprehensible is usually supposed to emanate from evil, the witches were believed to be possessed of devilish arts. As also every non-Christian God was, in the eyes of the Christian, the opponent of the Christian God, the witches were considered to worship the Enemy of Salvation, in other words, the Devil. The greater number of writers, however, obtained the evidence at first hand, and it must therefore be accepted although the statements do not bear the construction put upon them. It is only by a careful comparison with the evidence of anthropology that the facts fall into their proper places and an organized religion stands revealed.

---

143. A good title for this passage would be

   A. Understanding Witches: A Study of Witchcraft
   B. The Salem Witch Trials
   C. The Gods of Witches
   D. The Assemblies and Rites

144. The first paragraph discusses the

   A. Christian beliefs
   B. rejection of witchcraft in Europe
   C. witches' Devil worshipping
   D. reincarnation of Beelzebub

READING
PART III

145. The word <u>contemporary</u> most nearly means

- A. present
- B. old-fashioned
- C. succeeding
- D. connecting

146. The author states that during past times, anything misunderstood was

- A. explained through biblical texts
- B. considered to be evil
- C. applauded due to its mystery
- D. thought to be an act of God

147. It is implied that witchcraft was

- A. in fact an organized religion
- B. child's play
- C. an obscure myth
- D. was not possible

148. The word <u>salvation</u> most nearly means

- A. destruction
- B. safety
- C. loss
- D. release

CONTINUE ON TO THE NEXT PAGE ➡

READING
PART III

Questions 149-152 refer to the following passage.

The range of the American bison extended over about one-third of the entire continent of North America. Starting almost at tide-water on the Atlantic coast, it extended westward through a vast tract of dense forest, across the Alleghany Mountain system to the prairies along the Mississippi, and southward to the Delta of that great stream. Although the great plains country of the West was the natural home of the species, where it flourished most abundantly, it also wandered south across Texas to the burning plains of northeastern Mexico, westward across the Rocky Mountains into New Mexico, Utah, and Idaho, and northward across a vast treeless waste to the bleak and inhospitable shores of the Great Slave Lake itself. It is more than probable that had the bison remained unmolested by man and uninfluenced by him, he would eventually have crossed the Sierra Nevada and the Coast Range and taken up his abode in the fertile valleys of the Pacific slope.

Had the bison remained for a few more centuries in undisturbed possession of his range, and with liberty to roam at will over the North American continent, it is almost certain that several distinctly recognizable varieties would have been produced. The buffalo of the hot regions in the extreme south would have become a short-haired animal like the gaur of India and the African buffalo. The individuals inhabiting the extreme north, in the vicinity of Great Slave Lake, for example, would have developed still longer hair, and taken on more of the dense hairiness of the musk ox. In the "wood" or "mountain buffalo" we already have a distinct foreshadowing of the changes which would have taken place in the individuals which made their permanent residence upon rugged mountains.

---

149. The main idea of this passage is

A. the habitat and effect of the American bison
B. surviving the Alleghany Mountain
C. hunting the buffalo
D. living with the bison

150. The word bleak most nearly means

A. warm
B. cold
C. grim
D. encouraging

151. This passage can most likely be found in a

A. history book
B. encyclopedia
C. science article
D. social science textbook

152. What can be inferred about the bison's hair?

A. It is generally short for females and longer for males.
B. It can adapt based on the temperature of the environment.
C. Bison tend to shed all of their hair during the summer.
D. All bison have long hair.

CONTINUE ON TO THE NEXT PAGE ➡

VOCABULARY
PART III (25 MIN)

VOCABULARY

DIRECTIONS: In this section, you will need to determine the choice that is closest in meaning to the underlined words provided below. Pick the answer choice that fits accordingly and fill in the appropriate letter on your answer sheet.

153. to adapt means to

A. change
B. reject
C. comply
D. consume

154. to loot means to

A. steal
B. cherish
C. praise
D. argue

155. to alleviate

A. worsen
B. dangerous
C. relieve
D. mock

156. concurred with the teacher

A. joked
B. agreed
C. fought
D. clashed

157. being too colloquial

A. informal
B. harsh
C. proper
D. worried

158. averting the problem

A. caused
B. prevented
C. aided
D. solved

CONTINUE ON TO THE NEXT PAGE →

VOCABULARY
PART III

159. an ubiquitous trend

   A. rare
   B. controversial
   C. universal
   D. worn out

160. to abhor

   A. succeed at
   B. hate
   C. fail
   D. enjoy

161. a strong advocate

   A. supply
   B. supporter
   C. ruler
   D. odor

162. contemporary drawings

   A. colorful
   B. modern
   C. ancient
   D. unique

163. to benefit

   A. help
   B. aid
   C. assist
   D. all the above

164. To have immunity

   A. strength
   B. willpower
   C. clarity
   D. resistance

165. querulous couples

   A. argumentative
   B. talkative
   C. perfect
   D. wholesome

166. the placid meadow

   A. violent
   B. peaceful
   C. cold
   D. never-ending

CONTINUE ON TO THE NEXT PAGE ➡

VOCABULARY
PART III

167. to emulate someone

    A. tease
    B. beg
    C. copy
    D. compliment

168. being meticulous

    A. careless
    B. jealous
    C. attentive
    D. stubborn

169. to be exempt

    A. exhausted
    B. infuriated
    C. annoyed
    D. excused

170. his opinions were conventional

    A. wrong
    B. outrageous
    C. common
    D. bland

171. to accomplish your dreams

    A. follow
    B. forget
    C. change
    D. achieve

172. a gullible teacher

    A. naive
    B. stubborn
    C. loving
    D. inferior

173. to exploit

    A. assist
    B. manipulate
    C. create
    D. absolve

174. to ostracize an individual

    A. compliment
    B. banish
    C. mock
    D. to confide

CONTINUE ON TO THE NEXT PAGE →

MATHEMATICS
PART IV (45 MIN)

CONCEPTS (24 Questions)

DIRECTIONS: Choose the answer that best fits the problem. You may use scratch paper while working on these problems.

175. $(-1)^4(-2)^3$

A. 8
B. -7
C. -8
D. -14

176. The number 19.99 rounded to the nearest hundredths is

A. 20
B. 19.99
C. 19.9
D. 19.00

177. $(\{3,5,9\} \cup \{1,4,6\}) \cap \{1,2,5\}$

A. {1, 5}
B. {1, 3, 5, 9}
C. {1, 2, 3, 4, 5}
D. {}

178. The measure of angle A in terms of B and C is

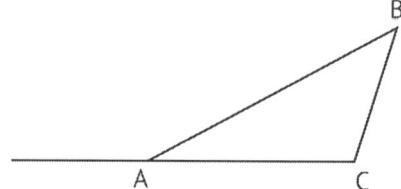

A. 180 - B - C
B. C + B - 180
C. B - C
D. B + C

179. Which of the following is not a polygon?

A. Circle
B. Triangle
C. Rectangle
D. Square

180. To multiply a number by one half, you can instead multiply the number by 5 and move the decimal point

A. one place to the right
B. one place to the left
C. two places to the right
D. two places to the left

CONTINUE ON TO THE NEXT PAGE →

181.

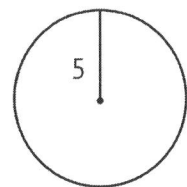

The area of the circle above is

A. 10π
B. 25π
C. 75
D. 5

182. Which of the following is **not** true?

A. $a(b + c) = ab + ac$
B. $\dfrac{b + c}{a} = \dfrac{b}{a} + \dfrac{c}{a}$
C. $\dfrac{a}{b + c} = \dfrac{a}{b} + \dfrac{a}{c}$
D. $a(b \div c) = \dfrac{ab}{1} \cdot \dfrac{1}{c}$

183. Which of the following shows the inverse property of multiplication?

A. $2^3 \cdot 3^2$
B. $1.4 \cdot \dfrac{5}{7}$
C. $3 \cdot 0$
D. $-1 \cdot 1$

184. As a fraction in simplest form, 0.358 is written as

A. $\dfrac{9}{25}$
B. $\dfrac{358}{100}$
C. $\dfrac{358}{1000}$
D. $\dfrac{179}{500}$

185. △ABC is similar to △DCE. Which of the following is false?

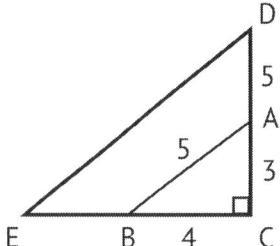

A. ∠ABC = ∠DEC
B. $\overline{AB}$ is parallel to $\overline{DE}$
C. $\overline{DE} = 2$
D. $\overline{EB} = 2.5$

CONTINUE ON TO THE NEXT PAGE ➡

MATHEMATICS PART IV

186. The associative property of multiplication states

A. $\frac{3}{5}(\frac{2}{5} + \frac{1}{5}) = \frac{6}{25} + \frac{3}{25}$

B. $\frac{3}{5}(\frac{2}{5} \cdot \frac{1}{5}) = (\frac{3}{5} \cdot \frac{2}{5})\frac{1}{5}$

C. $\frac{3}{5} \cdot \frac{1}{5} = \frac{1}{5} \cdot \frac{3}{5}$

D. $\frac{3}{5} \cdot \frac{2}{5} \cdot \frac{1}{5} = \frac{3}{5} \cdot \frac{2}{5} \cdot \frac{1}{5}$

187. The greatest common factor of 36 and 24 is

A. 12
B. 24
C. 72
D. 6

188. The prime factorization of 153 is

A. $(3)^2 \cdot 17$
B. $9 \cdot 17$
C. $51 \cdot 3$
D. $153 \cdot 1$

189. If Noah has *n* nickels, what is the value of his money in dollars?

A. $0.05n$
B. $2n$
C. $10n$
D. $0.1n$

190. A square can be all of the following *except*

A. rectangle
B. rhombus
C. trapezoid
D. parallelogram

191. The square root of 250 is between

A. 14 and 15
B. 15 and 16
C. 50 and 200
D. 10 and 20

192. How many multiples of 3 are there between $\frac{22}{7}$ and 29.60?

A. 5
B. 6
C. 7
D. 8

193. Which of the following has the greatest value?

A. $\frac{4}{5}$
B. $\frac{5}{6}$
C. $\frac{17}{20}$
D. 0.82

CONTINUE ON TO THE NEXT PAGE ➡

MATHEMATICS
PART IV

194. The ratio of 4.5 yards to 9 inches is

A. 1 to 2
B. 18 to 1
C. 4.5 to 9
D. 3 to 2

195. Which of the following is equal to $33\frac{1}{3}\%$?

A. $\frac{33}{100}$

B. $\frac{21}{60}$

C. $\frac{300}{1000}$

D. $0.\overline{33}$

196. Which of the following is not true?

A. $0 > 5$
B. $5 > -3$
C. $0.30 > 0.02$
D. $50 = 50$

197. Which of the following is correctly written in scientific notation?

A. $750 = 7.5 \cdot 10^3$
B. $0.075 = 7.5 \cdot 10^{-2}$
C. $750{,}000 = 7.5 \cdot 10^4$
D. $0.00075 = 7.5 \cdot 10^{-3}$

198. The least common multiple of 10 and 25 is

A. 5
B. 25
C. 50
D. 100

CONTINUE ON TO THE NEXT PAGE ➡

MATHEMATICS
PART IV

PROBLEM SOLVING QUESTIONS (40 Questions)

199. An amusement park sold 150 adult tickets for $5.25 each and 320 tickets for children for $3.10 each. How much profit did the amusement park make?

A. $2,467.50
B. $1,475.00
C. $2,145.00
D. $1,779.50

200. If $-3x + 2 = 59$, then $x =$

A. 19
B. -19
C. $20\frac{1}{3}$
D. $-20\frac{1}{3}$

201. A taxi charges $5 dollars for the first mile and $0.50 per mile after the first mile. If Jimmy wanted to travel 3 miles with a taxi, how much would the taxi ride cost?

A. $7.50
B. $15.00
C. $6.00
D. $7.00

202. Solve: $5 - (-3) + (-2) - (3)$

A. -3
B. 3
C. 7
D. 13

203. Dylan pays $36 per month for his internet. How much did he pay per day on the month of April (30 days = 1 month)?

A. $3.60
B. $432
C. $1.20
D. $1,080

204. Solve: $\frac{1}{6} \cdot \frac{2}{7} \cdot \frac{1}{3} =$

A. $\frac{1}{63}$
B. $\frac{2}{42}$
C. $\frac{1}{126}$
D. $\frac{1}{4}$

CONTINUE ON TO THE NEXT PAGE ➡

205. If the 8% discount on a car was $200, what is the cost of purchasing the car without the discount?

A. $2,600
B. $2,500
C. $2,300
D. $2,400

206. What is the surface area of this rectangular solid?

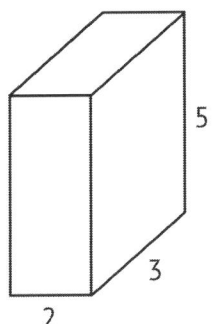

A. 30
B. 62
C. 60
D. 32

207. Solve: 0.32 + 6.3 + 0.058 =

A. 9.558
B. 7.20
C. 6.678
D. 15.30

208. Timothy paid $63.42 on a loan with a simple interest of 3%. How much did Timothy borrow?

A. $2,114
B. $65.322
C. $19.02
D. $211.40

209. Solve: $16 - 5\frac{5}{9}$

A. $10\frac{4}{9}$
B. $11\frac{4}{9}$
C. $11\frac{5}{9}$
D. $10\frac{5}{9}$

MATHEMATICS
PART IV

210. If 15 is subtracted from an integer and the result is $\frac{3}{4}$ of that integer, then what is $\frac{3}{4}$ the integer?

A. 60
B. 45
C. 30
D. 15

211. Solve: $9\frac{5}{6} - 6\frac{7}{8}$

A. $3\frac{35}{48}$
B. $3\frac{1}{2}$
C. $3\frac{1}{24}$
D. $2\frac{23}{24}$

212. If A = 4 and B = 7, then 4A - 6B =

A. -23
B. 4
C. -26
D. 36

213. The product of 11 and 13 is 7 less than N. What is N?

A. 136
B. 150
C. 80
D. 64

214. Solve: $37\overline{)42{,}311}$

A. 1,144 R54
B. 1,144 R20
C. 1,143 R20
D. 1,143 R54

215. If a tree has a shadow of 91 feet long and a 7-foot man has a shadow 13 feet long, then what is the height of the tree?

A. 91 feet
B. 97 feet
C. 169 feet
D. 49 feet

CONTINUE ON TO THE NEXT PAGE ➡

MATHEMATICS
PART IV

216. Solve for x: $5x + 2 < 9x + 6$

- A. $x > 0$
- B. $x = 1$
- C. $x < -1$
- D. $x > -1$

217. How many $2\frac{2}{3}$ feet long boards can be cut from a board that is $16\frac{2}{5}$ feet long?

- A. 13
- B. 7
- C. 6
- D. 8

218. Solve: $79.51 \cdot 0.043 =$

- A. 3.41893
- B. 34.1893
- C. 0.341893
- D. 341.893

219. If $5(7x - 8) = 135$, then $x =$

- A. 98
- B. 5
- C. 10
- D. 3

220. If $15x - 6 = 4x + 60$, then x equals

- A. 6
- B. 4.125
- C. 5
- D. 4.91

221. If $\frac{7}{8}x = 56$, then $x =$

- A. 56
- B. 49
- C. 64
- D. 65

222. 27.32, 27.35, 27.38, 27.41, ___
What number should come next in this sequence?

- A. 57.41
- B. 30.41
- C. 27.71
- D. 27.44

CONTINUE ON TO THE NEXT PAGE ➡

MATHEMATICS PART IV

223.

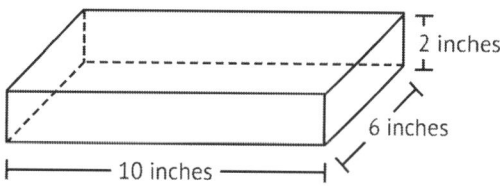

What is the volume, in cubic inches, of the rectangular prism?

A. 18 cubic inches
B. 120 cubic inches
C. 60 cubic inches
D. 184 cubic inches

224. What will a 24 ft by 18 ft rectangular rug cost at $5 a square yard?

A. $2,160
B. $720
C. $240
D. $80

225. Solve: 37,825 • 504 =

A. 19,114,200
B. 20,000,000
C. 19,063,296
D. 19,063,800

226. If the perimeter of a rectangle is 34 units and the length of one of the sides is 8 units, then what is the area of the respective rectangle?

A. 34 units^2
B. 72 units^2
C. 144 units^2
D. 288 units^2

227. Solve: $3.03 \overline{)3.9087}$

A. 1.28
B. 1.29
C. 1.30
D. 1.03

228. Seven years ago, Carroll's father was 4 times as old as Carroll. How old is her father now if Carroll is now 16?

A. 43 years old
B. 36 years old
C. 57 years old
D. 64 years old

229. If x% of 64 is 24, then x =

A. 38%
B. 83%
C. 27%
D. 37.5%

CONTINUE ON TO THE NEXT PAGE ➡

MATHEMATICS
PART IV

230. An object has a mass of 21.5 milligrams. What is the object's mass in grams?

A. 0.0215 g
B. 0.215 g
C. 2.15 g
D. 21.5 g

231.

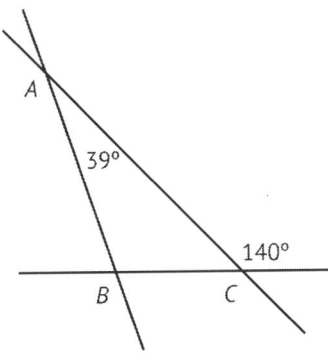

What is the degree measure of ∡ABC?

A. 101°
B. 140°
C. 40°
D. 141°

232. If A = 4, B = 7, C = 6, then $\frac{2BCA}{3AB}$ =

A. 1
B. 4
C. 6
D. 9

233. The ratio of boys to girls in a certain school is 1:4. If there are 80 girls in the school, how many boys are there?

A. 320
B. 40
C. 20
D. 100

234. If $\sqrt{x+3}$ = 15, then x =

A. 222
B. 225
C. 228
D. 144

235. Solve for x: $x^2 + 16 = 137$

A. 9
B. 10
C. 11
D. 12

236. If 10x - 50 < 50, then what could be a possible value of x?

A. 9
B. 10
C. 14
D. 17

CONTINUE ON TO THE NEXT PAGE ➡

MATHEMATICS
PART IV

237. The average of 3, 4, 10, 9, and 4 is

   A. 3
   B. 5
   C. 30
   D. 6

238. 80 is 80% of what number?

   A. 80
   B. 110
   C. 100
   D. 64

LANGUAGE
PART V (25 MIN)

USAGE

DIRECTIONS: For Questions 239-278, choose the sentence that contains an error in punctuation, capitalization, or usage. If there is no error present, select answer choice D.

239. A. At the meeting, the lawyer said, "My client finds fault with all those who have ignored his rights as an employee".
  B. The Olympic weightlifting trainer tried lifting the car with all his might; however, the car did not budge.
  C. The room was dimly lit and the old lady quietly recollected nostalgic thoughts of her childhood at Mamie Fay High School.
  D. No Mistakes

240. A. Ever since ever since he started painting, Danielle's sister would watch her paint.
  B. The Giant Armadillo is the land mammal with the most amount of teeth.
  C. Morphemes are the smallest unit of meaning and phonemes are the smallest unit of sound.
  D. No Mistakes

241. A. Because our telephone bill was too high, Dad called our service and complained.
  B. Rammstein is the most popular metal band in Germany; in fact, many know of the band's name without being a fan.
  C. In response to Ms. Bet's question, Jason made a joke and asked if she knew what the answer was?
  D. No Mistakes

242. A. John Little was a great mathematician and at the age of eight was able to calculate the summation of the first hundred numbers.
  B. Edgar Allan Poe, a famous writer, married his cousin when she was thirteen years old.
  C. After failing my test, I had lied on my bed for several hours.
  D. No Mistakes

CONTINUE ON TO THE NEXT PAGE ➡

LANGUAGE
PART V

243. A. Colleges and universities are two words that seem synonymous; however, colleges are usually smaller.
  B. Every time I visit my grandparent's place, grandma stuffs me with a lot of food.
  C. Gold and silver are two metals that are not very reactive making them able to withstand rust and great for using on coins.
  D. No Mistakes

244. A. After brushing my teeth, I like to wash my face.
  B. Valentine's Day is a day that originates from celebrating Saint Valentinus.
  C. Our eyes can only observe a specific range of the color spectrum but other animals can see much more.
  D. No Mistakes

245. A. Stephanie's room was filled with books and by the looks of it, she seemed like a studious person.
  B. Misao Okawa is the oldest living person according to the Guinness World Records.
  C. It was the first day of school and I knew people avoided associating to me since I forgot to take off my pajamas.
  D. No Mistakes

246. A. My dog preferred eating at my house, but preferred playing at my friend Suzanne's house.
  B. Social media has made us so interconnected that we can get to any other person just by viewing about 10 profiles from person to person.
  C. Each of the girls on the team were allowed to have Gatorade as a part of their warm up.
  D. No Mistakes

247. A. Playing helps develop several mammal's ligaments and muscles.
  B. New Delhi is the capital of India.
  C. They consistently got meatballs with spaghetti for lunch on Fridays.
  D. No Mistakes

248. A. Many illiterate adults who have never understood a language well enough can practice to improve their speech.
  B. Hair and fur are both made up of the same protein, Keratin.
  C. The teacher announced that anyone caught cheating on the test will be immediately suspended for the remainder of the class.
  D. No Mistakes

CONTINUE ON TO THE NEXT PAGE ➡

LANGUAGE
PART V

249.
A. The Cadillac parked outside had a ticket on its window.
B. Parkinson's Disease is a disorder of the central nervous system which disrupts normal movements.
C. The four girls were having a sleepover and they decided a scary movie would be the best way to have fun.
D. No Mistakes

250.
A. The deciduous trees of the Appalachian Mountains remain dormant in the winter by losing green leaves.
B. Either his friends or Vlad were at the university studying for the Italian final.
C. Cows usually stand up when it is hot and lay down when it is cool.
D. No Mistakes

251.
A. Albert really wanted a chance to go to Harvard Law, but he feared his grades were not up to par.
B. The lab procedure required us to contact our professor, Mr. Duilio, and submit a six page report on the experiment in class.
C. Ivan the Terrible was the first ruler to be crowned the tsar of All of the Russians.
D. No Mistakes

252.
A. Dogs mature much more quickly than humans do and the average life of a dog is 7 years.
B. The modern piano has 88 keys of which 52 are white and 36 are black.
C. Timothy believed his mindset was stronger than Edwin since Timothy could study for a longer amount of time.
D. No Mistakes

253.
A. The hardness of cement is much more than wood making it more reliable for roads.
B. Deoxyribonucleic Acid has a half-life of about 521 years which means that it can be identified for a very long time even after death.
C. She was great gymnast with a lot of flexibility and a lot of optimism.
D. No Mistakes

254.
A. My teacher asked, "What's wrong with the homework?"
B. Between you and I, clearly I am the smarter one.
C. The Grand Canyon could be further seen from The Grand Canyon Skywalk, a platform with glass as the base for visibility.
D. No Mistakes

CONTINUE ON TO THE NEXT PAGE ➡

LANGUAGE
PART V

255.
- A. I wish I did not have to do as much work as I need to.
- B. Tyrannosaurus Rex is the most common dinosaur that comes to mind when talking about the Jurassic era.
- C. Next year, I will be assigned three classes with the additional standard schedule: biology, chemistry, and spanish.
- D. No Mistakes

256.
- A. The tallest presidents were Abraham Lincoln and Lyndon B. Johnson; they were both 76 inches tall.
- B. Even though he never played football, whenever Albert, who was unusually athletic, sees an opponent, he was easily able to get past him.
- C. I thought school was open today, but I did not realize today was Christmas.
- D. No Mistakes

257.
- A. Amanda's lawyer said, "You have to plead guilty for the court to be in your favor."
- B. Seismometers are instruments that can measure the possibility of an earthquake from a nearby location.
- C. Noah was more happy when he got his present for Christmas than when he got his present on his birthday.
- D. No Mistakes

258.
- A. Roy asked ",What in the world are you doing with that banana peel?"
- B. Fahim's mom did not allow him to take a break from his school even though he had the flu.
- C. I am lactose intolerant and so I have a hard time digesting the sugars in dairy products such as cheese, milk, and ice cream.
- D. No Mistakes

259.
- A. That red pair of sandals are my favorite.
- B. By believing Harley, the test was way harder than what we had studied for.
- C. The doctor could not detect the tumor within the patient; he was accused of being too laid back to notice.
- D. No Mistakes

260.
- A. We have two kidneys in our body to help filter out excretory material from the blood.
- B. The First amendment of the United States is one of the most important amendments giving up the freedom of speech.
- C. The hormones that stimulate sexual characteristics are testosterone and estrogen.
- D. No Mistakes

CONTINUE ON TO THE NEXT PAGE ➡

LANGUAGE
PART V

261. A. Mexico has the world's largest population of Spanish speaking people.
B. The louse, insects that are great travelers and remain at the scalp, are a nuisance to everyone.
C. The Little People of America classify any adult under 58 inches as being a dwarf.
D. No Mistakes

262. A. Whenever Mother asks us to get groceries, we make a list on a piece of paper.
B. Down syndrome is a genetic condition with an extra copy of a chromosome in the 21st position.
C. If I had swam at a faster rate, I could have won the swimming competition.
D. No Mistakes

263. A. My sister believed that her hair was more luscious and longer than her friend Maria.
B. Many say that long term effects of energy drinks are detrimental to the heart.
C. Bears actually do not hibernate in the winter, but rather slow down with minimal activity.
D. No Mistakes

264. A. Women would often adopt pseudonyms as a replacement to their original names so that their gender would not show; being a male was more advantageous when writing a book.
B. Rain has never fallen on the the town of Calma, Chile in the Atamaca Desert.
C. The U.S. Senate is part of the legislative branch and with the House of Representatives make up the U.S. Congress.
D. No Mistakes

265. A. Although Jupiter is considered much bigger than the earth, the Sun is actually the biggest object accounting for most of Solar System's mass.
B. Thurl Ravenscroft sang the song "You're a Mean One, Mr. Grinch."
C. One should avoid swimming near the beach because of dangerous animals: sharks and jellyfish.
D. No Mistakes

266. A. A normal deck of cards has four symbols each with its own respective meaning: diamond, wealth; clover, luck; hearts, love; and spade, death.
B. The professor, a great lecturer gave a presentation on vector subspaces.
C. Dad is strict about curfew so I should return home before 8 p.m.
D. No Mistakes

CONTINUE ON TO THE NEXT PAGE ➡

LANGUAGE
PART V

267.
- A. On 1836, Samuel F.B. Morse, an American artist, with couple of others were able to develop the Morse Code.
- B. I wouldv'e been able to do the task my teacher assigned me, but I was too sick yesterday.
- C. A troop is a group of monkeys or kangaroos.
- D. No Mistakes

268.
- A. Among my two dogs, Fluffy is the biggest one.
- B. If we can stabilize the nuclear fusion reaction that happens in the Sun, we can obtain almost an unlimited source of energy.
- C. The hottest temperature recorded in the United States was 134 degrees Fahrenheit.
- D. No Mistakes

269.
- A. Adrenaline is a hormone that increases blood flow and oxygen delivery to the muscles in times of stress.
- B. The cat with their friends was able to get the mouse out from its hiding spot.
- C. My father always got a can of Monster before going to work.
- D. No Mistakes

270.
- A. The song "Who Let the Dogs out?" became popular as soon as it was released on July 26, 2000.
- B. Regular polygons have sides that are all equal and angles that are all equal as well.
- C. Greek mythology is a polytheistic belief and Zeus is the main god.
- D. No Mistakes

271.
- A. I was expecting to get a call home from my bad behavior in school, but Ms. Corneta was lenient.
- B. From the statistics of this trend we expect a rise in three percent of the stocks from Bank of China.
- C. Royal Dansk is my favorite brand of cookies.
- D. No Mistakes

272.
- A. You should try to use your time wisely in order to prepare for any challenge.
- B. Mathematics is a hard subject for many so my teacher recommended I stay after school for practice.
- C. Miss Fernando's son and Miss Johnson's daughter were in a fight and her child got hurt.
- D. No Mistakes

CONTINUE ON TO THE NEXT PAGE ➡

LANGUAGE
PART V

273. A. Hermione and Ron are two characters in J.K. Rowling's series of books known as Harry Potter.
   B. The inch is bigger than the centimeter; two and a half times bigger.
   C. The Internet and the phone show that the rise of technology has allowed a much faster rate of communication than ever before.
   D. No Mistakes

274. A. Darwin is often regarded the first to establish a theory on evolution, but it is Lamarck who proposed the theory of natural selection.
   B. The oldest president to be elected was Ronald Reagan at the age of 69.
   C. The slogan "Just Do It" was created by Dan Weeden.
   D. No Mistakes

275. A. Buddhism and Hinduism share many similarities among which one of them is reincarnation.
   B. Most glue works by attaching to surfaces and hardening within them, it does not work well on polyethylene glycol.
   C. That the conditions were met was more important than any of the monetary values exchanged.
   D. No Mistakes

276. A. The New York Jets is a football team that got its name from the Mets.
   B. After practicing many questions on cellular respiration, I was able to do good on my biology test.
   C. The skeletons of sharks are made up of cartilage, a more flexible and less dense materials than bone
   D. No Mistakes

277. A. Orville and Wilbur Wright were the first creators of the airplane.
   B. Acupuncture is an alternative treatment to pain in the back.
   C. O'Reilly believe he had much less glasses of drinks compared to his friends.
   D. No Mistakes

278. A. The principle yelled at Erin for cutting class multiple times.
   B. The Statue of Liberty faces southeast and was strategically placed for incoming boats and ships.
   C. Having 20/20 vision means that what one sees in 20 feet is also what the normal person sees within 20 feet.
   D. No Mistakes

CONTINUE ON TO THE NEXT PAGE →

LANGUAGE
PART V

SPELLING

DIRECTIONS: For questions 279-288, find the sentence that contains a spelling error. If there is no error present, select answer choice D.

279. A. The Taj Mahal was a great achievement by the Mughal Empire of India.
     B. Stein had a great threshhold for pain.
     C. As a part of the committee, we have to understand problems by working together with our colleagues.
     D. No mistakes

280. A. The candy was known to be irresistible, but as soon as Matthew tried a piece, he immediately regurgitated.
     B. The Caribbean is a great place for a vacation.
     C. I find the Lost Battalion Cemetary a scary place to visit.
     D. No mistakes

281. A. My teacher announced, "Unfortunatley I will not be able to make it tomorrow to class."
     B. Urine contains urea, a metabolic waste product converted from ammonia by the liver.
     C. There isn't much noticeable difference between the two lollipops.
     D. No mistakes

282. A. Make sure that whereever you go, you are happy.
     B. The occurrence of any individual's birth and genetic makeup is a miracle.
     C. Politicians are often seen as liars, but there are some who want the success of their country.
     D. No mistakes

283. A. I was able to get acquainted with my boss as soon as he hired me for the job.
     B. An energy pyramid shows the hierarchy of animals: the bottom being the producers and the top being the tertiary consumer.
     C. "Fahrenheit 451" is a book about a society that normally burns books.
     D. No mistakes

CONTINUE ON TO THE NEXT PAGE →

LANGUAGE
PART V

284.
- **A.** The possession of narcotics in the state of New York is a high offense.
- **B.** Melanie seem to get the gist of the idea of how the government works.
- **C.** The existance of trees is important for the survival of the animals in the environment.
- **D.** No mistakes

285.
- **A.** Please fill out the questionnaire and hand it in at the end of class.
- **B.** The pharoah is the king of ancient Egypt.
- **C.** Do you want a receipt with what you have ordered?
- **D.** No mistakes

286.
- **A.** He had forgotten to note down any predictions for the unforseen events that would come later on.
- **B.** My friend preferred being indoors than going outside and partying.
- **C.** I have received many anonymous letters, probably from my colleagues, about how my position at the office was too high.
- **D.** No mistakes

287.
- **A.** My brother got a tattoo of a tongue on his shoulder and my parents disapproved.
- **B.** Please remember to take a packet and complete it for the break.
- **C.** The colonists fought with resistance against the British forces.
- **D.** No mistakes

288.
- **A.** To be successful, one must make plans to achieve his or her goals.
- **B.** The Byzantine Empire seized parts of land from the Persian Empire.
- **C.** I have a tendency to be fidgety so when my brother yelled out 'suprise', I shook violently.
- **D.** No mistakes

CONTINUE ON TO THE NEXT PAGE ➡

LANGUAGE
PART V

COMPOSITION

DIRECTIONS: For questions 289-298, follow the directions for each question and select the best answer choice.

289. Choose the best word or words to join the thoughts together.

    The findings show that his DNA was at the crime scene; _____, we can conclude that he was involved in the murder.

    A. moreover
    B. however
    C. thus
    D. None of these

290. Choose the best word or words to join the thoughts together.

    They purchased a new video game system. _____, they were able to play what graphics never seen before.

    A. Furthermore
    B. However
    C. Subsequently
    D. None of these

291. Choose the best word or words to join the thoughts together.

    William became a great basketball player by_____

    A. carefully practicing his movements everyday.
    B. practicing his movements carefully everyday.
    C. practicing carefully his movements everyday.
    D. carefully practicing everyday his movements.

CONTINUE ON TO THE NEXT PAGE ➡

LANGUAGE
PART V

292. Which of these expresses the idea most clearly?

A. Tesla was a great innovator of electricity within technology although criticized for being a maniac.
B. Although criticized for being a maniac, electricity within technology was an by innovation by Tesla.
C. Although criticized for being a maniac, the people did not realize Tesla's innovation of electricity within technology.
D. Although criticized for being a maniac, Tesla was a great innovator of electricity within technology.

293. Which of these expresses the idea most clearly?

A. In 2003 Xavier High School defeated Robertson High School in a basketball game, even so, they did not win again until 2011.
B. In 2003 Xavier High School defeated Robertson High School in a basketball game; but it did not win again until 2011.
C. In 2003 Xavier High School defeated Robertson High School in a basketball game, but it did not win again until 2011.
D. In 2003 Xavier High School defeated Robertson High School in a basketball game, it did not win again until 2011.

294. Choose the pair of sentences that best develops this topic sentence.

The development of agriculture was key to growth in human populations.

A. By herding cattle, humans use domestication to help increase agriculture.
B. Humans used to hunt, but now can plant.
C. New inventions have allowed products to move to new places.
D. The increased use of specialized tools for harvesting has allowed exponential surplus of food.

295. Which of the following sentences offers least support to the topic "Actions speak louder than words"?

A. Martin Luther King Jr. led boycotts to show how he disapproved of segregation.
B. Mahatma Gandhi led the Salt March which was a peaceful protest against Great Britain.
C. Michael could no longer put up with how Samantha kept him out of the group; he confronted her.
D. Peter was too scared to let anyone know about how he felt.

CONTINUE ON TO THE NEXT PAGE ➡

LANGUAGE
PART V

296. Which of these best fits under the topic "Violence is not the answer"?

A. The only way to fix Paul's bad behavior was to give him detention.
B. After Brandon had thrown his phone because it was malfunctioning, he had to get a new battery.
C. The Allies had won World War 1, but many countries suffered damages.
D. Mom did not let my little brother play with his toys so he had a temper tantrum.

297. Which sentence does not belong in the paragraph?

(1) Humans are believed to be the smartest primates. (2) Among all the primates, humans are the most social. (3) Usually primates have the highest-ranking male as the leader of the group. (4) In fact a recent study showed that the higher the number of individuals in a social group, the higher the intelligence of the species.

A. Sentence 1
B. Sentence 2
C. Sentence 3
D. Sentence 4

298. Where should the sentence "It is important to never jump to conclusions" be placed in the paragraph below?

(1) The scientific method is a revolutionary strategy to prove a hypothesis after multiple tests at every possible angle. (2) Instead, one must use reasoning from a methodical approach. (3) This will ensure that the conclusion is not just from thin air.

A. Before sentence 1
B. Between sentence 1 & 2
C. Between sentence 2 & 3
D. None of the above

CONTINUE ON TO THE NEXT PAGE ➡

HSPT PRACTICE TEST 3
ANSWER KEY

ENGLISH

Verbal Skills (Part I)

1. D	11. B	21. C	31. A	41. A	51. C
2. C	12. B	22. A	32. D	42. C	52. D
3. B	13. C	23. A	33. A	43. C	53. D
4. A	14. C	24. B	34. C	44. B	54. D
5. A	15. C	25. D	35. B	45. A	55. B
6. A	16. B	26. C	36. D	46. A	56. C
7. B	17. C	27. A	37. A	47. A	57. C
8. D	18. B	28. A	38. B	48. C	58. C
9. C	19. B	29. A	39. B	49. A	59. D
10. D	20. A	30. C	40. B	50. B	60. A

Reading (Part III)

113. A	128. A	143. A	158. B
114. C	129. C	144. C	159. C
115. A	130. B	145. A	160. B
116. D	131. D	146. B	161. B
117. B	132. C	147. A	162. B
118. A	133. B	148. B	163. D
119. C	134. A	149. A	164. D
120. B	135. D	150. C	165. A
121. A	136. A	151. B	166. B
122. B	137. B	152. B	167. C
123. B	138. A	153. A	168. C
124. D	139. A	154. A	169. D
125. C	140. C	155. C	170. C
126. B	141. A	156. B	171. A
127. A	142. B	157. A	172. A
			173. B
			174. B

Language (Part V)

239. A	249. B	259. B	269. B	279. B	289. A
240. A	250. B	260. B	270. A	280. C	290. B
241. C	251. C	261. B	271. B	281. A	291. A
242. C	252. C	262. C	272. C	282. A	292. D
243. B	253. B	263. A	273. B	283. D	293. C
244. C	254. B	264. D	274. D	284. C	294. D
245. C	255. C	265. D	275. B	285. B	295. D
246. C	256. B	266. B	276. B	286. A	296. B
247. A	257. C	267. B	277. C	287. D	297. A
248. A	258. A	268. A	278. A	288. C	298. B

ARGO BROTHERS

To calculate your score and watch video tutorials, visit our web site: www.einstein-academy.com/catholic

MATHEMATICS

Quantitative (Part II)

61. D	74. A	87. C	100. C
62. D	75. C	88. B	101. D
63. B	76. D	89. C	102. B
64. B	77. D	90. C	103. A
65. A	78. C	91. A	104. D
66. B	79. D	92. D	105. D
67. C	80. B	93. D	106. A
68. C	81. B	94. B	107. B
69. C	82. A	95. C	108. A
70. D	83. A	96. C	109. A
71. B	84. D	97. C	110. C
72. C	85. C	98. C	111. A
73. B	86. A	99. D	112. B

Mathematics (Part IV)

175. C	188. A	201. C	214. C	227. B
176. B	189. A	202. B	215. D	228. A
177. A	190. C	203. C	216. D	229. D
178. D	191. B	204. A	217. C	230. A
179. A	192. D	205. B	218. A	231. A
180. B	193. C	206. A	219. B	232. B
181. B	194. B	207. C	220. A	233. C
182. C	195. D	208. A	221. C	234. A
183. B	196. A	209. A	222. D	235. C
184. D	197. B	210. A	223. B	236. A
185. C	198. C	211. D	224. C	237. D
186. B	199. D	212. C	225. D	238. C
187. A	200. B	213. B	226. B	

ANSWER EXPLANATIONS

VERBAL SECTION

1. **The correct answer is D.**
   Loathing, hate, and animosity are all synonyms of each other that have negative connotations. Lovely, is a word with a positive connotation and means the opposite of the other three.

2. **The correct answer is C.**
   Enlarge, minimize, and decrease are all words that refer to size. Strengthen is the only word that does not refer to size.

3. **The correct answer is B.**
   A play follows a script while a movie follows a screenplay.

4. **The correct answer is A.**
   Gavin is farsighted and all farsighted people wear glasses. Since Gavin is farsighted, Gavin must wear glasses. Therefore, the third statement is true.

5. **The correct answer is A.**
   Congruent means to be in agreement with, or identical in form or shape.

6. **The correct answer is A.**
   A grocery store employee is a clerk, while an office employee is a secretary.

7. **The correct answer is B.**
   Haughty, snobbish, and condescending are all synonyms of each other while humble is an antonym of these words. Therefore, answer choice B does not belong with the others.

8. **The correct answer is D.**
   Speech is actualized by hearing, and a picture is actualized by seeing.

9. **The correct answer is C.**
   A penny, nickel, and quarter are all denominations that can be represented by only a coin. A dollar can be represented by a coin or paper money.

10. **The correct answer is D.**
    Abrupt means unexpected or sudden.

11. **The correct answer is B.**
    Fortuitous means happening by chance or by luck.

12. **The correct answer is B.**
    A teacher works in a classroom whereas a researcher works in a lab.

13. **The correct answer is C.**
    Severe, mild, and slight all refer to a certain degree of severity. Amazing does not fall into this category.

14. **The correct answer is C.**
    Drugs are bought at the pharmacy whereas bread is bought at the bakery.

15. **The correct answer is C.**
    The piano is played with your fingers while the flute is played with your fingers as well as your mouth.

16. **The correct answer is B.**
    Josh can ride faster than Jack, and Jack can ride faster than Jill. This implies that Josh must be faster than Jill. Therefore, the third statement is false.

17. **The correct answer is C.**
    Astute means to have an ability to accurately assess situations or people and turn this into one's advantage. Clever would be a synonym.

ANSWER EXPLANATIONS

18. **The correct answer is B.**
    Innovative is an adjective that describes a product or idea that features new methods; something that is original.

19. **The correct answer is B.**
    Wane means to decrease in vigor, or weaken.

20. **The correct answer is A.**
    A notebook is placed in your schoolbag whereas your clothes are placed in luggage.

21. **The correct answer is C.**
    The sky is the natural opposite to the ground while the ceiling is the artificial opposite to the floor.

22. **The correct answer is A.**
    Abominable means to cause moral revulsion, or to be hateful.

23. **The correct answer is A.**
    Point C is north of point B and and point A is south of point B. This implies that point C is north of point A. Point C is also south of point D. This implies that point D is north of point A. Therefore, the third statement is true.

24. **The correct answer is B.**
    Alleviate, mitigate, and dampen are all synonyms of each other that mean to ease up or release the tension. Aggravate is an antonym that means to exasperate the situation.

25. **The correct answer is D.**
    Lucid means expressed clearly. Coherent would be a synonym for this.

26. **The correct answer is C.**
    River A is longer than river B, and river B is shorter than river C. Both rivers A, and C are longer than B, however, it is unknown as to what their relationship is to each other. Therefore, the third statement is uncertain.

27. **The correct answer is A.**
    Ostracize means to exclude from a group or society, or shun.

28. **The correct answer is A.**
    Alleviate means to make less severe, or relieve.

29. **The correct answer is A.**
    Red is the color of anger, and green is the color of jealousy.

30. **The correct answer is C.**
    Empathy means to be able to understand and share the feeling of another.

31. **The correct answer is A.**
    Hostile means unfriendly or antagonistic; the opposite would be peaceful.

32. **The correct answer is D.**
    Homework, test, and classwork are all tasks that need to be completed for school. The teacher, however is not a task that needs to be completed.

33. **The correct answer is A.**
    A textbook, autobiography, and document are all written manuscripts, whereas a recording is not.

ANSWER EXPLANATIONS

34. The correct answer is C.
Amiable is an adjective that means to have a friendly and pleasant manner; the opposite would be disagreeable.

35. The correct answer is B.
If Rafael scored more points than Jeff, and Jeff scored more points than Rachel, this must mean that Rachel scored the fewest amount of points out of the three. Therefore, the third statement is false.

36. The correct answer is D.
Appalled means to be in great dismay or horrified; the opposite would be encouraged.

37. The correct answer is A.
Miscellaneous means to be of various types or from different sources. Varied would be a synonym for this.

38. The correct answer is B.
Annihilate means to destroy utterly; the opposite would be to not destroy but create.

39. The correct answer is B.
Gullible means to be easily persuadable to believe something; the opposite would be suspicious.

40. The correct answer is B.
Shampoo, conditioner, and soap are all bathroom products that are applied during a shower. Detergent on the other hand is not applied during a shower and therefore does not belong with the other three words.

41. The correct answer is A.
Character, setting, and plot are all elements of a story. A book includes all of these elements and therefore does not fit with the other three.

42. The correct answer is C.
A fireplace is brighter than both a lamp, and a lighter according to the first two statements. However, nothing else is said connecting the relationship between a lamp and a lighter, therefore, the third statement is uncertain.

43. The correct answer is C.
A painting, sculpture, and photograph are all forms of art, whereas an artist creates the art.

44. The correct answer is B.
Timid means to show a lack of courage or confidence. Shy would be a synonym for this.

45. The correct answer is A.
Tranquil means free from disturbance; the opposite would be disturbed.

46. The correct answer is A.
If Kingsley reads more than Pamela, and Pamela reads more than Casey, this implies that Kingsley reads more than Casey. Therefore, the third statement is true.

47. The correct answer is A.
Opaque means to not be able to see through; the opposite would be transparent.

48. The correct answer is C.
Malice means to have the intention or desire to do evil; the opposite would be benevolence.

49. The correct answer is A.
If a hole is deeper than an opening, and an opening is deeper than a gap, this must mean that a hole is deeper than a gap. Therefore, the third statement is true.

ANSWER EXPLANATIONS

50. **The correct answer is B.**
    Abigail scored higher than Jill. Jill scored higher than Betty, who in turn scored higher than Jen. This must mean that Abigail scored higher than Jen. Therefore, the third statement is false.

51. **The correct answer is C.**
    Consensus means to come to a general agreement; the opposite would be to be in disagreement.

52. **The correct answer is D.**
    Shoes, pants, and a shirt are all necessary articles of clothing that you wear. Jewelry is an accessory.

53. **The correct answer is D.**
    A clown, juggler, and mime are all acts that happen in a circus. Therefore, circus is the odd word out of the four words.

54. **The correct answer is D.**
    Dexterous means to demonstrate skill especially with your hands.

55. **The correct answer is B.**
    Decisive means to settle an issue and to be able to make decisions quickly; the opposite would be halfhearted.

56. **The correct answer is C.**
    Exhilarate means to make someone feel very happy; the opposite would be to disgust someone.

57. **The correct answer is C.**
    Glasses are used to help vision whereas hearing aids are used to help transmission of sound.

58. **The correct answer is C.**
    Established means to be in existence for a long time, or recognized.

59. **The correct answer is D.**
    Garage, bedroom, and living room are all interior components of a house whereas a backyard is part of the exterior.

60. **The correct answer is A.**
    Dangerous, vicious, and savage are all synonyms of each other that refer to something that can cause harm. To be harmless would be the opposite.

QUANTITATIVE SECTION

61. **The correct answer is D.**
    Recall that the word "of" means to multiply and the word "is" is an equal sign. Convert the 30% into a decimal since the number 60 needs to be multiplied by 30%.
    .30 • 60 = 18.
    The question asks for 5 more than the above number. 18 + 5 = 23.

62. **The correct answer is D.**
    Multiply 30 by $\frac{5}{6}$ which gives 25. 7 plus 25 is 32.

ANSWER EXPLANATIONS

63. **The correct answer is B.**
    The numbers in the series go according to the pattern; subtract 7, add 3, subtract 7, add 3 and so on. The difference between the two numbers previous to the blank is 3. Therefore, to get from 64 to the blank, 7 needs to be subtracted from 64. This gives 57.

64. **The correct answer is B.**
    Examine each of the figures and determine how much of each figure is shaded in. In figure A, 2 out of 6 equal parts are shaded. In figure B, 1 out of 3 equal parts are shaded. In figure C, 1 out of 2 equal parts are shaded. Therefore, figure C is shaded more than A and B.

65. **The correct answer is A.**
    Convert the fractions and percents into decimals.
    (A) $\frac{9}{10} = 0.9$
    (B) $93\% = 0.93$
    (C) $0.3 \cdot 3.14 = 0.942$

    Looking at the answer choices, only answer choice A is true. 0.93 is greater than 0.9 but less than 0.942.

66. **The correct answer is B.**
    Evaluate each of the statements given. Statement A comes out to 2.5 Statement B comes out to 2.5 and statement C comes out to 25. Therefore, C > A = B.

67. **The correct answer is C.**
    The numbers in this series go according to the pattern; add 4, subtract 2, add 4, subtract 2 and so on. The last two numbers have a difference of 2, so the next number should be 4 more than the previous. 43 is four more than 39, and is the answer.

68. **The correct answer is C.**
    Examine the numbers in the series. Notice that 1, 27, 64, and 125 are all cubes of a number. 1 is 1 cubed, 27 is 3 cubed, 64 is 4 cubed and 125 is 5 cubed. The blank must be 2 cubed, which is 8.

69. **The correct answer is C.**
    Multiply 65 by $\frac{2}{5}$ which gives 26. 26 multiplied 4 is 104.

70. **The correct answer is D.**
    Simplify each of the statements into decimal form. Statement B simplifies to 0.66. Statement C can already be seen to be less than .01 because $\frac{13}{20}$ is less than 1, and less than 1% is less than .01. Therefore, C is smaller than both A and B.

71. **The correct answer is B.**
    The numbers in this series are each decreasing by 0.125. 0.375 - 0.125 = 0.250.

72. **The correct answer is C.**
    Angle A must be greater than B or C because both angles B and C are noticeably acute, while A is obtuse.

ANSWER EXPLANATIONS

73. The correct answer is B.
Look at the difference between each consecutive letter. There are two letters in between consecutive numbers in the series. The next letter should contain an "R." The numbers in the series are decreasing by 3 which each number, which means the next number should be 80. This gives "R80."

74. The correct answer is A.
The numbers in this series add a certain amount for two consecutive numbers. For the first two, it is 2, for the next two, it is 4, for the next two it is 6, and for the last two is 8. This means for the next two, 10 should be added. This gives 52 as the next number.

75. The correct answer is C.
Evaluate each of the statements given. Statement A simplifies to $5y - 5x$. Statement B simplifies to $7x - 7y$. Statement C simplifies to $7x - 7y$. It is seen that both B and C are the same so they are equal. This eliminates answer choice B and C. If x is less than y, then $5y - 5x$ must be greater than $7x - 7y$.

76. The correct answer is D.
Set up the equation given in the question. It is saying $x - 0.09x = 182$. This simplifies to $0.91x - 182$. Divide by 0.91 on both sides to get $x = 200$.

77. The correct answer is D.
Simplify the statements into decimal form. Statement B simplifies to repeating decimal $3.\overline{33}$. This means that answer choices B and C are equal, therefore D is the right answer.

78. The correct answer is C.
Find the length of DG. Draw a line connecting E to C. From E to the line going from D to G, the distance has to be 3 because AB is equal to 6 and half that is 3. This forms a 3-4-5 triangle. From D to the line connecting E to C the distance would be 4. This gives a total length of DG to be 7, and AB to be 6.

79. The correct answer is D.
The numbers in this series should be looked at in sets of two. The first number multiplied by 4 gives 20. The 3rd number multiplied by 4 gives 12 and so on. The blank is in an odd position so the number previous to it is four times smaller. 14 times 4 is 42.

80. The correct answer is B.
The numbers in this series go according to the pattern; multiply by 3, multiply by 1, multiply by 3, multiply by 1 and so on. Therefore, the next three numbers should be multiplied by 3, then 1, and then 3 again. This gives answer choice B.

81. The correct answer is B.
Find out the measurement of angle C. Angle C is equal to 180 - 60 - 40 which gives 80°. This means that the side opposite to it has to be the largest in the triangle. Angle A is the second largest so BC should be the second longest. Therefore answer choice B is correct.

82. The correct answer is A.
5 times 5 is 25. 4 less than 25 is 21. 21 multiplied by the reciprocal of $\frac{3}{7}, \frac{7}{3}$ is 49.

ANSWER EXPLANATIONS

83. The correct answer is A.
Count the number of acute angles in each of the figures. Figure A has 1, figure B has 5, figure C has 4, and figure D has 1. Therefore, B has more acute angles than A and D combined.

84. The correct answer is D.
$$\frac{5}{4} \cdot x = 5 \cdot 2$$
$$\frac{5}{4}x = 10$$
$$5x = 40$$
$$x = 8$$

85. The correct answer is C.
Evaluate each of the statements given. Statement A simplifies to 180. Statement B simplifies to 330. Statement C simplifies to 900. Therefore, C > B > A.

86. The correct answer is A.
8 more than 5 is 13. 13 multiplied by 4 is 52.

87. The correct answer is C.
Find the average of the numbers given. Find the average by adding 12, 90, 69, and 41 and then dividing the sum by 4. This gives 53. The difference between 53 and 22 is 31.

88. The correct answer is B.
Evaluate the statements given. Statement A simplifies to 32. Statement B simplifies to 66 and statement C simplifies to 48. Therefore, B is the largest.

89. The correct answer is C.
The numbers in this series are doubling with each consecutive number. Multiply 16 by 2 and get 32 as the correct answer.

90. The correct answer is C.
Examine the figures and determine the portion of each figure that is shaded in. In figure A, 2 out of 3 equal parts are shaded in. In figure B, 2 out of 3 equal parts are shaded in. In figure C, 1 out of 4 unequal parts are shaded in, however, it can be seen that a total of $\frac{1}{3}$ is still shaded in. Therefore, C is less shaded in than A and B.

91. The correct answer is A.
Each consecutive number in this series is increasing by 7. 58 + 7 is 65.

92. The correct answer is D.
$\frac{1}{4}$ of 36 can be found by multiplying each other, which is 9. 9 less than 9 is 0.

93. The correct answer is D.
Examine the three figures and determine the amount shaded in each figure. Figure A has 1 of 4 equal parts shaded. Figure B has 2 of 8 equal parts shaded in.. Figure C has 6 of 16 equal parts shaded. None of the answers above match these portions.

94. The correct answer is B.
$\frac{5}{9}$ of 81 is 45. 6 more than 45 is 51.
51 + 19 is 70.

95. The correct answer is C.
Set up an equation where you subtract $0.35x$, where x = the number, from $1.05x$, and equate to 35. Subtract $1.05x$ and $.35x$ to get $0.7x = 35$. Divide both sides by 0.7 to solve for x. This gives that x is 50.

ANSWER EXPLANATIONS

96. The correct answer is C.
Evaluate the statements given. Statement A is equal to -8 Statement B is equal to -16 and statement C is equal to 16. From the answer choices, only option C makes sense. The absolute value of C, which is 16 is greater than -8 which is greater than -16.

97. The correct answer is C.
The product of 4 and 9 is 36. 5 times 36 is 180. 180 + 7 is 187.

98. The correct answer is C.
Evaluate the statements given. The first statement is equal to 43.2. The second statement is equal to 30. The third statement is equal to 30. Therefore B = C < A.

99. The correct answer is D.
The triangle that can be seen in the figure is a 45-45-90 triangle. Therefore, The sides opposite to the 45 degree angles are equivalent. Since there is a rectangle in the figure, opposite sides in a rectangle are also equal. Therefore, side A and B are equal. Additionally, side C is the hypotenuse of the triangle so it is the longest side of the triangle.

100. The correct answer is C.
Each consecutive number in this series is adding one less than was added to the previous number. First 3 is added, then 2, then 1, then 0. Since the numbers added are being decreased by 1, the next number added should be -1, which when done, gives -3 as the answer.

101. The correct answer is D.
The numbers in this series go according to the pattern; add 3, subtract 2, add 3, subtract 2 and so on. The last two numbers in the series have a difference of 3, so the next number should be 2 less than the last. 108 - 2 is 106.

102. The correct answer is B.
Examine each consecutive number in this series. The pattern is to multiply by 0.6 from the previous term. Therefore, $0.1296 \cdot 0.6 = 0.07776$.

103. The correct answer is A.
$\frac{5}{8} \cdot 32 = 20$

104. The correct answer is D.
$\frac{1}{3}$ of 36 is 12. 12 multiplied by 5 is 60.

105. The correct answer is D.
Each two consecutive numbers are in roman numerals or numerals. The last two numbers was a numeral followed by a roman numeral, so the answer choice should be a roman numeral. The numbers in this series are adding 4 to each consecutive number. The last number is 21, so the next number should be 25. Therefore, answer choice D is correct.

106. The correct answer is A.
Each consecutive number in this series is being divided by 5. 4 divided by 5 is $\frac{4}{5}$ which divided by 5 is $\frac{4}{25}$ and so on. 125 times 5 is 625, so the answer is A.

286

ANSWER EXPLANATIONS

107. The correct answer is B.
Line segment BD must be greater than AB according to the dimensions of a cylinder. Line segments AB, BD, and AD make up a triangle, with segment AD being the hypotenuse. In a triangle, no one line can be longer than the sum of the other two lines. Therefore, B is correct.

108. The correct answer is A.
The numbers in this series go according to the pattern; subtract 6, add 4, subtract 6, add 4 and so on. The difference between the last two numbers is 4, so the next number needs to be 6 smaller than the previous. This gives 23.

109. The correct answer is A.
$\frac{1}{6}$ of 84 is found by multiplying the two numbers. This gives 14. 4 less than 14 is 10.

110. The correct answer is C.
The numbers in this series are repeated the amount of times as the number. 1 is repeated once, 2 is repeated twice, 3 is repeated three times. and 4 should be repeated 4 times. In the problem, 4 is repeated 3 times so one 4 is missing. The next two numbers after 4, should both be 5 as 4 has already been repeated 4 times.

111. The correct answer is A.
To find the answer, set up an equation. Let the number represent x. The equation is, $x(\frac{3}{7}) = \frac{7}{3}$. Multiply $\frac{7}{3}$ on both sides to get $\frac{9}{49}$ for x.

112. The correct answer is B.
To find the number, multiply 6 by the reciprocal of $\frac{3}{8}$, which is $\frac{8}{3}$. This gives 16. 25% of a number would be $\frac{1}{4}$ of a number, so one fourth of 16 is 4.

READING SECTION

113. The correct answer is A.
The passage discusses how fossils are formed, and how their discovery is useful to gather information of the past from these imprints. Choice A is the only answer that grasps this idea.

114. The correct answer is C.
The definition of the word *meager* is most closely related to something that is lacking in quantity. *Insignificant* is the only answer choice that is similar in meaning to this definition.

115. The correct answer is A.
The main idea of the passage discusses the formation of fossils as well as their use. Of the answer choices, only choice A represents this idea appropriately.

116. The correct answer is D.
In the introductory sentence of the passage, it is stated that fossils are the remains of animals and plants that have been buried and preserved for long periods of time.

117. The correct answer is B.
In the first sentence of the second paragraph, the author mentions that though the Great Auk and Rytina are extinct, their bones would not be considered to be fossils.

ANSWER EXPLANATIONS

118. **The correct answer is A.**
Using context clues, it can be inferred that *petrification* is somehow related to the idea of being turned to stone. *Crystallization* is the only answer choice that fits the description of the definition.

119. **The correct answer is C.**
In the final sentence of the passage, the author mentions that a great deal of important information about past plants and animals have been gathered from imprints found in fossils.

120. **The correct answer is B.**
In the third paragraph, it is stated that imprints provide information of plants and animals that were previously considered to be lost.

121. **The correct answer is A.**
When the author mentions Siberian Mammoths in the second paragraph, the example is used after the mention of that it is not essential for organisms to be replaced by another mineral to be considered a fossil.

122. **The correct answer is B.**
The passage contains a great deal of scientific information about the classification and use of fossils.

123. **The correct answer is B.**
The main idea of the passage is the United States' understanding of the German threat and its preparation to defend and react to a nuclear attack. Choice B best supports this idea.

124. **The correct answer is D.**
In the first paragraph, it is stated that German scientists informed the United States of German experiments on developing nuclear weapons.

125. **The correct answer is C.**
The author states in the first paragraph that after the warnings by German scientists, fears were confirmed in 1939 when Germany stopped sales of uranium ore.

126. **The correct answer is B.**
In both the first and second paragraph, it can be inferred that uranium is the primary cause of concern of the Germans' attempts to create nuclear weapons. In the first paragraph, it was confirmed that Germany was attempting cataclysmic bombs by preserving uranium.

127. **The correct answer is A.**
Using context clues. its can be inferred that *cataclysmic* is synonymous to dangerous. The only word that has a similar definition is *deadly*.

128. **The correct answer is A.**
In the third paragraph, it is stated that President Roosevelt appointed the S-1 Committee to determine if the United States could develop nuclear weaponry.

129. **The correct answer is C.**
As stated in the beginning of the third paragraph, the report written by the Committee for Military Application of Uranium Detonation encouraged American leaders to become more serious about nuclear weaponry.

ANSWER EXPLANATIONS

130. The correct answer is B.
In the second paragraph, it is found that plutonium-239 would provide the United State with an additional source of material for nuclear weapons.

131. The correct answer is D.
Using context clues, the word constitute most likely refers to development, as mentioned in the sentence written previously. Choice D would be the best answer.

132. The correct answer is C.
In the second paragraph, it is stated that after Germany occupied Belgium, the Belgians turned over their uranium ore to the United States.

133. The correct answer is B.
In the first half of the paragraph, the passage describes a princess that struggles to sleep under a pea due to her high sensitivity. Choice B best describes this idea.

134. The correct answer is A.
Soon after the story of the princess and the pea, the author delves into the idea of the possible psychological aspects as to why she could not sleep. This can lead the reader to assume that the story was given to introduce an idea in psychology.

135. The correct answer is D.
In the first paragraph, the author states numerous details of the princess' upbringing, including a variety of illnesses, consultation by doctors and being brought up as an only child.

136. The correct answer is A.
Using context clues based on her upbringing, it can be inferred that the princess was considered to be a very fragile individual. Choice A is the best fit for this word.

137. The correct answer is B.
The details of the first paragraph's description on the background of the princess' childhood transitions to the discussion of childhood training in the second paragraph.

138. The correct answer is A.
In the final sentence of the first paragraph, it is stated that any mental issues that are overlooked in childhood can inevitably be passed onto adult life.

139. The correct answer is A.
By substituting the answer choices with the word *insensibly*, it can be determined through process of elimination that the answer choice must be *gradually*.

140. The correct answer is C.
The end of the first paragraph discusses the importance of addressing childhood mental hygiene. The consequence would be such issues leading onto adult life.

141. The correct answer is A.
In the final sentences, it is stated that physical disturbances are linked to mental and nervous unrest. If a doctor is to check on physical issues, mental examinations must be made as well.

142. The correct answer is B.
As stated in the final paragraph, the author states that the doctor must make thorough examinations that are both physical and mental.

ANSWER EXPLANATIONS

143. The correct answer is A.
The main idea of this passage is how witches are perceived by others based on their beliefs and customs. Choice A is the best answer for this.

144. The correct answer is C.
The first paragraph discusses the witches' prayers and thanks to the Devil. Thus, it goes over their worshipping of the Devil.

145. The correct answer is A.
The word *contemporary* can be best defined as modern. *Present* would be the best word to represent the answer.

146. The correct answer is B.
In the beginning of the second paragraph, the author states that anything that could not be explained by the knowledge at hand was considered to be evil and part of the devilish arts.

147. The correct answer is A.
In the final sentence of the passage, the author mentions that the customs of witchcraft lead many to believe that it holds its proper place as an organized religion.

148. The correct answer is B.
The word *salvation* can be defined as being saved from harm or ruin. Choice B best represents this definition.

149. The correct answer is A.
The passage mostly discusses the natural environment of the American bison, and its possible effects on the area had it not been targeted by hunters.

150. The correct answer is C.
Using context clues, it can be inferred that the word *bleak* must be similar in meaning to the word inhospitable. The word choice that best fits the description is *grim*.

151. The correct answer is B.
The passage discusses the habitat of the American bison. As it does not discuss the full history of the bison, nor its scientific significance on the prairies, the passage would most likely be found in an encyclopedia.

152. The correct answer is B.
In the second paragraph, it is stated that while buffalo in the hot regions have short hair, buffalo that occupy much colder areas have longer hair. It can be inferred that bison hair grows depending on the temperature of the environment.

153. The correct answer is A.
Adapt means to make suitable for a new use or purpose. Change is a synonym.

154. The correct answer is A.
To loot means to steal goods from a place, usually during a war or riot.

155. The correct answer is C.
Alleviate means to make suffering less severe, or to relieve.

156. The correct answer is B.
To concur means to be of the same opinion or agree.

157. The correct answer is A.
Colloquial refers to language that is used in ordinary or familiar conversation. It is not formal or literary.

ANSWER EXPLANATIONS

158. The correct answer is B.
To avert means to prevent or ward off.

159. The correct answer is C.
To be ubiquitous means to be present or found everywhere, universal.

160. The correct answer is B.
To abhor means to regard with disgust and hatred.

161. The correct answer is B.
An advocate is a person who publicly supports or recommends a particular cause or policy.

162. The correct answer is B.
Contemporary means belonging to or occurring in the present; modern.

163. The correct answer is D.
To benefit means to receive an advantage or gain. Assist, help, and aid are all synonyms.

164. The correct answer is D.
Immunity means to be protected or exempt from something.

165. The correct answer is A.
To be querulous means to complain in a petulant or whining manner; argumentative.

166. The correct answer is B.
Placid means not easily upset or excited. Peaceful would be a synonym for this.

167. The correct answer is C.
To emulate means to match or imitate.

168. The correct answer is C.
Meticulous means to show great attention to detail. It means to be careful and precise.

169. The correct answer is D.
To be exempt means to be free from an obligation or liability imposed on others. Excused is a synonym.

170. The correct answer is C.
Conventional means to follow traditional forms and genres, or common.

171. The correct answer is A.
To accomplish means to complete successfully or achieve.

172. The correct answer is A.
Gullible means to be easily persuaded to believe something, or naive.

173. The correct answer is B.
To exploit means to use in an unfair or selfish way by manipulation.

174. The correct answer is B.
To ostracize means to exclude from a society or group. Banish would be a synonym for this.

MATH SECTION

175. The correct answer is C.
-1 to the fourth power is equal to $-1 \cdot -1 \cdot -1 \cdot -1$ which is equal to 1. (Any number raised to an even exponent will always result in a positive number.) -2 raised to the 3rd power is equal to -8.
$1 \cdot -8 = -8$

176. The correct answer is B.
Look at the number next to the hundredths position in the number. There is no number, so assume that there is a 0. Since 0 is less than 5, we round down. The number stays as is.

ANSWER EXPLANATIONS

177. The correct answer is A.
The first symbol asks for the union of the two sets. The union of two sets includes all numbers of both sets. The union of the sets would be {1, 3, 4, 5, 6, 9}. The second symbol asks for the intersection of the two sets; in other words, which numbers belong to both sets. The numbers in both sets are 1 and 5. Therefore, A is the right answer.

178. The correct answer is D.
The question asks for the measure of angle A. If you recall the Exterior Angle Rule of triangles, it states that the exterior angle is equal to the sum of the two non-adjacent interior angles. In this question, B and C are the two non-adjacent interior angles, and if we simply add them we will get the measure of angle A. Therefore, the measure of angle A is B + C.

179. The correct answer is A.
A polygon is any shape that is bounded by a finite number of straight line segments. A circle has infinite straight line segments.

180. The correct answer is B.
The best way to approach this problem is to use a hypothetical number.

Example: $10 \cdot \frac{1}{2} = 5$

Instead of multiplying by $\frac{1}{2}$ the question asks us to instead multiply the hypothetical number by 5 and move the decimal point. $10 \cdot 5 = 50$, however we know the answer is 5. If we move the decimal point one point to the left, we get 5.0, therefore the correct answer choice is B.

181. The correct answer is B.
The area of a circle is equal to $A = \pi r^2$. The radius is 5 and 5 squared is 25. This gives 25π.

182. The correct answer is C.
Answer choice A is true because of the distributive property, $a(b + c) = ab + ac$. Choice B is also true because fractions can be broken up with the same denominator and added as separate fractions. Choice D is true because, since dividing is equal to multiplying by the reciprocal, b dividing by c is equal to $\frac{b}{c}$. When this is multiplied by a, this gives $\frac{ab}{c}$ which can be equated to $\frac{ab}{1} \cdot \frac{1}{c}$.

$\frac{a}{b} + \frac{a}{c}$ is not the same as $\frac{a}{b} + c$, therefore answer choice C is not true.

183. The correct answer is B.
The inverse property of multiplication says that when a number is multiplied by its inverse, it equals one. The inverse of $\frac{5}{7}$ is $\frac{7}{5}$ which is equal to 1.4.

184. The correct answer is D.
The decimal 0.358 can be written as $\frac{358}{1000}$. The numerator and denominator can both be divided by 2 and simplified to $\frac{179}{500}$.

ANSWER EXPLANATIONS

185. The correct answer is C.
Since triangles ABC and DCE are similar, it also means their angles are the same making answer choice A correct. Answer choice B and C are also correct. Choice C states DE = 2 but if side AB measures 4, side DE should be greater than 4 because triangle DCE has longer lengths.

186. The correct answer is B.
The associative property says that you can add or multiply numbers no matter how they are grouped. Choice B shows multiplication of fractions in two different groups and orders.

187. The correct answer is A.
The factors of 36 are 1, 2, 3, 4, 6, 9, 12, 18, and 36. The factors of 24 are 1, 2, 3, 4, 6, 8, 12, and 24. The greatest common factor is 12 between them.

188. The correct answer is A.
This question can be solved by process of elimination. In choices B, C, and D, all the numbers can be factored further by prime numbers. 9 is divisible by 3, 51 is divisible by 3 and 17, and 153 is divisible by 3, along with other numbers. Only choice A makes sense.

189. The correct answer is A.
One nickel is equal to .05 dollars, so if he has n nickels, he has $.05n$ dollars.

190. The correct answer is C.
A square is a special form of a rectangle. A parallelogram is a special form of rectangle where opposite sides are parallel. A trapezoid has only 2 parallel sides, the other two sides intersect if continued, therefore a trapezoid cannot be a square.

191. The correct answer is B.
The square of 15 is 225 and the square of 16 is 256 so the square root of 250 lies between 15 and 16.

192. The correct answer is D.
Count the multiples of 3 between $\frac{22}{7}$ and 29.60. They are 6, 9, 12, 15, 18, 21, 24, 27. There are 8 multiples of 3 between these numbers.

193. The correct answer is C.
Simplify each of the fractions into decimal form. The first fraction simplifies to 0.8. The second fraction simplifies to repeating decimal 0.8333, the third fraction simplifies to 0.85. Therefore, choice C is correct.

194. The correct answer is B.
There are 36 inches in a yard. 4.5 yards is equal to 4.5 • 36 = 162 inches. 9 times 18 is equal to 162 yards. Therefore the ratio is 18 to 1.

195. The correct answer is D.
$33\frac{1}{3}$ % is equivalent to 0.3333, a repeating decimal. The only answer choice to have a repeating decimal is answer choice D.

196. The correct answer is A.
0 is less than 5, however answer choice A states 0 is greater than 5 which is false.

197. The correct answer is B.
$7.5 \times 10^3 = 7,500$ not 750
$7.5 \times 10^{-2} = 0.075$
$7.5 \times 10^4 = 75,000$ not 750,000
$7.5 \times 10^{-3} = 0.0075$ not 0.00075
Answer choice B is correctly written in scientific notation.

ANSWER EXPLANATIONS

198. The correct answer is C.
The first few multiples of 10 are 10, 20, 30, 40, and 50. The first multiples of 25 are 25, and 50. 50 is the least common multiple.

Problem solving questions

199. The correct answer is D.
150 • $5.25= $787.50
320 • $3.10= $992.00
$787.50 + $992.00= $1,779.50

200. The correct answer is B.
Subtract 2 on both sides to get -3x = 57. Divide by -3 on both sides to get x = -19.

201. The correct answer is C.
If Jimmy wanted to travel 3 miles total, there would be a 5 dollar charge for the first mile, 50 cents for the next mile, and 50 cents for the last mile. $5 + $0.50 + $0.50 = $6.00

202. The correct answer is B.
5 - (-3) =8
8 + -2 =6
6 - 3 = 3

203. The correct answer is C.
If Dylan paid 36 dollars for his internet, each day he spends $\frac{36}{30}$ which is $1.20 per day.

204. The correct answer is A.
Simply multiply the three fractions to get $\frac{2}{126}$. Simplify the fraction by dividing the numerator and denominator by 2 to get $\frac{1}{63}$, which is answer choice A.

205. The correct answer is B.
Set up an equation to represent the problem. Let x represent the original price of the car. The equation is 0.08x = 200. Divide 200 by 0.08 to get 2,500.

206. The correct answer is A.
The formula to find the surface area of a rectangular solid is $A = 2(wl + hl + hw)$ where w is the width, l is the length and h is the height.
$A= 2((3•5) + (2•5) + (2•3)) = 62$, answer choice A.

207. The correct answer is C.
Add across
0.32 + 6.3 = 6.62
6.62 + 0.058 = 6.678.

208. The correct answer is A.
Timothy paid $63.42 on a loan that had a simple interest of 3%. To find out how much Timothy borrowed, we can divide $63.42 by 0.03 to give us $2,114.
Another way to approach this problem, is to try each of the answer choices and multiply by 3% to see which answer choice gives us $63.42. Fortunately, in this problem, answer choices B and C can be immediately eliminated because the amount is too low and does not make sense. Hint: If you do not know how to properly set up an equation from a word problem, try to use the guess and check strategy.

ANSWER EXPLANATIONS

209. The correct answer is A.
Convert both numbers into improper fractions with the same denominator. 16 becomes $\frac{144}{9}$ and the mixed number becomes $\frac{50}{9}$.
$\frac{144}{9} - \frac{50}{9}$ is $\frac{94}{9}$. This simplifies to $10\frac{4}{9}$.

210. The correct answer is A.
For these types of problems try to set up an equation.
The equation here is $x - 15 = \frac{3}{4}x$
Add 15 to both sides of the equation to get $x = \frac{3}{4}x + 15$.
Subtract $\frac{3}{4}x$ on both sides to get $\frac{1}{4}x = 15$.
Cross multiply to get $x = 60$.
The integer is 60, therefore the correct answer choice is A.

211. The correct answer is D.
Convert each of the mixed numbers into improper fractions. The first mixed number converts to $\frac{59}{6}$. The second converts to $\frac{55}{8}$. Find the least common denominator for both 6 and 8. This is 24. Multiply the top and bottom of the first fraction by 4 and of the second fraction by 3. This gives $\frac{236}{24}$ and $\frac{165}{24}$. Subtract the two to get $\frac{71}{24}$. This simplifies to 2 and $\frac{23}{24}$ which is choice D.

212. The correct answer is C.
Plug in A = 4 and B = 7 into the equation. This gives 4(4) - 6(7) which is 16 - 42 which is -26.

213. The correct answer is B.
Set up the equation 11 • 13 = N - 7. This is 143 = N - 7.
N = 150.

214. The correct answer is C.
$$\begin{array}{r} 1143 \;\; r\, 20 \\ 37\overline{)42{,}311} \\ -37 \\ \hline 53 \\ 37 \\ \hline 161 \\ 148 \\ \hline 131 \\ 111 \\ \hline 20 \end{array}$$

215. The correct answer is D.
Set up a ratio. The ratio is the height of the shadow over the height of the object. The ratio of the man is $\frac{13}{7}$ and the ratio of the tree is $\frac{91}{x}$, where x represents the height of the tree. Set the ratios equal to each other, $\frac{13}{7} = \frac{91}{x}$. Multiply both sides by x and $\frac{7}{13}$ to isolate x. This gives $x = \frac{637}{13}$
x = 49 feet

216. The correct answer is D.
Subtract 2 on both sides to get $5x < 9x + 4$.
Subtract 9x on both sides to get $-4x < 4$.
Divide by -4 on both sides to get $x > -1$.
(Remember, when dividing by a negative number, you must flip the sign.)

ANSWER EXPLANATIONS

217. The correct answer is C.
Convert both mixed numbers into improper fractions. The first becomes $\frac{8}{3}$. The second becomes $\frac{82}{5}$. Since division is needed, multiplying by the reciprocal is possible. Dividing $\frac{82}{5}$ by $\frac{8}{3}$ is the same as multiplying $\frac{82}{5}$ by $\frac{3}{8}$. This gives $\frac{246}{40}$ which is approximately 6.15, so we can have 6 long boards in total.

218. The correct answer is A.
It is not necessary to multiply the two numbers. Simply look at the decimal positions of both numbers. Choice D cannot be correct because we are multiplying by less than 1, so the number cannot get larger. Choice B cannot be correct because it is approximately half of the first number. The number being multiplied has a first digit in the hundredths place. Choice C is not correct because if that were the answer, the first digit of the second number would need to be in the thousandths place. Choice A is correct because if 79.51 is approximated to 100, the answer would be 4.3 The closest answer choice is A.

219. The correct answer is B.
Divide by 5 on both sides to simplify to $7x - 8 = 27$. Add 8 on both sides to get $7x = 35$. Divide by 7 on both sides to get $x = 5$.

220. The correct answer is A.
Subtract $4x$ on both sides to get $11x - 6 = 60$. Add 6 on both sides to get $11x = 66$. Divide by 11 on both sides to get $x = 6$.

221. The correct answer is C.
Multiply by $\frac{8}{7}$ on both sides to isolate x. This gives $x = 64$.

222. The correct answer is D.
The sequence is adding .03 with each consecutive number.
27.41 + .03 = 27.44

223. The correct answer is B.
The volume of a rectangular prism can be found by the equation $V = l \cdot w \cdot h$. This comes out to 10 • 6 • 2 in this problem. This is equal to 120 cubic inches.

224. The correct answer is C.
There are three feet in a yard. Divide 24 and 18 by 3 to get 8 and 6 respectively. Find the area of the rug by multiplying 8 by 6 to get 48 square yards. If each square yard is 5 dollars, multiply 48 by 5 to get 240 dollars.

225. The correct answer is D.
It is seen that the digit in the ones place of both numbers is a 4 and 5. 4 times 5 is 20. The number in the ones place needs to be a 0. This eliminates choice C.
A shortcut to doing this problem would be to multiply the number in the hundreds place and onward. For the first number, it is 825 and for the second it is 504. Multiplying these two out gives 415,800. It is for certain that the number in the hundreds place is an "8" by this method, therefore, the answer is D. Alternatively, you can simply multiply the original numbers in this problem but the method listed above may save you some time.

ANSWER EXPLANATIONS

226. The correct answer is B.
If the perimeter is 34 and one of the sides is 8, find out how much the other side is. The two sides of length 8 have a total length of 16 added up. This leaves 18 for the other two sides. 18 divided by 2 is 9. The sides of the rectangle are 9 and 8, and 9 times 8 is 72.

227. The correct answer is B.
3.03 can go into 3.90 1 time. This leaves a remainder of 0.87. The next digit, 8 can be brought down and the decimal moved one spot to the right. 3.03 can go into 8.78, 2 times. This leaves a remainder of 2.72. Bring the 7 down and move the decimal one spot to the right. 3.03 can go into 27.27 exactly 9 times. Therefore, the correct answer choice is B.

228. The correct answer is A.
If Carroll is now 16, 7 years ago she was 9 years old. If her father was four times her age then, he was 36 years old. 7 years later, he would be 43 years old.

229. The correct answer is D.
Set up an equation. $x(64) = 24$. Divide by 64 on both sides to get $\frac{24}{64}$ which simplifies to $\frac{3}{8}$ which is 37.5%.

230. The correct answer is A.
To convert milligrams to grams, move the decimal place over 3 times, since milli represents 10^{-3}. This becomes 0.0215 g.

231. The correct answer is A.
Find the supplement of angle C by subtracting 140 from 180 to get 40°. Add 39 to 40 to get 79° for those two angles. The last angle added to the other two angles must equal to 180° since the addition of all angles in a triangle must add up to 180° 180 - 79 = 101.

232. The correct answer is B.
Plug in the numbers for the letters in the fraction. The fraction becomes
$$\frac{(2(7)(6)(4))}{(3(4)(7))}.$$
This becomes $\frac{336}{84}$ which simplifies to 4.

233. The correct answer is C.
If the ratio of boys to girls in a school is 1 : 4, this means that there are 4 times as many girls as boys in the school. Divide 80 by 4 and get that there are 20 boys in the school.

234. The correct answer is A.
Square both sides to get $x + 3 = 225$. Subtract 3 on both sides to get $x = 222$.

235. The correct answer is C.
Subtract 16 on both sides to get $x^2 = 121$. The square root of 121 is 11.

236. The correct answer is A.
Solve the inequality by first adding 50 to both sides. The inequality becomes $10x < 100$. Divide by 10 on both sides to get $x < 10$. The choice that satisfies this is choice A.

ANSWER EXPLANATIONS

237. The correct answer is D.
Add up the numbers 3, 4, 10, 9, and 4 to get 30 and divide that by the amount of numbers, 5, to get 6.

238. The correct answer is C.
Divide 80 by the percentage .80, to get that 80 is 80% of 100.

LANGUAGE SECTION

239. The correct answer is A.
Periods go within quotations at the end.

240. The correct answer is A.
The error is due to the relative pronoun. Danielle's sister is a female and therefore the pronoun *he* is incorrect. *He* should be replaced with she.

241. The correct answer is C.
The following sentence is not a question but rather a declarative sentence. Therefore, the question mark is incorrect.

242. The correct answer is C.
Here, the word "lied" should be "lain" since lied is part of the perfect tense and means to not tell the truth. On the other hand, lain is to sit back or recline and is also part of the perfect tense. A past participle should come after the perfect tense. Here, there is an error with the verb tense.

243. The correct answer is B.
The word grandma should be lower cased if "my" precedes it. If there is no personal possessive such as "my," then it is capital as it should have been here.

244. The correct answer is C.
A comma is necessary before the conjunction but.

245. The correct answer is C.
Here, there is an error with appropriate preposition. Instead of "associating to" it should be "associating with."

246. The correct answer is C.
This is an error in subject verb agreement. Each makes the subject singular even if it refers to multiple nouns and therefore the verb should be "was" instead of "were."

247. The correct answer is A.
The apostrophe should go after the s in the word mammals since the sentence refers to several mammals. When the subject is plural and there needs to be a distinction from singular possession. Singular apostrophes have the punctuation in between the noun and the s.

248. The correct answer is A.
There is an error in redundancy since illiterate is the same as not understanding a language well enough.

249. The correct answer is B.
Disease should not be capitalized.

250. The correct answer is B.
This is an error in subject verb agreement. Vlad makes the subject singular since it comes before the verb and therefore the verb should be "was" instead of "were." This rule applies to situations involving "Either....or..." and "Neither...nor..."

251. The correct answer is C.
All should not be capital.

ANSWER EXPLANATIONS

252. The correct answer is C.
Here, the error is with the comparison of Timothy's mindset compared to Edwin. It should have mentioned "Edwin's mindset" as a correct comparison.

253. The correct answer is B.
Here, the error is with the comparison of the hardness of cement compared to wood. It should have mentioned "wood's hardness" as a correct comparison.

254. The correct answer is B.
Here there is an error in subjective form versus objective form. Since the subject is already "I", the phrase "Between you and I" should be "Between you and me."

255. The correct answer is C.
Spanish should be capitalized.

256. The correct answer is B.
Here, the word "was" should be "is" since sees as a verb is in the present tense. Here, there is an error with the verb tense.

257. The correct answer is C.
The correct comparative form of happy is happier, not "more happy." This goes under the comparative and superlative category.

258. The correct answer is A.
Commas should go before the quotations in the starting of a dialogue.

259. The correct answer is B.
The error is due to the dangling modifier. Here, the subject or the person doing the action in the sentence is "we" and so it should come after the comma because "we" is the people doing the believing.

260. The correct answer is B.
Amendment should be capitalized since it is part of the title of an important law.

261. The correct answer is B.
This is an error in subject verb agreement. Louse makes the subject singular therefore the verb should be "is" instead of "are." Also "insects" should become "an insect." Another way to fix this is to change louse into its plural form lice.

262. The correct answer is C.
Here, the word "swam" should be "swum" since it follows the word had, which is part of the perfect tense. A past participle should come after the perfect tense. Here, there is an error with the verb tense.

263. The correct answer is A.
Here, the error is with the comparison of the hair of the sister compared to Maria. It should have mentioned "Maria's hair" as a correct comparison.

264. The correct answer is D.
No mistakes.

265. The correct answer is D.
No mistakes.

266. The correct answer is B.
There should be a comma after the word lecturer.

267. The correct answer is B.
The correct contraction is would've.

ANSWER EXPLANATIONS

268. The correct answer is A.
The correct comparative form of big is bigger, not "biggest." This goes under the comparative and superlative category and here it is comparing two things. This is why "er" should come after the adjective rather than "est."

269. The correct answer is B.
The error is due to pronoun antecedent. The cat is a singular noun and therefore the pronoun their is incorrect. It should be replaced with its/his/her.

270. The correct answer is A.
Out is part the tile and should be capitalized. Articles such as the is only capitalized at the beginning of titles.

271. The correct answer is B.
There should be a comma after trend.

272. The correct answer is C.
Here there is an error in pronoun vagueness. One cannot tell who the child refers to.

273. The correct answer is B.
A semicolon separates two independent clause and therefore the phrase after the colon makes this incorrect. The semicolon can be replaced by a colon to make the sentence correct since it is the colon that separates an independent clauses with a following expansion and has the highest freedom in terms of its use compared to other punctuations.

274. The correct answer is D.
No mistakes.

275. The correct answer is B.
A comma separates two independent clauses but it needs a conjunction such as "and." The comma can be replaced by a semicolon to make the sentence correct since it is the semicolon (or colon) that separates two independent clauses without a conjunction.

276. The correct answer is B.
There is an error with adverb and adjective mismatch. Good is an adjective, but here it should be replaced by the word well since it describes did, the verb.

277. The correct answer is C.
The verb tense is incorrect and the word less should be replaced with fewer.

278. The correct answer is A.
Principle means a rule, but it should be replaced with principal which means head master.

279. The correct answer is B.
The correct spelling is threshold.

280. The correct answer is C.
The correct spelling is Cemetery.

281. The correct answer is A.
The correct spelling is unfortunately.

282. The correct answer is A.
The correct spelling is wherever.

283. The correct answer is D.
No mistakes.

284. The correct answer is C.
The correct spelling is existence.

ANSWER EXPLANATIONS

ARGO BROTHERS

285. The correct answer is B.
The correct spelling is Pharaoh.

286. The correct answer is A.
The correct spelling is unforeseen.

287. The correct answer is D.
No mistakes.

288. The correct answer is C.
The correct spelling is surprise.

289. The correct answer is A.
The correct transition word should allow the last sentences to be a concluding result and the only word that does that is thus from the choices given.

290. The correct answer is B.
The correct transition word should allow the two sentences to be in a cause and effect relationship and the only word that does that is subsequently from the choices given.

291. The correct answer is A.
Carefully should come before the verb since it is an adverb.

292. The correct answer is D.
This sentence should be placed in active voice with no dangling modifiers. For these kind of questions, try to have a dependent clause followed by an independent clause.

293. The correct answer is C.
For these kind of questions, look for the correct punctuation from previous rules. Only the comma in the two independent clauses with the conjunction "but" makes the sentence correct.

294. The correct answer is D.
The essential idea here is how agriculture supports human growth and it is done so by the tools to increase harvesting.

295. The correct answer is D.
Answer choice D goes against the main idea.

296. The correct answer is B.
Choice B best shows how when someone is violent, there isn't success at the end.

297. The correct answer is A.
There was no mention of dominance of males in the other sentences.

298. The correct answer is B.
Instead follows right after this sentence providing a fluid transition.

TACHS
PRACTICE TESTS

ARGO BROTHERS

EXAM 1
TACHS

ARGO BROTHERS

To calculate your score and watch video tutorials, visit
our web site: www.einstein-academy.com/catholic

TACHS PRACTICE TEST 1
ANSWER SHEET

Reading (Part I)

1. Ⓐ Ⓑ Ⓒ Ⓓ
2. Ⓙ Ⓚ Ⓛ Ⓜ
3. Ⓐ Ⓑ Ⓒ Ⓓ
4. Ⓙ Ⓚ Ⓛ Ⓜ
5. Ⓐ Ⓑ Ⓒ Ⓓ
6. Ⓙ Ⓚ Ⓛ Ⓜ
7. Ⓐ Ⓑ Ⓒ Ⓓ
8. Ⓙ Ⓚ Ⓛ Ⓜ
9. Ⓐ Ⓑ Ⓒ Ⓓ
10. Ⓙ Ⓚ Ⓛ Ⓜ
11. Ⓐ Ⓑ Ⓒ Ⓓ
12. Ⓙ Ⓚ Ⓛ Ⓜ
13. Ⓐ Ⓑ Ⓒ Ⓓ
14. Ⓙ Ⓚ Ⓛ Ⓜ
15. Ⓐ Ⓑ Ⓒ Ⓓ
16. Ⓙ Ⓚ Ⓛ Ⓜ
17. Ⓐ Ⓑ Ⓒ Ⓓ
18. Ⓙ Ⓚ Ⓛ Ⓜ
19. Ⓐ Ⓑ Ⓒ Ⓓ
20. Ⓙ Ⓚ Ⓛ Ⓜ

Reading (Part I)

21. Ⓐ Ⓑ Ⓒ Ⓓ
22. Ⓙ Ⓚ Ⓛ Ⓜ
23. Ⓐ Ⓑ Ⓒ Ⓓ
24. Ⓙ Ⓚ Ⓛ Ⓜ
25. Ⓐ Ⓑ Ⓒ Ⓓ
26. Ⓙ Ⓚ Ⓛ Ⓜ
27. Ⓐ Ⓑ Ⓒ Ⓓ
28. Ⓙ Ⓚ Ⓛ Ⓜ
29. Ⓐ Ⓑ Ⓒ Ⓓ
30. Ⓙ Ⓚ Ⓛ Ⓜ
31. Ⓐ Ⓑ Ⓒ Ⓓ
32. Ⓙ Ⓚ Ⓛ Ⓜ
33. Ⓐ Ⓑ Ⓒ Ⓓ
34. Ⓙ Ⓚ Ⓛ Ⓜ
35. Ⓐ Ⓑ Ⓒ Ⓓ
36. Ⓙ Ⓚ Ⓛ Ⓜ
37. Ⓐ Ⓑ Ⓒ Ⓓ
38. Ⓙ Ⓚ Ⓛ Ⓜ
39. Ⓐ Ⓑ Ⓒ Ⓓ
40. Ⓙ Ⓚ Ⓛ Ⓜ
41. Ⓐ Ⓑ Ⓒ Ⓓ
42. Ⓙ Ⓚ Ⓛ Ⓜ
43. Ⓐ Ⓑ Ⓒ Ⓓ
44. Ⓙ Ⓚ Ⓛ Ⓜ
45. Ⓐ Ⓑ Ⓒ Ⓓ
46. Ⓙ Ⓚ Ⓛ Ⓜ
47. Ⓐ Ⓑ Ⓒ Ⓓ
48. Ⓙ Ⓚ Ⓛ Ⓜ
49. Ⓐ Ⓑ Ⓒ Ⓓ
50. Ⓙ Ⓚ Ⓛ Ⓜ

Language (Part I)

1. Ⓐ Ⓑ Ⓒ Ⓓ
2. Ⓙ Ⓚ Ⓛ Ⓜ
3. Ⓐ Ⓑ Ⓒ Ⓓ
4. Ⓙ Ⓚ Ⓛ Ⓜ
5. Ⓐ Ⓑ Ⓒ Ⓓ
6. Ⓙ Ⓚ Ⓛ Ⓜ
7. Ⓐ Ⓑ Ⓒ Ⓓ
8. Ⓙ Ⓚ Ⓛ Ⓜ
9. Ⓐ Ⓑ Ⓒ Ⓓ
10. Ⓙ Ⓚ Ⓛ Ⓜ
11. Ⓐ Ⓑ Ⓒ Ⓓ
12. Ⓙ Ⓚ Ⓛ Ⓜ
13. Ⓐ Ⓑ Ⓒ Ⓓ
14. Ⓙ Ⓚ Ⓛ Ⓜ
15. Ⓐ Ⓑ Ⓒ Ⓓ
16. Ⓙ Ⓚ Ⓛ Ⓜ
17. Ⓐ Ⓑ Ⓒ Ⓓ
18. Ⓙ Ⓚ Ⓛ Ⓜ
19. Ⓐ Ⓑ Ⓒ Ⓓ
20. Ⓙ Ⓚ Ⓛ Ⓜ
21. Ⓐ Ⓑ Ⓒ Ⓓ
22. Ⓙ Ⓚ Ⓛ Ⓜ
23. Ⓐ Ⓑ Ⓒ Ⓓ
24. Ⓙ Ⓚ Ⓛ Ⓜ
25. Ⓐ Ⓑ Ⓒ Ⓓ
26. Ⓙ Ⓚ Ⓛ Ⓜ
27. Ⓐ Ⓑ Ⓒ Ⓓ
28. Ⓙ Ⓚ Ⓛ Ⓜ
29. Ⓐ Ⓑ Ⓒ Ⓓ
30. Ⓙ Ⓚ Ⓛ Ⓜ
31. Ⓐ Ⓑ Ⓒ Ⓓ
32. Ⓙ Ⓚ Ⓛ Ⓜ
33. Ⓐ Ⓑ Ⓒ Ⓓ
34. Ⓙ Ⓚ Ⓛ Ⓜ
35. Ⓐ Ⓑ Ⓒ Ⓓ
36. Ⓙ Ⓚ Ⓛ Ⓜ
37. Ⓐ Ⓑ Ⓒ Ⓓ
38. Ⓙ Ⓚ Ⓛ Ⓜ
39. Ⓐ Ⓑ Ⓒ Ⓓ
40. Ⓙ Ⓚ Ⓛ Ⓜ

Math (Part I)

1. Ⓐ Ⓑ Ⓒ Ⓓ
2. Ⓙ Ⓚ Ⓛ Ⓜ
3. Ⓐ Ⓑ Ⓒ Ⓓ
4. Ⓙ Ⓚ Ⓛ Ⓜ
5. Ⓐ Ⓑ Ⓒ Ⓓ
6. Ⓙ Ⓚ Ⓛ Ⓜ
7. Ⓐ Ⓑ Ⓒ Ⓓ
8. Ⓙ Ⓚ Ⓛ Ⓜ
9. Ⓐ Ⓑ Ⓒ Ⓓ
10. Ⓙ Ⓚ Ⓛ Ⓜ
11. Ⓐ Ⓑ Ⓒ Ⓓ
12. Ⓙ Ⓚ Ⓛ Ⓜ
13. Ⓐ Ⓑ Ⓒ Ⓓ
14. Ⓙ Ⓚ Ⓛ Ⓜ
15. Ⓐ Ⓑ Ⓒ Ⓓ
16. Ⓙ Ⓚ Ⓛ Ⓜ
17. Ⓐ Ⓑ Ⓒ Ⓓ
18. Ⓙ Ⓚ Ⓛ Ⓜ
19. Ⓐ Ⓑ Ⓒ Ⓓ
20. Ⓙ Ⓚ Ⓛ Ⓜ
21. Ⓐ Ⓑ Ⓒ Ⓓ
22. Ⓙ Ⓚ Ⓛ Ⓜ
23. Ⓐ Ⓑ Ⓒ Ⓓ
24. Ⓙ Ⓚ Ⓛ Ⓜ
25. Ⓐ Ⓑ Ⓒ Ⓓ
26. Ⓙ Ⓚ Ⓛ Ⓜ
27. Ⓐ Ⓑ Ⓒ Ⓓ
28. Ⓙ Ⓚ Ⓛ Ⓜ
29. Ⓐ Ⓑ Ⓒ Ⓓ
30. Ⓙ Ⓚ Ⓛ Ⓜ
31. Ⓐ Ⓑ Ⓒ Ⓓ
32. Ⓙ Ⓚ Ⓛ Ⓜ

Math (Part II)

33. Ⓐ Ⓑ Ⓒ Ⓓ
34. Ⓙ Ⓚ Ⓛ Ⓜ
35. Ⓐ Ⓑ Ⓒ Ⓓ
36. Ⓙ Ⓚ Ⓛ Ⓜ
37. Ⓐ Ⓑ Ⓒ Ⓓ
38. Ⓙ Ⓚ Ⓛ Ⓜ
39. Ⓐ Ⓑ Ⓒ Ⓓ
40. Ⓙ Ⓚ Ⓛ Ⓜ
41. Ⓐ Ⓑ Ⓒ Ⓓ
42. Ⓙ Ⓚ Ⓛ Ⓜ
43. Ⓐ Ⓑ Ⓒ Ⓓ
44. Ⓙ Ⓚ Ⓛ Ⓜ
45. Ⓐ Ⓑ Ⓒ Ⓓ
46. Ⓙ Ⓚ Ⓛ Ⓜ
47. Ⓐ Ⓑ Ⓒ Ⓓ
48. Ⓙ Ⓚ Ⓛ Ⓜ
49. Ⓐ Ⓑ Ⓒ Ⓓ
50. Ⓙ Ⓚ Ⓛ Ⓜ

Language (Part II)

41. Ⓐ Ⓑ Ⓒ Ⓓ
42. Ⓙ Ⓚ Ⓛ Ⓜ
43. Ⓐ Ⓑ Ⓒ Ⓓ
44. Ⓙ Ⓚ Ⓛ Ⓜ
45. Ⓐ Ⓑ Ⓒ Ⓓ
46. Ⓙ Ⓚ Ⓛ Ⓜ
47. Ⓐ Ⓑ Ⓒ Ⓓ
48. Ⓙ Ⓚ Ⓛ Ⓜ
49. Ⓐ Ⓑ Ⓒ Ⓓ
50. Ⓙ Ⓚ Ⓛ Ⓜ

Ability (Part I)

1. Ⓐ Ⓑ Ⓒ Ⓓ
2. Ⓙ Ⓚ Ⓛ Ⓜ
3. Ⓐ Ⓑ Ⓒ Ⓓ
4. Ⓙ Ⓚ Ⓛ Ⓜ
5. Ⓐ Ⓑ Ⓒ Ⓓ
6. Ⓙ Ⓚ Ⓛ Ⓜ
7. Ⓐ Ⓑ Ⓒ Ⓓ
8. Ⓙ Ⓚ Ⓛ Ⓜ
9. Ⓐ Ⓑ Ⓒ Ⓓ
10. Ⓙ Ⓚ Ⓛ Ⓜ
11. Ⓐ Ⓑ Ⓒ Ⓓ
12. Ⓙ Ⓚ Ⓛ Ⓜ
13. Ⓐ Ⓑ Ⓒ Ⓓ
14. Ⓙ Ⓚ Ⓛ Ⓜ
15. Ⓐ Ⓑ Ⓒ Ⓓ
16. Ⓙ Ⓚ Ⓛ Ⓜ
17. Ⓐ Ⓑ Ⓒ Ⓓ
18. Ⓙ Ⓚ Ⓛ Ⓜ
19. Ⓐ Ⓑ Ⓒ Ⓓ
20. Ⓙ Ⓚ Ⓛ Ⓜ
21. Ⓐ Ⓑ Ⓒ Ⓓ
22. Ⓙ Ⓚ Ⓛ Ⓜ
23. Ⓐ Ⓑ Ⓒ Ⓓ
24. Ⓙ Ⓚ Ⓛ Ⓜ
25. Ⓐ Ⓑ Ⓒ Ⓓ
26. Ⓙ Ⓚ Ⓛ Ⓜ
27. Ⓐ Ⓑ Ⓒ Ⓓ
28. Ⓙ Ⓚ Ⓛ Ⓜ
29. Ⓐ Ⓑ Ⓒ Ⓓ
30. Ⓙ Ⓚ Ⓛ Ⓜ
31. Ⓐ Ⓑ Ⓒ Ⓓ
32. Ⓙ Ⓚ Ⓛ Ⓜ
33. Ⓐ Ⓑ Ⓒ Ⓓ
34. Ⓙ Ⓚ Ⓛ Ⓜ
35. Ⓐ Ⓑ Ⓒ Ⓓ
36. Ⓙ Ⓚ Ⓛ Ⓜ
37. Ⓐ Ⓑ Ⓒ Ⓓ
38. Ⓙ Ⓚ Ⓛ Ⓜ
39. Ⓐ Ⓑ Ⓒ Ⓓ
40. Ⓙ Ⓚ Ⓛ Ⓜ

Ability (Part II)

41. Ⓐ Ⓑ Ⓒ Ⓓ
42. Ⓙ Ⓚ Ⓛ Ⓜ
43. Ⓐ Ⓑ Ⓒ Ⓓ
44. Ⓙ Ⓚ Ⓛ Ⓜ
45. Ⓐ Ⓑ Ⓒ Ⓓ
46. Ⓙ Ⓚ Ⓛ Ⓜ
47. Ⓐ Ⓑ Ⓒ Ⓓ
48. Ⓙ Ⓚ Ⓛ Ⓜ
49. Ⓐ Ⓑ Ⓒ Ⓓ
50. Ⓙ Ⓚ Ⓛ Ⓜ

READING
PART I (10 MIN)

DIRECTIONS: In this section, you will need to determine the choice that is closest in meaning to the underlined words provided below. Pick the answer choice that fits accordingly and fill in the appropriate letter on your answer sheet.

1. A <u>miser</u>

   A. penny-pincher
   B. secret
   C. misunderstanding
   D. discovery

2. A <u>virtue</u> is a

   J. high praise
   K. decoration
   L. virus
   M. good quality

3. He has <u>vigor</u>

   A. desire
   B. strength
   C. awareness
   D. respect

4. To <u>conform</u>

   J. fit in
   K. dislike
   L. conclude
   M. disobey

5. A strong <u>advocate</u>

   A. supply
   B. supporter
   C. ruler
   D. odor

6. What a <u>meek</u> girl

   J. corrupt
   K. tired
   L. quarrelsome
   M. quiet

7. To have <u>copious</u> amounts

   A. minimal
   B. full
   C. abundant
   D. free

8. An <u>impartial</u> jury

   J. different
   K. modern
   L. vulnerable
   M. fair

CONTINUE ON TO THE NEXT PAGE ➡

READING
PART I

9. Contemporary art

   A. colorful
   B. unique
   C. ancient
   D. modern

10. A daunting message

    J. helpful
    K. clear
    L. wordy
    M. intimidating

11. To expedite the process

    A. praise
    B. use
    C. understand
    D. speed-up

12. A subtle hint

    J. indirect
    K. practical
    L. useful
    M. essential

13. A pacifist is a

    A. bully
    B. hard worker
    C. peacemaker
    D. resister

14. To embellish your home

    J. clean
    K. sell
    L. decorate
    M. purchase

15. An extraneous task

    A. difficult
    B. not essential
    C. boring
    D. obvious

16. A competent player

    J. competitive
    K. agreeable
    L. skilled
    M. terrible

17. To feel altruistic

    A. compassionate
    B. disdain
    C. unemotional
    D. secretive

18. A burgeoning of religions

    J. desecration
    K. rapid growth
    L. repealing
    M. purifying

CONTINUE ON TO THE NEXT PAGE ➡

READING
PART I

19. A <u>nefarious</u> old man

    A. corrupt
    B. depraved
    C. fiendish
    D. all of the above

20. To <u>garner</u> evidence

    J. tamper
    K. discover
    L. lose
    M. acquire

CONTINUE ON TO THE NEXT PAGE ➡

READING
PART II (25 MIN)

DIRECTIONS: Read the passages below and pick the answer choices that fit accordingly. Fill in the appropriate letter on your answer sheet.

Read the following passage and answer questions 21 - 25.

"Destruction of the Tea in Boston", otherwise known as the The Boston Tea Party, was an iconic event of the American Revolution. The action took place in defiance of the Tea Act, which the American colonist felt violated their rights of "no taxation without representation." The colonists believed they should have only been taxed by their own elected leaders, and not the British government in which their ideas were not being represented. On December 16, 1773, after a meeting, a few dozen protesting colonists dressed as Mohawk Indians boarded ships carrying the supplies and threw entire chests full of tea into the Boston Harbor, ruining the tea. Such an act of brazenness was received with quite harsh response from the British government and helped spark the aftermath events that led to the American Revolution.

21. Based on the passage, what led to the Boston Tea Party?

    A. extremely delicious tea
    B. low cost of tea
    C. unfair taxation
    D. celebration for the American Revolution

22. What would be an appropriate title for this passage?

    J. The American Revolution
    K. No Taxation Without Representation
    L. The Tea Act
    M. The Boston Tea Party

23. The author indicates that the colonists

    A. did not want representation in the British government
    B. were drunkards
    C. were unsatisfied with the British government
    D. felt apathetic towards the new taxes

24. In the passage, the word *brazenness* can be best described as

    J. cowardly
    K. orderly
    L. bold
    M. embarrassing

CONTINUE ON TO THE NEXT PAGE ➡

READING
PART II

25. What did the colonists do in protest of the Tea Act?

    A. calmly rally in front of the Boston Harbor
    B. bring Mohawk Indians to the meeting
    C. throw the tea into the water
    D. ask the British government for representation

CONTINUE ON TO THE NEXT PAGE ➡

READING
PART II

Read the following passage and answer questions 26 - 30.

Vincent van Gogh is now considered one of the most well-known artists in the world. However, such recognition was not always evident, as he has become the exemplar for the title "tortured artist." Van Gogh was born into a religious family in Holland, and held many occupations before his life as an artist, including as an art dealer and even a missionary in a coal mining company. Over time, his interest in art began to grow, and at the age of 27, van Gogh enrolled in the Academie Royale des Beaux-Arts in Belgium. The following year, he had his heart broken in Amsterdam, and began painting. He was now completely dedicated to art, studying color theory and the works of other artists. However, his paintings proved unsuccessful and were difficult to sell; many critiqued that the tone of his art was dark, the complete opposite of "Impressionism." Van Gogh decided to move to France, where he used more color in his paintings, but was still unable to sell any works. Never feeling fully appreciated after producing an estimated 900 paintings, Vincent van Gogh took his own life in 1890. Ironically, nearly two decades after his death, his art was shown across the world, influencing generations of artists.

26. According to the passage, art influenced by "Impressionism" contained

   J. underlying dark tones
   K. bright and vivid colors
   L. landscapes
   M. portraits

27. In the passage, the word *occupation* most nearly means

   A. home
   B. profession
   C. situation
   D. artstyle

28. What was a major cause for van Gogh to begin painting?

   J. his love of painting
   K. a need for fame
   L. boredom
   M. a broken heart

29. Why did van Gogh initially have trouble with his paintings?

   A. They were too dark.
   B. He was only painting portraits.
   C. They were too vivid.
   D. He was not famous enough.

CONTINUE ON TO THE NEXT PAGE ➡

READING
PART II

30. Van Gogh was known as a "tortured artist" because he was

- **J.** well-known in the industry
- **K.** in physical pain
- **L.** frustrated with his art
- **M.** lonely

READING
PART II

Read the following passage and answer questions 31 - 35.

The phenomena lightning and thunder have been the topic of conversation in many stories and mythologies. Many cultures have created gods as the personification of the forces; the Greek believed in Zeus, the lightning-bolt wielding god of the sky and thunder, while the Vikings worshipped the hammer-wielding Thor, son of Odin. But is it truly a god that throws lightning throughout the sky and deafens ears with the roar of thunder? Science says otherwise. Lightning is actually caused by positive and negative charges that grow large enough to create a spark. This usually occurs between two differently charged regions of clouds, seen by lightning in the sky, but can also occur between clouds and the ground, causing lightning strikes. Thunder claps, on the other hand, are caused by lightning. When a bolt of lightning travels to the ground, a hole in the air is opened, creating a sound wave. And why do we see lightning before we hear the thunder? Because light travels faster than sound!

31. Another word for *personification* is

    J. representation
    K. element
    L. god
    M. sound

32. The author mentioned Zeus and Thor to

    A. talk about his favorite gods
    B. explain the role they play in the weather
    C. to introduce how religion affects weather
    D. make the passage appear more interesting

33. According to the passage, thunder is caused by

    J. lightning-bolts thrown by the gods
    K. a deafening of the ears
    L. a hole in the air that is opened by lightning
    M. a person clapping really hard

34. Lightning strikes occur when

    A. there are charges between two regions of clouds
    B. people worship deities
    C. science says so
    D. there are charges between clouds and the ground

35. According to the passage, thunder is heard after lightning because

    J. they are irrelevant to one another
    K. of holes in the sky
    L. light travels slower than sound
    M. sound travels slower than light

CONTINUE ON TO THE NEXT PAGE ➡

READING PART II

40. A major component of color is

    A. darkness
    B. perception
    C. light
    D. absorption

READING
PART II

Read the following passage and answer questions 36 - 40.

The sky can be described as blue, trees as a combination of brown and green, and rocks as grey. When one looks around, color is one of the most appropriate ways to describe sight. But where do these colors come from? Most objects receive their colors from light that shines upon them. Light can be thought of as waves, and there are many various wavelengths that pertain to it. Objects reflect certain wavelengths while absorbing others. Other objects, such as the sun, produce various spectrums of light. In addition, objects that are black absorb all wavelengths of light. The key to color must then be light. In order to see an object, light must be shined on it. Think about sitting in a completely dark room. Can you distinguish the color of any object? The key to seeing colors however, is a characteristic within us. There are certain wavelengths that can be perceived, and objects reflecting the correct ones will portray the color that we then see. Those whose perceptions are limited are known to be "colorblind." However, the opposite can occur, too. There are certain animals that can see even a greater number of colors than humans. While humans see three distinct colors - and the combinations of such colors - butterflies can see five!

36. Colors are distinguished by certain wavelengths that are

   A. absorbed by the object
   B. reflected by the object
   C. chosen by the object
   D. considered correct

37. A black table

   J. emits all wavelengths
   K. can be seen in the dark
   L. reflects certain wavelengths of light
   M. absorbs all wavelengths of light

38. According to the passage, a colorblind dog cannot see certain colors because it

   A. cannot perceive certain wavelengths
   B. has poor focus of vision
   C. absorbs all colors
   D. chooses not to reflect those wavelengths

39. The word *portray* most nearly means

   J. show
   K. confuse
   L. obscure
   M. mix up

CONTINUE ON TO THE NEXT PAGE ➡

318

READING
PART II

40. A major component of color is

- **A.** darkness
- **B.** perception
- **C.** light
- **D.** absorption

READING PART II

Read the following passage and answer questions 41 - 45.

In ancient India, a social system was developed in which people were divided into different occupational groups, and has pervaded through Indian society for decades. Known in English as the caste system, the structure consists of two concepts, varna and jati. Varna, meaning color, was the groundwork of classifying people into the four social tiers: priest Brahmins, warrior Ksatriyas, tradesman Vaishyas and lower Shudras. On the other hand, jati, translated as caste or birth, is hereditary, and fixed at the time of birth. The jati system can be considered as a subset of varna, and those born in the system were restricted in their food, marriage and overall sociaizing with "jatis" of differing classes. Those considered below the caste, called the dalit or Untouchables, were ostracized and segregated to no end. Such discrimination included prohibition of eating with other classes, entering village temples, and using common village paths. The extremities also comprised of bonded labor and separate burial grounds. Fortunately, the practice of untouchability was abolished by the national constitution of India in 1950. Despite this act, prejudice against the dalits continues.

41. An appropriate title for the passage can be

    J. The History of Ancient India
    K. The Untouchables
    L. The Caste System of India
    M. Varna and Jati: Indian Society

42. The word *ostracized* can best be defined as

    A. exclusion
    B. welcoming
    C. ratification
    D. approval

43. The literal meaning of the term *jati* is

    J. color
    K. birth
    L. hereditary
    M. society

44. The dalits were discriminated for

    A. birth outside of the caste system
    B. laziness
    C. supreme power
    D. indulgence

45. The practice of untouchability is

    J. no longer an issue in India
    K. frowned upon by all
    L. continuing despite its abolishment
    M. no longer relevant

CONTINUE ON TO THE NEXT PAGE ➡

READING
PART II

Read the following passage and answer questions 46 - 50.

Hades, brother of Zeus and the Greek God of the Underworld, instantly fell in love with the beautiful Persephone when he saw her. Asking his brother for help, Hades plotted her kidnapping. One day, while Persephone was playing in a valley, she was distracted by a narcissus flower plotted there by Zeus. Running off to see the beautiful flower, she fell through a hole in the ground and was instantly transported to the Underworld. When her mother, Demeter, Goddess of Nature, noticed her daughter's disappearance, she spent nine days and nine nights searching for Persephone. When Demeter finally came to the conclusion that the God of the Underworld had indeed abducted her daughter, she begged Hades to release Persephone. With the distress of the loss of her daughter, the Goddess of Nature forwent her duties, causing most plant life to die off. Realizing the devastating effects, Zeus consulted with Hades to agree allowing Persephone to live on earth for six months every year. The seasons were associated with Persephone, for when she returned to earth, her mother was again rejoiced with happiness. Thus, the idea of the coming of Winter and Spring was born.

46. The word *abducted* most nearly means

    A. seize
    B. give up
    C. release
    D. remove

47. In order to capture Persephone, Hades

    J. plotted a flower to distract her
    K. asked Zeus for help
    L. attacked Demeter
    M. hid amongst trees

48. One of Demeter's roles as the Goddess of Nature is to

    A. tend to plant life
    B. rule the Underworld
    C. plant flowers
    D. search for Persephone

49. Hades agreed to release Persephone

    J. indefinitely
    K. after Demeter asked him nicely
    L. on the condition that she return for six months every year
    M. because she was upset

50. It can be inferred that the approach of Winter is caused by

    A. Persephone's return to her mother
    B. Demeter taking off for vacation
    C. the tilt of the Earth's rotational axis away from the sun
    D. Persephone returning to the Underworld

CONTINUE ON TO THE NEXT PAGE →

LANGUAGE
PART I (23 MIN)

DIRECTIONS: In this section, you will need to determine the errors that are found in the sentences. Pick the answer choice that highlights the mistake and fill in the appropriate letter on your answer sheet. If no mistake is present, choose the last answer choice.

Directions: Look for <u>punctuation</u> mistakes.

1. A. The boys and girls need to
   B. be told what is going on, can
   C. you let them know?
   D. *(No mistakes)*

2. J. We will not hike too far
   K. down the trail. It will get dark
   L. within a few hours.
   M. *(No mistakes)*

3. A. Once the boy received his puppy
   B. as a present he knew he would
   C. never be lonely again.
   D. *(No mistakes)*

4. J. Arnold Schwarzenegger, is mostly known
   K. for his various roles in action movies.
   L. However, *Pumping Iron* is his best film yet.
   M. *(No mistakes)*

5. A. The restaurant has run out of food
   B. once again; the owner needs to
   C. do a better job grocery shopping.
   D. *(No mistakes)*

6. J. The list of places you must visit are
   K. as follows, New York City, Los Angeles
   L. and Hollywood. You have to go there.
   M. *(No mistakes)*

7. A. Pluto is no longer considered a true
   B. planet due to its size and location in
   C. space. Actually it is now called a dwarf planet.
   D. *(No mistakes)*

8. J. Joanne really needs help with
   K. her homework? Is there no one available
   L. to tutor her at this hour?
   M. *(No mistakes)*

9. A. Henry cannot wait for Halloween this
   B. year. He will be dressing as Jack
   C. Skellington his favorite cartoon character.
   D. *(No mistakes)*

10. J. Jack tripped while climbing the hill
    K. to fetch a pail of water and began
    L. tumbling down the hill.
    M. *(No mistakes)*

CONTINUE ON TO THE NEXT PAGE ➡

322

LANGUAGE
PART I

Directions: Look for <u>spelling</u> mistakes.

11. A Johnny took a peice of that pie
    B. without asking his mother whether
    C. it was ready to be eaten.
    D. *(No mistakes)*

12. J. My brother has decided to not return
    K. there collectible cards until he is
    L. compensated for his broken toy car.
    M. *(No mistakes)*

13. A. The class has not won the arguement
    B. just yet. The teacher will not make her
    C. final decision on the test date until Friday.
    D. *(No mistakes)*

14. J. The young girl was so embarassed by
    K. her ripped dress that she ran home
    L. and cried for two hours.
    M. *(No mistakes)*

15. A. I need to you look at the test papers
    B. very closely. Please seperate them in
    C. order of grade and subject.
    D. *(No mistakes)*

16. J. Russell believed in himself as he
    K. launched off the diving board and
    L. speared into the pool below.
    M. *(No mistakes)*

17. A. The slow loris, while sporting an
    B. adorable face, is quite dangerous.
    C. Its elbows contain poison.
    D. *(No mistakes)*

18. J. Are you boys ready for the game
    K. tommorrow? You have trained for an
    L. entire season for this moment.
    M. *(No mistakes)*

19. A. They will recieve a parcel early
    B. tomorrow morning with instructions
    C. for the following day's mission.
    D. *(No mistakes)*

20. J. Continue on this path at your own
    K. leisure. New securities have been
    L. placed on the trail.
    M. *(No mistakes)*

CONTINUE ON TO THE NEXT PAGE ➡

LANGUAGE
PART I

Directions: Look for usage mistakes

21. A. He clearly misunderstood the question
    B. since he continued to squint at
    C. the one teacher.
    D. *(No mistakes)*

22. J. There are dozens of many varieties of
    K. greek yogurt being sold at the market
    L. at a bargained price now.
    M. *(No mistakes)*

23. A. When you finish your training tomorrow,
    B. you will begin to understand its true
    C. value and importance.
    D. *(No mistakes)*

24. J. As soon as the vase hit the ground,
    K. it broke, shattering into hundreds of
    L. small shards.
    M. *(No mistakes)*

25. A. Its too soon to know whether or not
    B. the choices made during last year's
    C. harvest were the correct ones.
    D. *(No mistakes)*

26. J. Honesty shall always forever be
    K. considered a great virtue, for not
    L. everyone can truly be trusted.
    M. *(No mistakes)*

27. A. We sat down and watched cautiously as
    B. the hunters picked up there weapons
    C. and set off to find the rest of the group.
    D. *(No mistakes)*

28. J. Shakespeare is considered to be one of
    K. the greatest writers of all time; his
    L. plays have been reenacted for centuries.
    M. *(No mistakes)*

29. A. Would you kindly cut the potatoes
    B. while I continue to almost prepare the
    C. rest of tonight's meal?
    D. *(No mistakes)*

30. J. Lily must never ever know about
    K. the preparations being made for her
    L. fifteenth birthday party next week.
    M. *(No mistakes)*

CONTINUE ON TO THE NEXT PAGE ➡

LANGUAGE
PART I

Direction: Look for <u>capitalization</u> mistakes.

31. A. The Fourth of July, otherwise known as
    B. independence day, is one of the most
    C. celebrated holidays in the summer.
    D. *(No mistakes)*

32. J. Julissa's current favorite read is
    K. Harper Lee's *To kill a Mockingbird*;
    L. it's Daniel's favorite, too.
    M. *(No mistakes)*

33. A. Martin Luther king, jr. is heralded as
    B. one of the most famous Civil Rights
    C. activists of his time.
    D. *(No mistakes)*

34. J. We have prepared enough food and
    K. water for any emergency that might
    L. occur on mount Everest.
    M. *(No mistakes)*

35. A. Although Vincent van Gogh is one of
    B. my favorite artists, I must say that
    C. Pablo Picasso was more talented.
    D. *(No mistakes)*

36. J. Currently the defending champion of
    K. the title "World's strongest man",
    L. Brian Shaw consumes over ten
    thousand calories.
    M. *(No mistakes)*

37. A. George Orwell has many notable novels,
    B. including, but not limited to, <u>1984</u> and
    C. his satire <u>Animal Farm</u>.
    D. *(No mistakes)*

38. J. I cannot wait to attend the "Burning Man"
    K. this year; I hear it's one of the greatest
    L. events after the Superbowl.
    M. *(No mistakes)*

39. A. while Terry was off fixing newly bought
    B. shed in the backyard, Kim decided to
    C. prepare a meal for when he finished.
    D. *(No mistakes)*

40. J. Losing all sense of control in his anger,
    K. my father yelled, "don't you ever set foot
    L. in this house, again!"
    M. *(No mistakes)*

CONTINUE ON TO THE NEXT PAGE ➡

LANGUAGE
PART II (7 MIN)

Directions: For questions 41-42, choose the best answer based on the following paragraph.

Excerpt from An Easy Introduction to the Game of Chess

(1) In chess, when a Pawn has been pushed forward into the adversary's royal line, it may be exchanged for the Queen, or any other Piece lost in the preceding part of the game. (2) As soon as a Pawn reaches any square on that line, it is to be taken off, the piece chosen placed on the square where it stood. (3) No piece, except the Knight, can pass over any Piece or Pawn. (4) The Pieces can take any of the Pieces or Pawns which stand in the line of their direction and must be placed on the square where the Piece or Pawn stands that is taken. (5) The Pawns, although they move forward, can only take Pieces or Pawns which stand on the squares diagonally before them. (6) You are not obliged to take any Piece or Pawn which is in your power but may decline it if you think proper. (7) The power of taking is reciprocal.

---

41. In sentence 2, where should the word "and" be placed?

- **A.** after "placed on the square"
- **B.** before "the piece"
- **C.** after "where"
- **D.** *(No mistakes)*

42. Which of the words in sentence 5 is an <u>adverb</u> describing?

- **J.** "although"
- **K.** "diagonally"
- **L.** "stand"
- **M.** "Pawns"

CONTINUE ON TO THE NEXT PAGE ➡

LANGUAGE
PART II

Directions: For questions 43-44, choose the best answer based on the following paragraph.

(1) The Great Famine, otherwise known as the Great Hunger, was a period of emigration in Ireland during the 1840s and 1850s due to massive starvation and spread of disease. (2) It was also known as the Irish Potato Famine, as roughly two-thirds of the population relied on the crop as their primary source of food. (3) Due to the famine, an estimated one million Irishmen perished while another million emigrated from Ireland, and that causing the population to diminish drastically. (4) The cause of the famine was found to be potato blight, a disease that destroyed potato crops throughout Europe during the time period. (5) The destruction caused by the famine acts as a catalyst for the Irish independence from the British Crown. (6) The Great Hunger is held with such significance that many experts have named the time period before the event "pre-Famine."

43. In sentence 3, which phrase should be removed?

    A. "and that"
    B. "due to"
    C. "emigrated from"
    D. *(No mistakes)*

44. Which of the words in sentence 5 is in the wrong tense?

    J. caused
    K. acts
    L. catalyst
    M. independence

CONTINUE ON TO THE NEXT PAGE ➡

LANGUAGE
PART II

Directions: For questions 45-47, choose the best answer based on the following paragraph.

(1) Halloween is one of the most celebrated holidays of the year. (2) Held annually on the last day of October, the celebration is observed by numerous countries, and is filled with amusing endeavors. (3) The activities include guising as famed fictional characters and trick-or-treating, playing pranks and carving jack-o'-lanterns from pumpkins. (4) In fact, many of these interests come from pagan traditions influenced by harvest festivals held by Celts. (5) However, Halloween has another name: "All Hallow's Eve" or "All Saints' Eve." (6) Such practices is considered to be religious observances held by Christians, and are held to dedicate the remembering of past hallows - or saints - and martyrs. (7) Practices include attending church and placing lighted candles on the graves of the departed. (8) A few also refrain from eating meat during Hallows' Eve, instead eat foods such as apples.

45. What is a <u>verb</u> used in sentence 2?

   A. "held"
   B. "last"
   C. "celebration"
   D. "amusing"

46. Which word in sentence 6 should be replaced?

   J. "such"
   K. "is"
   L. "and"
   M. "remembering"

47. What is wrong with sentence 8?

   A. wrong tense
   B. misspelled word
   C. sentence fragment
   D. *(No mistakes)*

CONTINUE ON TO THE NEXT PAGE ➡

LANGUAGE
PART II

Directions: For questions 48-50, choose the best answer based on the following paragraph.

Excerpt from House Rats and Mice

(1) The rat is the worst pest in the world. (2) From it's home among filth it visits dwellings and storerooms to pollute and destroy human food. (3) It carries bubonic plague and many other diseases fatal to man and has been responsible for more untimely deaths among human beings than all the wars of history. (4) In the United States, rats and mice each year destroys crops and other property valued at over $200 million. (5) This destruction is equivalent to the gross earnings of an army of over 200,000 men. (6) On many a farm, if the grain eaten and wasted by rats and mice could be sold, the proceeds would more than pay all the farmer's taxes. (7) The common brown rat breeds six to ten times a year and produces an average of ten young at a litter. (8) Young females breed when only three or four months old.

48. What is the <u>adjective</u> in sentence 1?

    J. "rat"
    K. "worst"
    L. "world"
    M. "pest"

49. Which word is incorrect in sentence 2?

    A. "it's"
    B. "among"
    C. "visits"
    D. *(No mistakes)*

50. What is wrong with sentence 4?

    J. the verb does not agree with the subject
    K. misspelled word
    L. adverb is used incorrectly
    M. *(No mistakes)*

CONTINUE ON TO THE NEXT PAGE ➡

MATH
PART I (33 MIN)

DIRECTIONS: Choose the answer that best fits the problem.

1. 3 - (-5) =

   A. 2
   B. -8
   C. 8
   D. -2

2. What is the greatest common factor of 12 and 18?

   J. 3
   K. 6
   L. 4
   M. 12

3. $4(3) - 4^2 =$

   A. 4
   B. -4
   C. 12
   D. 20

4. $\frac{2}{3} - \frac{1}{4} =$

   J. $\frac{1}{3}$
   K. $\frac{1}{12}$
   L. $\frac{5}{12}$
   M. $\frac{5}{15}$

5. The following chart shows how John divided his savings for his trip to New York.

   What fraction of his savings is he going to spend on hotel rent and travel?

   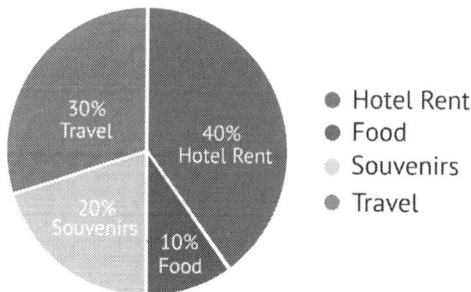

   A. $\frac{7}{10}$
   B. $\frac{1}{2}$
   C. $\frac{3}{10}$
   D. $\frac{3}{5}$

CONTINUE ON TO THE NEXT PAGE ➡

MATH
PART I

6. Which of the following is a prime number?

   J. 1
   K. 9
   L. 21
   M. 17

7. $(3)(-4)(5) =$

   A. 60
   B. 48
   C. -60
   D. -40

8. If $9 - x = 32$, then what is the value of x?

   J. 41
   K. 23
   L. -41
   M. -23

9. Find the least common multiple of 4, 12 and 15.

   A. 24
   B. 30
   C. 60
   D. 72

10. $\frac{2}{5} \div \frac{7}{10} =$

    J. $\frac{1}{5}$
    K. $\frac{4}{7}$
    L. $\frac{3}{10}$
    M. $\frac{1}{2}$

11. Evaluate $2x - 3y^2$, if $x = 3$ and $y = -2$

    A. 18
    B. 0
    C. -6
    D. 12

12. How many more marbles does Michael have than Shannon?

    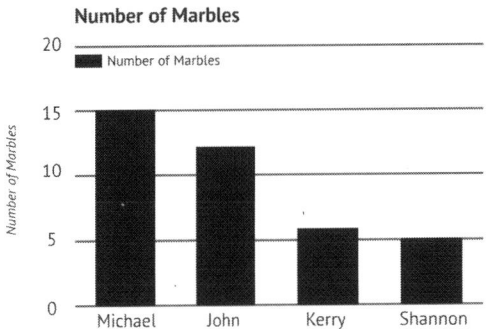

    J. 3
    K. 7
    L. 10
    M. 12

CONTINUE ON TO THE NEXT PAGE ➡

MATH
PART I

13. 62.5% =

- A. $\frac{3}{8}$
- B. $\frac{7}{10}$
- C. $\frac{5}{8}$
- D. $\frac{6}{7}$

14. A certain leather jacket went up for sale at a price of $56.14. If the discount was 30% off, what was the original price of the jacket?

- J. $16.84
- K. $39.30
- L. $187.13
- M. $80.20

15. A recipe for chocolate cake requires eight eggs for every two cups of milk added. If Justin only has 1.5 cups of milk, how many eggs must he add to bake the cake?

- A. 6
- B. 3
- C. 12
- D. 9

16. A yellow school bus can fit exactly 24 students for trips to the zoo. If there are 590 students going on the trip to the zoo, what is the least number of buses need to be rented to accommodate all of the students?

- J. 25
- K. 13
- L. 20
- M. 10

17. The following data shows the Millennium Academy school lunch menu. Ali has $20.00 and has decided to buy two sandwiches, one apple and one bag of potato chips.

How much change will he receive?

Item	Price
Sandwich	$3.50
Milk	$1.25
Apple	$0.75
Potato Chips	$1.50

- A. $9.25
- B. $13.00
- C. $10.75
- D. $11.25

CONTINUE ON TO THE NEXT PAGE ➡

MATH
PART I

18. Writer Julia Hammond has written $\frac{4}{5}$ of her new novel, *To Be Alive Again*. If she has written 728 pages, what does she expect the full length of her novel to be?

    J. 910 pages
    K. 580 pages
    L. 840 pages
    M. 950 pages

19. What is 40% of 210?

    A. 84
    B. 240
    C. 180
    D. 164

20. Which of the following is **not** a prime number?

    J. 2
    K. 13
    L. 23
    M. 39

21. The least common denominator of $\frac{3}{5}$, $\frac{1}{6}$ and $\frac{23}{50}$ is

    A. 30
    B. 100
    C. 300
    D. 3000

22. A phone call charges $2.50 for the first minute and $0.75 for each additional 30 seconds. Joe made a call that lasted nine minutes. How much will he be charged?

    J. $3.25
    K. $8.50
    L. $14.50
    M. $16.00

23. Michelle runs at an average speed of eight miles per hour. If her school is 28 miles away, and she leaves her home at 6:00am, when will she arrive to school?

    A. 9:30am
    B. 7:45am
    C. 9:00am
    D. 10:15am

CONTINUE ON TO THE NEXT PAGE ➡

MATH
PART I

24. Triangle *ABC* has side lengths of 3 and 8. What is the largest possible perimeter for the triangle if the third side is an integer?

- J. 19
- K. 14
- L. 21
- M. 24

25. Arrange the following fractions in order of greatest to least:

$$\frac{1}{3}, \frac{2}{5}, \frac{3}{8}$$

- A. $\frac{1}{3}, \frac{2}{5}, \frac{3}{8}$
- B. $\frac{1}{3}, \frac{3}{8}, \frac{2}{5}$
- C. $\frac{2}{5}, \frac{3}{8}, \frac{1}{3}$
- D. $\frac{3}{8}, \frac{2}{5}, \frac{1}{3}$

26. Merry decides to sell his collectible figures at a comic book store. He is able to sell two Darth Vader figures for $42.50 each and one Saruman figure for $8.25. After paying 20% of his sales to the owner of the store, how much does Merry take home?

- J. $93.25
- K. $74.60
- L. $85.00
- M. $111.90

27. Kim wants to buy twenty dolls. If the price of each doll is $0.72, what will be the final cost?

- A. $14.40
- B. $15.00
- C. $12.80
- D. $20.00

28. What is 0.0000000304 in scientific notation?

- J. $3.04 \cdot 10^8$
- K. $3.04 \cdot 10^{-10}$
- L. $3.04 \cdot 10^{-8}$
- M. $3.04 \cdot 10^{10}$

CONTINUE ON TO THE NEXT PAGE ➡

29. A bag contains 4 green marbles, 6 red marbles, 12 blue marbles and 3 black marbles. What is the probability of picking a blue or black marble at random?

A. $\frac{3}{25}$

B. $\frac{12}{25}$

C. $\frac{3}{5}$

D. $\frac{4}{5}$

30. The following graph depicts the final results of a questionnaire on favorite colors. If there were 48 participants, what percentage of voters chose black as their favorite color?

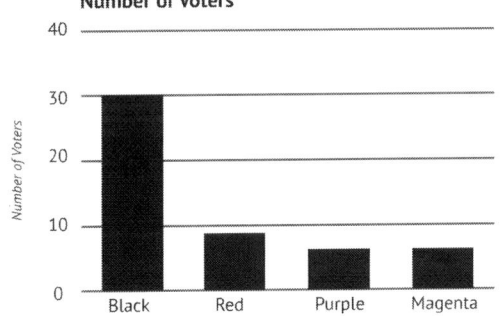

J. 75%
K. 62.5%
L. 50%
M. 75%

31. $15^2 =$

A. 30
B. 200
C. 150
D. 225

32. How many more BMWs were sold than Rolls Royce in the year 1995?

Item	1994	1995	1996	Total
Mercedes	200	150	310	660
BMW	15	310	?	468
Rolls Royce	165	?	213	420
Ferrari	52	78	90	220

J. 240
K. 268
L. 160
M. 212

MATH
PART II (7 MIN)

DIRECTIONS: In this section, you will need to estimate all your answers. There is no scratch work allowed. Do not determine exact answers. Pick the answer choice that fits accordingly and fill in the appropriate letter on your answer sheet.

33. The closest estimate of $15.89 - $12.32 is _____.

    A. $3
    B. $2
    C. $4
    D. $5

34. The closest estimate of 19.89 x 192.74 is _____.

    J. 3000
    K. 4000
    L. 3500
    M. 4500

35. The closest estimate of 5,132 + 10,978 is _____.

    A. 16,000
    B. 18,000
    C. 15,000
    D. 17,000

36. The closest estimate of 409 ÷ 12 is _____.

    J. 40
    K. 35
    L. 50
    M. 45

37. The number 99.954 rounded to the nearest hundredths place is _____.

    A. 99.94
    B. 99.00
    C. 99.95
    D. 99.90

38. The number 669.995 rounded to the nearest hundredths place is _____.

    J. 669.99
    K. 670.00
    L. 669.00
    M. 669.995

CONTINUE ON TO THE NEXT PAGE ➡

MATH
PART II

39. The number 10,003 rounded to the nearest tens is _____.

   A. 10,010
   B. 10,000
   C. 10,100
   D. 10,003

40. The closest estimate of 504 x 392 is _____.

   J. 150,000
   K. 15,000
   L. 10,000
   M. 200,000

41. The closest estimate of 72 + 19 - 109 + 52 is _____.

   A. 40
   B. 30
   C. 50
   D. 20

42. The number 6.284 rounded to the nearest tenths place is _____.

   J. 6.28
   K. 6.29
   L. 6.2
   M. 6.3

43. The closest estimate of 7,623 - 2,942 is _____.

   A. 5,000
   B. 4,000
   C. 3,500
   D. 5,500

44. The closest estimate of 105(22 - 11) is _____.

   J. 9,000
   K. 1,000
   L. 2,000
   M. 800

45. Sally drove the car at an average rate of 98 miles per hour for 111.2 hours during her road trip. Approximately how many miles did she drive her car?

   A. 9,000
   B. 10,000
   C. 8,000
   D. 12,000

CONTINUE ON TO THE NEXT PAGE ➡

MATH
PART II

46. A sale on a basket of fruit began on Monday at noon. If 9,182 baskets were sold in a matter of 11 hours, which is the closest estimate to the average number of baskets sold per hour?

- J. 800
- K. 900
- L. 1,000
- M. 1,100

47. The closest estimate of 9,186 - 4,113 is _____.

- A. 6,000
- B. 5,000
- C. 4,000
- D. 7,000

48. The number 34.995 rounded to the nearest hundredths place is _____.

- J. 35.00
- K. 34.99
- L. 34.995
- M. 35.10

49. The number 8,321.543 rounded to the nearest thousandths place is _____.

- A. 8,000.000
- B. 8,321.540
- C. 8,321.543
- D. 8,321.500

50. John originally had 3,098 cards in his collection. Jenny gave him an additional 8,923 cards. Approximately how many cards does John now own?

- J. 10,000
- K. 12,000
- L. 11,000
- M. 9,000

CONTINUE ON TO THE NEXT PAGE ➡

ABILITY
PART I (25 MIN)

ARGO BROTHERS

DIRECTIONS: In this section, you will need to recognize certain similarities. Pick the answer choice that best matches with the three shapes provided for each question and fill in the appropriate letter on your answer sheet.
TIME LIMIT: 32 minutes for the entire ability section.

CONTINUE ON TO THE NEXT PAGE ➡

339

ABILITY
PART I

5.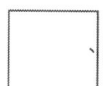

   A.   B.   C.

   D.   E.

6.

   J.   K.    L.

   M.   N.

7.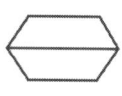

   A.   B.   C.

   D.   E.

8.

   J.    K. 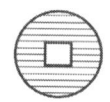   L.

   M.   N.

9.

   A.   B.   C.

   D.   E.

10.

    J.   K.   L.

    M.    N.

CONTINUE ON TO THE NEXT PAGE ➡

ABILITY
PART I

11.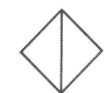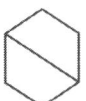

   A.  B.  C.

   D.  E.

12.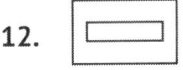

   J.   K.   L.

   M.   N.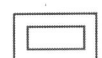

13.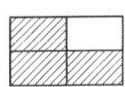

   A.   B.   C.

   D. 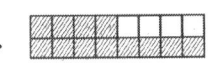 E.

14.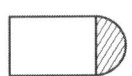

   J.  K. 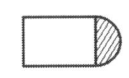 L.

   M.   N.

15.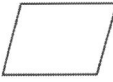

   A.  B.  C.

   D.   E.

16.

   J.   K.   L.

   M.   N.

CONTINUE ON TO THE NEXT PAGE →

ABILITY
PART I

17.

   A. B. C.

   D. E.

20.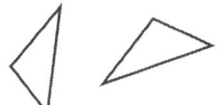

   J. K. L.

   M. N.

18.

   J. K. L.

   M. N.

19.

   A. B. C.

   D. E.

CONTINUE ON TO THE NEXT PAGE ➡

ABILITY
PART I

DIRECTIONS: There is a particular change made on the first shape to result in the second shape. Follow the same rule to determine how the third shape will change.

21.

22.

23.

24.

ABILITY
PART I

25.

    A. ◇ B. ▭ C. ▢

    D. ▭ E. ▪

26.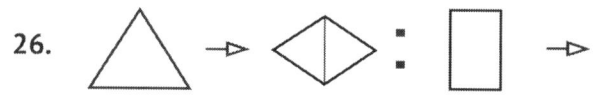

    J. ▭ K. ▯ L. ▯

    M. ▭ N. ▭

27.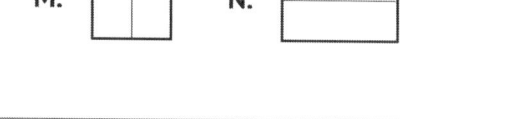

    A. △ B. ⬠ C. ⌂

    D. ◇ E. ○

28.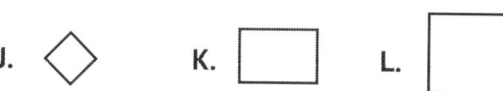

    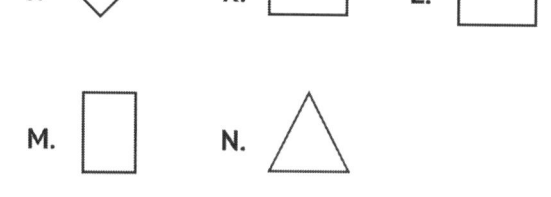

    J. ◇ K. ▭ L. ▢

    M. ▭ N. △

29.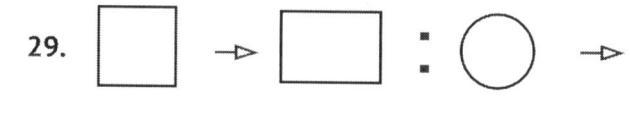

    A. ● B. ⬭ C. ⬭

    D. ▪ E. ◇

30.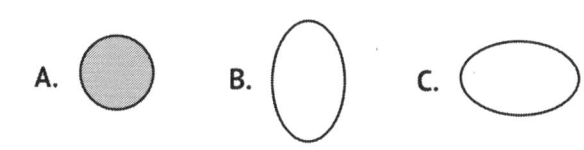

    J. ▲ K. △ L. ●

    M. ○ N. ▪

CONTINUE ON TO THE NEXT PAGE ➡

ABILITY
PART I

31.  :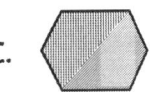

32.

33.

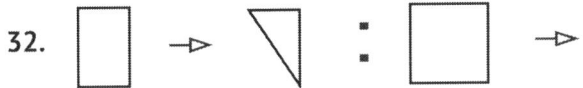

34.

35.

36.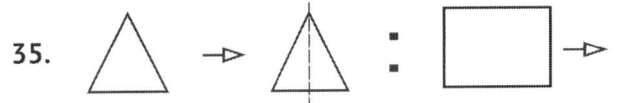

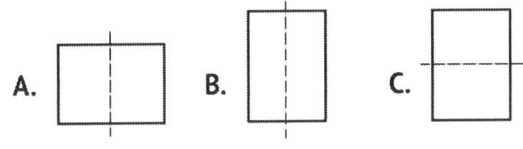

CONTINUE ON TO THE NEXT PAGE ➡

ABILITY
PART I

37.

A. B. C.

D. E.

38.

J. K. L.

M. N.

39.

A. B. C.

D. E.

40.

J. K. L.

M. N.

CONTINUE ON TO THE NEXT PAGE ➡

ABILITY
PART II (7 MIN)

DIRECTIONS: The second figure represents a change made on the first figure. What would be the resulting figure if the second figure was unfolded?

41.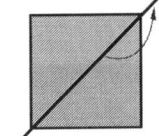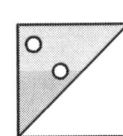

A. 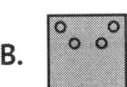 B. C.

D. 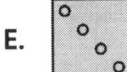 E.

42.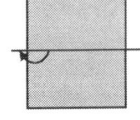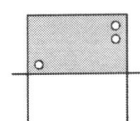

J.  K. L.

M. N.

43.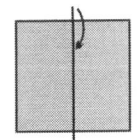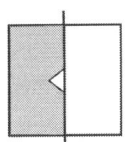

A. 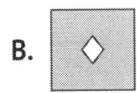 B. C.

D. 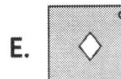 E.

44.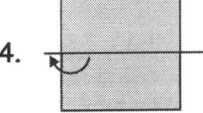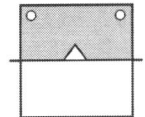

J. 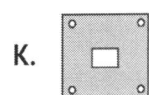 K. L.

M. 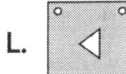 N.

CONTINUE ON TO THE NEXT PAGE ➡

ABILITY
PART II

45.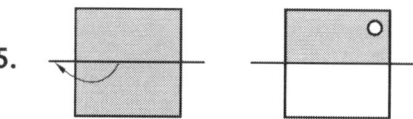

A.  B.   C.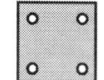

D.   E.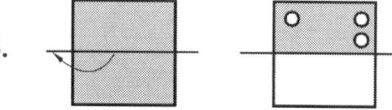

46.

J. 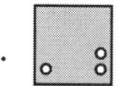 K.   L.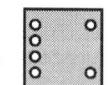

M.   N.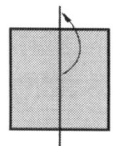

47.

A. 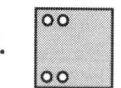 B.   C.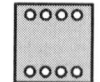

D.   E.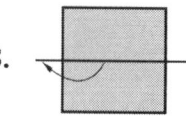

48.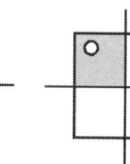

J. 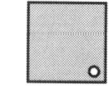 K. 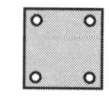 L.

M.   N.

49.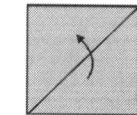

A. 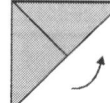 B. 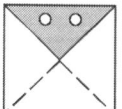 C.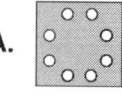

D.  E.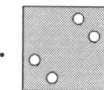

50.

J. 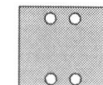 K. 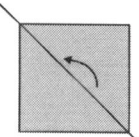 L.

M.  N.

TACHS PRACTICE TEST 1
ANSWER KEY

ENGLISH

Reading (Part I)

1. A
2. M
3. B
4. J
5. B
6. M
7. C
8. M
9. D
10. M
11. D
12. J
13. C
14. L
15. B
16. L
17. A
18. K
19. D
20. M

Reading (Part II)

21. C
22. M
23. C
24. L
25. C
26. K
27. B
28. M
29. A
30. L
31. J
32. D
33. L
34. D
35. M
36. B
37. M
38. A
39. J
40. C
41. L
42. A
43. K
44. A
45. L
46. A
47. K
48. A
49. L
50. D

Language (Part I)

1. B
2. M
3. B
4. J
5. D
6. K
7. C
8. K
9. C
10. M
11. A
12. K
13. A
14. J
15. B
16. M
17. D
18. K
19. A
20. M
21. C
22. J
23. D
24. M
25. A
26. J
27. B
28. M
29. B
30. J
31. B
32. K
33. A
34. L
35. D
36. K
37. D
38. M
39. A
40. K

Language (Part II)

41. B
42. L
43. A
44. K
45. A
46. K
47. C
48. K
49. A
50. J

ARGO BROTHERS

To calculate your score and watch video tutorials, visit our web site: www.einstein-academy.com/catholic

MATHEMATICS

Mathematics (Part I)

1. C
2. K
3. B
4. M
5. A
6. M
7. C
8. M
9. C
10. K
11. C
12. L
13. C
14. M
15. A
16. J
17. C
18. J
19. A
20. M
21. C
22. L
23. A
24. L
25. C
26. K
27. A
28. L
29. C
30. K
31. D
32. K

Mathematics (Part II)

33. C
34. K
35. A
36. J
37. C
38. K
39. B
40. M
41. B
42. M
43. A
44. K
45. B
46. J
47. B
48. J
49. C
50. K

ABILITY

Ability (Part I)

1. C
2. N
3. B
4. K
5. E
6. N
7. B
8. L
9. D
10. L
11. C
12. M
13. D
14. K
15. C
16. J
17. C
18. K
19. B
20. K
21. A
22. L
23. C
24. L
25. B
26. J
27. A
28. L
29. C
30. J
31. B
32. N
33. B
34. K
35. A
36. L
37. B
38. K
39. C
40. K

Ability (Part II)

41. E
42. L
43. B
44. J
45. A
46. L
47. D
48. K
49. C
50. K

ANSWER EXPLANATIONS

READING SECTION
The following 20 questions can be fully understood with the vocabulary section attached with the book.

1. **The correct answer is A.**
   A miser is an individual who likes to spend little money as possible. A synonym for miser would be a penny-pincher.

2. **The correct answer is M.**
   To have virtue means to have high moral standards. A synonym for virtue would be high praise or goodness.

3. **The correct answer is B.**
   To have vigor means to have strength or sturdiness, therefore, the correct answer choice is B, strength.

4. **The correct answer is J.**
   To conform is to comply or behave according to social standards. The best answer that represents the word conform is answer choice J, to fit in.

5. **The correct answer is B.**
   Someone who is an advocate is a supporter.

6. **The correct answer is M.**
   To be meek is to be quiet or gentle.

7. **The correct answer is C.**
   Synonyms of copious are abundant, plentiful and ample. Therefore, the correct answer choice is C.

8. **The correct answer is M.**
   To be impartial is to be fair and just.

9. **The correct answer is D.**
   A contemporary piece of work refers to a modern piece of work.

10. **The correct answer is M.**
    To be daunting is to be difficult or unsettling. The best answer choice that resembles the word daunting is answer choice M, intimidating.

11. **The correct answer is D.**
    To expedite something is to quicken, therefore, speed-up is the best answer choice.

12. **The correct answer is J.**
    Subtle means muted or subdued. Indirect best fits this.

13. **The correct answer is C.**
    Pacifist is a person who does not approve of violence. A peacemaker best fits this.

14. **The correct answer is L.**
    Embellish means to make more attractive. Decorate best fits this.

15. **The correct answer is B.**
    Extraneous means irrelevant. Not essential best fits this.

16. **The correct answer is L.**
    Competent means capable. Skilled best fits this.

17. **The correct answer is A.**
    Altruistic means to be selfless or kind. Compassionate best fits this.

ANSWER EXPLANATIONS

18. **The correct answer is K.**
    Burgeoning means to flourish and thrive. Rapid growth best fits this.

19. **The correct answer is D.**
    Synonyms of nefarious are corrupt, depraved and fiendish. The correct answer choice is D, all of the above.

20. **The correct answer is M.**
    Garner means to collect. Acquire best fits this.

21. **The correct answer is C.**
    The colonists felt that the taxes were unfair according to the phrase "no taxation without representation." Also the passage states that the colonists should have been only taxed by their own elected leaders.

22. **The correct answer is M.**
    The main idea of the passage involves the Boston Tea Party and the events that led up to it.

23. **The correct answer is C.**
    This answer correlates with question number 21. The answer for 21 was C which showed that the colonists "felt violated" and were unsatisfied with extra taxes.

24. **The correct answer is L.**
    If the word brazenness is replaced with boldness, the sentence makes sense. Here, it can be seen that the act of throwing tea resulted in later British hostility which means that the colonists defied the taxes. The defiance is a clear indication of boldness.

25. **The correct answer is C.**
    The Tea Act was a tax by the British. The entire passage devotes information on the

29. **The correct answer is A.**
    This can be understood from question 27 where the art critics claimed that van Gogh's paintings were too dark.

30. **The correct answer is L.**
    An understanding of the whole passage in general will help with this question. Van Gogh was never really appreciated even though he was one of the greatest artists. This can be seen near the end of the passage.

31. **The correct answer is J.**
    Again, using context clues, replace each of the choices with the word personification. Representation fits personification since religion tries to represent what lightning is.

32. **The correct answer is D.**
    From the passage above, answer choices B and C are automatically eliminated since religion does not play a role in weather. We do not know if Zeus and Thor are the author's favorite gods so answer choice D is best fit for this question.

33. **The correct answer is L.**
    The passage states that thunder claps are caused by lightning and "when a bolt of lightning travels to the ground, a hole in the air is opened."

34. **The correct answer is D.**
    Referring to lines 7-9, we can eliminate answer choice B and C. The passage states that lightning can be caused by two different charged regions of clouds, however, **lightning strikes** are only caused between the clouds and the ground. Therefore, the correct answer choice is D.

352

ANSWER EXPLANATIONS

35. The correct answer is M.
The last two lines of the passage shows this to be true. "And why do we see lightning before we hear thunder? Because light travels faster than sound!"

36. The correct answer is B.
The passage states that "most objects receive their colors from light that shines upon them." Therefore, the correct answer choice is B.

37. The correct answer is M.
The gist of the passage suggests that the color one perceives seems that way since it absorbs all other colors and reflects that one color. The passage states that "black absorb all wave lengths of light."

38. The correct answer is A.
The "key to seeing colors...is a characteristic within us. There are certain wavelengths that can be perceived." Perception here is the word that makes this answer correct.

39. The correct answer is J.
Use context clues and process of elimination. Here, a good word to replace portray is show. From the answer choices, interpret best matches show.

40. The correct answer is C.
Using question 38 and the idea of the passage in general, one can understand that the only way something is truly seen is if they is light and if we can PERCEIVE it.

41. The correct answer is L.
This is a main idea question. The passage talks about the caste system in India and its social structure.

42. The correct answer is A.
Before looking at the answer choices, find a word that replaces ostracized. In the sentence used, it should have a similar meaning to segregated, a negative connotation. Exclusion matches that from all the choices given.

43. The correct answer is K.
The passage mentions that a jati is "translated as caste or birth."

44. The correct answer is A.
The caste system was based on birth. A dali, also called an Untouchable, was "considered below the caste system." This shows that they were belittled for being outside the social standards.

45. The correct answer is L.
The last sentence provides the reasoning behind the answer to this question. The passage states: "...the practice of untouchability was abolished...despite this act, prejudice against the dalits continue."

46. The correct answer is A.
Earlier in the passage, it says that Hades was trying to kidnap Persephone. Kidnap and abducted are synonyms, so you should look for a word that means kidnap. The word seize most closely fits this.

47. The correct answer is K.
In lines 2-3 in the passage, it is said "Asking his brother for help, Hades plotted her kidnapping." Clearly, Hades needed Zeus's help to capture Persephone.

ANSWER EXPLANATIONS

48. **The correct answer is A.**
    In lines 9-10 in the passage, it states, "With the distress of her daughter, the Goddess of Nature forgoed her duties, causing most plant life to die off." The last portion of this sentence is key, because when Demeter relieved herself of her duties, the plants died. This implies that her job was to tend to plant life.

49. **The correct answer is L.**
    In lines 10-11, it is said "Zeus consulted with Hades to agree allowing Persephone to live on earth for six months of every year." This was the condition in which Persephone was allowed to return.

50. **The correct answer is D.**
    It can be inferred from the last three sentences of the passage that, while Persephone is in the Underworld, that is when Demeter doesn't take care of the plants, and when Persephone is on earth, she does take care of the plants. Winter arrives when the plants are not being taken care of and spring arrives when the plants are being taken care of.

LANGUAGE SECTION

1. **The correct answer is B.**
   Two independent clauses cannot be separated just by a comma. A semicolon here would be a better fit.

2. **The correct answer is M.**
   No mistakes.

3. **The correct answer is B.**
   A comma is necessary before "he" to separate the dependent clause from the independent clause.

4. **The correct answer is J.**
   The comma is unnecessary between the subject, Arnold Schwarzenegger, and the verb, is.

5. **The correct answer is D.**
   No mistakes.

6. **The correct answer is K.**
   After "as follows," a comma is incorrect and should be replaced with a colon since there is a list.

7. **The correct answer is C.**
   After the word actually, there should be a comma.

8. **The correct answer is K.**
   The first sentence is not a question, so to place a question mark is incorrect.

9. **The correct answer is C.**
   After the word Skellington, there should be a comma to separate out the phrase "his favorite cartoon character."

10. **The correct answer is M.**
    No mistakes.

11. **The correct answer is A.**
    The correct spelling is piece.

12. **The correct answer is K.**
    The correct spelling is their.

ANSWER EXPLANATIONS

13. **The correct answer is A.**
    The correct spelling is argument.

14. **The correct answer is J.**
    The correct spelling is embarrassed.

15. **The correct answer is B.**
    The correct spelling is separate.

16. **The correct answer is M.**
    No mistakes.

17. **The correct answer is D.**
    No mistakes.

18. **The correct answer is K.**
    The correct spelling is tomorrow.

19. **The correct answer is A.**
    The correct spelling is receive. The general rule is I before E except after C.

20. **The correct answer is M.**
    No mistakes.

21. **The correct answer is C.**
    The word "one" is unnecessary.

22. **The correct answer is J.**
    Dozens become redundant with the word varieties.

23. **The correct answer is D.**
    No mistakes.

24. **The correct answer is M.**
    No mistakes.

25. **The correct answer is A.**
    "Its" is the possessive form, which is the incorrect use. The contraction of the phrase "it is" - "it's" is the appropriate form.

26. **The correct answer is J.**
    The words "forever" and "always" are synonymous. Using both in the same context is redundant.

27. **The correct answer is B.**
    "There" should be "their" since the former indicates location and the latter indicates possession.

28. **The correct answer is M.**
    No mistakes.

29. **The correct answer is B.**
    The word "almost" is unnecessary.

30. **The correct answer is J.**
    The word "ever" is unnecessary.

31. **The correct answer is B.**
    "Independence Day" should be capitalized.

32. **The correct answer is K.**
    "Kill" is part of the title and should be capitalized. Prepositions and conjunctions on the other hand are not capitalized in the names of titles.

33. **The correct answer is A.**
    "Jr." is part of his name and should be capitalized.

34. **The correct answer is L.**
    "Mount Everest" is part of the mountain's name and should be capitalized.

35. **The correct answer is D.**
    No mistakes. Van is lower case when in between sentences.

36. **The correct answer is K.**
    "World's Strongest Man" is part of a title and should be capitalized.

ANSWER EXPLANATIONS

37. **The correct answer is D.**
    No mistakes.

38. **The correct answer is M.**
    No mistakes.

39. **The correct answer is A.**
    "While" is capitalized since it's at the beginning of a sentence.
    The beginning word of a quotation in dialogue should be capitalized and in this case it should be "don't."

40. **The correct answer is K.**
    The beginning word of a quotation in dialogue should be capitalized and in this case it should be "don't."

41. **The correct answer is B.**
    Here, the word "and" should separate the two independent clauses and the second independent clause starts with the word the "piece."

42. **The correct answer is L.**
    An adverb usually describes a verb and in this case the adverb, "diagonally," describes "stand," the verb.

43. **The correct answer is A.**
    "And that" is unnecessary and makes the sentence much easier to read.

44. **The correct answer is K.**
    The verb acts is in present tense, but the sentence itself is in past tense.

45. **The correct answer is A.**
    A verb is an action in the sentence and here it is the word held.

46. **The correct answer is K.**
    Such practices, the subject, is plural and needs to have the verb "are" after it. This is why "is" is wrong.

47. **The correct answer is C.**
    "Instead eat food such as apples" is a clause that creates a sentence fragment. The conjunction "and" should be added before the word "instead."

48. **The correct answer is K.**
    An adjective describes hey now and here the noun is animal. The word "worst" describes animal and so it is the adjective.

49. **The correct answer is A.**
    "It's" should be "its" since the contraction can be replaced with "it is", but its shows possession. The position of home must be shown through the word its.

50. **The correct answer is J.**
    The subject is rats and mice and this is plural so the correct verb should be "destroy" instead of "destroys."

MATH SECTION

1. **The correct answer is C.**
   Subtracting a negative number is the same thing as adding the positive version of the number. $3 - (-5) = 3 + 5 = 8$.

2. **The correct answer is K.**
   6 is the highest number which can be divided from 18 and 12.

3. **The correct answer is B.**
   $= 4(3) - 4^2$
   $= 4(3) - 16$
   $= 12 - 16$
   $= -4$

ANSWER EXPLANATIONS

4. **The correct answer is M.**
   The least common denominator of 3 and 4 is 12.
   $$\frac{2}{3} - \frac{1}{4} = \frac{8}{12} - \frac{3}{12} = \frac{5}{12}$$

5. **The correct answer is A.**
   The total percentage for hotel rent and travel is 40% + 30% = 70%. 70% is the equivalent of 70 out of 100 which is also $\frac{70}{100}$. This simplified gives $\frac{7}{10}$.

6. **The correct answer is M.**
   The number 1 is neither prime nor composite. Since 9 and 21 have a factor of 3 which is not one or itself, they are both composite. This leaves us with 17.

7. **The correct answer is C.**
   3 • -4 = -12. -12 • 5 = -60.

8. **The correct answer is M.**
   Subtract 9 from both sides and then divide by -1 in front of the x.
   9 - x = 32
   - x = 23
   x = -23

9. **The correct answer is C.**
   60 is the smallest number that has factors of 4, 12, and 15.

10. **The correct answer is K.**
    When dividing fractions, switch the division to multiplication and flip the fraction on the right side of the division sign. The new operation is $\frac{2}{5} \cdot \frac{10}{7} = \frac{20}{35}$.
    When simplified, the result is $\frac{4}{7}$.

11. **The correct answer is C.**
    Plug in the values to get 2(3) - 3(-2)2. By following PEMDAS, you should get 2(3) - 3(4) = 6 - 12 = -6.

12. **The correct answer is L.**
    Michael has 15 marbles and Shannon has 5 marbles. The difference is 10 marbles.

13. **The correct answer is C.**
    62.5% = $\frac{62.5}{100}$. However, decimals are not allowed in simplest terms in a fraction. Multiply top and bottom by 10 to get $\frac{625}{1000}$. By dividing by 25 and then by 5, one gets $\frac{5}{8}$.

14. **The correct answer is M.**
    If the discount was 30% off, one has to pay 70% of the jacket. One can use a proportion $\frac{70}{100} = \frac{\$56.14}{x}$ and solve for x, the original cost. By cross multiplying and isolating x, you get $80.20. The easier way is to do this is $56.14 ÷ 0.70 = $80.20.

15. **The correct answer is A.**
    One can use a proportion $\frac{8}{2} = \frac{x}{1.5}$ and solve for x, the number of eggs needed 1.5 cups of milk. By cross multiplying and isolating x, one will get 6.

ANSWER EXPLANATIONS

16. The correct answer is J.
To find how many buses are needed for all the students, do 590 ÷ 24. This gives 24 with some remainder. The remaining students will need an extra bus so the answer is 25.

17. The correct answer is C.
The total cost of the items that Ali purchased is 2($3.50) + $0.75 + $1.50 = $9.25. The change can be determined by subtracting this value from $20.00 and this gives $10.75.

18. The correct answer is J.
One can use a proportion $\frac{4}{5} = \frac{728}{x}$ and solve for x, the total. By cross multiplying and isolating x, you get 910 pages. The easier way is to do this is 728 ÷ 0.8 = 910.

19. The correct answer is A.
One can use a proportion, but easiest way is to do 40% of 120 = 0.40 × 210 = 84. "Of" means to multiply.

20. The correct answer is M.
A prime number only has factor of one and itself. 39 is composite (opposite of prime) since it can be divided by 3 and 13.

21. The correct answer is C.
300 is the lowest number which has 6, 5, and 50 as its factors.

22. The correct answer is L.
Since the initial minute is paid for by $2.50, the rate charge only applies to 8 minutes. There are two 30 second intervals in every minute when the $0.75 rate is charged.
= $2.50 + (9 - 1)(2)($0.75)
= $2.50 + (8)(2)($0.75)
= $2.50 + $12.00
= $14.50

23. The correct answer is A.
Using distance equals rate times time, the number of hours it took Michelle to run can be determined. Since then rate is 8 mph and the distance is 28 miles, the hours of commute is $\frac{28}{8}$ = 3.5 hours. This is also 3 hour and 30 min and when added to 6:00 a.m. generates 9:30 a.m.

24. The correct answer is L.
For all triangles, the third side must be smaller than the sum and larger than the difference of the other two sides. So, the third side must be less than 11, but bigger than 5. In order to have the largest possible perimeter, the possible side must be chosen. The integer 10 maximizes the perimeter. 8 + 3 + 10 = 21.

25. The correct answer is C.
Looking back at the fraction, decimal and per centage conversion chart, $\frac{1}{3}$ = 0.333, $\frac{2}{5}$ = 0.400, $\frac{3}{8}$ = 0.375. The decimal values in order of least to greatest is 0.333, 0.400, 0.375.

26. The correct answer is K.
The total profit of the toy is 2($42.50) + $8.25. However, Merry makes 80% of the profit since he sells it through a store owner for 20%. That is 0.8 • $93.25 = $74.60.

27. The correct answer is A.
Since Kim is buying 20 dolls and each dog is $0.72, multiply to get $14.40.

ANSWER EXPLANATIONS

28. The correct answer is L.
The number of spaces needed to move the decimal to the right of 3 is eight. Since the number is less than 1, the exponent should be negative 8. Remember that the mantissa has to be in between 1 and 10 (3.04).

29. The correct answer is C.
The concept in this problem tests probability. Whenever there is an "or" in probability, it signifies to add the two chances together. The probability of picking blue and black together is 15 out of 25 because there are 15 blue and black marbles together out of 25 the total number of marbles. This simplified gives $\frac{3}{5}$.

30. The correct answer is K.
30 have chosen black out of 48 total. The fraction simplified with the division done properly gives a value of 0.625. This turned to a percent is 62.5%. The problem can also be done through proportion where the total is represented by 100: $\frac{30}{48} = \frac{x}{100}$ and $x = 62.5$.

31. The correct answer is D.
15 squared is 15 times 15 which equals 225.

32. The correct answer is K.
The number of cars for Rolls Royce in 1995 is missing. To find this, add all the years of the Rolls Royce and subtract this from the total number of Rolls Royce. This is $420 - (165 + 213) = 42$. Then subtract this from 310 to get 268.

33. The correct answer is C.
Round each of these values to the nearest dollar. This makes the new difference $16 - $12 = $4.

34. The correct answer is K.
Round the operation to $20 \cdot 190 = 3,800$. The closest answer is 4,000.

35. The correct answer is A.
Round each of these values to the nearest thousand. This makes the new addition $5,000 + 11,000 = 16,000$.

36. The correct answer is J.
Round the number 409 to 400 and the number 12 to 10.
$$\frac{400}{10} = 40$$

37. The correct answer is C.
Here, 5 is in the hundredths place. The number to the right of it is 4 which means the 5 should remain with 4 becoming dropped to zero.

38. The correct answer is K.
Here, the 9 to the right is in the hundredths place. The number to the right of it is 5 which means the 9 should go up. Since 9 goes up to 10, it rounds the 9 to the left up to 10, and this happens until the 6 in the tens place then rounds to 7.

ANSWER EXPLANATIONS

39. **The correct answer is B.**
    Here, the rightmost 0 is in the tens place. The number to the right of it is 3 which means the 0 should remain with 3 becoming dropped to zero.

40. **The correct answer is M.**
    Round each of these values to the nearest hundred. This makes the new multiplication 500 • 400 = 200,000.

41. **The correct answer is B.**
    Round each of these values to the nearest tens. This makes the new operation 70 + 20 - 110 + 50 = 30.

42. **The correct answer is M.**
    Here, 8 is in the tenths place. The number to the right of it is 4 which means the 8 should remain with 4 becoming dropped to zero.

43. **The correct answer is A.**
    Based on the answers provided, round the numbers to the closest thousands place. This makes the new operation 8,000 - 3,000 = 5,000.

44. **The correct answer is K.**
    22-11 is 11. Round to 10 and multiply by 100, which is 105 rounded to the nearest hundred. This gives 1,000.

45. **The correct answer is B.**
    This can be solved by understanding the formula distance equals rate times time. The problem gives us the time traveled and the rate so we multiply. Rounding each to the nearest hundred and multiplying gives choice B.

46. **The correct answer is J.**
    The term "per" indicates division. Here, one has to round carefully by paying attention to how the values are rounded. If one rounds the operation to 9,000 ÷ 10 the answer is 900. But notice the that the drop from 11 to 10 was much more of a significant change than the the drop from the 9,182 to 9,000. So the answer should be smaller which is choice J.

47. **The correct answer is B.**
    Round each of these values to the nearest thousand. This makes the new difference 9,000 - 4,000 = 5,000.

48. **The correct answer is J.**
    Here, the 9 to the right is in the hundredths place. The number to the right of it is 5 which means the 9 should go up. Since 9 goes up to 10, it rounds the 9 to the left up to 10, and this then rounds the 4 to 5.

49. **The correct answer is C.**
    The number to the right of 3, which is in the thousandths place is 0. Since it is 0, leave the number as is.

50. **The correct answer is K.**
    John had a certain amount of cards and received more cards so addition is involved. All of the multiple choice answers have a value at the thousands place, so round the numbers given to the nearest thousand. This makes the operation 3,000 + 9,000 = 12,000.

ANSWER EXPLANATIONS

ABILITY SECTION

1. **The correct answer choice is C.**
   All three figures have five sides.

2. **The correct answer choice is N.**
   All three figures have only straight sides.

3. **The correct answer choice is B.**
   All three figures have only straight sides and are surrounded by a diagonally shaded border facing the same direction.

4. **The correct answer choice is K.**
   All three figures are shaded horizontally.

5. **The correct answer choice is E.**
   All three figures are perfect polygons.

6. **The correct answer choice is N.**
   The figures are increasing in the number of sides by one.

7. **The correct answer choice is B.**
   All three figures contain a bisecting line (cuts the shape in half).

8. **The correct answer choice is L.**
   All three figures are shaded horizontally with a non-shaded diamond figure in the center.

9. **The correct answer choice is D.**
   All three figures have one small circle attached to a vertex.

10. **The correct answer choice is L.**
    All three figures contain either a horizontally or vertically centered oval.

11. **The correct answer choice is C.**
    All three figures contain a bisecting line (cuts the shape in half).

12. **The correct answer choice is M.**
    All three figures contain a smaller similar figure in their centers.

13. **The correct answer choice is D.**
    All three figures are shaded three-fourths of the way.

14. **The correct answer choice is K.**
    All three figures contain one semi-circle that is shaded in diagonally in the same direction. Answer J is shaded in the wrong direction.

15. **The correct answer choice is C.**
    All three figures have only straight sides.

16. **The correct answer choice is J.**
    All three figures have only curved edges.

17. **The correct answer choice is C.**
    All three figures have six sides.

18. **The correct answer choice is K.**
    All three figures have shaded figures that have one less side than the original figure.

19. **The correct answer choice is B.**
    All three figures are solid polygons that are broken into equal pieces.

20. **The correct answer choice is K.**
    All three figures are scalene triangles.

21. **The correct answer choice is A.**
    The first figure increased its number of sides by one.

22. **The correct answer choice is L.**
    The first figure added a solid shaded circle to its center.

ANSWER EXPLANATIONS

23. **The correct answer choice is C.**
    The first figure added a diagonal and fully shaded the top half.

24. **The correct answer choice is L.**
    The first figure added a vertical line through its center and was flipped horizontally.

25. **The correct answer choice is B.**
    The first figure was rotated clockwise by 90°.

26. **The correct answer choice is J.**
    The first figure was rotated counter-clockwise by 90° and was attached to its mirror image.

27. **The correct answer choice is A.**
    The first figure decreased its total number of sides by 1.

28. **The correct answer choice is L.**
    The first figure was bisected and rotated clockwise by 90°.

29. **The correct answer choice is C.**
    The first figure was stretched horizontally.

30. The first figure removed the outer shape.
    The correct answer choice is J.

31. The first figure was shaded a solid color.
    The correct answer choice is B.

32. **The correct answer choice is N.**
    The first figure was bisected diagonally.

33. **The correct answer choice is B.**
    The first figure was bisected horizontally, and reflected. The top half was shaded vertically and the bottom half was shaded a solid color.

34. **The correct answer choice is K.**
    The first figure decreased its total number of sides by 2.

35. **The correct answer choice is A.**
    A vertical dotted line was drawn through the center of the first figure.

36. **The correct answer choice is L.**
    Two diagonal lines were drawn through the first figure.

37. **The correct answer choice is B.**
    The first figure was changed into its perfect polygon form.

38. **The correct answer choice is K.**
    A triangle was added to the right side of the first figure.

39. **The correct answer choice is C.**
    The first figure was reflected horizontally and shaded in.

40. **The correct answer choice is K.**
    The first figure was reflected diagonally and was shaded vertically.

41. The correct answer choice is E.
42. The correct answer choice is L.
43. The correct answer choice is B.
44. The correct answer choice is J.
45. The correct answer choice is A.
46. The correct answer choice is L.
47. The correct answer choice is D.
48. The correct answer choice is K.
49. The correct answer choice is C.
50. **The correct answer choice is K.**

EXAM 2
TACHS

ARGO BROTHERS

To calculate your score and watch video tutorials, visit our web site: www.einstein-academy.com/catholic

READING
PART I (10 MIN)

DIRECTIONS: In this section, you will need to determine the choice that is closest in meaning to the underlined words provided below. Pick the answer choice that fits accordingly and fill in the appropriate letter on your answer sheet.

1. A reproachful person

   A. unique
   B. disapproving
   C. cunning
   D. arrogant

2. To greatly benefit

   J. help
   K. aid
   L. assist
   M. all the above

3. Remnants of war

   A. soldiers
   B. weapons
   C. exclusions
   D. remainders

4. An edible plant

   J. green
   K. tall
   L. eatable
   M. carnivorous

5. A candid statement

   A. bland
   B. false
   C. honest
   D. dispensable

6. To cleave

   J. clean
   K. push
   L. cut
   M. sleep

7. A great advocate

   A. leader
   B. teacher
   C. supporter
   D. opponent

8. A recurrent theme

   J. deceptive
   K. valuable
   L. reappearing
   M. uncommon

CONTINUE ON TO THE NEXT PAGE ➡

READING
PART I

9. Trite remark

   A. banal
   B. common
   C. cliche
   D. all of the above

10. To coalesce quickly

    J. aggregate
    K. burn
    L. spread
    M. submerge

11. The dynamic character

    A. suspenseful
    B. dramatic
    C. changing
    D. brave

12. An antithetical opinion

    J. argumentative
    K. opposite
    L. justifiable
    M. rhetorical

13. Significant studies

    A. important
    B. esoteric
    C. formidable
    D. all of the above

14. A relentless battle

    J. peaceful
    K. dangerous
    L. continuous
    M. temporary

15. To have immunity

    A. strength
    B. willpower
    C. clarity
    D. resistance

16. To be sophisticated

    J. special
    K. advanced
    L. extricate
    M. resourceful

17. An antiquated book

    A. outdated
    B. informational
    C. opinionated
    D. extravagant

18. The avaricious lion

    J. hungry
    K. enormous
    L. malicious
    M. greedy

CONTINUE ON TO THE NEXT PAGE ➡

READING
PART I

19. It is <u>crucial</u>

    A. essential
    B. significant
    C. important
    D. all of the above

---

20. <u>Querulous</u> couples

    J. argumentative
    K. talkative
    L. perfect
    M. wholesome

READING
PART II (25 MIN)

DIRECTIONS: Read the passages below and pick the answer choices that fit accordingly. Fill in the appropriate letter on your answer sheet.

Read the following passage and answer questions 21 - 25.

Excerpt from An Introduction to Astronomy

The present age is known as the age of science. Never before have so many men been actively engaged in the pursuit of science, and never before have its results contributed so enormously to the ordinary affairs of life. If all its present-day applications were suddenly and for a considerable time removed, the results would be disastrous. With the stopping of trains and steamboats, the food supply in cities would soon fail, and there would be no fuel with which to heat the buildings. Water could no longer be pumped, and devastating fires might follow. If people escaped to the country, they would perish in large numbers because without modern machinery not enough food could be raised to supply the population. In fact, the more the subject is considered, the more clearly it is seen that at the present time the lives of civilized men are in a thousand ways directly dependent on the things produced by science.

---

21. What would be an appropriate title for this passage?

    A. Science
    B. Technology: The Uses of Science
    C. Civilization and Water
    D. Disaster Strikes

22. Which of the following is another example the author would use to describe his point?

    J. Without water, the crops would all die.
    K. If there were no refrigerators, gathered supplies of foods would spoil.
    L. If cars were not invented, people would have to walk to work.
    M. With no television, people would become bored.

23. The word *perish* can best be described as

    A. preserve
    B. grow
    C. wither
    D. revive

24. The author would agree that science

    J. is important in changing the way humankind faces nature
    K. is not an important aspect of civilization
    L. is helpful, but not needed
    M. causes destruction

CONTINUE ON TO THE NEXT PAGE ➡

READING
PART II

25. It can be assumed that without the use of machinery

   A. mankind would not have progressed as far
   B. people would simply gather more food
   C. there would be no change
   D. life would be comfortable

CONTINUE ON TO THE NEXT PAGE ➡

READING
PART II

Read the following passage and answer questions 26 - 30.

Excerpt from The Automobilist Abroad

We have progressed appreciably beyond the days of the old horseless carriage, which, it will be remembered, retained even the dashboard. The control of a restive horse, a cranky boat, or even a trolley-car on rails is difficult enough for the inexperienced, and there are many who would quail before making the attempt. But to the novice in charge of an automobile, some serious damage is likely enough to occur within an incredibly short space of time, particularly if he does not take into account the tremendous force and power which he controls merely by the moving of a tiny lever, or by the depressing of a pedal. There are those who doubt the utility of the automobile, as there have been scoffers at most new things under the sun; and there have been critics who have derided it for its "seven deadlysins," as there have been others who have praised its "Christian graces." A motor-car is a fearsome thing - when it goes, it goes, and when it doesn't, something, or many things, are wrong. However, everyone remembers what a weirdly ungraceful thing the first safety bicycle was. So, too, is the gaudy painted-up early locomotive.

26. It can be assumed that the author feels that automobiles are

   J. unnecessary
   K. a new technology to be appreciated
   L. dangerous
   M. useless

27. Controlling a horse, boat or trolly-car is

   A. far more difficult than an automobile
   B. more fun
   C. underappreciated
   D. easier than driving cars

28. In the passage, the word *retained* most nearly means

   J. disregarded
   K. recalled
   L. lost
   M. needed

29. The general views on the use of automobiles are

   A. misleading
   B. positive
   C. negative
   D. evenly matched

CONTINUE ON TO THE NEXT PAGE →

READING
PART II

30. The bicycle is mentioned at the end of the passage to

  J. give an example of something that was once doubted
  K. bring an alternative method of transportation
  L. express the author's love for biking
  M. denounce the use of automobiles

READING
PART II

Read the following passage and answer questions 31 - 35.

Excerpt from The Human Side of Animals

The art of concealment or camouflage is one of the newest and most highly developed techniques of modern warfare. But the animals have been masters of it for ages. The lives of most of them are passed in constant conflict. Those which have enemies from which they cannot escape by rapidity of motion must be able to hide or disguise themselves. Those which hunt for a living must be able to approach their prey without unnecessary noise or attention to themselves. It is very remarkable how Nature helps the wild creatures to disguise themselves by colouring them with various shades and tints best calculated to enable them to escape enemies or to entrap prey. In the art of camouflage—an art which affects the form, colour, and attitude of animals—Nature has worked along two different roads. One is easy and direct, the other circuitous and difficult. The easy way is that of protective resemblance is pure and simple, where the animal's colour, form, or attitude becomes like that of its habitat. In which case the animal becomes one with its environment and thus is enabled to go about unnoticed by its enemies or by its prey. The other way is that of bluff, and it includes all inoffensive animals which are capable of assuming attitudes and colours that terrify and frighten.

---

31. According to the passage, animals use camouflage to

A. hide or disguise themselves
B. play tricks on humans
C. climb up trees
D. gather fruit

32. An example of "protective resemblance" would be

J. sharks using the scent of blood to find their prey
K. a brown moth sitting on a tree trunk
L. a zebra hiding underwater
M. a bear waiting in a cave

33. An example of "bluff" camouflage would be

A. a rattlesnake using its poisonous fangs
B. a porcupine's needles
C. a chameleon blending into the grass
D. a man wearing a bear suit to scare off dogs

34. An appropriate title for this passage would be

J. Hiding in Nature
K. The Art of Protection
L. Changing Colors
M. Survival of the Fittest

CONTINUE ON TO THE NEXT PAGE ➡

READING
PART II

35. From the passage, the word *circuitous* most nearly means

   A. straightforward
   B. indirect
   C. simple
   D. sincere

READING
PART II

Read the following passage and answer questions 36 - 40.

Excerpt from <u>Beethoven</u>

If Bach is the mathematician of music, as it has been understood, Beethoven is its philosopher. In his work the philosophic spirit comes to the front. In his music, Beethoven adds a wide mental grasp, an altruistic spirit, that seeks to help humanity on the upward path. He addresses the intellect of mankind. Up to Beethoven's time musicians in general (Bach is always an exception) performed their work without the aid of an intellect for the most part; they worked by intuition. In everything outside their art they were like children. Beethoven was the first one having the independence to think for himself—the first to have ideas on subjects unconnected with his art. It was he who established the dignity of the artist over that of the simply well-born. His entire life was a protest against the pretensions of birth over mind. His predecessors, to a great extent subjugated by their social superiors, sought only to please. Nothing further was expected of them. This mental attitude is apparent in their work. The language of the courtier is usually polished, but will never have the virility that characterizes the speech of the free man. As with all valuable things, however, Beethoven's music is not to be enjoyed for nothing.

---

36. From the passage, the word *intuition* most nearly means

    J. instinct
    K. intellect
    L. guile
    M. perception

37. The author first mentions Bach in the beginning of the passage to

    A. commend the better musician
    B. offer a comparison of two famous artists
    C. explain why Beethoven is better
    D. show his distaste for the artist's music

38. Beethoven was able to stand out due to his ability to

    J. use intuition in his music
    K. think for himself
    L. copy the works of Bach
    M. speak up against intellectuals

39. The word *predecessors* in this passage refers to

    A. previous artists
    B. Beethoven's parents
    C. independent thinkers
    D. philosophers

CONTINUE ON TO THE NEXT PAGE ➡

40. It can be implied that Beethoven wrote his music to

- **J.** only please listeners
- **K.** bring a deeper understanding to his work
- **L.** compete with other musicians
- **M.** generate fame

READING
PART II

Read the following passage and answer questions 41 - 45.

Excerpt from Myths and Legends of Ancient Greece and Rome

Before entering upon the many strange beliefs of the ancient Greeks, and the extraordinary number of gods they worshipped, we must first consider what kind of beings these divinities were. In appearance, the gods were supposed to resemble mortals, whom they far surpassed in beauty, grandeur, and strength. They were also more commanding in stature, height being considered by the Greeks an attribute of beauty in man or woman. They resembled human beings in their feelings and habits, intermarrying and having children, and requiring daily nourishment to recruit their strength, and refreshing sleep to restore their energies. Their blood, a bright ethereal fluid called Ichor, never caused disease, and, when shed, had the power of producing new life. The Greeks believed that the mental qualifications of their gods were of a much higher order than those of men, but nevertheless, as we shall see, they were not considered to be exempt from human passions, and we frequently behold them actuated by revenge, deceit, and jealousy. They, however, always punish the evil-doer, and visit with dire calamities any immoral mortal who dares to neglect their worship or despise their rites.

41. The best title for this passage would be

   A. Greek Mythology
   B. Understanding Greek Gods
   C. Worshipping Deities in Ancient Times
   D. The Immortals

42. The Greek gods resembled

   J. a perfect version of humans
   K. incomprehensible beings
   L. monsters
   M. humans with higher qualities

43. The gods described in the passage would never

   A. marry and have children
   B. be jealous of others
   C. die from disease
   D. punish those they opposed

44. In the passage, the word *nourishment* most nearly means

   J. worship
   K. food
   L. starvation
   M. supplies

CONTINUE ON TO THE NEXT PAGE ➡

READING
PART II

45. It is implied that the Greeks worshipped gods that were considered to be

- **A.** flawless
- **B.** corrupt
- **C.** personal
- **D.** ordinary

READING
PART II

Read the following passage and answer questions 46 - 50.

Sandwiches may be made from one of three or four kinds of bread; whole wheat bread, Boston brown or oatmeal bread, white bread and rye bread made into square, deep loaves; in fact, all bread used for sandwiches should be made especially for the purpose, so that the slices may be in good form, and sufficiently large to cut into fancy shapes. The butter may be used plain, slightly softened or it may be seasoned and flavored with just a suspicion of paprika, a little white pepper, and a few drops of Worcestershire sauce. For ordinary sandwiches use the bread without toasting. For canapés, toast is to be preferred. Sandwiches are principally used for buffet lunches or evening sociables, where only a light, substantial lunch is required. In these days they are made in great varieties. Almost all sorts of meat, if properly seasoned, may be made into delicious sandwiches. If the meat is slightly moistened with cream or olive oil, sandwiches for traveling, provided each one is carefully wrapped in oiled paper, will keep fresh three or four days. The small French rolls may have the centres scooped out, the spaces filled with chicken salad or chopped oysters, and served as sandwiches. The rolls may be made especially for that purpose, not more than two inches long and one and a half inches wide. With coffee, they make an attractive meal easily served.

46. According to the passage, sandwiches should be served

   J. at any time of the day
   K. only during breaks
   L. usually during buffet lunches
   M. to children for dinner

47. The author suggests the breads used for sandwiches because

   A. they retain good form
   B. they have the best taste
   C. sandwiches can only be made from them
   D. they are his favorite breads

48. The tone of the passage is

   J. enthusiastic
   K. apathetic
   L. disinterested
   M. skeptical

49. Sandwiches can remain fresh for days if

   A. the meat is cooked properly
   B. they are properly wrapped in oiled paper
   C. paprika is added
   D. they are sufficiently sized

CONTINUE ON TO THE NEXT PAGE ➡

READING
PART II

50. The French rolls can be used

  J. as the primary sandwich for lunch
  K. to hold chicken salad
  L. to eat with any meat
  M. as toast

LANGUAGE
PART I (23 MIN)

DIRECTIONS: In this section, you will need to determine the errors that are found in the sentences. Pick the answer choice that highlights the mistake and fill in the appropriate letter on your answer sheet. If no mistake is present, choose the last answer choice.

Directions: Look for mistakes in <u>spelling</u>.

1. A. The preservation of trees
   B. is of utmost importance for
   C. the surviveal of native chimpanzees.
   D. (No mistakes)

2. J. Turkish is a language that is
   K. a combination of Arabic
   L. and Pershan influences.
   M. (No mistakes)

3. A. As an affluent businessman,
   B. John received many awards
   C. for his accomplishments.
   D. (No mistakes)

4. J. It too was a great
   K. priviledge for Cassie
   L. to join the team.
   M. (No mistakes)

5. A. The teacher faced great
   B. embarrasment after being
   C. fired by the principal.
   D. (No mistakes)

6. J. Alchemy is
   K. considered a
   L. pseudoscience.
   M. (No mistakes)

7. A. The jewelery was stolen
   B. from the thrift
   C. shop near downtown.
   D. (No mistakes)

8. J. Our leisure time involves
   K. meditation, acupuncture,
   L. and therapuetic massage.
   M. (No mistakes)

9. A. The teacher told
   B. us not to mispell
   C. the word "knives."
   D. (No mistakes)

10. J. Many scientists emphasize the gills of
    K. early mammalian embryos as a key
    L. evolutionery relationship to fishes.
    M. (No mistakes)

CONTINUE ON TO THE NEXT PAGE ➡

LANGUAGE
PART I

Directions: Look for mistakes in <u>capitalization</u>.

11.
   A. According to astrology,
   B. Saturn is considered by
   C. many to be an ill omen.
   D. *(No mistakes)*

12.
   J. The pope is the
   K. worldwide leader of the
   L. Catholic Church.
   M. *(No mistakes)*

13.
   A. My Mom told us
   B. not to go outside, but
   C. Grandpa helped change her mind.
   D. *(No mistakes)*

14.
   J. A prominent figure in Hollywood,
   K. Robert Downey Jr. was the
   L. actor playing ironman.
   M. *(No mistakes)*

15.
   A. The high specific heat of water
   B. makes it an excellent property of
   C. maintaining temperature in all organisms.
   D. *(No Mistakes)*

16.
   J. The book *To Kill*
   K. *a mockingbird* involves
   L. the time during the Great Depression.
   M. *(No mistakes)*

17.
   A. Known for its busy streets,
   B. the City of New York has more
   C. people than 39 out of the 50 states.
   D. *(No mistakes)*

18.
   J. Professor Jones asked,
   K. "Who let the mice
   L. out of the Klein laboratory?"
   M. *(No mistakes)*

19.
   A. Summer and Winter
   B. are the two extremes
   C. of all the seasons.
   D. *(No mistakes)*

20.
   J. Tourists who visit
   K. New York City should
   L. travel to Central park.
   M. *(No mistakes)*

CONTINUE ON TO THE NEXT PAGE ➡

383

LANGUAGE
PART I

Directions: Look for <u>punctuation</u> mistakes.

21. A. While doing her homework Sarah felt
    B. obliged to do the extra credit
    C. that her teacher assigned.
    D. *(No mistakes)*

22. J. The experiment illustrates the
    K. correlation. Thus we can
    L. establish a great discovery.
    M. *(No mistakes)*

23. A. Although a great lecturer
    B. Robert had a hard time
    C. elevating his voice.
    D. *(No mistakes)*

24. J. Sufism is a mystical idea
    K. of Islam, it encompasses
    L. many different sects.
    M. *(No mistakes)*

25. A. Even though dominance is restricted for
    B. males in most mammals, hyenas have
    C. females as the leaders of the pack.
    D. *(No mistakes)*

26. J. Garrett Robinson once said,
    K. "I will never surrender
    L. to a corrupt government".
    M. *(No mistakes)*

27. A. Robert asked who was
    B. at the conference
    C. meeting with Diana?
    D. *(No mistakes)*

28. J. My mom told me to
    K. get the following fish,
    L. eggs, and milk.
    M. *(No mistakes)*

29. A. Plasma is considered the
    B. hottest state of matter and
    C. solid is considered the coolest.
    D. *(No mistakes)*

30. J. Einstein is famous for his theory
    K. of relativity; and his theories have
    L. corrected Newtonian physics.
    M. *(No mistakes)*

CONTINUE ON TO THE NEXT PAGE ➡

LANGUAGE
PART I

Directions: Look for mistakes in usage.

31. A. After running the
     B. marathon, her parents gave
     C. Emily her drink.
     D. *(No mistakes)*

32. J. If you travel to the
     K. Saharan desert, one will find
     L. it difficult under extreme conditions.
     M. *(No mistakes)*

33. A. The hammer is
     B. a useful tool for
     C. attaching nails to wood.
     D. *(No mistakes)*

34. J. Each of the girls
     K. played on the team
     L. and gave their best shot.
     M. *(No mistakes)*

35. A. The teacher allowed us
     B. both to skip homework
     C. or to have extra break.
     D. *(No mistakes)*

36. J. The school of fish
     K. make it difficult for
     L. sharks to spot prey.
     M. *(No mistakes)*

37. A. The conversation between
     B. my teacher and I does not
     C. involve you whatsoever.
     D. *(No mistakes)*

38. J. I have ran 3 miles
     K. in order to prepare
     L. for my school track team.
     M. *(No mistakes)*

39. A. Alot of casualties
     B. occurred during both
     C. World War 1 and World War 2.
     D. *(No mistakes)*

40. J. Every child must
     K. learn to cope without
     L. his or her mother after maturity.
     M. *(No mistakes)*

CONTINUE ON TO THE NEXT PAGE ➡

LANGUAGE
PART II (7 MIN)

Directions: For questions 41-42, choose the best answer based on the following paragraph.

Excerpt from Japanese Fairy Tales

(1) Long, long ago there lived in Japan a brave warrior known to all as Tawara Toda, or "My Lord Bag of Rice." (2) His true name was Fujiwara Hidesato, and there is a very interesting story of how he came to change his name. (3) One day he sallied forth in search of adventures, for he had the nature of a warrior and could not bear to be idle. (4) So he buckled on his two swords, took his huge bow in his hand, and started out. (5) He had not gone far when he came to the bridge of Seta-no-Karashi spanning one end of the beautiful Lake Biwa. (6) No sooner had he set foot on the bridge then he saw lying right across his path a huge serpent-dragon. (7) It's body was so big that it looked like the trunk of a large pine tree and it took up the whole width of the bridge. (8) One of its huge claws rested on the parapet of one side of the bridge, while its tail lay right against the other. (9) The monster seemed to be asleep, and as it breathed, fire and smoke came out of its nostrils.

41. Which of the words in sentence 2 is an underlined adjective?

    A. "name"
    B. "how"
    C. "change"
    D. "interesting"

42. Which of the words in sentence 7 is wrongly used?

    J. "It's"
    K. "looked"
    L. "trunk"
    M. "took"

CONTINUE ON TO THE NEXT PAGE ➡

LANGUAGE
PART II

Directions: For questions 43-44, choose the best answer based on the following paragraph.

(1) Nutrients can be defined as the major component in foods that provide the essential nourishment that living organisms require for growth and survival. (2) The primary organic nutrients are categorized under the term "macronutrients," and provide the main source of energy to carry out the functions of life. (3) They consist of carbohydrates, fats and protein. Carbohydrates are made up of different forms of sugars; their fundamental role is to provide the body's main source of fuel for numerous activities, including brain function and physical movement. (4) Fats are needed to act as a cushion for body organs, keep the body temperature stable and absorb certain nutrients. (5) They can also be used as a secondary source of energy when the body no longer has carbohydrates. (6) Lastly, proteins are essential in the repair of body tissue which also including muscles, the structure of red blood cells, and the regulation of enzymes and hormones.

43. What is a <u>verb</u> in sentence 2?

    A. "primary"
    B. "are categorized"
    C. "term"
    D. "source"

44. Which of the following phrases may be removed from sentence 6?

    J. "Lastly"
    K. "essential in the"
    L. "which also"
    M. "regulation of enzymes"

CONTINUE ON TO THE NEXT PAGE ➡

LANGUAGE
PART II

Directions: For questions 45-47, choose the best answer based on the following paragraph.

(1) Santa Claus lives in the Laughing Valley, where stands the big, rambling castle in which his toys are manufactured. (2) His workmen, happily selected from the pixies and fairies, live with him, and everyone is as busy as can be from one year's end to another. (3) It is called the Laughing Valley because everything there is happy. (4) The wind whistles merrily in the trees and the violets and wild flowers look smilingly up from their green nests. (5) To laugh one needs to be happy; to be happy one needs to be content. (6) Throughout the Laughing Valley of Santa Claus contentment reigns supreme. (7) One would thing that our good old Santa Claus, who devotes his days to making children happy, would have no enemies on all the earth. (8) As a matter of fact, for a long period of time he encountered nothing but love wherever he might go. (9) But the Daemons who live in the mountain caves grew to hate Santa Claus very much, and all for the simple reason that he made children happy.

45. Which of the words in sentence 2 is an <u>adverb</u>?

- A. "workment"
- B. "happily"
- C. "pixies"
- D. "busy"

46. After what word in sentence 6 should a comma be added?

- J. "Throughout"
- K. "Valley"
- L. "Claus"
- M. "contentment"

47. Which of the following words in sentence 7 is wrongly used?

- A. "One"
- B. "thing"
- C. "devotes"
- D. "all"

CONTINUE ON TO THE NEXT PAGE ➡

LANGUAGE
PART II

Directions: For questions 48-50, choose the best answer based on the following paragraph.

(1) Breeders of every class of horse, saving only those who breed the Shetland pony and the few who aim at getting ponies for polo, have for generations made it their goal to obtain increased height. (2) There is nothing to be urged against this policy insofar as certain breeds are concerned. (3) The sixteen-hand thoroughbred with his greater stride is more likely to win races than the horse of fifteen two. (4) The sixteen-hand carriage horse, other qualities being equal, brings a better price than one of less stature. (5) Thus there is excellent reason for our efforts to increase the height of our most valuable breeds the long period that has elapsed since we were last called upon to put forward our military strength has allowed us to lose sight of the great importance of other qualities. (6) However, increased height in the horse does not necessarily involved increased strength in all directions, such as greater weight-carrying power and more endurance.

48. In sentence 1, what is the <u>adjective</u> "every" describing?

   J. "Breeders"
   K. "class"
   L. "horse"
   M. "those"

49. What is wrong with sentence 5?

   A. sentence fragment
   B. wrong tense
   C. misspelled word
   D. *(No mistakes)*

50. Which <u>verb</u> in sentence 6 is in the wrong tense?

   J. "increased"
   K. "does"
   L. "involved"
   M. "carrying"

CONTINUE ON TO THE NEXT PAGE ➡

MATH
PART I (33 MIN)

DIRECTIONS: Choose the answer that best fits the problem.

1. $1.\overline{3}$ written as a fraction is ___ ?

   A. $1\frac{3}{10}$
   B. $1\frac{33}{100}$
   C. $\frac{4}{3}$
   D. $\frac{13}{10}$

2. Based on the table, how many more hours did Mark spend on studying for his Geometry class than for his Spanish class?

   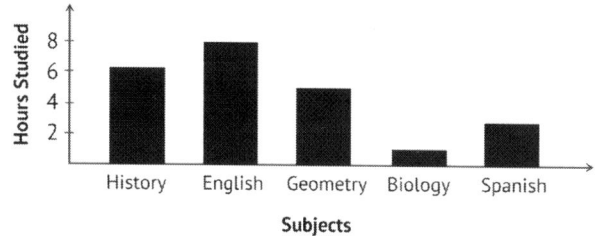

   J. 4 hours
   K. 2 hours
   L. 3 hours
   M. 5 hours

3. $\frac{3}{5} + \frac{7}{8}$ is equal to ___ ?

   A. $\frac{10}{13}$
   B. $\frac{59}{40}$
   C. $\frac{1}{2}$
   D. $\frac{71}{40}$

4. Which of the following is *not* a prime number?

   J. 71
   K. 31
   L. 91
   M. 41

5. Ms. Nina is setting a school trip for 150 students. If each bus can hold 28 students, and she already has 2 buses ready, how many more will she need?

   A. 5
   B. 2
   C. 3
   D. 4

CONTINUE ON TO THE NEXT PAGE ➡

MATH
PART I

6. The chart below shows the prices of certain items in the school cafeteria. Based on the chart, if Colin decides to buy 2 cartons of milk, 1 hamburger, and a bottle of water, how much would he have to pay?

Item	Price
Egg	$1.08
Milk	$2.01
Hamburger	$3.49
Cheeseburger	$3.71
Water Bottle	$1.13

   J. $8.64
   K. $8.63
   L. $8.53
   M. $8.54

7. What is the least common denominator of $\frac{1}{3}, \frac{7}{6}$, and $\frac{2}{9}$?

   A. 24
   B. 9
   C. 18
   D. 36

8. A shirt has a starting value of 5 dollars and increases by 20 percent every year. What is the price of the shirt after 2 years?

   J. $7.20
   K. $6.00
   L. $7.00
   M. $6.20

9. What is the decimal equivalent of $\frac{3}{4}$?

   A. 0.5
   B. 0.25
   C. 0.75
   D. 0.10

10. Abraham works for a store with the following menu. If a customer were to get cheesecake, ice cream and popcorn, how much would the customer pay?

Item	Price
Popcorn	$1.05
Waffles	$3.14
Pancakes	$3.19
Chicken	$2.90
Cheesecake	$4.30
Ice Cream	$2.10

    J. $7.35
    K. $7.45
    L. $8.35
    M. $8.45

11. What is the greatest common factor of 125 and 625?

    A. 125
    B. 25
    C. 5
    D. 625

CONTINUE ON TO THE NEXT PAGE ➡

MATH
PART I

12. What is 9% of 9%?

    J. .0081
    K. 8.1%
    L. .81
    M. 81%

13. If Sam finished $\frac{3}{11}$ of his homework assignment which included doing 9 tasks, how many tasks does he have left to finish?

    A. 112
    B. 33
    C. 8
    D. 24

14. $15 \div \frac{5}{6}$

    J. 18
    K. $\frac{1}{2}$
    L. 5
    M. $\frac{75}{6}$

15. Solve $7y^2 - x$ if $y = -3$ and $x = -1$

    A. -62
    B. 63
    C. 62
    D. 64

16. $(-2)(-2)(7)(-3)$

    J. 84
    K. -84
    L. 72
    M. -42

17. $5 + (-(-64))$

    A. 61
    B. -61
    C. 69
    D. -69

18. If $3x + 5 = 80$, find $2x + 10$.

    J. 60
    K. 70
    L. 50
    M. 25

CONTINUE ON TO THE NEXT PAGE ➡

19. Based on the graph, between which two years did the museum experience the greatest change in the number of people who attended?

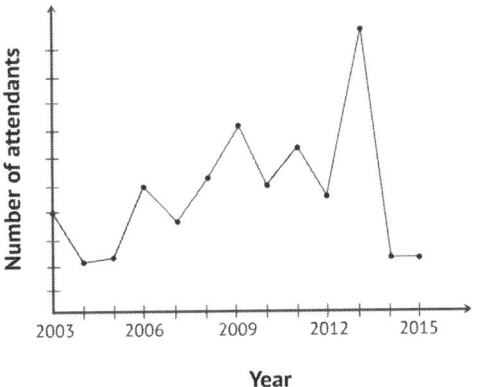

A. 2007 - 2008
B. 2012 - 2013
C. 2009 - 2010
D. 2013 - 2014

20.

Number of people	3	2	7	0	4	3
Ratings	0	1	2	3	4	5

The table above gives the results of a group of people who rated a movie from 0 -5. What is the average rate given by the group?

J. 2.50
K. 2.47
L. 3.17
M. 3

Use the following table to answer questions 21 and 22.

21. Which histogram best fits the data according to table below?

Height	Cumulative Frequency (Number of people)
41 - 50	0
41 - 60	3
41 - 70	7
41 - 80	9

A.
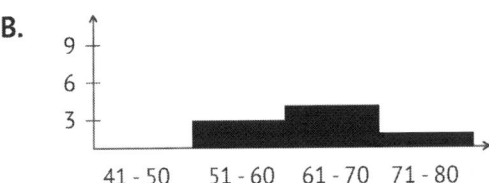

B.
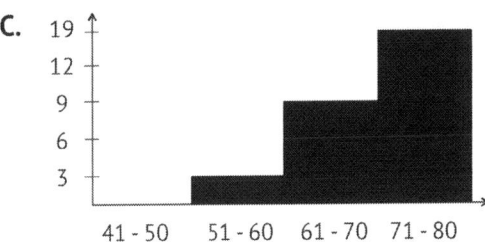

C.

D.
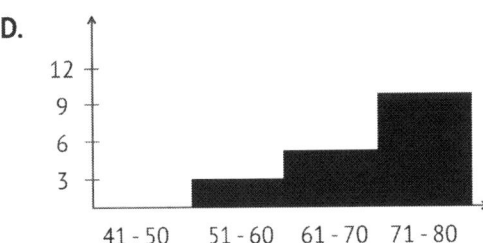

CONTINUE ON TO THE NEXT PAGE →

MATH
PART I

22. Referring to the table above, what is the total number of people?

J. 9
K. 19
L. 15
M. 5

23. The following graph showing the scatter plot of a trend between the average salary and the SAT score for a certain sample size.

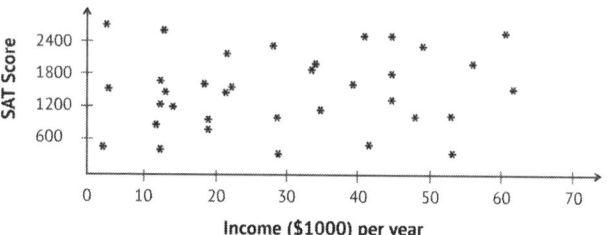

Looking at the scatter plot, what is the best <u>interpretation</u> of the graph?

A. More of the sample make under $40 than do over.
B. The higher income correlates to higher SAT score.
C. There is no clear relationship between the two.
D. Rich people are good test-takers.

24.

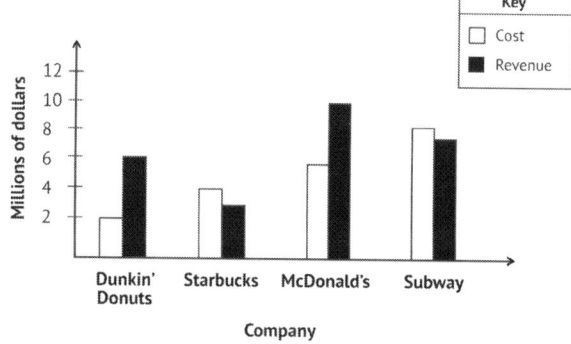

Which company experienced the greatest loss as a percent change?

J. Dunkin' Donuts
K. Starbucks
L. McDonald's
M. Subway

25. The height of a building on a blueprint is 4 inches. If the actual height of the building is 30 feet, what is the ratio of the blueprint to the actual height of the building?

A. 1:80
B. 1:90
C. 4:30
D. 30:4

MATH
PART I

26. 9.09090909090909........% =

J. $\frac{9}{100}$

K. $\frac{1}{11}$

L. $\frac{9}{10}$

M. $\frac{1}{12}$

27. Julissa plans to buy a used car for $2,500 from a store. The tax is 8 percent, but after Julissa submits a coupon, she is able to bring the price down by 10 percent. How much did she pay for the car?

A. $2,498
B. $2,400
C. $2,430
D. $2,470

28. If the price of a pencil is $0.13, what will be the price if Mary wants to buy 17 of these pencils?

J. $2.21
K. $2.71
L. $2.31
M. $22.10

29. The following circle graph shows the percentages of the types of candies preferred by Howard High School seniors. If there was a total of 270 seniors who like Skittles, then how many seniors are there in Howard High School?

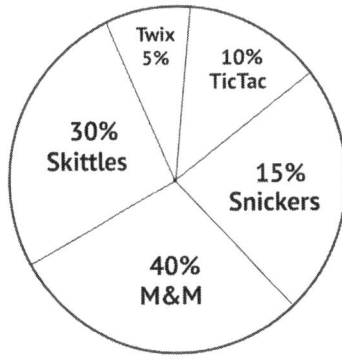

A. 300
B. 910
C. 900
D. 91

30. A certain game has a deck of cards with 1 that is red, 7 that are green, 5 that are blue, and 2 that are yellow. If choosing each one is equally likely, what is the probability that Sam will choose a green or blue card?

J. $\frac{7}{15}$

K. $\frac{5}{15}$

L. $\frac{4}{5}$

M. $\frac{2}{3}$

CONTINUE ON TO THE NEXT PAGE ➡

MATH
PART I

31. $17^2 - 4^3$

- **A.** 129
- **B.** 225
- **C.** 277
- **D.** 15^2

32.

Gas Prices	
Regular	$2.00
Premium	$2.25
Unloaded	$2.50

The prices in the table above show the different types of gas offered at a gas station and the prices of the gas per gallon. If Emily has $50, what is the least amount of gas, in gallons, she can purchase subtracted from the greatest amount of gas, in gallons, she can purchase?

- **J.** 2 gallons
- **K.** 3 gallons
- **L.** 5 gallons
- **M.** 20 gallons

CONTINUE ON TO THE NEXT PAGE ➡

MATH
PART II (7 MIN)

DIRECTIONS: In this section, you will need to estimate all your answers. There is no scratch work allowed. Do not determine exact answers. Pick the answer choice that fits accordingly and fill in the appropriate letter on your answer sheet.

33. The closest estimate of 573 + 231 is _____.

- **A.** 700
- **B.** 810
- **C.** 790
- **D.** 800

34. The closest estimate of $\frac{725}{6}$ is _____.

- **J.** 200
- **K.** 150
- **L.** 100
- **M.** 50

35. The closest estimate of 17,984 - 9,782 is _____.

- **A.** 8,000
- **B.** 7,000
- **C.** 8,500
- **D.** 7,500

36. The number 5,679 rounded to the nearest thousands place is _____.

- **J.** 5,700
- **K.** 5,680
- **L.** 6,000
- **M.** 5,000

37. The number 8.291 rounded to the nearest tenth place is _____.

- **A.** 8.2
- **B.** 8
- **C.** 8.29
- **D.** 8.3

38. The closest estimate of $11.97 + $45.54 + $7.23 to the nearest dollar is _____.

- **J.** $64
- **K.** $65
- **L.** $66
- **M.** $63

CONTINUE ON TO THE NEXT PAGE ➡

MATH
PART II

39. The number 9.2679 rounded to the nearest thousandth place is _____.

- A. 9.3679
- B. 9.268
- C. 9.267
- D. 9.27

40. The closest estimate of 199,999 x 32 is _____.

- J. 5,900,000
- K. 7,000,000
- L. 6,500,000
- M. 6,000,000

41. The number 123,546 rounded to the nearest thousands place is _____.

- A. 124,000
- B. 123,000
- C. 122,000
- D. 121,000

42. The closest estimate of 2,489 / 11 is _____.

- J. 300
- K. 200
- L. 250
- M. 350

43. The total number of cars that drive past the Raphael Bridge yearly is 10,756. The total number of trucks that pass the same bridge yearly is 1,232. What is the approximate difference between the two amounts?

- A. 10,500
- B. 9,500
- C. 9,000
- D. 10,000

44. The closest estimate of 13.9 - 35.6 is _____.

- J. -24
- K. -23
- L. -22
- M. -21

45. The number 6.25 rounded to the nearest tenths place is _____.

- A. 6.3
- B. 6.2
- C. 6.25
- D. 6

CONTINUE ON TO THE NEXT PAGE ➡

MATH
PART II

46. The number 1.987 rounded to the nearest tenths place is _____.

- J. 1.97
- K. 1.98
- L. 1.99
- M. 2

47. Last year, Danielle had an average score of 23.7 shots per game on her basketball team. This year, she scored an average of 32.2 shots per game. Which is the closest estimate to the average of the two years?

- A. 30
- B. 20
- C. 22
- D. 19

48. The closest estimate of 1,125 x 567 is _____.

- J. 700,000
- K. 600,000
- L. 550,000
- M. 500,000

49. If George drove a total of 3,577 miles within 103 hours, what is the best estimate for his average speed within his travel?

- A. 30
- B. 35
- C. 40
- D. 45

50. Sally originally had 2,808 stamps in her collection. Joe gave her an additional 9,923 stamps. Approximately how many stamps does Sally now own?

- J. 10,000
- K. 11,000
- L. 12,000
- M. 13,000

CONTINUE ON TO THE NEXT PAGE ➡

ABILITY
PART I (25 MIN)

DIRECTIONS: In this section, you will need to recognize certain similarities. Pick the answer choice that best matches with the three shapes provided for each question and fill in the appropriate letter on your answer sheet.
TIME LIMIT: 32 minutes for the entire ability section.

1.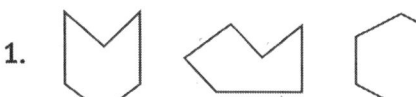

   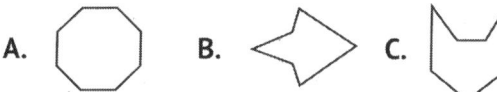

2.

3.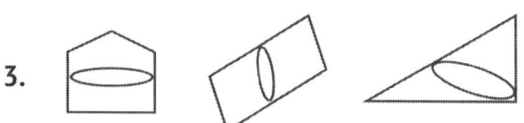

4.

   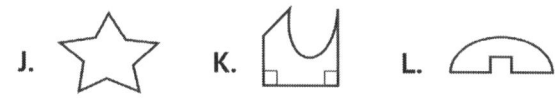

CONTINUE ON TO THE NEXT PAGE ➡

ABILITY
PART I

5.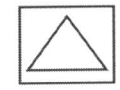

A.  B.  C.

D.  E.

8.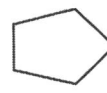

J. 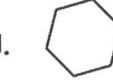 K. 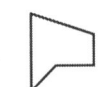 L.

M. N.

6.

J.  K.  L.

M.  N.

9.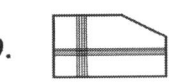

A. 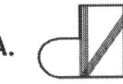 B.  C.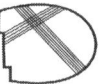

D.   E.

7.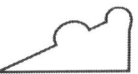

A.  B.  C.

D.  E.

10.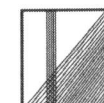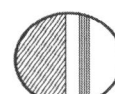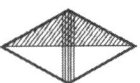

J. 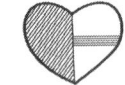 K. L.

M.  N.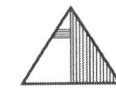

CONTINUE ON TO THE NEXT PAGE ➡

ABILITY
PART I

11.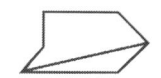

   A.  B.  C.

   D. E.

12.

   J.  K.  L.

   M.  N.

13.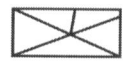

   A. B. C.

   D. E.

14.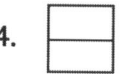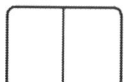

   J.  K. 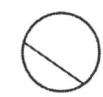 L.

   M. 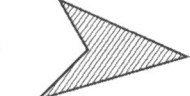 N.

15.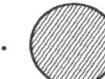

   A. 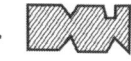 B. C.

   D.  E.

16.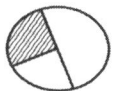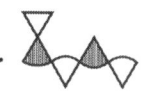

   J.  K. 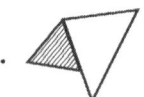 L.

   M. N.

CONTINUE ON TO THE NEXT PAGE ➡

ABILITY
PART I

17.

A. 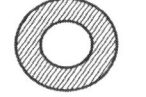 B.  C.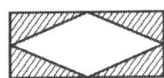

D. 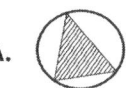 E.

18.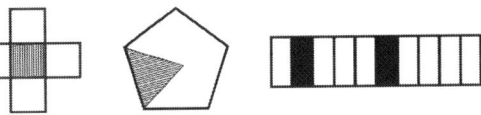

J.   K. 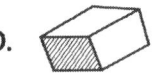 L.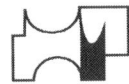

M. N.

19.

A. B. C.

D. E.

20.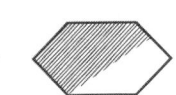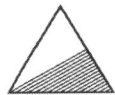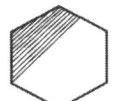

J. 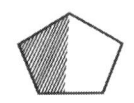 K. 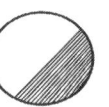 L.

M. 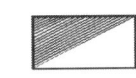 N.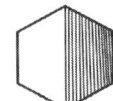

CONTINUE ON TO THE NEXT PAGE ➡

ABILITY
PART I

DIRECTIONS: There is a particular change made on the first shape to result in the second shape. Follow the same rule to determine how the third shape will change.

ABILITY
PART I

25.

26.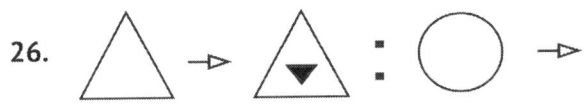

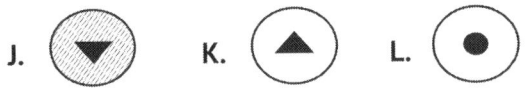

27.

28.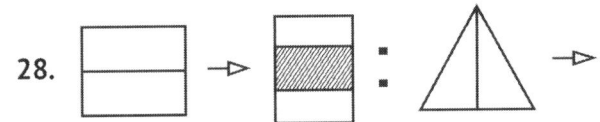

29.

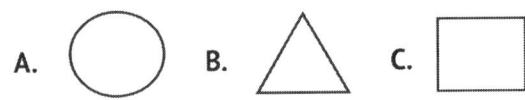

30.

CONTINUE ON TO THE NEXT PAGE ➡

ABILITY
PART I

ABILITY
PART I

37.

A. B. C.

D. E.

38.

J. K. L.

M. N.

39.

A. B. C.

D. E.

40.

J. K. L.

M. N.

CONTINUE ON TO THE NEXT PAGE ➡

ABILITY
PART II (7 MIN)

DIRECTIONS: The second figure represents a change made on the first figure. What would be the resulting figure if the second figure was unfolded?

41.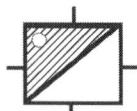

A. 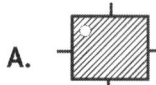 B. 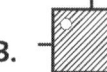 C.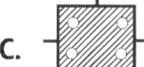

D. 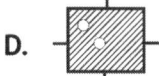 E.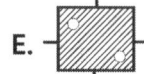

43.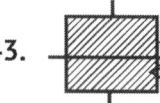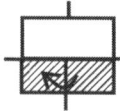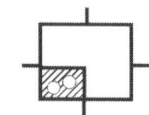

A. 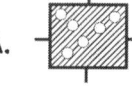 B. 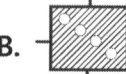 C.

D.   E.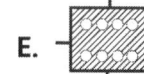

42.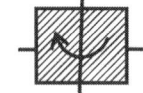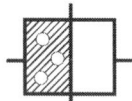

J. 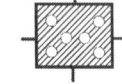 K. 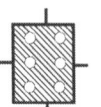 L.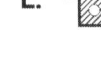

M. 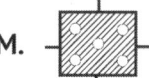 N.

44.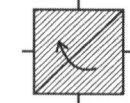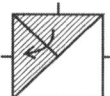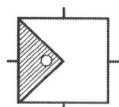

J.   K. L.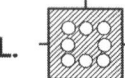

M.   N.

CONTINUE ON TO THE NEXT PAGE ➡

ABILITY
PART II

45.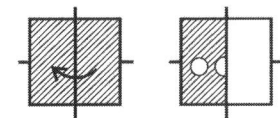

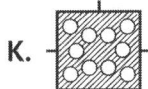 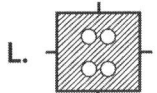

48.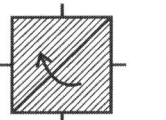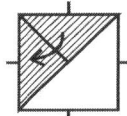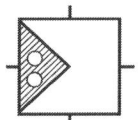

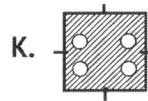 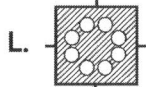

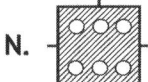

46.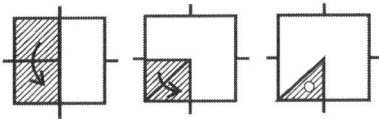

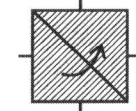 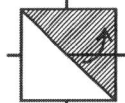 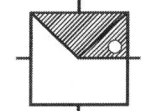

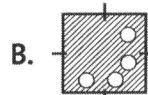 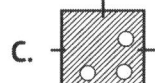

49.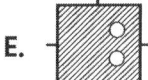

47.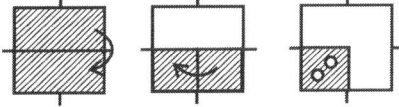

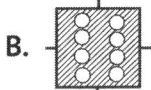

50.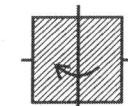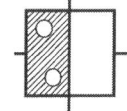

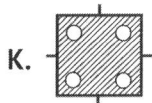 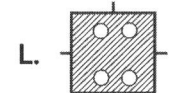

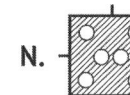

409

TACHS PRACTICE TEST 2
ANSWER KEY

ENGLISH

Reading (Part I)

1. B
2. M
3. D
4. L
5. C
6. L
7. C
8. L
9. D
10. J
11. C
12. K
13. A
14. L
15. D
16. K
17. A
18. J
19. D
20. J

Reading (Part II)

21. B
22. K
23. C
24. J
25. A
26. K
27. D
28. K
29. D
30. J
31. A
32. K
33. D
34. J
35. B
36. J
37. B
38. K
39. A
40. K
41. B
42. M
43. C
44. K
45. C
46. L
47. A
48. J
49. B
50. K

ARGO BROTHERS

To calculate your score and watch video tutorials, visit our web site:
www.einstein-academy.com/catholic

Language (Part I)

1. C
2. L
3. D
4. K
5. B
6. M
7. A
8. L
9. B
10. L
11. D
12. J
13. A
14. L
15. D
16. K
17. B
18. M
19. A
20. L
21. A
22. K
23. A
24. K
25. D
26. L
27. C
28. K
29. D
30. K
31. B
32. K
33. D
34. L
35. C
36. K
37. B
38. J
39. A
40. M

Language (Part II)

41. D
42. J
43. B
44. L
45. B
46. L
47. B
48. K
49. A
50. L

MATHEMATICS

Mathematics (Part I)

1. C
2. K
3. B
4. L
5. D
6. J
7. C
8. J
9. C
10. K
11. A
12. J
13. D
14. J
15. D
16. K
17. C
18. J
19. D
20. K
21. B
22. J
23. C
24. K
25. D
26. K
27. C
28. J
29. C
30. L
31. B
32. L

Mathematics (Part II)

33. D
34. L
35. A
36. L
37. D
38. K
39. B
40. M
41. A
42. L
43. B
44. L
45. A
46. M
47. A
48. K
49. B
50. M

ABILITY

Ability (Part I)

1. B
2. N
3. C
4. M
5. C
6. J
7. D
8. K
9. E
10. L
11. A
12. L
13. A
14. L
15. C
16. L
17. B
18. M
19. B
20. J
21. A
22. L
23. B
24. N
25. D
26. L
27. B
28. K
29. E
30. M
31. E
32. J
33. A
34. N
35. C
36. K
37. B
38. L
39. E
40. J

Ability (Part II)

41. E
42. J
43. C
44. M
45. B
46. N
47. A
48. L
49. B
50. M

ANSWER EXPLANATIONS

READING SECTION
The following 20 questions can be fully understood with the vocabulary section attached with the book.

1. **The correct answer is B.**
   Reproach means to express disapproval. Critical best fits this.

2. **The correct answer is M.**
   Benefit means to profit or have an advantage. Gain best fits this.

3. **The correct answer is D.**
   Remnant means a remaining quantity of something. Remainder best fits this.

4. **The correct answer is L.**
   Edible means consumable. Eatable best fits this.

5. **The correct answer is C.**
   Candid means to be truthful or frank. Honest best fits this.

6. **The correct answer is L.**
   Cleave means to sever. Cut best fits this.

7. **The correct answer is C.**
   Advocate means to publicly promote. Supporter best fits this

8. **The correct answer is L.**
   Recurrent means something that occurs again and again. Reappearing best fits this.

9. **The correct answer is D.**
   Trite means overused or lacking originality. Banal, common and cliché all fit this.

10. **The correct answer is J.**
    Coalesce means to bring together. Aggregate, which means to combine, best fits this.

11. **The correct answer is C.**
    Dynamic means constantly changing. Changing best fits this.

12. **The correct answer is K.**
    Antithetical means to be directly opposing. Opposite best fits this.

13. **The correct answer is A.**
    Significant means noteworthy. Important best fits this.

14. **The correct answer is L.**
    Relentless means constant. Continuous best fits this.

15. **The correct answer is D.**
    Immunity means protection or exemption from something. Resistance best fits this.

16. **The correct answer is K.**
    Sophisticated means complex. Advanced best fits this.

17. **The correct answer is A.**
    Antiquated means old-fashioned. Outdated best fits this.

18. **The correct answer is J.**
    Avaricious means to be very materialistic. Greedy best fits this.

19. **The correct answer is D.**
    Crucial means to be of great importance. Essential. Significant and important all best fit this.

ANSWER EXPLANATIONS

20. **The correct answer is J.**
    Querulous means to be irritable. Argumentative best fits this.

21. **The correct answer is B.**
    The main idea of the passage involves science so choices C and D are automatically incorrect. Choice B is better because the specific uses of science are constantly brought up as examples of improvement.

22. **The correct answer is K.**
    The passage's main idea is about how technology makes our lives easier and how without it, we would have a hard time functioning and surviving. This correlates with choice K.

23. **The correct answer is C.**
    If the word perish is replaced with wither, the sentence makes sense. Here, there needs to be a negative connotation because the people are suffering without technology.

24. **The correct answer is J.**
    The general idea of the fact that technology is a huge benefit for mankind. This helps us thrive from the natural resources we already have.

25. **The correct answer is A.**
    This idea again here is that technology has "contributed so enormously to the ordinary affairs of life" that we would not have progressed as much in terms of growth without its use.

26. **The correct answer is K.**
    The gist of the passage is that new technology is often criticized at first, but it is this new aspect that makes it special. This can be seen from the author's statement that "a motor car is a fearsome thing."

27. **The correct answer is D.**
    The second and third line of the passage shows that D is the correct answer. A horse, boat, and trolley car are "difficult for the inexperienced....But to the novice in charge of an automobile, serious damage is likely enough to occur."

28. **The correct answer is K.**
    Using context clues, replace each other the choices with the word retained in the passage. Here, something has to describe the idea of remembering.

29. **The correct answer is D.**
    The sentence that starts with "There are those who doubt..." shows that there are critics of automobiles, but there are also others who have praised it.

30. **The correct answer is J.**
    The explanation for 26 correlates with this question. New vehicles at first are criticized and then later on appreciated.

31. **The correct answer is A.**
    In sentence 4 of the passage, it says, "Those which have enemies from which they cannot escape by rapidity of motion must be able to hide or disguise themselves." This is to say that animals that use camouflage, help them escape predators by hiding themselves.

32. **The correct answer is K.**
    The passage indicates that protective resemblance is when an animal mimics the habitat in which it lives on. This is best illustrated by choice K.

33. **The correct answer is D.**
    The last sentence of the passage states that a bluff camouflage is one that intends to terrify. A man wearing a bear suit is doing this type of camouflage to terrify the dog.

ANSWER EXPLANATIONS

34. The correct answer is J.
The general idea of the passage is to either conceal with the environment or mimic a living threatening animal. Here, it is like hiding with both the living and nonliving aspects of nature.

35. The correct answer is B.
Using context clues, replace each other the choices with the word circuitous. Here, it has to describe something opposite easy and direct which would be the equivalent of difficult.

36. The correct answer is J.
Again, using context clues, replace each of the choices with the word intuition. The word has to be antithetical to intellect which is knowledge that is acquired externally. Therefore, instinct have to do what's something that is more from the inside.

37. The correct answer is B.
The authors make a comparison between Beethoven and Bach. Bach is more mathematical whereas Beethoven is more philosophical.

38. The correct answer is K.
The passage states that " Beethoven was the first one having the independence to think for himself."

39. The correct answer is A.
The definition of predecessor as someone who has held a position previously. In this case, Beethoven's predecessors were musicians before him who thought only to please others around than themselves.

40. The correct answer is K.
It can be implied that Beethoven made music only for himself." This is implied because it says in lines 8, "it was he who established the dignity of the artist." Additionally it says "His predecessors, to a great extent subjugated by their social superiors, sought only to please." His predecessors made music to please others, but he made music to please himself.

41. The correct answer is B.
The main idea of the passage is to give the attributes of the Greek gods. The passage talks about the Greek Gods human-like characteristics, as well as their ethereal qualities, therefore helping us understand these Gods.

42. The correct answer is M.
The passage indicates that the gods were very human like in character, but with higher powers.

43. The correct answer is C.
The passage states that the gods' blood, which was called Ichor, "never caused disease."

44. The correct answer is K.
Use context clues and process of elimination. Here, a good word to replace nourishment is food.

45. The correct answer is C.
The gods "were not considered to be exempt from human passions." this illustrates that humans often made the gods personal.

46. The correct answer is L.
The passage states that "...sandwiches are principally used for buffet lunches or evening sociables."

ANSWER EXPLANATIONS

47. The correct answer is A.
The second sentence of the passage indicates that the following types of bread should be used so that it retains good form.

48. The correct answer is J.
The author of the passage shows his/her interest in the making of a sandwich and details mouth-watering aspects and appreciation for different styles of the culinary arts of a sandwich.

49. The correct answer is B.
The passage states that they can remain fresh if "each one is carefully wrapped in oiled paper." (Lines 10-11)

50. The correct answer is K.
The second to last sentence states that french toast may have a space to fill with chicken salad or chopped oysters.

LANGUAGE SECTION

1. The correct answer is C.
The correct spelling is survival.

2. The correct answer is L.
The correct spelling is Persian.

3. The correct answer is D.
No mistakes.

4. The correct answer is K.
The correct spelling is privilege.

5. The correct answer is B.
The correct spelling is embarrassment.

6. The correct answer is M.
No mistakes.

7. The correct answer is A.
The correct spelling is jewelry.

8. The correct answer is L.
The correct spelling is therapeutic.

9. The correct answer is B.
The correct spelling is misspell.

10. The correct answer is L.
The correct spelling is evolutionary.

11. The correct answer is D.
No mistakes.

12. The correct answer is J.
A noble title is capitalized so here the word Pope needs to be capital. The same is true for a title before a name such as Doctor John.

13. The correct answer is A.
The word mom should be lower cased if "my" precedes it. If there is no personal possessive such as "my," then it is usually capital.

14. The correct answer is L.
Ironman should be capitalized since it is a name.

15. The correct answer is D.
No mistakes.

16. The correct answer is K.
The nouns in the title of a work of literature or media all need to be capital whereas the conjunctions and prepositions within are lowercase. Here, the word mockingbird should be capitalized.

17. The correct answer is B.
The word city should be lower case since it is not included with the name. However, if the "city" came after New York, it would then be capitalized.

ANSWER EXPLANATIONS

18. The correct answer is M.
No mistakes.

19. The correct answer is A.
Seasons are not capitalized when they are within a sentence. In this case, winter is incorrectly capitalized.

20. The correct answer is L.
The word park should be capitalized since it comes after a name of an important place. This follows the same idea as question 17.

21. The correct answer is A.
There should be a comma in between "homework" and "Sarah" because the first part is a dependent clause and after it is an independent clause.

22. The correct answer is K.
A comma is necessary after the word thus since it is a transitional word. Other transitional words include however, hence, therefore, and etc.

23. The correct answer is A.
There should be a comma after "lecturer" because the first part is a noun phrase describing the subject in the independent clause that comes after.

24. The correct answer is K.
A comma cannot separate two independent clauses without a conjunction. The comma should either be replaced by a semicolon or a period.

25. The correct answer is D.
No mistakes.

26. The correct answer is L.
Periods and commas at the end of quotations always go within.

27. The correct answer is C.
The following sentence is not a question and therefore should not have "?".

28. The correct answer is K.
There should be a colon after the word following because it introduces a list.

29. The correct answer is D.
No mistakes.

30. The correct answer is K.
A semicolon makes the conjunction redundant. Here, it would have been better if the semicolon with a comma.

31. The correct answer is B.
This is an error in dangling modifier. The phrase before the comma should correspond to the subject in the independent clause. Here, it is Emily who ran the marathon so she should come after the comma.

32. The correct answer is K.
In the first part of the sentence, the pronoun "you" is used. You need to stay consistent with the pronouns. In the second part of the sentence, "one" is used, and is therefore, incorrect because it is not consistent with the first part of the sentence. Additionally, if you use "one" for the first part of the sentence, the word travel should be "travels" according to subject verb agreement. Since it isn't "travels," "you" is the correct pronoun.

33. The correct answer is D.
No mistakes.

34. The correct answer is L.
The word each makes the subject singular so the pronoun their, which is plural, is an incorrect replacement. Instead, it should be her and this is an error in pronoun antecedent.

ANSWER EXPLANATIONS

35. **The correct answer is C.**
    This is an error an appropriate preposition and conjunction. The word both indicates that there should be in and following the first noun or pronoun after it. Here, the word "or" is incorrect.

36. **The correct answer is K.**
    The subject of the following sentence is school and it is singular. Therefore, the verb should be makes. This is an error in subject verb agreement.

37. **The correct answer is B**
    Here, the word "I" should be "me" since me is an objective form of I. The "teacher and I" are not the subject in the sentence; it is actually "the conversation."

38. **The correct answer is J.**
    Here, the word "ran" should be "run" since it follows the word have, which is part of the perfect tense. A past participle should come after the perfect tense. Here, there is an error with the verb tense.

39. **The correct answer is A.**
    "A lot" is two separate words. This question may not belong here since it has to do with spelling. We will review this question in person.

40. **The correct answer is M.**
    No mistakes.

41. **The correct answer is D.**
    An adjective describes hey now and here the noun is story. The word "interesting" describes story and so it is the adjective.

42. **The correct answer is J.**
    "It's" should be "Its" since the contraction can be replaced with "it is", but "Its" shows possession. The possession of body must be shown through the word its.

43. **The correct answer is B.**
    A verb is an action in the sentence and here it is the word "are" with the helping verb "categorized."

44. **The correct answer is L.**
    Since there is already the word "including", the phrase "which also" is redundant.

45. **The correct answer is B.**
    An adverb usually describes a verb and in this case the adverb, happily, describes selected, the verb.

46. **The correct answer is L.**
    There should be a comma after "Claus" because the first part is a phrase describing the subject, contentment, in the independent clause that comes after.

47. **The correct answer is B.**
    The word "thing" should be "think."

48. **The correct answer is K.**
    The adjective "every" comes before the noun "class" so every describes class.

49. **The correct answer is A.**
    A comma is necessary after the word thus since it is a transitional word.

50. **The correct answer is L.**
    The sentence should be in the present tense and the verb "involved" should be "involve."

ANSWER EXPLANATIONS

MATH SECTION

1. **The correct answer is C.**
   Convert each of the multiple choices into decimal values and one will find that $\frac{4}{3}$ = 1.3333.... with the 3's repeating.

2. **The correct answer is K.**
   Mark spent 5 hours studying geometry and 3 hours studying Spanish. The difference is 2.

3. **The correct answer is B.**
   The least common denominator of 5 and 8 is 40. $\frac{3}{5} + \frac{7}{8} = \frac{24}{40} + \frac{35}{40} = \frac{59}{40}$

4. **The correct answer is L.**
   91 is divisible by 13 and 7 and so it has more than a factor of itself and 1. Therefore, it is not prime.

5. **The correct answer is D.**
   If Ms. Nina already has two buses and each bus holds 28 students, she currently has seats for 56 students. 150 - 56 gives 94 students left over. The operation from here is to divide 94 by 28 to find the bare minimum number of buses needed. This gives a value between 3 and 4, meaning there are some leftover students and so there should be 4 buses that are needed additionally.

6. **The correct answer is J.**
   The total cost of the items that Colin purchased is 2($2.01) + $3.49 + $1.13 = $8.64.

7. **The correct answer is C.**
   18 is the smallest number that has factors of 3, 6, and 9.

8. **The correct answer is J.**
   If the increase was 20%, one has to pay 120% of the jacket every year. One can use a proportion $\frac{120}{100} = \frac{\$5}{x}$ and solve for x, the cost of the first year. By cross multiplying and isolating x, you get $6. Repeat this process to get $7.20 as the second proportion. The easier way is to do this is $5 • 1.20 • 1.20.

9. **The correct answer is C.**
   You should know that the value of $\frac{1}{4}$ is 0.25 and 3 times that is 0.75.

10. **The correct answer is K.**
    The total cost of the items that the customer purchased is $4.30 + $2.10 + $1.05 = $7.45.

11. **The correct answer is A.**
    125 is the highest number which can be divided from 125 and 625.

12. **The correct answer is J.**
    The word "of" means to multiply. 9% as a decimal is .09 and .09 x .09 = .0081.

13. **The correct answer is D.**
    One can use a proportion $\frac{3}{11} = \frac{9}{x}$ and solve for x, the total number of assignments. By cross multiplying and isolating x, you get 33 pages. But the problem asks how many pages were left over. 33 - 9 equals 24.

14. **The correct answer is J.**
    When dividing fractions, switch the division to multiplication and flip the fraction on the right side of the division sign. The new operation is $\frac{15}{1} • \frac{6}{5} = \frac{90}{5}$. When simplified, the result is 18.

ANSWER EXPLANATIONS

15. **The correct answer is D.**
    Plug in the values to get $7(-3)^2 - -1$. By following PEMDAS, you should get $7(9) + 1 = 64$.

16. **The correct answer is K.**
    There are three negatives and one positive being multiplied. Two negatives make a positive when multiplied and that multiplied by a negative makes a resulting negative number. 2 times 2 times 7 times 3 is 84 and the answer should be negative.

17. **The correct answer is C.**
    2 negative signs next to each other make a positive. The operation becomes 5 plus positive 64 which is 69.

18. **The correct answer is J.**
    Solve for x by first subtracting 5 from both sides and dividing by 3. This gives the value of x is 25. $2(25) + 10 = 60$.

19. **The correct answer is D.**
    The greatest change is indicated by the steep slope which is between the years 2013 and 2014.

20. **The correct answer is K.**
    Average is determined by taking the total and dividing by the frequency. Here the total is the addition of all the rating is $3(0) + 2(1) + 7(2) + 0(3) + 4(4) + 3(5) = 47$. The frequency is the total number of people which is 19. $47 \div 19$ which is around 2.47.

21. **The correct answer is B.**
    One has to be careful with this problem since it is cumulative chart and the histogram is not. Calculate the number of people that are between 51-60 inches by taking the difference of the first two. This gives a value of 3. By continuing this, one will find 4 people in between 61-70 inches and 2 in between 71-80.

22. **The correct answer is J.**
    The last row gives the total number of people since the data is cumulative.

23. **The correct answer is C.**
    The data points are too scattered to make a conclusion so there is no connection.

24. **The correct answer is K.**
    The only two companies that experienced a loss were Starbucks and Subway since they paid more (cost) than they made profit (revenue). The percent change formula is $\frac{(\text{original} - \text{new})}{(\text{original})} \cdot 100\%$. Doing this for both will give a higher magnitude of percent change for Starbucks even though the amount of decrease is the same for both. This is because Starbucks started out with a lower cost.

25. **The correct answer is D.**
    First convert 30 feet to inches by multiplying by 12. This generates a value of 360 inches. Thee ratio of 4 inches to 360 inches can be simplified to 1 to 90 by dividing top and bottom by 4.

ANSWER EXPLANATIONS

26. **The correct answer is K.**
    Convert each of the multiple choices into decimal values and one will find that $\frac{1}{11}$ = 0.090909090.... with the 0 and 9 repeating. Simply multiply by 100 to get the correct percentage.

27. **The correct answer is C.**
    If the tax was 8%, one has to pay 108% of the original price of the car. One can use a proportion $\frac{108}{100} = \frac{\$2500}{x}$ and solve for x, the cost of the taxed car. By cross multiplying and isolating x, you get $2700. Repeat this process to get the discounted price. The easier way is to do this is $2500 • 1.08 • 0.90.

28. **The correct answer is J.**
    This problem involves multiplication. $0.13 • 17 = $2.21.

29. **The correct answer is C.**
    One can use a proportion $\frac{30\%}{100\%} = \frac{270}{x}$ and solve for x, the total percent. By cross multiplying and isolating x, one will get 900.

30. **The correct answer is L.**
    The concept in this problem tests probability. Whenever there is an "or" in probability, it signifies to add the two chances together. The probability of picking blue and green together is 12 out of 15 because there are 12 blue and black marbles together out of 15 the total number of marbles. This simplified gives $\frac{4}{5}$.

31. **The correct answer is B.**
    Follow the rules of PEMDAS.
    17^2 = 289 and 4^3 = 64.
    289 - 64 = 225 The difference is 225.

32. **The correct answer is L.**
    The greatest amount of gallons Emily can purchase is if she gets regular gas. That amount is 50 ÷ 2 which is 25 gallons. The least amount of gallons she can purchase is if she gets unloaded gas. That amount is 50 ÷ 2.5 = 20 gallons. The difference is 5.

33. **The correct answer is D.**
    Here, one has to round carefully by paying attention to the multiple choice. All the choices when considered together have a number in the tens or hundreds place. It is best to round to the nearest tens. This makes the new addition 570 + 230 = 800.

34. **The correct answer is L.**
    Round the operation to 700 ÷ 10 = 70. Since the denominator was increased much more compare to the numerator, the number should be bigger and so the answer is 100.

35. **The correct answer is A.**
    Round each of these values to the nearest thousand. This makes the new difference 18,000 - 10,000 = 8,000.

36. **The correct answer is L.**
    Here, 5 is in the thousands place. The number to the right of it is 6, which means the 5 should increase to 6 and all the numbers after it should change to 0.

ANSWER EXPLANATIONS

37. **The correct answer is D.**
    Here, 2 is in the tenths place. The number to the right of it is 9, which means the 2 should increase to 3 and all the numbers after it should change to 0.

38. **The correct answer is K.**
    Round each of these values to the nearest dollar. This makes the new addition $12 + $46 + $7 = $65.

39. **The correct answer is B.**
    Here, 7 is in the thousandths place. The number to the right of it is 9, which means the 7 should increase to 8 and all the numbers after it should change to 0.

40. **The correct answer is M.**
    Round the operation to 200,000 • 30 = 6,000,000.

41. **The correct answer is A.**
    Here, 3 is in the thousands place. The number to the right of it is 5, which means the 3 should increase to 4 and all the numbers after it should change to 0.

42. **The correct answer is L.**
    Round the operation to 2,500 ÷ 10 = 250.

43. **The correct answer is B.**
    Here, one has to round carefully by paying attention to the multiple choice. All the choices when considered together have a number in the hundreds place or higher. It is best to round to the nearest hundred. This makes the new difference 10,800 - 1,200 = 9,600 which is closest to B.

44. **The correct answer is L.**
    Round the operation to the nearest whole number. This makes the difference 14 - 36 = -22.

45. **The correct answer is A.**
    Here, 2 is in the tenths place. The number to the right of it is 5, which means the 2 should increase to 3 and all the numbers after it should change to 0.

46. **The correct answer is M.**
    Here, the 9 is in the tenths place. The number to the right of it is 8 which means the 9 should go up. Since 9 goes up to 10, it rounds the 1 to the left up to 2, and every other number after becomes 0 making the final answer 2.

47. **The correct answer is A.**
    Round the operation for the average to the nearest whole number. This is (24 + 32) ÷ 2 = 66 ÷ 2 = 33. This is closest to choice A.

48. **The correct answer is K.**
    Round the operation to 1,000 • 600 = 600,000.

49. **The correct answer is B.**
    This can be solved by understanding the formula distance equals rate times time. The problem gives us the time traveled and the distance so we divide the two to find the distance. Rounding each to the nearest hundred gives 3,600 ÷ 100 = 36, which is closest to choice B.

50. **The correct answer is M.**
    The word additional indicates that one has to add. Round each number to the nearest thousand and this makes the operation 3,000 + 10,000 = 13,000.

ANSWER EXPLANATIONS

ABILITY SECTION

1. **The correct answer is B.**
   All of the shapes are hexagons.

2. **The correct answer is N.**
   All the shapes have curves and no sides.

3. **The correct answer is C.**
   All the shapes have only one oval within two or more sides.

4. **The correct answer is M.**
   All the shapes contain one right angle.

5. **The correct answer is C.**
   All the shapes contain an N sided figure in the inside and N+1 four sided figure on the outside.

6. **The correct answer is J.**
   All the three figures contain 3 acute angles.

7. **The correct answer is D.**
   All the shapes contain two curves and the rest are straight sides.

8. **The correct answer is K.**
   All the shapes are pentagons.

9. **The correct answer is E.**
   All the diagonals Criss-Cross to make four segmented lines.

10. **The correct answer is L.**
    Half the figures are shaded and the other half has a vertical strip.

11. **The correct answer is A.**
    An angle is connected to another angle by a diagonal.

12. **The correct answer is L.**
    All the figures are parallelograms.

13. **The correct answer is A.**
    All the figures connect the center of the figure through the angles of the figure.

14. **The correct answer is L.**
    All the figures should be divided into two equal parts.

15. **The correct answer is C.**
    All the figures contain one reflex angle.

16. **The correct answer is L.**
    All the figures contain only arcs.

17. **The correct answer is B.**
    All the shapes are decagons.

18. **The correct answer is M.**
    One fifth of the figure is shaded.

19. **The correct answer is B.**
    One half of the figure is shaded with a smaller version of it inscribed within the figure.

20. **The correct answer is J.**
    An angle is connected to a side and that portion is shaded.

21. **The correct answer is A.**
    The figure is split in half.

22. **The correct answer is L.**
    The figure is placed within a figure with one more side around it.

ANSWER EXPLANATIONS

23. **The correct answer is B.**
    The inside figure is turned fully 180° and inscribed within the figure. The inside figure is also turned darker.

24. **The correct answer is N.**
    The figure is rotated 180° and the left side of the resulting figure is shaded.

25. **The correct answer is D.**
    The n sided figure is lowered by one side.

26. **The correct answer is L.**
    The upside down version of the original figure is placed within and is shaded in.

27. **The correct answer is B.**
    Three fourths of the original figure remains.

28. **The correct answer is K.**
    The half versions of the original figure are separated and placed with a rectangle in the middle of the line of separation.

29. **The correct answer is E.**
    The figure is increased by one side.

30. **The correct answer is M.**
    The bottom half of the figure is rotated 180° and the top half is unshaded compared to its original figure. The bottom remains shaded in.

31. **The correct answer is E.**
    The bottom half is moved to the top and the top half is moved to the bottom.

32. **The correct answer is J.**
    All the reflex angles are turned into angles less than 180°.

33. **The correct answer is A.**
    The figure is rotated 180° and there is an anti-diagnol. There should be no shading.

34. **The correct answer is N.**
    One dot is made into four connected dots so one square should be made into four connected squares. The resulting figures should all be vertical.

35. **The correct answer is C.**
    The figure is rotated 90° counterclockwise.

36. **The correct answer is K.**
    The borders of the figure is made bolder.

37. **The correct answer is B.**
    A n sided figure is lowered by two sides and the new figure is shaded.

38. **The correct answer is L.**
    The bottom half of the figure is placed on top after it is rotated 180° and the top figures placed in the bottom. The bottom figure is also opposite in terms of shading of the original figure.

39. **The correct answer is E.**
    The figure is split in half and the two halves are placed side-by-side facing away from each other with a semicircle cut from each of the halves on the left and right side.

40. **The correct answer is J.**
    The figure is reflected along the arrow with a smaller version of it nearby.

41. **The correct answer is E.**
42. **The correct answer is J.**
43. **The correct answer is C.**
44. **The correct answer is M.**
45. **The correct answer is B.**
46. **The correct answer is N.**
47. **The correct answer is A.**
48. **The correct answer is L.**
49. **The correct answer is B.**
50. **The correct answer is M.**

EXAM 3
TACHS

ARGO BROTHERS

To calculate your score and watch video tutorials, visit
our web site: www.einstein-academy.com/catholic

TACHS PRACTICE TEST 3
ANSWER SHEET

Reading (Part I)

1. Ⓐ Ⓑ Ⓒ Ⓓ
2. Ⓙ Ⓚ Ⓛ Ⓜ
3. Ⓐ Ⓑ Ⓒ Ⓓ
4. Ⓙ Ⓚ Ⓛ Ⓜ
5. Ⓐ Ⓑ Ⓒ Ⓓ
6. Ⓙ Ⓚ Ⓛ Ⓜ
7. Ⓐ Ⓑ Ⓒ Ⓓ
8. Ⓙ Ⓚ Ⓛ Ⓜ
9. Ⓐ Ⓑ Ⓒ Ⓓ
10. Ⓙ Ⓚ Ⓛ Ⓜ
11. Ⓐ Ⓑ Ⓒ Ⓓ
12. Ⓙ Ⓚ Ⓛ Ⓜ
13. Ⓐ Ⓑ Ⓒ Ⓓ
14. Ⓙ Ⓚ Ⓛ Ⓜ
15. Ⓐ Ⓑ Ⓒ Ⓓ
16. Ⓙ Ⓚ Ⓛ Ⓜ
17. Ⓐ Ⓑ Ⓒ Ⓓ
18. Ⓙ Ⓚ Ⓛ Ⓜ
19. Ⓐ Ⓑ Ⓒ Ⓓ
20. Ⓙ Ⓚ Ⓛ Ⓜ

Reading (Part I)

21. Ⓐ Ⓑ Ⓒ Ⓓ
22. Ⓙ Ⓚ Ⓛ Ⓜ
23. Ⓐ Ⓑ Ⓒ Ⓓ
24. Ⓙ Ⓚ Ⓛ Ⓜ
25. Ⓐ Ⓑ Ⓒ Ⓓ
26. Ⓙ Ⓚ Ⓛ Ⓜ
27. Ⓐ Ⓑ Ⓒ Ⓓ
28. Ⓙ Ⓚ Ⓛ Ⓜ
29. Ⓐ Ⓑ Ⓒ Ⓓ
30. Ⓙ Ⓚ Ⓛ Ⓜ
31. Ⓐ Ⓑ Ⓒ Ⓓ
32. Ⓙ Ⓚ Ⓛ Ⓜ
33. Ⓐ Ⓑ Ⓒ Ⓓ
34. Ⓙ Ⓚ Ⓛ Ⓜ
35. Ⓐ Ⓑ Ⓒ Ⓓ
36. Ⓙ Ⓚ Ⓛ Ⓜ
37. Ⓐ Ⓑ Ⓒ Ⓓ
38. Ⓙ Ⓚ Ⓛ Ⓜ
39. Ⓐ Ⓑ Ⓒ Ⓓ
40. Ⓙ Ⓚ Ⓛ Ⓜ
41. Ⓐ Ⓑ Ⓒ Ⓓ
42. Ⓙ Ⓚ Ⓛ Ⓜ
43. Ⓐ Ⓑ Ⓒ Ⓓ
44. Ⓙ Ⓚ Ⓛ Ⓜ
45. Ⓐ Ⓑ Ⓒ Ⓓ
46. Ⓙ Ⓚ Ⓛ Ⓜ
47. Ⓐ Ⓑ Ⓒ Ⓓ
48. Ⓙ Ⓚ Ⓛ Ⓜ
49. Ⓐ Ⓑ Ⓒ Ⓓ
50. Ⓙ Ⓚ Ⓛ Ⓜ

Language (Part I)

1. Ⓐ Ⓑ Ⓒ Ⓓ
2. Ⓙ Ⓚ Ⓛ Ⓜ
3. Ⓐ Ⓑ Ⓒ Ⓓ
4. Ⓙ Ⓚ Ⓛ Ⓜ
5. Ⓐ Ⓑ Ⓒ Ⓓ
6. Ⓙ Ⓚ Ⓛ Ⓜ
7. Ⓐ Ⓑ Ⓒ Ⓓ
8. Ⓙ Ⓚ Ⓛ Ⓜ
9. Ⓐ Ⓑ Ⓒ Ⓓ
10. Ⓙ Ⓚ Ⓛ Ⓜ
11. Ⓐ Ⓑ Ⓒ Ⓓ
12. Ⓙ Ⓚ Ⓛ Ⓜ
13. Ⓐ Ⓑ Ⓒ Ⓓ
14. Ⓙ Ⓚ Ⓛ Ⓜ
15. Ⓐ Ⓑ Ⓒ Ⓓ
16. Ⓙ Ⓚ Ⓛ Ⓜ
17. Ⓐ Ⓑ Ⓒ Ⓓ
18. Ⓙ Ⓚ Ⓛ Ⓜ
19. Ⓐ Ⓑ Ⓒ Ⓓ
20. Ⓙ Ⓚ Ⓛ Ⓜ
21. Ⓐ Ⓑ Ⓒ Ⓓ
22. Ⓙ Ⓚ Ⓛ Ⓜ
23. Ⓐ Ⓑ Ⓒ Ⓓ
24. Ⓙ Ⓚ Ⓛ Ⓜ
25. Ⓐ Ⓑ Ⓒ Ⓓ
26. Ⓙ Ⓚ Ⓛ Ⓜ
27. Ⓐ Ⓑ Ⓒ Ⓓ
28. Ⓙ Ⓚ Ⓛ Ⓜ
29. Ⓐ Ⓑ Ⓒ Ⓓ
30. Ⓙ Ⓚ Ⓛ Ⓜ
31. Ⓐ Ⓑ Ⓒ Ⓓ
32. Ⓙ Ⓚ Ⓛ Ⓜ
33. Ⓐ Ⓑ Ⓒ Ⓓ
34. Ⓙ Ⓚ Ⓛ Ⓜ
35. Ⓐ Ⓑ Ⓒ Ⓓ
36. Ⓙ Ⓚ Ⓛ Ⓜ
37. Ⓐ Ⓑ Ⓒ Ⓓ
38. Ⓙ Ⓚ Ⓛ Ⓜ
39. Ⓐ Ⓑ Ⓒ Ⓓ
40. Ⓙ Ⓚ Ⓛ Ⓜ

Math (Part I)

1. Ⓐ Ⓑ Ⓒ Ⓓ
2. Ⓙ Ⓚ Ⓛ Ⓜ
3. Ⓐ Ⓑ Ⓒ Ⓓ
4. Ⓙ Ⓚ Ⓛ Ⓜ
5. Ⓐ Ⓑ Ⓒ Ⓓ
6. Ⓙ Ⓚ Ⓛ Ⓜ
7. Ⓐ Ⓑ Ⓒ Ⓓ
8. Ⓙ Ⓚ Ⓛ Ⓜ
9. Ⓐ Ⓑ Ⓒ Ⓓ
10. Ⓙ Ⓚ Ⓛ Ⓜ
11. Ⓐ Ⓑ Ⓒ Ⓓ
12. Ⓙ Ⓚ Ⓛ Ⓜ
13. Ⓐ Ⓑ Ⓒ Ⓓ
14. Ⓙ Ⓚ Ⓛ Ⓜ
15. Ⓐ Ⓑ Ⓒ Ⓓ
16. Ⓙ Ⓚ Ⓛ Ⓜ
17. Ⓐ Ⓑ Ⓒ Ⓓ
18. Ⓙ Ⓚ Ⓛ Ⓜ
19. Ⓐ Ⓑ Ⓒ Ⓓ
20. Ⓙ Ⓚ Ⓛ Ⓜ
21. Ⓐ Ⓑ Ⓒ Ⓓ
22. Ⓙ Ⓚ Ⓛ Ⓜ
23. Ⓐ Ⓑ Ⓒ Ⓓ
24. Ⓙ Ⓚ Ⓛ Ⓜ
25. Ⓐ Ⓑ Ⓒ Ⓓ
26. Ⓙ Ⓚ Ⓛ Ⓜ
27. Ⓐ Ⓑ Ⓒ Ⓓ
28. Ⓙ Ⓚ Ⓛ Ⓜ
29. Ⓐ Ⓑ Ⓒ Ⓓ
30. Ⓙ Ⓚ Ⓛ Ⓜ
31. Ⓐ Ⓑ Ⓒ Ⓓ
32. Ⓙ Ⓚ Ⓛ Ⓜ

Math (Part II)

33. Ⓐ Ⓑ Ⓒ Ⓓ
34. Ⓙ Ⓚ Ⓛ Ⓜ
35. Ⓐ Ⓑ Ⓒ Ⓓ
36. Ⓙ Ⓚ Ⓛ Ⓜ
37. Ⓐ Ⓑ Ⓒ Ⓓ
38. Ⓙ Ⓚ Ⓛ Ⓜ
39. Ⓐ Ⓑ Ⓒ Ⓓ
40. Ⓙ Ⓚ Ⓛ Ⓜ
41. Ⓐ Ⓑ Ⓒ Ⓓ
42. Ⓙ Ⓚ Ⓛ Ⓜ
43. Ⓐ Ⓑ Ⓒ Ⓓ
44. Ⓙ Ⓚ Ⓛ Ⓜ
45. Ⓐ Ⓑ Ⓒ Ⓓ
46. Ⓙ Ⓚ Ⓛ Ⓜ
47. Ⓐ Ⓑ Ⓒ Ⓓ
48. Ⓙ Ⓚ Ⓛ Ⓜ
49. Ⓐ Ⓑ Ⓒ Ⓓ
50. Ⓙ Ⓚ Ⓛ Ⓜ

Language (Part II)

41. Ⓐ Ⓑ Ⓒ Ⓓ
42. Ⓙ Ⓚ Ⓛ Ⓜ
43. Ⓐ Ⓑ Ⓒ Ⓓ
44. Ⓙ Ⓚ Ⓛ Ⓜ
45. Ⓐ Ⓑ Ⓒ Ⓓ
46. Ⓙ Ⓚ Ⓛ Ⓜ
47. Ⓐ Ⓑ Ⓒ Ⓓ
48. Ⓙ Ⓚ Ⓛ Ⓜ
49. Ⓐ Ⓑ Ⓒ Ⓓ
50. Ⓙ Ⓚ Ⓛ Ⓜ

Ability (Part I)

1. Ⓐ Ⓑ Ⓒ Ⓓ
2. Ⓙ Ⓚ Ⓛ Ⓜ
3. Ⓐ Ⓑ Ⓒ Ⓓ
4. Ⓙ Ⓚ Ⓛ Ⓜ
5. Ⓐ Ⓑ Ⓒ Ⓓ
6. Ⓙ Ⓚ Ⓛ Ⓜ
7. Ⓐ Ⓑ Ⓒ Ⓓ
8. Ⓙ Ⓚ Ⓛ Ⓜ
9. Ⓐ Ⓑ Ⓒ Ⓓ
10. Ⓙ Ⓚ Ⓛ Ⓜ
11. Ⓐ Ⓑ Ⓒ Ⓓ
12. Ⓙ Ⓚ Ⓛ Ⓜ
13. Ⓐ Ⓑ Ⓒ Ⓓ
14. Ⓙ Ⓚ Ⓛ Ⓜ
15. Ⓐ Ⓑ Ⓒ Ⓓ
16. Ⓙ Ⓚ Ⓛ Ⓜ
17. Ⓐ Ⓑ Ⓒ Ⓓ
18. Ⓙ Ⓚ Ⓛ Ⓜ
19. Ⓐ Ⓑ Ⓒ Ⓓ
20. Ⓙ Ⓚ Ⓛ Ⓜ
21. Ⓐ Ⓑ Ⓒ Ⓓ
22. Ⓙ Ⓚ Ⓛ Ⓜ
23. Ⓐ Ⓑ Ⓒ Ⓓ
24. Ⓙ Ⓚ Ⓛ Ⓜ
25. Ⓐ Ⓑ Ⓒ Ⓓ
26. Ⓙ Ⓚ Ⓛ Ⓜ
27. Ⓐ Ⓑ Ⓒ Ⓓ
28. Ⓙ Ⓚ Ⓛ Ⓜ
29. Ⓐ Ⓑ Ⓒ Ⓓ
30. Ⓙ Ⓚ Ⓛ Ⓜ
31. Ⓐ Ⓑ Ⓒ Ⓓ
32. Ⓙ Ⓚ Ⓛ Ⓜ
33. Ⓐ Ⓑ Ⓒ Ⓓ
34. Ⓙ Ⓚ Ⓛ Ⓜ
35. Ⓐ Ⓑ Ⓒ Ⓓ
36. Ⓙ Ⓚ Ⓛ Ⓜ
37. Ⓐ Ⓑ Ⓒ Ⓓ
38. Ⓙ Ⓚ Ⓛ Ⓜ
39. Ⓐ Ⓑ Ⓒ Ⓓ
40. Ⓙ Ⓚ Ⓛ Ⓜ

Ability (Part II)

41. Ⓐ Ⓑ Ⓒ Ⓓ
42. Ⓙ Ⓚ Ⓛ Ⓜ
43. Ⓐ Ⓑ Ⓒ Ⓓ
44. Ⓙ Ⓚ Ⓛ Ⓜ
45. Ⓐ Ⓑ Ⓒ Ⓓ
46. Ⓙ Ⓚ Ⓛ Ⓜ
47. Ⓐ Ⓑ Ⓒ Ⓓ
48. Ⓙ Ⓚ Ⓛ Ⓜ
49. Ⓐ Ⓑ Ⓒ Ⓓ
50. Ⓙ Ⓚ Ⓛ Ⓜ

READING
PART I (10 MIN)

DIRECTIONS: In this section, you will need to determine the choice that is closest in meaning to the underlined words provided below. Pick the answer choice that fits accordingly and fill in the appropriate letter on your answer sheet.

1. A benign tumor
   A. harmful
   B. big
   C. harmless
   D. growing

2. Being blatant
   J. obvious
   K. kind
   L. dangerous
   M. understanding

3. A helpless mendicant
   A. mourner
   B. beggar
   C. traveler
   D. laborer

4. An astute student
   J. failing
   K. careless
   L. misbehaved
   M. intelligent

5. Candid photography
   A. natural
   B. painted
   C. posed
   D. artistic

6. Feeling reckless
   J. bold
   K. careless
   L. caring
   M. careful

7. To console someone
   A. surprise
   B. comfort
   C. hurt
   D. confuse

8. A gullible parent
   J. naive
   K. stubborn
   L. loving
   M. inferior

CONTINUE ON TO THE NEXT PAGE ➡

READING
PART I

9. Showing extreme valor

   A. determination
   B. patience
   C. fear
   D. courage

10. A potent potion

    J. weak
    K. useless
    L. powerful
    M. magical

11. Performing laudable actions

    A. poor
    B. dishonorable
    C. praiseworthy
    D. hasty

12. Pugnacious little animals

    J. friendly
    K. aggressive
    L. extremely cute
    M. fearful

13. A diminutive beast

    A. monstrous
    B. grandiose
    C. little
    D. aggressive

14. The travails of life

    J. joy
    K. mysteries
    L. greed
    M. hardship

15. An opulent piece

    A. disastrous
    B. disorganized
    C. lavish
    D. creative

16. Altruistic behavior

    J. sporadic
    K. selfless
    L. territorial
    M. infectious

17. Giving sagacious advice

    A. ridiculous
    B. cold-hearted
    C. wise
    D. false

18. Irate behavior

    J. agitated
    K. calm
    L. angry
    M. lewd

CONTINUE ON TO THE NEXT PAGE →

429

READING
PART I

19. The <u>placid</u> waters

    A. violent
    B. peaceful
    C. cold
    D. never-ending

20. Being <u>meticulous</u>

    J. careless
    K. jealous
    L. attentive
    M. stubborn

CONTINUE ON TO THE NEXT PAGE ➡

READING
PART II (25 MIN)

DIRECTIONS: Read the passages below and pick the answer choices that fit accordingly. Fill in the appropriate letter on your answer sheet.

Read the following passage and answer questions 21 - 25.

In undertaking a study of insects, it is important to know something about what they are, their general nature, appearance, habits and development." The insects comprise the largest group of animals on the globe. There are about four times as many distinctive kinds of insects as all other kinds of animals combined. Insects vary greatly in size; some are as large as small birds, while others are so miniscule that a thousand placed in one pile would not equal the size of a pea. Insects are commonly spoken of as "bugs." This term, however, is properly used only when referring to the one order of insects which includes the sap and blood-sucking insects such as the chinch bug, bed-bug, squash bug, and the like. Then too, there are many so-called "bugs" which are not insects at all. Spiders, centipedes, crawfishes and even earthworms are often spoken of as bugs. Insects are variously formed, but as a rule, they usually have three and only three pairs of legs, one pair of feelers, one pair of large eyes, and one or two pairs of wings. The body is divided into a head, thorax and abdomen.

21. According the the passage, a bug can best be described as

    A. an insect
    B. a blood-sucker
    C. a spider
    D. an abdomen

22. In the passage, the word *distinctive* most nearly means

    J. similar
    K. many
    L. different
    M. proper

23. One of the characteristics of insects are

    A. four pairs of legs
    B. two pairs of large eyes
    C. one pair of feelers
    D. four pairs of wings

24. In the passage, the word *miniscule* most nearly means

    J. small
    K. large
    L. disgusting
    M. irrelevant

CONTINUE ON TO THE NEXT PAGE ➡

432

25. The three parts of the insect's body are the head, abdomen and

   A. feelers
   B. wings
   C. legs
   D. thorax

READING
PART II

Read the following passage and answer questions 26 - 30.

A large majority of people speak of a "criminal" as if the word had a clearly defined meaning and as if humans were divided by a plain and distinct line into the criminal and the virtuous. As a matter of fact, there is no such division, and from the nature of things, there never can be such a line. Strictly speaking, a crime is an act tabooed by the law of the land, and one which is considered sufficiently serious to warrant providing penalties for its commission. It does not necessarily follow that this act is either good or bad; the punishment follows for the violation of the law and not necessarily for any moral transgression. No doubt most of the things forbidden by the penal code are such as are injurious to the organized society of the time and place, and are usually of such a character as for a long period of time, and in most countries, have been classed as criminal. But even then it does not always follow that the violator of the law is not a person of higher type than the majority who are directly and indirectly responsible for the law.

26. What would be an appropriate title for this passage?

   J. What is Crime?
   K. Detectives and Mystery
   L. Man and Law
   M. Punishing Criminals

27. Most people believe there is a distinct division between the virtuous and the

   A. doubtful
   B. law
   C. code
   D. criminal

28. In the passage, the word *tabooed* most nearly means

   J. allowed
   K. limited
   L. forbidden
   M. closed

29. According to the passage, a law-breaker is not necessarily

   A. evil
   B. either good or bad
   C. a rebel
   D. correct

CONTINUE ON TO THE NEXT PAGE →

READING
PART II

30. Laws are usually made to prevent acts that are

- **J.** damaging to society
- **K.** helpful
- **L.** unjust
- **M.** harmless

READING
PART II

Read the following passage and answer questions 31 - 35.

Bushido, or "the way," was the understanding of samurai moral values that focus on loyalty, honor and the mastery of the martial arts, similar to the idea of chivalry that was so well known to the knights of the Middle Ages. The samurai were considered to be the highest point of military nobility in medieval Japan. They were the middle and upper rankings of the feudal Japanese military officers, and were seen as the peak of military tactics and strategy, numbering less than one-tenth of the country's population. The samurai were prided in their katana swords, which became of great significance and a symbol of a man's honor. They began as well-equipped and armed supporters of wealthy individuals. Over time, their use as extremely effective warriors helped their daimyos, or lords, rise in military power over Japan's emperors during the 12th century. Their title as "those who serve" lasted for centuries until the mid 1800's. The samurai would command the Japanese government until the eventual abolition of the feudal system which resulted in the deaths of most sword-bearers.

---

31. The term *samurai* most likely means

- **A.** the way
- **B.** honor
- **C.** those who serve
- **D.** lord

32. Daimyos were considered to be

- **J.** leaders of the samurai
- **K.** runaways
- **L.** emperors
- **M.** warriors

33. According to the passage, the samurai draw a parallel to

- **A.** villagers
- **B.** horsemen
- **C.** Vikings
- **D.** knights

34. The katana was a symbol of a samurai's

- **J.** wealth
- **K.** strength
- **L.** honor
- **M.** martial prowess

CONTINUE ON TO THE NEXT PAGE ➡

READING
PART II

35. The word *abolition* most nearly means

- **A.** approval
- **B.** overthrow
- **C.** beginning
- **D.** establishment

READING
PART II

Read the following passage and answer questions 36 - 40.

Excerpt from Are the Planets Inhabited?

The first wonder that men had concerning the heavenly bodies was an obvious one: lights. There was a greater light to rule the day; a lesser light to rule the night, and there were the stars also. In those days, there seemed an immense difference between the earth upon which men stood, and the bright objects that shone down upon it from the heavens above. The earth seemed to be vast, dark, and motionless. The celestial lights seemed to be small, and moved, and shone. The earth was then regarded as the fixed center of the universe, but the Copernican theory has since deprived it of this pride of place. Yet from another point of view the new conception of its position involves a promotion, since the earth itself is now regarded as a heavenly body of the same order as some of those which shine down upon us. It is amongst them, and it too moves and shines—shines, as some of them do, by reflecting the light of the sun. Could we transport ourselves to a neighboring world, the earth would seem a star, not distinguishable in kind from the rest. But as men discerned this, they began to ask: "Since this world from a distant standpoint must appear as a star, would not a star, if we could get near enough to it, show itself also as a world?"

---

36. According to the passage, the Copernican theory disproved that

    J. There are other worlds other than the earth.
    K. The earth is at the center of the universe.
    L. Humans are the only lifeforms.
    M. Light is found everywhere.

37. What would be an appropriate title for this passage?

    A. Light and Other Worlds
    B. The Humans of Earth
    C. Copernican Theory
    D. Celestial Lights

38. It can be inferred from the concluding sentence that

    J. men are alone in the universe
    K. light travels faster than sound
    L. there may be other worlds other than earth
    M. there is only darkness in other planets

39. In the passage, the word *discerned* most nearly means

    A. misinterpreted
    B. overlooked
    C. neglected
    D. realized

CONTINUE ON TO THE NEXT PAGE ➡

READING
PART II

40. When first looking to the sky, men were most amazed by

   J. light from stars
   K. other planets
   L. clouds
   M. the moon

READING
PART II

Read the following passage and answer questions 41 - 45.

For thousands of years before men had any accurate and exact knowledge of the changes of material things, they had thought about these changes and regarded them as revelations of spiritual truths. They built on them theories of things in heaven and earth, and used them in manufactures, arts, and handicrafts. From such, the accurate and systematic study of the changes which material things undergo is called chemistry. The forerunner of chemistry originating as early as 640 BC is the art known as alchemy. It can be described as the superficial examination of these changes, the speculative systems founded on that examination. Certainly alchemy had a long life, for chemistry did not begin until about the middle of the 18th century. No branch of science has had so long a period of incubation as chemistry. There must be some extraordinary difficulty in the way of disentangling the steps of those changes wherein substances of one kind are produced from substances totally unlike them.

41. In the passage, the word *forerunner* most nearly means

   A. jogger
   B. result
   C. ancestor
   D. descendant

42. Unlike chemistry, the study of alchemy is based on

   J. guesswork
   K. truth
   L. proof
   M. studying

43. In the passage, the word *superficial* most nearly means

   A. complete
   B. serious
   C. inaccurate
   D. detailed

44. Chemistry is the study of

   J. the movement of materials
   K. changes of material things
   L. the composition of materials
   M. the heavens

CONTINUE ON TO THE NEXT PAGE ➡

READING PART II

45. According to the passage, which study did chemistry originate from?

- A. alchemy
- B. biology
- C. arts
- D. speculation

READING
PART II

Read the following passage and answer questions 46 - 50.

Excerpt from "Day of Infamy" speech by Franklin Delano Roosevelt

Yesterday, December 7th, 1941 — a date which will live in infamy — the United States of America was suddenly and deliberately attacked by naval and air forces of the Empire of Japan. The United States was at peace with that nation and, at the solicitation of Japan, was still in conversation with its government and its emperor looking toward the maintenance of peace in the Pacific. Indeed, one hour after Japanese air squadrons had commenced bombing in the American island of Oahu, the Japanese ambassador to the United States and his colleague delivered to our Secretary of State a formal reply to a recent American message. And while this reply stated that it seemed useless to continue the existing diplomatic negotiations, it contained no threat or hint of war or of armed attack. It will be recorded that the distance of Hawaii from Japan makes it obvious that the attack was deliberately planned many days or even weeks ago. During the intervening time, the Japanese government has deliberately sought to deceive the United States by false statements and expressions of hope for continued peace.

---

46. In the passage, the word *infamy* most nearly means

    J. pride
    K. dishonor
    L. respect
    M. approval

47. It was determined that the Japanese attack was deliberate based on

    A. naval intel
    B. German information
    C. the proximity of Hawaii and Japan
    D. Japanese statements

48. After the attack, the Japanese sought to

    J. find peace with the US
    K. declare war
    L. maintain its economy
    M. send aid and support

49. Based on the passage, the attack was

    A. justifiable
    B. unprejudiced
    C. baseless
    D. reasonable

CONTINUE ON TO THE NEXT PAGE ➡

READING
PART II

50. The aftermath of the event in Oahu led to

- **J.** an end of peace
- **K.** greater trade negotiations
- **L.** a formal reply from the US
- **M.** talks of diplomacy

CONTINUE ON TO THE NEXT PAGE ➡

LANGUAGE
PART I (23 MIN)

DIRECTIONS: In this section, you will need to determine the errors that are found in the sentences. Pick the answer choice that highlights the mistake and fill in the appropriate letter on your answer sheet. If no mistake is present, choose the last answer choice.

Directions: Look for mistakes in <u>spelling</u>.

1.
   A. functional
   B. fortress
   C. mygrate
   D. marriage
   E. *(No mistakes)*

2.
   J. problematic
   K. possess
   L. unanimously
   M. discreet
   N. *(No mistakes)*

3.
   A. endanger
   B. qualifies
   C. efforts
   D. afforts
   E. *(No mistakes)*

4.
   J. acommodate
   K. amateur
   L. apparent
   M. acquit
   N. *(No mistakes)*

5.
   A. calendar
   B. beleive
   C. heir
   D. collectible
   E. *(No mistakes)*

6.
   J. cemetary
   K. committed
   L. acquire
   M. consensus
   N. *(No mistakes)*

7.
   A. fiery
   B. gauge
   C. greatful
   D. exceed
   E. *(No mistakes)*

8.
   J. guarantee
   K. harrass
   L. humorous
   M. independent
   N. *(No mistakes)*

9.
   A. hierarchy
   B. intelligence
   C. mispell
   D. miniscule
   E. *(No mistakes)*

10.
   J. miniature
   K. medieval
   L. maneuver
   M. millenium
   N. *(No mistakes)*

CONTINUE ON TO THE NEXT PAGE ➡

LANGUAGE
PART I

Directions: Look for mistakes in <u>capitalization</u>.

11. A. My friend and I
    B. went to arizona
    C. for summer vacation.
    D. *(No mistakes)*

12. J. We are learning
    K. about the astronaut
    L. who landed on the Moon.
    M. *(No mistakes)*

13. A. The d.e.a. is tasked
    B. with combating drug smuggling
    C. and use within the United States.
    D. *(No mistakes)*

14. J. I saw Dad and Uncle Bob
    K. at the movies eating
    L. popcorn and hotdogs.
    M. *(No mistakes)*

15. A. I cannot wait
    B. for Summer so I
    C. can play outside in the sun.
    D. *(No mistakes)*

16. J. I studied algebra and biology
    K. this morning because
    L. I have an exam later this evening.
    M. *(No mistakes)*

17. A. President carter was
    B. the 39th President of
    C. the United States.
    D. *(No mistakes)*

18. J. These features include
    K. caller id, long distance
    L. and call waiting.
    M. *(No mistakes)*

19. A. When I was a kid,
    B. I thought I would
    C. be a Doctor.
    D. *(No mistakes)*

20. J. Justin Bieber is
    K. my favorite
    L. Canadian singer.
    M. *(No mistakes)*

CONTINUE ON TO THE NEXT PAGE ➡

LANGUAGE
PART I

Directions: Look for punctuation mistakes.

21. A. Ms. Alvarez was happy
    B. because the boys debate team
    C. won a championship.
    D. *(No mistakes)*

22. J. Lindsey worked a long and
    K. tiring shift at work. However she
    L. made a ton of money.
    M. *(No mistakes)*

23. A. John is a highly athletic
    B. student. He plays basketball
    C. soccer, and football.
    D. *(No mistakes)*

24. J. It is nearly half past six,
    K. we cannot reach the
    L. town before dark.
    M. *(No mistakes)*

25. A. I need an assistant who can do
    B. the following; answer phone calls,
    C. write reports, and input data.
    D. *(No mistakes)*

26. J. We won the game last night. Did
    K. you also know that we never
    L. lost a game before.
    M. *(No mistakes)*

27. A. "Reflecting back on it," he said,
    B. "she didn't expect to do
    C. this well on the exam."
    D. *(No mistakes)*

28. J. Its wise to take a flashlight
    K. and a first aid kit when
    L. you go camping in the dark.
    M. *(No mistakes)*

29. A. The pilot announced
    B. "Please fasten your seatbelts
    C. and enjoy the trip."
    D. *(No mistakes)*

30. J. We are moving to Memphis
    K. Texas because our father
    L. started a new job there.
    M. *(No mistakes)*

CONTINUE ON TO THE NEXT PAGE ➡

LANGUAGE
PART I

Directions: Look for mistakes in usage.

31. A. There are a very good surgeon
    B. who works at the hospital
    C. down the block.
    D. *(No mistakes)*

32. J. Chocolate has not always
    K. been the common confectionary
    L. we experience today.
    M. *(No mistakes)*

33. A. I wanted too go to
    B. the zoo with my friend
    C. but he was busy.
    D. *(No mistakes)*

34. J. On Black Friday,
    K. I would like to buy
    L. two pears of shoes.
    M. *(No mistakes)*

35. A. Michelle plays the piano poor,
    B. but is determined to get better so
    C. she practices every week.
    D. *(No mistakes)*

36. J. Writing the book is a
    K. difficult task which requires
    L. time and energy.
    M. *(No mistakes)*

37. A. Cancer cells differ from normal cells in
    B. many ways that allow them to grow
    C. out of control and become invasive.
    D. *(No mistakes)*

38. J. A cooperative differs from a corporation
    K. in that it has members, not shareholders,
    L. and they share decision-making authority.
    M. *(No mistakes)*

39. A. Sometimes we have to
    B. except change if we
    C. want to move forward.
    D. *(No mistakes)*

40. J. All officers working in this building
    K. must carry his badge and
    L. identification papers.
    M. *(No mistakes)*

CONTINUE ON TO THE NEXT PAGE →

447

LANGUAGE
PART II (7 MIN)

Directions: For questions 41-42, choose the best answer based on the following paragraph.

Excerpt from "Day of Infamy" speech by Franklin Delano Roosevelt

Yesterday, December 7th, 1941 – a date which will live in infamy – the United States of America was suddenly and deliberately attacked by naval and air forces of the Empire of Japan. The United States was at peace with that nation and, at the solicitation of Japan, was still in conversation with its government and its emperor looking toward the maintenance of peace in the Pacific. Indeed, one hour after Japanese air squadrons had commenced bombing in the American island of Oahu, the Japanese ambassador to the United States and his colleague delivered to our Secretary of State a formal reply to a recent American message. And while this reply stated that it seemed useless to continue the existing diplomatic negotiations, it contained no threat or hint of war or of armed attack. It will be recorded that the distance of Hawaii from Japan makes it obvious that the attack was deliberately planned many days or even weeks ago. During the intervening time, the Japanese government has deliberately sought to deceive the United States by false

41. In sentence 2, where should the word "and" be placed?

   A. after "Experience"
   B. before "seem to prove"
   C. after "to prove"
   D. needs no correction

42. Which of the words in sentence 6 is a <u>verb</u>?

   J. "severest"
   K. "assault"
   L. "eradicate"
   M. "mortal"

CONTINUE ON TO THE NEXT PAGE ➡

LANGUAGE
PART II

Directions: For questions 43-44, choose the best answer based on the following paragraph.

Excerpt from The Philosophy of Moral Feelings

(1) Man is to be contemplated as an intellectual and moral being. (2) By his intellectual powers, he acquires the knowledge of facts, observes their connections, and traces the conclusions which arise out of them. (3) These mental operations, however, even in a high state of cultivation, may be directed entirely to truths of an extrinsic kind. (4) That is, to such as do not exert any influence either on the moral condition of the individual, or on his relations to other sentient beings. (5) So they may exist in an eminent degree in the man who lives only for himself, and feels little beyond the personal wants, or the selfish enjoyments of the hour that is passing over him. (6) But, when we contemplate man as a moral being, new relations open on our view, and these are of mightier importance. (7) We find him occupying a place in a great system of moral government, in which he has an important station to fill and high duties to perform.

43. In sentence 2, which of the following words is an <u>adjective</u>?

    A. "intellectual"
    B. "acquire"
    C. "knowledge"
    D. "connections"

44. In sentence 5, which phrase should be removed?

    J. "So"
    K. "may exist"
    L. "to other sentient beings"
    M. *(No mistakes)*

CONTINUE ON TO THE NEXT PAGE ➡

449

LANGUAGE
PART II

Directions: For questions 45-47, choose the best answer based on the following paragraph.

(1) Before attempting to define psychology, it will be helpful to make some inquiry into the nature of science in general. (2) Science is knowledge; it is what we ultimately know. (3) For a bit of knowledge to become a part of science, its relation to other bits of knowledge must be found. (4) In botany, for example, bits of knowledge about plants do not make a science of botany. (5) To have a science of botany, we must not only know about leaves, roots, flowers, and seeds, but we must know the relations of these parts and of all the parts of a plant to one another. (6) In other words, in science, we must not only know, we must not only have knowledge, but we must know the significance of the knowledge, must know its meaning. (7) This is only another way of saying that we must have knowledge and know its relation to other knowledge. (8) A scientist is one who has learn to organize his knowledge. (9) The main difference between a scientist and one who is not a scientist is that the scientist sees the significance of facts, while the non-scientific man sees facts as more or less unrelated things.

45. In sentence 2, which of the following words is an <u>adverb</u>?

A. "knowledge"
B. "is"
C. "ultimately"
D. "know"

46. What is the issue with sentence 6?

J. wrong tense
K. improper use of pronoun
L. sentence fragment
M. *(No mistakes)*

47. Which of the following <u>verbs</u> in sentence 8 is in the wrong tense?

A. "is"
B. "learn"
C. "to organize
D. *(No mistakes)*

CONTINUE ON TO THE NEXT PAGE ➡

LANGUAGE
PART II

Directions: For questions 48-50, choose the best answer based on the following paragraph.

(1) Before attempting to define psychology, it will be helpful to make some inquiry into the nature of science in general. (2) Science is knowledge; it is what we ultimately know. (3) For a bit of knowledge to become a part of science, its relation to other bits of knowledge must be found. (4) In botany, for example, bits of knowledge about plants do not make a science of botany. (5) To have a science of botany, we must not only know about leaves, roots, flowers, and seeds, but we must know the relations of these parts and of all the parts of a plant to one another. (6) In other words, in science, we must not only know, we must not only haveknowledge, but we must know the significance of the knowledge, must know its meaning. (7) This is only another way of saying that we must have knowledge and know its relation to other knowledge. (8) A scientist is one who has learn to organize his knowledge. (9) The main difference between a scientist and one who is not a scientist is that the scientist sees the significance of facts, while the non-scientific man sees facts as more or less unrelated things.

48. What is the tense of sentence 1?

   J. present
   K. past
   L. future
   M. perfect past

49. What is wrong with sentence 6?

   A. misspelled word
   B. adverb is used incorrectly
   C. wrong tense
   D. *(No mistakes)*

50. Which of the following words in sentence 7 is misspelled?

   J. "colossal"
   K. "conciet"
   L. "cataloging"
   M. "instinct"

CONTINUE ON TO THE NEXT PAGE ➡

MATH
PART I (33 MIN)

DIRECTIONS: Choose the answer that best fits the problem.

1. Which of the following is a prime number?

   A. 27
   B. 33
   C. 57
   D. 59

2. 4 - (-4) + (-3) =

   J. -3
   K. 3
   L. 5
   M. 11

3. Which of the following is not a multiple of 6?

   A. 36
   B. 72
   C. 90
   D. 94

4. What is the difference between $\frac{8}{9}$ and $\frac{1}{3}$?

   J. $\frac{5}{9}$
   K. $\frac{7}{9}$
   L. $\frac{7}{3}$
   M. $\frac{2}{9}$

5. What is the least common multiple of 12, 15 and 120?

   A. 2
   B. 60
   C. 120
   D. 240

6. What is 30% of 420?

   J. 12.6
   K. 126
   L. 294
   M. 1,400

CONTINUE ON TO THE NEXT PAGE ➡

MATH
PART I

7. Jack wants to purchase fifty-five pencils. The store sells pencils in packages, where each package has 5 pencils. Each package costs $0.89. How much will Jack spend at the store? (Assume there is no tax.)

   A. $4.45
   B. $8.90
   C. $9.79
   D. $48.95

8. Change $5\frac{3}{8}$ to a decimal.

   J. 5.580
   K. 5.625
   L. 5.375
   M. 5.675

9. It takes George 3 minutes to read 300 words. If each page in a book that he is reading has 750 words, how long will it take George to read 6 pages?

   A. 30 minutes
   B. 45 minutes
   C. 60 minutes
   D. 90 minutes

10. John works 40 hours a week, and his monthly salary in June was $4,000. In the month of July, John got a 4% raise on his monthly salary. In the month of July, what was John's hourly rate?

    Note: Assume there are four weeks in a month

    J. $25
    K. $26
    L. $40
    M. $100

11. Helena would like to buy a clarinet. The clarinet costs $320. She currently has $210 saved. If she receives a $10 a week allowance, how many weeks will it take for Helena to save enough money to buy the clarinet?

    A. 9 weeks
    B. 10 weeks
    C. 11 weeks
    D. 12 weeks

12. The height of a building on a blueprint is 4 inches. If the actual height of the building is 20 feet, what is the ratio of the blueprint to the actual height of the building?

    J. 1:5
    K. 1:60
    L. 60:1
    M. 5:1

CONTINUE ON TO THE NEXT PAGE ➡

MATH
PART I

13. Ashley works at Company Z and receives a salary of $1500 per week. Her friend Joanna who works at Company Y, gets 15% more per week. How much more money does Joanna make than Ashley, weekly?

  A. $150
  B. $225
  C. $100
  D. $1,725

14. It takes 3 cats 3 minutes to catch 3 mice. How many cats are needed to catch 99 mice in 99 minutes?

  J. 3
  K. 6
  L. 33
  M. 99

15. A yellow cab has a base fare of $3.50 per ride plus $0.20 for each $\frac{1}{4}$ of mile ridden. If a yellow cab costs $22.50, how many miles long was the ride?

  A. 23.75 miles
  B. 42.5 miles
  C. 47.5 miles
  D. 112.5 miles

16. A computer originally priced at $550.50 is on sale for 20% off. Kevin used a 5% discount coupon which was applied to the sales price. How much did Kevin pay for the computer? (Assume there is no tax.)

  J. $412.88
  K. $418.38
  L. $440.40
  M. $522.98

17. In Ms. Daniel's class there are 30 kids. If there are twice as many boys as there are girls in the English club, then what percentage of the English club are boys?

  A. 33.3%
  B. 10%
  C. 20%
  D. $66.\overline{66}$%

18. There are 45 plastic ducks in a bag. If there are black, green, blue, and purple plastic ducks and $\frac{1}{3}$ of the plastic ducks are black, $\frac{1}{5}$ of the plastic ducks are blue, one third of the number of black plastic ducks are green, then how many purple plastic ducks are in the bag?

  J. 6
  K. 15
  L. 16
  M. 21

CONTINUE ON TO THE NEXT PAGE ➡

19.

Gas Prices	
Regular	$3.00
Premium	$3.50
Unloaded	$4.00

The prices in the table above show the different types of gas offered at a gas station and the prices of the gas per gallon. If Anna has $120, what is the least amount of gas, in gallons, she can purchase subtracted from the greatest amount of gas, in gallons, she can purchase?

A. 5 gallons
B. 10 gallons
C. 15 gallons
D. 20 gallons

20. The mean weekly salary of 9 teachers in a school is $1,000. If there are 9 teachers and 11 assistant principals and the mean weekly salary for assistant principals and teachers is $1,275, what is the mean salary of the assistant principals?

J. $1,100
K. $1,500
L. $1,137.50
M. $1,300

21.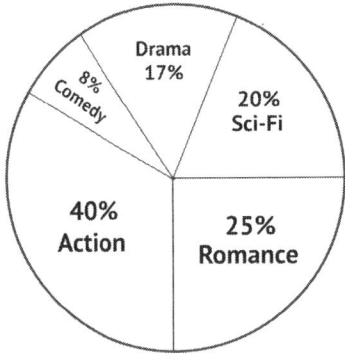

There are 15,000 teens whose favorite genre is comedy. How many teens have a favorite genre of action?

A. 75,000
B. 41,250
C. 52,500
D. 56,250

CONTINUE ON TO THE NEXT PAGE ➡

MATH
PART I

Use the following graph to answer questions 22 and 23.

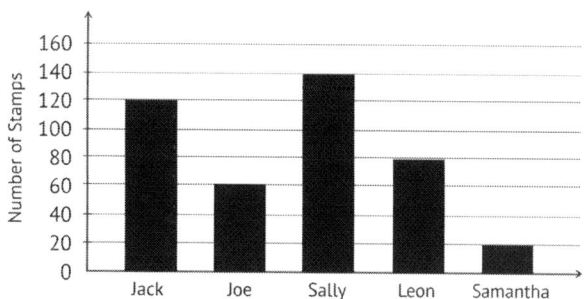

22. Jack, Joe, Sally, Leon and Samantha are collecting stamps as a hobby. What is the average amount of stamps these five friends have together?

    J. 80 stamps
    K. 84 stamps
    L. 105 stamps
    M. 420 stamps

23. If Samantha buys another sixty stamps, then what is the average amount of stamps these five friends have together?

    A. 80 stamps
    B. 84 stamps
    C. 96 stamps
    D. 480 stamps

Use the chart below to answer questions 24 and 25.

	Number of students enrolled
College X	◇◇◇◇◇
College Y	◇◇◇◇
College Z	◇◇◇◇
College B	◇◇◇◇◇◇◇◇◇
College A	◇◇

◇ = 500 people

24. How many students were enrolled at College B?

    J. 500 students
    K. 1,000 students
    L. 5,000 students
    M. 10,000 students

25. How many more students were enrolled at College Y than College A?

    A. 500 students
    B. 1,000 students
    C. 1,500 students
    D. 2,000 students

CONTINUE ON TO THE NEXT PAGE ➡

26.

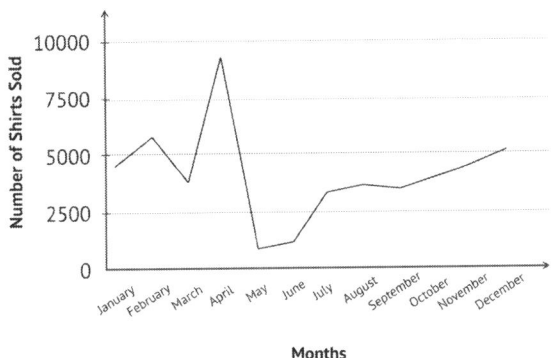

Based on the graph above, between which two months did this store experience the greatest change in the number of shirts sold?

J. February to March
K. March to April
L. April to May
M. January to February

Use the table below to answer questions 27 and 28.

Item	Unit Price
Shirt	$19.99
Pants	$29.99
Socks	$3.99
Hat	$5.99

27. Pamela goes into the store and buys two shirts and one pair of pants. She hands the cashier a hundred dollar bill. How much change will Pamela get back?

A. $42.03
B. $32.03
C. $67.97
D. $30.03

28. Shannon purchases three hats, two pairs of pants and one shirt. She uses a 10% discount coupon on the entire purchase. How much does Shannon owe the cashier?
(Assume there is no tax.)

J. $88.15
K. $97.94
L. $86.15
M. $97.15

CONTINUE ON TO THE NEXT PAGE ➡

MATH
PART I

29.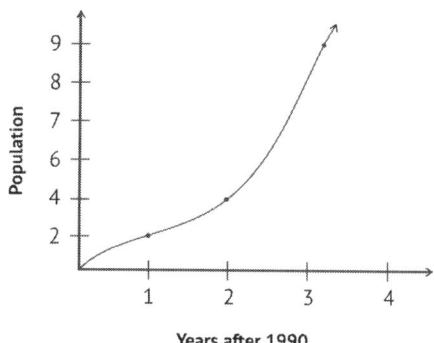

Years after 1990

The following graph shows the population of fish in a certain time after the year 1990. What would be the best approximate for the number of fish in 1995?

A. 16
B. 25
C. 9
D. 15

30.

The graph above shows the number of books Hasan has at home. About what percent of the books are math?

J. 4%
K. 15%
L. 20%
M. 25%

31. Maspeth High School

	Freshman	Sophomore	Junior	Senior	Total
Algebra	53	....	....	12	148
Geometry	21	35	35	....	....
Trigonometry	———	5	7	....	57
Total	77	104	———	77	———

How many more seniors are there that take trigonometry than juniors that take algebra?

A. 42
B. 19
C. 23
D. 3

32. A certain survey revealed that out of 50 people, 20 like cats and 37 like dogs. How many like both cats and dogs?

J. 0
K. 44
L. 17
M. 7

CONTINUE ON TO THE NEXT PAGE ➡

458

MATH
PART II (7 MIN)

DIRECTIONS: In this section, you will need to estimate all your answers. There is no scratch work allowed. Do not determine exact answers. Pick the answer choice that fits accordingly and fill in the appropriate letter on your answer sheet.

33. The closest estimate of 621 + 281 is _____.

    A. 800
    B. 900
    C. 950
    D. 1000

34. The closest estimate of 99,783 - 1005 is _____.

    J. 98,000
    K. 98,500
    L. 99,000
    M. 100,000

35. The closest estimate of
    4(4.9 + 5.1) - 2(9.9 - 2.1) is _____.

    A. 22
    B. 24
    C. 26
    D. 30

36. John is a computer programmer and he can approximately type 97 words per minute. At this rate, how many minutes would it take John to type 900 words?

    J. 8 minutes
    K. 9 minutes
    L. 10 minutes
    M. 90 minutes

37. The closest estimate of $\frac{589}{6}$ is _____.

    A. 80
    B. 90
    C. 100
    D. 110

38. The number 8,601 rounded to the nearest thousands place is _____.

    J. 8,000
    K. 8,600
    L. 8,700
    M. 9,000

CONTINUE ON TO THE NEXT PAGE →

MATH
PART II

39. The number 0.291 rounded to the nearest tenths place is _____.

A. .2
B. 0
C. 0.29
D. 0.3

40. The number 123,546 rounded to the nearest tens place is _____.

J. 124,000
K. 123,000
L. 123,540
M. 123,550

41. The closest estimate of $.97 + $40.23 + $8.93 to the nearest dollar is _____.

A. $49
B. $50
C. $51
D. $52

42. If Mike drove a total of 8,777 miles within 107 hours, what is the best estimate for his average speed within his travel?

J. 90
K. 95
L. 100
M. 105

43. Lilly originally had 9,808 stamps in her collection. She gave 7,002 stamps to her friend Joe. Approximately how many stamps does Lilly now own?

A. 1,000 stamps
B. 2,000 stamps
C. 3,000 stamps
D. 4,000 stamps

44. The closest estimate of 1,115 x 487 is _____.

J. 400,000
K. 500,000
L. 600,000
M. 700,000

45. Mike scored a 99.5 on his first exam and 49.5 on his second exam. What was Mike's test score average?

A. 50
B. 65
C. 75
D. 85

CONTINUE ON TO THE NEXT PAGE ➡

MATH PART II

46. The closest estimate of 98(45-35) is ____.

- J. 800
- K. 1000
- L. 2000
- M. 9000

47. The closest estimate of $(7.125)^2$ is ____.

- A. 47
- B. 49
- C. 50
- D. 65

48. The closest estimate of $\frac{3,479}{11}$ is ____.

- J. 200
- K. 300
- L. 350
- M. 400

49. Joe donates 5% of his annual salary to a charity of his choosing every year. Last year, his annual salary was $97,099. Approximately, how much money did Joe give to a charity last year?

- A. $2,000
- B. $3,000
- C. $5,000
- D. $10,000

50. Michael drove 8,981 miles with his car in a period of one year. Jake drove 19,002 miles with his car in a period of one year. Approximately, how many more miles did Jake drive than Michael?

- J. 10,000 miles
- K. 11,000 miles
- L. 12,000 miles
- M. 30,000 miles

CONTINUE ON TO THE NEXT PAGE ➡

ABILITY
PART I (25 MIN)

DIRECTIONS: In this section, you will need to recognize certain similarities. Pick the answer choice that best matches with the three shapes provided for each question and fill in the appropriate letter on your answer sheet.
TIME LIMIT: 32 minutes for the entire ability section.

1.

A.   B.   C.

D.   E.

2.

J.   K.   L.

M.   N.

3.

A.   B.   C.

D.   E.

4.

J.   K.   L.

M.   N.

CONTINUE ON TO THE NEXT PAGE ➡

462

ABILITY
PART I

5.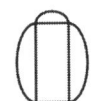

A.  B.  C.

D.  E.

6.

J.  K. 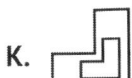 L.

M.  N.

7.

A.  B.  C. (teardrop)

D.  E.

8.

J.  K.  L. (parallelogram)

M. (rectangle) N.

9.

A. 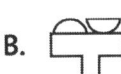 B. (shape) C. (shape)

D.  E. (shape)

10.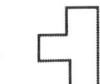

J. 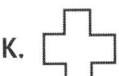 K.  L. (triangle)

M. (shape) N.

CONTINUE ON TO THE NEXT PAGE ➡

ABILITY
PART I

11.

   A.   B.   C.

   D.   E.

12.

   J.   K.  L.

   M.   N.

13.

   A. B. C.

   D. E.

14.

   J. 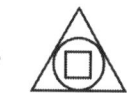 K. 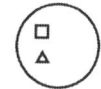 L.

   M.   N.

15.

   A. 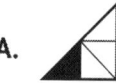 B.   C.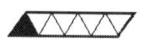

   D. 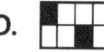 E.

16.

   J.  K.  L.

   M. 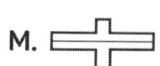 N.

CONTINUE ON TO THE NEXT PAGE ➡

ABILITY
PART I

ABILITY
PART I

DIRECTIONS: In this section, you will need to recognize certain similarities. Pick the answer choice that best matches with the three shapes provided for each question and fill in the appropriate letter on your answer sheet.

21.

22.

23.

24.

CONTINUE ON TO THE NEXT PAGE ➡

ABILITY
PART I

ABILITY
PART I

31.

32.

33.

34.

35.

36.

ABILITY
PART I

37.

A. B. C.

D. E.

38.

J. K. L.

M. N.

39.

A. B. C.

D. E.

40.

J. K. L.

M. N.

CONTINUE ON TO THE NEXT PAGE ➡

ABILITY
PART II (7 MIN)

DIRECTIONS: The second figure represents a change made on the first figure. What would be the resulting figure if the second figure was unfolded?

41.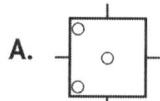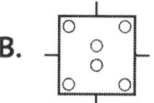

A. 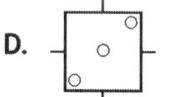 B. 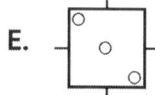 C. (square with 3 dots at bottom)

D. (square with 2 dots) E. (square with 2 dots)

42. (three figures)

J. K. L.

M. N.

43. 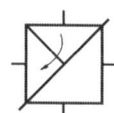 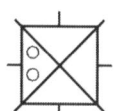 (square with X)

A. 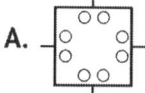 B. 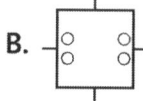 C.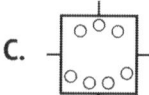

D. E.

44. (two figures)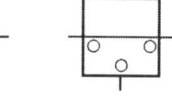

J. K. 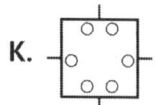 L.

M. N.

CONTINUE ON TO THE NEXT PAGE ➡

ABILITY
PART I

45.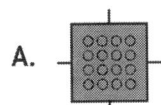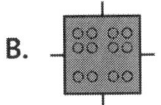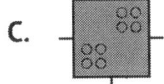

A. 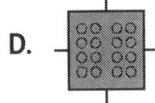 B. 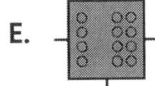 C.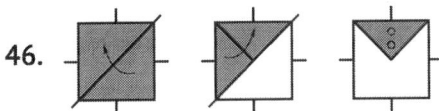

D. 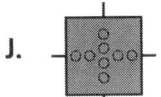 E.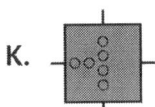

46.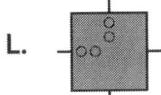

J. 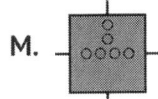 K. 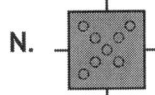 L.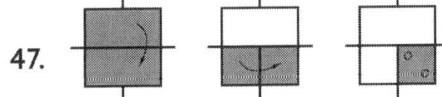

M. 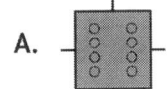 N.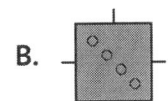

47.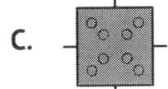

A. 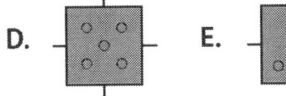 B. 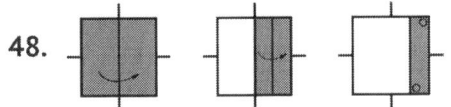 C.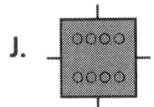

D. 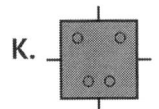 E.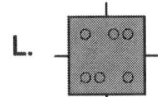

48.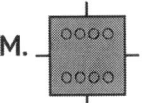

J. 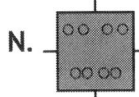 K. 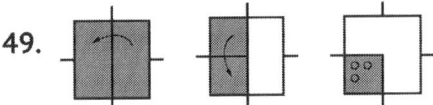 L.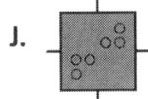

M. 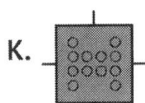 N.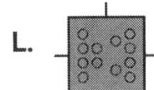

49.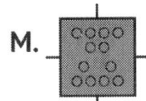

J. 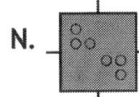 K. 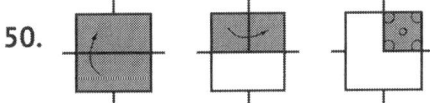 L.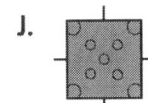

M. 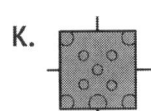 N.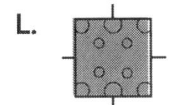

50.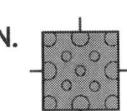

TACHS PRACTICE TEST 3
ANSWER KEY

ENGLISH

Reading (Part I)

1. C
2. J
3. B
4. M
5. A
6. K
7. B
8. J
9. D
10. L
11. C
12. K
13. C
14. M
15. C
16. K
17. C
18. L
19. B
20. K

Reading (Part II)

21. B
22. L
23. C
24. J
25. D
26. J
27. D
28. L
29. B
30. J
31. C
32. J
33. D
34. L
35. B
36. K
37. A
38. L
39. D
40. J
41. C
42. J
43. C
44. K
45. A
46. K
47. C
48. J
49. C
50. J

Language (Part I)

1. C
2. N
3. D
4. J
5. B
6. J
7. C
8. K
9. C
10. M
11. B
12. L
13. A
14. M
15. B
16. M
17. A
18. K
19. C
20. M
21. B
22. K
23. B
24. J
25. B
26. L
27. D
28. J
29. A
30. J
31. A
32. M
33. A
34. L
35. A
36. J
37. D
38. M
39. B
40. K

Language (Part II)

41. A
42. L
43. A
44. J
45. C
46. K
47. B
48. J
49. D
50. K

ARGO BROTHERS

To calculate your score and watch video tutorials, visit our web site: www.einstein-academy.com/catholic

MATHEMATICS

Mathematics (Part I)

1. D
2. L
3. D
4. J
5. C
6. K
7. C
8. L
9. B
10. K
11. C
12. K
13. B
14. J
15. A
16. K
17. D
18. J
19. B
20. K
21. D
22. K
23. C
24. L
25. B
26. L
27. D
28. J
29. B
30. L
31. C
32. M

Mathematics (Part II)

33. B
34. L
35. B
36. K
37. C
38. M
39. D
40. M
41. B
42. J
43. C
44. K
45. C
46. K
47. C
48. L
49. C
50. J

ABILITY

Ability (Part I)

1. E
2. L
3. B
4. J
5. D
6. J
7. C
8. K
9. B
10. J
11. D
12. N
13. C
14. K
15. C
16. N
17. A
18. N
19. E
20. K
21. A
22. M
23. A
24. L
25. B
26. N
27. B
28. K
29. D
30. L
31. B
32. J
33. C
34. M
35. D
36. K
37. C
38. M
39. E
40. L

Ability (Part II)

41. B
42. L
43. A
44. M
45. D
46. J
47. C
48. N
49. B
50. N

ANSWER EXPLANATIONS

READING SECTION
The following 20 questions can be fully understood with the vocabulary section attached with the book.

1. **The correct answer is C**
   Benign means gentle, or not harmful to the environment. Harmless best fits this.

2. **The correct answer is J.**
   To be blatant means to be done openly and unashamedly or to be done lacking subtlety. Obvious is a synonym.

3. **The correct answer is B**.
   Mendicant is a noun that refers to a beggar.

4. **The correct answer is M.**
   To be astute means to have or show an ability to accurately assess situations or people and turn this to one's advantage. Intelligent best fits this definition.

5. **The correct answer is A**.
   Candid is an adjective that describes someone or something that is truthful and straightforward. With reference to photography, it means taken informally without the subject's knowledge, or natural.

6. **The correct answer is K**.
   Reckless is an adjective that describes something that is done without thinking or caring about the consequences of an action. Careless is a synonym for this.

7. **The correct answer is B.**
   To console means to comfort someone at a time of grief or disappointment.

8. **The correct answer is J.**
   Gullible means to be easily persuaded to believe something. Naive best fits this.

9. **The correct answer is D.**
   To show valor means to show great courage in the face of danger. Courage is a synonym.

10. **The correct answer is L.**
    Potent means to have great power or influence. Powerful is a synonym for this.

11. **The correct answer is C**.
    Laudable is an adjective that describes something that is deserving of praise and commendation. Praiseworthy is a synonym.

12. **The correct answer is K**
    Pugnacious means to be eager or quick to argue, quarrel, or fight. Aggressive best fits this.

13. **The correct answer is C.**
    Diminutive means extremely or unusually small. Little best fits this.

14. **The correct answer is M.**
    Travail means painful or laborious effort. Hardship best fits this.

15. **The correct answer is C.**
    Opulent is an adjective that describes something ostentatiously rich and luxurious. Lavish is a synonym for this.

16. **The correct answer is K.**
    Altruistic means to show a disinterested and selfless concern for the well-being of others.

ANSWER EXPLANATIONS

17. The correct answer is C.
Sagacious means to have or show keen mental discernment and good judgement. Wise is a synonym for this.

18. The correct answer is L.
Irate means to be characterized by great anger. Angry is a synonym.

19. The correct answer is B.
Placid means not easily upset or excited, or calm and peaceful.

20. The correct answer is K.
To be meticulous means to show great attention to detail, and to be very careful. Attentive is a synonym.

21. The correct answer is B.
The passage states that the term "bug" is only properly used when talking about blood sucking insects.

22. The correct answer is L.
Using context clues, plug in the answer choices into the sentence and get an idea for which word best fits. Here, something has to describe various types of bugs and "different" fits that.

23. The correct answer is C.
The second to last sentence gives what the characteristics of an insect are. One of the characteristics include one pair of feelers.

24. The correct answer is J.
Using context clues, replace each answer choice with the word miniscule. The word "small" best fits this. "Mini" in front of the word further gives us a clue to the meaning.

25. The correct answer is D.
The last sentence summarizes the parts of an insect which include the head, the thorax, and the abdomen.

26. The correct answer is J.
The main idea of the passage involves crime and the aspects behind it.

27. The correct answer is D.
The first sentence says that there is an assumed clear division of line between the criminal and the virtuous.

28. The correct answer is L.
If the word tabooed is replaced with forbidden, the sentence makes sense. Here, it can be seen that a crime is outlawed by laws. This shows how forbidden is the answer.

29. The correct answer is B.
The passage states that "this does not necessarily follow that the act is either good or bad."

30. The correct answer is J.
According to the passage, things are usually forbidden since they are "injurious to the organized society."

31. The correct answer is C.
In the third to last line, the passage states, "Their title as 'those who serve' lasted for centuries until the mid 1800's."

32. The correct answer is J.
In the passage, before the word Daimyos, it mentions that the extremely effective warriors, which were the samurai, helped their Lords gain power. The Daimyos were their lords, or leaders.

ANSWER EXPLANATIONS

33. **The correct answer is D.**
    The first sentence states that the chivalry is similar to that of a knight.

34. **The correct answer is L.**
    The passage states that the katana is "a symbol of a man's honor."

35. **The correct answer is B.**
    The "abolition" led to the death of many sword-bearers according to the last sentence. The sword bearers were the samurai, so in this context the samurai were probably being overthrown.

36. **The correct answer is K.**
    The passage states that the Copernican theory deprives the pride of the earth being the center of the universe.

37. **The correct answer is A.**
    The entirety of the passage suggest that light seems to distinguish between stars and earth. It then draws a parallel between the two.

38. **The correct answer is L.**
    From the previous sentence, men ponder at the fact that the Earth may not be so special after all. This may be because there are other worlds other than Earth and it is not necessarily at the center as people used to think.

39. **The correct answer is D.**
    Using context clues, plug each answer choice into the sentence. You are looking for a word that describes a thought against a previously accepted idea. The word "realized" best fits this.

40. **The correct answer is J.**
    The first sentence states that men were amazed at the sight of light from heavenly bodies.

41. **The correct answer is C.**
    The sentence with forerunner indicates an early version of chemistry so ancestor is the best answer.

42. **The correct answer is J.**
    The passage states that alchemy was a superficial examination. Superficial means something appearing to be true until it is closely examined, therefore, the best fit answer is J, guesswork.

43. **The correct answer is C.**
    Using context clues, superficial should be similar to the word speculative and so inaccurate is the best answer since alchemy was based on guesswork.

44. **The correct answer is K.**
    The last sentence summarizes what chemistry is. It refers to "changes wherein substances of one kind are produced from substances totally unlike them."

45. **The correct answer is A.**
    The answer to 41 justifies this answer.

46. **The correct answer is K.**
    The first sentence states that the US was attacked and this suggests infamy is related to dishonor.

47. **The correct answer is C.**
    The second to last sentence states that the recorded distance made it obvious that the attack was deliberate.

48. **The correct answer is J.**
    The last sentence states that Japan sought to deceive the U.S., but wanted also to give "hope for continued peace."

ANSWER EXPLANATIONS

49. The correct answer is C.
It was deliberate and originally, the U.S. and Japan had a peaceful relationship. Therefore, the attack was uncalled for.

50. The correct answer is J.
The second sentence states that the U.S. was at peace with Japan, but because of the deliberate attack this has changed.

LANGUAGE SECTION

1. The correct answer is C.
The correct spelling is migrate.

2. The correct answer is N.
No mistakes.

3. The correct answer is D.
The correct spelling is efforts.

4. The correct answer is J.
The correct spelling is accommodate.

5. The correct answer is B.
The correct spelling is believe.

6. The correct answer is J.
The correct spelling is cemetery.

7. The correct answer is C.
The correct spelling is grateful.

8. The correct answer is K.
The correct spelling is harass.

9. The correct answer is C.
The correct spelling is misspell.

10. The correct answer is M.
The correct spelling is millennium.

11. The correct answer is B.
The word "Arizona" should be capitalized sinceit is the name of a state.

12. The correct answer is L.
The moon and the sun are not capitalized unless they are placed with other capitalized celestial bodies.

13. The correct answer is A.
The acronym "D.E.A" should be capitalized since it is the name of an organization.

14. The correct answer is M.
No mistakes.

15. The correct answer is B.
The word 'summer" is not capitalized and neither is any of the other seasons.

16. The correct answer is M.
No mistakes.

17. The correct answer is A.
The name "Carter" should be capitalized.

18. The correct answer is K.
The acronym "I.D" should be capitalized.

19. The correct answer is C.
The word "doctor" is not capitalized unless it is placed before a name and acts as a title.

20. The correct answer is M.
No mistakes.

21. The correct answer is B.
For possession, the word "boys" should have an apostrophe "s" since it is their debate team.

ANSWER EXPLANATIONS

22. **The correct answer is K.**
    With a sentence beginning with however, thus, or therefore, there should be a comma after however.

23. **The correct answer is B.**
    Since this is a list of more than two, there should be a comma after every item. In this case, there should be a comma between basketball and soccer.

24. **The correct answer is J.**
    Two independent clauses cannot be separated just by a comma. A semicolon here would be a better fit.

25. **The correct answer is B.**
    A semicolon separates two independent clauses, but in this case the ending phrase is not a complete sentence. Since it is a list, it would be better to put a colon before the items and after the word following.

26. **The correct answer is L.**
    The second portion of the sentence is a question so it should end with a question mark.

27. **The correct answer is D.**
    No mistakes.

28. **The correct answer is J.**
    "Its" should be "It's" since the contraction can be replaced with "it is", but its shows possession.

29. **The correct answer is A.**
    The word before the beginning word of a quotation in dialogue should have a comma after it. As a general rule, punctuation with the exception of colon and semicolon go before the quotation at the beginning and within the quotation at the end.

30. **The correct answer is J.**
    Between city and state, there should always be a comma. Here, a comma is necessary after Memphis.

31. **The correct answer is A.**
    The subject is very good surgeon and since this is singular the correct verb is "is" instead of "are."

32. **The correct answer is M.**
    No mistakes.

33. **The correct answer is A.**
    The incorrect word "too" is used. "Too" refers to when there is an excess of something, but here it should be the word "to" since it is referencing a location.

34. **The correct answer is L.**
    The incorrect word "pears" is used. "Pairs" refer to the fruits, but here it should be the word "pairs" since it is referencing to two of something.

35. **The correct answer is A.**
    The incorrect word "poor" is used. "Poor" is an adjective, but hereit should be the word "poorly" since it is referencing to how the piano is being played, making it an adverb.

36. **The correct answer is J.**
    The article "the" is used for specific nouns. Since the sentences generalizing the hard work put into a book the correct article should be "a" in front of book.

37. **The correct answer is D.**
    No mistakes.

38. **The correct answer is M.**
    No mistakes.

ANSWER EXPLANATIONS

39. The correct answer is B.
The incorrect word "except" is used. "Except" is used when something goes against conventional ideas, but here it should be the word "accept" since it is referencing to receiving or taking something.

40. The correct answer is K.
The pronoun "his" is wrong because the antecedent is officers and the best replacement for officers is "their."

41. The correct answer is A.
Substitute the word "and" for each choice. The sentence flows the best with choice A.

42. The correct answer is L.
A verb indicates an action and here eradicate is an action.

43. The correct answer is A.
An adjective describes a noun and here intellectual, the adjective, describes the noun, powers.

44. The correct answer is J.
So is used usually as a conjunction between two sentences and since this sentence starts off after a period, so is unnecessary.

45. The correct answer is C.
An adverb describes a verb and usually ends with "ly." Here, ultimately describes the verb, know.

46. The correct answer is K.
The sentence should have "and we" before "must know its meaning." This creates a more fluid sentence because of parallelism. Without it, the pronoun is missing.

47. The correct answer is B.
The perfect tense is used and should have the past participle of learn which is learned.

48. The correct answer is J.
The verb "is" indicates present tense.

49. The correct answer is D.
No mistakes.

50. The correct answer is K.
The correct spelling is conceit.

MATH SECTION

1. The correct answer is D.
59 is the only number that has factors of one and itself from the answer choices.

2. The correct answer is L.
Two negatives make a positive and a positive and a negative make a negative. The operation can be written as 4 + 4 - 3 = 5.

3. The correct answer is D.
94 is not divisible by 6.

4. The correct answer is J.
$\frac{1}{3}$ needs to have a common denominator of nine so multiply top and bottom by 3. This rewrites the operation as $\frac{8}{9} - \frac{3}{9} = \frac{5}{9}$

5. The correct answer is C.
120 is the smallest number for which 12, 15, 120 are factors of.

6. The correct answer is K.
30% of 420 = 0.30 • 420 = 126.

ANSWER EXPLANATIONS

7. The correct answer is C.
1 Package = 5 Pencils
11 Packages = 55 pencils
If each package costs $0.89, multiply by 11 to get $9.79

8. The correct answer is L.
$\frac{3}{8}$ turned to a decimal is 3 ÷ 8 which is 0.375.
This added to 5 gives 5.375.

9. The correct answer is B.
If it takes George 3 minutes to read 300 words, and each page has 750 words, then it takes George 7.5 minutes to read a single page. To calculate how long George needs to read 6 pages, simply multiply 7.5 • 6 which results in 45 minutes.

10. The correct answer is K.
A 4% raise of $4,000 is the equivalent of $4,000 + 0.04($4,000) = $4,160. Since the question states there are 4 weeks in a month, we can calculate John works 160 hours per month.
$\frac{\$4,160}{160}$ is equal to $26.

11. The correct answer is C.
One can make an equation and solve for x, the number of weeks: $320 = $210 + 10x$. This give choice C, 11 weeks to obtain $110.

12. The correct answer is K.
Convert 20 feet to inches.
20 • 12 = 240 inches.
The new ratio is 4 inches to 240 inches, and simplified is 1 to 60.

13. The correct answer is B.
15% of $1,500 = 0.15 • $1,500 = $225, the amount of money Joanna gets more than Ashley.

14. The correct answer is J.
If it takes 3 cats, 3 minutes, to catch 3 mice, this means that on average, it takes 1 cat, 3 minutes to catch 1 mouse. In order to catch 99 mice in 99 minutes, you would still need 3 cats.

15. The correct answer is A.
Since $0.20 is charged per quarter mile, $0.80 is charged per 1 full mile. One can make an equation and solve for x, the number of miles: $22.50 = $3.50 + 0.80x$. Subtract 3.50 on both sides and then divide by 0.80.

16. The correct answer is K.
20% discount off the original price is the same as 80% of the original price which is 0.80 • $550.50 = $440.40. A 5% coupon will allow a 5% drop which is 95% of the sale price. The final calculation would be 0.95 • $440.40 = $418.38.

17. The correct answer is D.
We know that for every 2 boys, there is 1 girl. The total in this case is not needed because the ratio for the number of boys to the total is 2 to 3 which is $66.\overline{66}\%$.

18. The correct answer is J.
$\frac{1}{3}$ of 45 is 15 and $\frac{1}{5}$ of 45 is 9. There are therefore 15 black and green ducks each and 9 blue ducks. 45 - 9 - 15 - 15 = 6.

ANSWER EXPLANATIONS

19. **The correct answer is B.**
The price per gallon is cheapest when it is $3. This divided from $120 is 40 gallons. The price per gallon is highest when it is $4. This divided from $120 is 30 gallons. The difference between the number of gallons between the highest and the lowest price is 10 gallons.

20. **The correct answer is K.**
The average is the total over the number of data points (number of teachers). Here, the total is 9 • $1000 = $9,000, total salary of the 9 teachers. The total salary for the 9 teachers and 11 assistant principal is 20 • $1,275 = $25,500. The difference between the two totals gives the total salary of the 11 assistant principal which is $16,500. Divide this by 11 to get the salary per assistant principals.

21. **The correct answer is D.**
One can use a proportion $\frac{8}{15,000} = \frac{40}{x}$
and solve for x. By cross multiplying and isolating x, one will get 75,000. An easy approach is to notice that 40% is 5 times 8% so simply multiply 15,000 by 5.

22. **The correct answer is K.**
The average is the total over the number of data points. Here, the total is 120 + 60 + 140 + 80 + 20 = 420. There are five data points so 420 ÷ 5 = 84.

23. **The correct answer is C.**
420 is just increased by 60 and the new division becomes 480 ÷ 5 = 96.

24. **The correct answer is L.**
College B is represented with 10 diamonds and since each diamond is worth 500 people, multiply the two numbers to find the total number of people which is 5,000.

25. **The correct answer is B.**
The difference between the two colleges is 4 diamonds - 2 diamonds which is 2 diamonds. One diamond is the equivalent of 500 students and so 2 times that is 1,000.

26. **The correct answer is L.**
The steepest slope indicates the greatest change and this is between April and May.

27. **The correct answer is D.**
The total price that Pamela would have to pay is 2($19.99) + $29.99 = $69.97. If Pamela pays 100 dollars, she should receive a change that is the difference between hundred and the cost which is $100.00 - $69.97 = $30.03.

28. **The correct answer is J.**
The total price that Shannon would have to pay without the discount is 3($5.99) + 2($29.99) + 1($19.99) = $97.94. A 10% discount is the equivalent of 90% of the original price. 90% of $97.94 = 0.90 • $97.94 = $ 88.146 which approximates to $88.15.

29. **The correct answer is B.**
Notice that the number of fish is increasing exponentially. The question asks you to find the population at year 1995, which is 5 years after 1990. Choice A is a trick answer.

ANSWER EXPLANATIONS

30. **The correct answer is L.**
    The total number of books is 19 and the total number of math books is 4. $\frac{4}{19}$ as a percentage is closest to 20%.

31. **The correct answer is C.**
    To find the number of seniors that are taking trigonometry, the table has to be filled out with the unknown values of the freshmen were also taking trigonometry. This can be done by doing 77 - 21 - 53 = 3.
    57 - 3 - 5 - 7 = 42, the number of seniors taking trigonometry. By doing the series of subtraction, one will find that the number of juniors taking algebra is 19. The difference is 23.

32. **The correct answer is M.**
    For this problem, it is useful to make a venn diagram with cats being one of the circle and dogs being the other. The middle will contain people who like both cats and dogs. The easier option is to add the number of people who like cats and dogs and subtracted from 50 to find those who like both. The results will show that 7 like both, 13 like cats only, and 30 like dogs only.

33. **The correct answer is B.**
    621 rounds down to 600
    281 rounds up to 300
    600 + 300 = 900

34. **The correct answer is L.**
    99,783 rounds up to 100,000
    1,005 rounds down to 1,000
    100,000 - 1,000 = 99,000

35. **The correct answer is B.**
    Round each of these values to the nearest ones. This makes the new expression:
    4(5 + 5) - 2(10 - 2)
    4(10) - 2(8)
    40 - 16
    = 24

36. **The correct answer is K.**
    The correct operation here is division since we are trying to find how many minutes it takes to type 900 words for John when he already types 97 words in 1 minute. Round 97 to 100 and the operation becomes 900 ÷ 100 = 9.

37. **The correct answer is C.**
    589 rounds up to 600
    $\frac{600}{6} = 100$

38. **The correct answer is M.**
    8,601 rounded to the nearest **thousands** place is 9,000.

39. **The correct answer is D.**
    0.291 rounded to the nearest **tenths** place is 0.3.

40. **The correct answer is M.**
    123,546 rounded to the nearest **tens** place is 123,550.

41. **The correct answer is B.**
    Round each of these values to the nearest dollar. This makes the new operation $1 + $40 + $9 = $50.

ANSWER EXPLANATIONS

42. **The correct answer is J.**
    8,777 rounds up to 9,000
    107 rounds down to 100.

    $\dfrac{9,000}{100} = 90$

43. **The correct answer is C.**
    10,000 - 7,000 = 3,000.

44. **The correct answer is K.**
    Round the operation to
    1,000 • 500 = 500,000.

45. **The correct answer is C.**
    99.5 rounds to 100
    49.5 rounds to 50.

    $\text{Average} = \dfrac{\text{Sum of Numbers}}{\text{\# of \#'s}}$

    $\text{Average} = \dfrac{150}{2}$

    Average = 75

46. **The correct answer is K.**
    Round each of the following numbers to the nearest tens. This changes the operation to 100(50 - 40) = 100(10) = 1,000.

47. **The correct answer is C.**
    Round 7.125 to 7. Seven squared is 49 and since we rounded down the number should be a little higher. This makes the answer 50.

48. **The correct answer is L.**
    3,479 rounds up to 3,500
    11 rounds down to 10

    $\dfrac{3,500}{10} = 350$

49. **The correct answer is C.**
    $97,099 rounds up to $100,000.
    $100,000 x 0.05 = $5,000

50. **The correct answer is J.**
    19,000 - 9,000 = 10,000.

ANSWER EXPLANATIONS

ABILITY SECTION

1. **The correct answer is E.**
   All the triangles are isosceles triangles.

2. **The correct answer is L.**
   All the shapes have two equal parts.

3. **The correct answer is B.**
   All the shapes contain one reflex angle.

4. **The correct answer is J.**
   All the shapes are heptagons.

5. **The correct answer is D.**
   All the shapes contain a polygon with some or one side with a semicircle.

6. **The correct answer is J.**
   There should be a smaller version of the figure with itself rotated 180°.

7. **The correct answer is C.**
   All the figures only contain two straight sides with everything else being curves.

8. **The correct answer is K.**
   All the shapes only contain one shade of diagonal.

9. **The correct answer is B.**
   The bottom should be a polygon while the top should be a curved figure or figures.

10. **The correct answer is J.**
    The figures have sides of 8.

11. **The correct answer is D.**
    All the shapes are not polygons.

12. **The correct answer is N.**
    The center should contain only a dot.

13. **The correct answer is C.**
    The figures are completely without sides.

14. **The correct answer is K.**
    Each of the figures contain a circle, a square, and a triangle with two of them being smaller and within the bigger one.

15. **The correct answer is C.**
    One eighth of the figure is shaded.

16. **The correct answer is N.**
    The figures are broken into two equal parts.

17. **The correct answer is A.**
    All of the figures contain one right angle.

18. **The correct answer is N.**
    All shapes contain only triangles.

19. **The correct answer is E.**
    The top figures should not be a polygon and the bottom should be a polygon.

20. **The correct answer is K.**
    The arrows point to reflex angles.

21. **The correct answer is A.**
    A two-sided curved figure becomes a 3 sided figure. There is an increase in sides.

22. **The correct answer is M.**
    The number of sides increase by 1.

23. **The correct answer is A.**
    The figure is split in half and reflected over the line of symmetry with the right figure shaded.

ANSWER EXPLANATIONS

24. The correct answer is L.
The number of sides is divided by 2.

25. The correct answer is B.
The figure is copied and shaded and placed to the right of the original figure.

26. The correct answer is N.
The figure is divided into 8 equal parts.

27. The correct answer is B.
The figure is rotated 180°.

28. The correct answer is K.
All reflex angles within the figure are connected and the area that is made is shaded.

29. The correct answer is D.
The reflex angle is extended and there is a dot indicating its original place.

30. The correct answer is L.
The figure is split along its line of symmetry and the bottom portion is flipped over. The top portion is shaded and there are two dots in an anti-diagonal fashion.

31. The correct answer is B.
One half of the figure is shaded in gray, one sixth of the figure is shaded in black, and the rest is unshaded.

32. The correct answer is J.
The number of sides of a polygon is increased by one.

33. The correct answer is C.
There should be three times as many figures as the original figure with two of them being unshaded and one of them being shaded.

34. The correct answer is N.
The left half of the figure is moved to the right and the right half is moved to the left with a semicircle in between. The right is then unshaded.

35. The correct answer is D.
The figure is rotated 180°.

36. The correct answer is K.
The figure is rotated 90° clockwise.

37. The correct answer is C.
The centerpiece of the original figure is placed on the bottom with the triangles assembled into a tessellation, alternating with grey and white triangles on top.

38. The correct answer is N.
There should be three times the original figure connected by loops and so 2 times 3 equals 6.

39. The correct answer is E.
Since one of the figure became three of the figures, three of the figures should be nine of the figures.

40. The correct answer is L.
The figure is rotated 90° counterclockwise.

41. The correct answer choice is **B.**
42. The correct answer choice is **L.**
43. The correct answer choice is **A.**
44. The correct answer choice is **M.**
45. The correct answer choice is **D.**
46. The correct answer choice is **J.**
47. The correct answer choice is **C.**
48. The correct answer choice is **N.**
49. The correct answer choice is **B.**
50. The correct answer choice is **N.**

VOCABULARY

VOCABULARY

The following vocabulary list contains the definition of the specified word and may include the different parts of speech of the word, the synonyms, and the antonyms associated with the general definition. The list is designed to be as concise as possible instead of being a comprehensive one. Do not solely use this as a study guide.

A

- Abrasive (adj.): irritating, grinding, eroding
  Other forms: abrasion
  Synonyms: annoying, pestilent, vexing, caustic, corrosive, marred, scarred
  Antonyms: comforting, relaxing, alleviating, emollient

- Abridge (v.): to shorten or to make smaller
  Other form: abridgement
  Synonyms: truncate, curtail
  Antonyms: augment, amplify

- Ambivalence (n.): being unsure of something or feeling of being pulled in two directions
  Other forms: ambivalent, ambivalently
  Synonyms: indecision, quandary, dilemma
  Antonyms: determined, absolute

- Acquiescent (adj.): reluctantly agreeable
  other forms: acquiesce, acquiescence
  Synonyms: compliant, agreeable, consent, concede
  Antonyms: disagreeing

- Acrimony (n.): words or behavior filled with harshness or anger
  Other forms: acrimonious, acrimoniously
  Synonyms: assail, assailant
  Antonyms: exalt, praise

- Advocate (v.): to plead for or speak in behalf of
  Other Forms: advocate (n.), advocacy
  Synonym: supporter
  Antonym: antagonistic

- Aesthetic (adj.): to do with art and beauty
  Other forms: aesthetics, aesthetically
  Synonyms: ethereal (heavenly beautiful), comely
  Antonyms: grotesque, hideous

- Alienate (v.): to push someone or cause to separate from people
  Other forms: alienation
  Synonyms: estrange, withdrawn, diverted
  Antonyms: reconcile, bring in, adopt

- Ambidextrous (adj.): able to use both hands with equal skill

- Amorphous (adj.): without form or shape
  Other forms:
  Synonyms: shapeless, unstructured
  Antonyms: shaping, structured, organized

- Anarchy (n.): a lack of order
  Other form: anarchist
  Synonyms: lawlessness, misrule
  Antonyms: law-abiding, orderly

VOCABULARY

- Anathema (n.): a religious curse; a thing or person being cursed
  Other forms: anathematize
  Synonyms: malediction, malison, execration, ban
  Antonyms: benediction, blessing

- Antiquated (adj.): too old to be useful
  Other forms: antique, antiquity
  Synonyms: archaic, obsolete, moribund, neolithic
  Antonyms: new, contemporary, modern

- Antithesis (n.): opposite
  Other forms: antithetical
  Synonyms: disparate (different), polar
  Antonyms: same, equal

- Ascendance (adj.): controlling power
  Other forms: ascendant, ascendancy
  Synonyms: dominance, hegemony, sovereignty, reign
  Antonyms: impotence, powerless

- Ascetic (n.): person who rejects physical comfort for self-discipline
  Other forms: ascetic (adj.)
  Synonym: hermit
  Antonym: hedonist

- Asperity (adj.): irritability
  Other forms: aspersion
  Synonyms: roughness, harshness, adversity (misfortune)
  Antonyms: soothing, alleviation

- Atrophy (v.): waste and wither away
  Other forms: atrophy (n.)
  Synonyms: wizened, whither
  Antonyms: grow, nourish

- Averse (adj.): wanting to avoid
  Synonyms: repelled, dislike
  Antonyms: penchant, attraction

B

- Baleful (adj.): dangerous
  Other form: balefully
  Synonyms: treacherous, hazard
  Antonyms: innocuous, harmless

- Bequeath (v.): to leave behind or hand through a will
  Other forms: bequeathal, bequest
  Synonym: transmit

[a] Blight (n.): widespread death
  Other forms: blight (v.), blighted
  Synonyms: decay, disease
  Antonyms: support, healthful

- Bombast (n.): speech or writing intended to impress; arrogant
  Other forms: bombastic
  Synonym: pompous

- Bourgeois (adj.): the middle class
  Other form: bourgeois the noun

- Bumptious (adj.): obnoxiously self-assertive
  Other forms: bumptiousness, bumptiously
  Synonyms: pushy, narcissistic
  Antonyms: modest, selfless

VOCABULARY

C

- Capacious (adj.): spacious
  Other form: capaciousness, capaciously
  Synonyms: large, roomy, space
  Antonyms: small, packed

- Celerity (n.): speed
  Other forms: accelerate
  Synonyms: alacrity, quickness
  Antonyms: slow, ponderous

- Circumscribe (v.): draw a line around
  Other forms: circumscribable, circumscription
  Synonyms: define limits, confine, restrict
  Antonyms: unbounded, free

- Circumspect (adj.): cautious
  Other forms: circumspectly, circumspection
  Synonyms: prudent, gingerly, alert
  Antonyms: heedless, unwary, careless, incautious

- Clemency (n.): mercy
  Other form: clement
  Synonyms: leniency, forbearance
  Antonyms: unforgiving, strict

- Coalesce (v.): grow together
  Other forms: coalescent, coalescence
  Synonyms: converge, fuse
  Antonyms: diverge, divisive

- Coerce (v.): to force someone by physically overpowering him/her
  Other forms: coercion, coercive
  Synonyms: cogent (convincingly forceful), compel, oblige, pressure

- Cordial (adj.): welcoming and gracious; friendly
  Other forms: cordiality, cordially
  Synonyms: friendly, amicable, amiable, camaraderie, fraternize
  Antonyms: enmity, antagonistic, adversary

- Condolence (n.): pity for someone else's loss
  Other forms: condole
  Synonym: contrite (sorry for past misdeeds)

- Contingent (adj.): dependent on circumstances
  Other forms: contingency, contingently
  Synonyms: circumstantial, conditional
  Antonyms: predetermined, uncircumstantial

- Contrite (adj.): sorry
  Other form: contrition
  Synonyms: penitent, lamentable
  Antonyms: unapologetic, unrepentant

- Conviction (n.): an opinion that is strongly held or the belief in the correctness of one's opinion
  Other forms: convicted
  Synonyms: bias, assurance, certainty
  Antonyms: dubious (doubt), uncertain

- Contemporary (adj.): modern
  Other form: contemporary the noun
  Synonyms: current, extant, novelty
  Antonyms: old, antiquated

- Copious (adj.): in large amounts
  Other form: copiousness
  Synonyms: abundant, myriad
  Antonyms: meager

VOCABULARY

- Corporation (n.): to do with a body of people or its physical representation
  Other forms: corporeal, corporealness, corporeally

- Cynical (adj.): believe that people are generally bad and selfish
  Other form: cynically
  Synonyms: pessimistic, peevish, captious
  Antonyms: hopeful, optimistic

D

- Debased (adj.): to lower in quality
  Other forms: debase
  Synonyms: relegate, ban, abase, demean, profane, vitiate,
  Antonyms: uplift, elevate, ennoble

- Debunk (v.): to expose as false
  Synonyms: confound, disprove, rebut
  Antonyms: confirm, validate, verify

- Daunted (adj.): dismayed
  Other forms: daunt, dauntless, dauntlessly
  Synonyms: disheartened, discouraged
  Antonyms: motivate, assist

- Decadence (n.): moral decay
  Other forms: decadent, decadently
  Synonyms: decline, indecency
  Antonyms: decorous, decorum

- Depleted (v.): used up
  Other forms: depletion, depletable
  Synonyms: drained, emptied
  Antonyms: fill up, saturate

- Deride (v.): make fun of
  Other form: derision
  Synonyms: ridicule, jeer, mock
  Antonyms: praise, acclaim

- Dilatory (adj.): causing lateness
  Other form: dilatorily
  Synonyms: delay, stalling

- Diminutive (adj.): unusually small
  Other forms: diminution
  Synonyms: tiny, minute
  Antonyms: gargantuan, enormous

- Discourse (n.): exchange of idea
  Other forms: discourse the verb
  Synonyms: conversation, discussion

- Disdain (n.): a feeling of contempt
  Other forms: disdain (v.), disdainful
  Synonyms: scorn, despite
  Antonyms: honor, respect

- Distended (adj.): swollen
  Other forms: distend, distension
  Synonyms: extended

- Dogmatic (adj.): sticking to widely accepted ideas
  Other forms: dogma, dogmatism
  Synonyms: orthodox, conformer
  Antonyms: heretic, unorthodox

VOCABULARY

E

- Eccentric (adj.): different from most,
  Other form: eccentricity
  Synonyms: idiosyncratic, individualistic, unique, anomaly
  Antonyms: conforming, homogenous

- Eclectic (adj.): choosing from many different resources
  Other forms: eclectically, eclecticism
  Synonyms: resourceful, assorted, heterogeneous
  Antonyms: limited, homogenous

- Efface (v.): to erase or wipe out
  Synonyms: expunge, evanescent (vanishing slowly)
  Antonyms: keep, hold onto

- El oquent (adj.): able to speak clearly and effectively
  Other forms: eloquently, eloquence
  Synonyms: articulate, voluble
  Antonyms: inarticulate, unvocal

- Efficacy (n.): the ability to produce desired results
  Other forms: efficacious, efficaciously
  Synonyms: efficiently, productiveness
  Antonyms: unproductive, inefficient

- Emissary (n.): someone who represents another
  Synonyms: delegate (giving responsibility), representative

- Endorse (v.): promote
  Other forms: endorsement,
  Synonyms: endorse, advocate
  Antonyms: admonish (warn), caution

- Erudition (n.): the knowledge acquired through years of study
  Other forms: erudite, eruditely
  Synonyms: experience, expertise
  Antonyms: novice, beginner

- Euphemism (n.): a word of phrase that's used to make an unpleasant idea sound better
  Other forms: euphemistic, euphemistically

- Exacerbate (v.): to make a situation worse
  Other forms: exacerbation
  Synonyms: worsen, vilify
  Antonyms: alleviate, extentuate

- Expurgate (v.): to remove offensive ideas
  Other forms: expurgation, expurgatory
  Synonym: censor

F

- Fabricate (v.): to synthesize or make up
  Other forms: fabricator, fabricated, fabricating
  Synonyms: invent, create, manufacture
  Antonyms: demount, disassemble, dismantle

- Facile (adj.): too shallow and not showing enough thought or effort; to easily done or scratch on the surface that does not show completeness
  Other forms: facilitate, facility
  Synonyms: superficial, easy, fake, facade, exterior, cursory
  Antonyms: interior, deep, profound, laborious (difficult)

VOCABULARY

- Fallacy (n.): the state of falsehood
  Other forms: fallacious, fallaciously
  Synonyms: misleading, lie, deception, mendacity
  Antonyms: veracity, reality, truth, fact

- Fastidious (adj.): difficult to please
  Other forms: fastidiousness, fastidiously
  Synonyms: truly, dainty, picky
  Antonyms: undemanding, unfastidious

- Felicitous (adj.): pleasing or fortunate
  Other form: felicity
  Synonyms: appropriate, suitable
  Antonyms: inopportune, irrelevant

- Flagrant (adj.): openly and obviously evil
  Other forms: flagrantly, flagrancy
  Synonyms: shameless, undisguised, brazen, evil, glaring, conspicuous, offensive, egregarious
  Antonyms: obscure, contained, camouflaged

- Flamboyant (adj.): over the top and showy
  Other form: flamboyantly
  Synonyms: glamorous, pretentious, garish, embellished, bodacious, gaudy, grandiose
  Antonyms: unnoticeable, unshowy

- Fledgling (n.): beginner
  Synonyms: novice, neophyte
  Antonyms: expert

- Flippancy (n.): treating a serious situation with arrogant humor and disrespect
  Other forms: flippant, flippantly
  Synonyms: facetious, witty, temerity, bold, audacious, brazen, puerile (childish), effrontery
  Antonyms: earnest, sincere, gravity, seriousness

- Foment (v.): to incite or to stir into action
  Other form: fomentation
  Synonyms: stimulus, abet, brew, provoke, rouse, instigate, kindle, incite, provoke, to cause, catalytic, engender

- Fortuitous (adj.): lucky and fortunate
  Other forms: fortuitously, fortuitousness
  Synonyms: providential, auspicious, serendipity
  Antonyms: ill-fated, unlucky, ominous, omen, portent

- Futile (adj.): hopelessly ineffective
  Other forms: futilely, futility
  Synonyms: useless, in vain
  Antonyms: effective

G

- Garner (v.): to collect
  Synonyms: accumulate, earn, gather
  Antonyms: scatter, disperse

- Girth (n.): the distance around an object
  Synonyms: circumference, perimeter

- Glutton (n.): a person who consumes large amounts of food or drink or is greedy; can also mean someone with great endurance
  Other forms: gluttony, gluttonous
  Synonyms: greedy, insatiable, selfish, avarice, cupidity (money)
  Antonyms: generous, giving, altruistic, magnanimous

VOCABULARY

- Gregarious (adj.): sociable and enjoying companionship
  Other forms: gregariousness, gregariously
  Synonyms: extroverted, sociable, convivial
  Antonyms: introverted, taciturn

- Guileless (adj.): truthful and honest
  Synonyms: straightforward, friendly, candid, candor
  Antonyms: cunning, deceitful, tricky, cajole

- Gullible (adj.): easily deceived
  Other form: gullibility
  Synonyms: simple, credulous
  Antonyms: sophisticated, skeptical, incredulous

H

- Hamper (v.): to interfere with movement of progress
  Synonyms: stymie, block, impede, hinder, thwart, inhibit
  Antonyms: permit, allow

- Haphazard (adj.): without plan or direction
  Other forms: haphazardly, haphazardness
  Synonyms: extemporaneous, unprepared, aimless
  Antonyms: planned, organized

- Harbor (v.): to provide refuge or hide
  Other forms: harborer, harborage
  Synonyms: salvage, save, assist, relief
  Antonyms: damage, destroy, harm, eradicate (exterminate/destroy), obliterate, pernicious(destructive), deleterious (harmful)

- Hardy (adj.): capable of withstanding harsh conditions
  Other forms: hardiness, hardily
  Synonyms: bold, brave, invincible
  Antonyms: weak, afraid

- Hedge (v.): to avoid giving clear answers
  Synonyms: garbled, evasive
  Antonym: incisive

- Hedonism (n.): belief that pleasure is the most important part of life
  Other forms: hedonist, hedonistic, hedonistically

- Heretic (n.): someone has an opinion that is in defiance of generally accepted ideas
  Other forms: heresy, heretical, heretically
  Synonyms: unorthodox, dissenter, iconoclast, pariah
  Antonyms: orthodox, conformer

- Hiatus (n.): a break in the continuity of process
  Synonyms: gap, interruption, pause
  Antonyms: continuity, incessant, perpetual

- Homage (n.): respect paid to someone or something
  Synonyms: tribute, honor, revere, lionize
  Antonyms: irreverent, disrespect, repudiate, castigate, objurgate

- Hyperbole (n.): extreme exaggeration; to emphasize something more than it actually is
  Synonyms: overstatement, embellishment, caricature, extravagant, stretched
  Antonyms: understatement, restrained

VOCABULARY

I

- Idolatry (n.): the worship of a person, thing, or institution as a god
  Other forms: idolater, idolize, idolatrous

- Imminent (adj.): about to take place
  Other forms: imminently, imminence
  Synonyms: soon, impending, looming
  Antonyms: late, recent

- Impartial (adj.): being fair
  Other form: impartiality
  Synonyms: equal, unbiased, unprejudiced
  Antonyms: biased, prejudiced

- Impetuous (adj): quick to make decisions
  Other forms: impetuosity, impetuously
  Synonyms: hasty, impulsive, unpredictable, erratic
  Antonyms: deliberate, planned, designed

- Imposter (n.): pretender
  Synonyms: imitate, copy, mimic, impersonate, emulate, quack, dissemble
  Antonyms: differ, diverge

- Impudence (n.): rudeness
  Other forms: impudent, impudently
  Synonyms: insolent, crudeness, disrespect
  Antonyms: respect, obedience, humility

- Inadvertent (adj.): unintentional
  Other forms: inadvertantly, inadvertence
  Synonyms: unplanned, accidental
  Antonyms: planned, deliberate, intentional

- Inaugurate (v.): to induct and or to begin
  Other forms: inauguration, inaugural
  Synonyms: initiate, start, begin
  Antonyms: end, finish, cease, consummate

- Inchoate (adj.): not fully developed
  Synonyms: rudimentary, nascent, fundamental, elementary
  Antonyms: ripe, mature

- Incompatible (adj.): not capable of existing together
  Other forms: incompatibility, incompatibly
  Synonyms: incongruous, incongruity, conflicting, inconsistent, atypical
  Antonyms: suitable, harmonious, compatible, analogous, equal, comparable

- Indict (v.): to charge with a crime
  Other form: indictment
  Synonyms: accuse, blame, impeach, defame, incriminate, culpable (guilty)
  Antonyms: absolve, acquit, exculpate, vindicate, exonerate, exculpate, absolve

- Indolent (adj.): lazy
  Other forms: indolence, indolently
  Synonyms: unmotivated, unenergetic
  Antonyms: driven, hardworking, industrious

- Infamy (n.): a bad reputation
  Other forms: infamous, infamously
  Synonyms: notoriety, disreputable, nefarious (evil)
  Antonyms: righteous, noble, goodly, eminent

VOCABULARY

- **Jubilant (adj.):** filled with joy
  Other forms: jubilation, jubilantly
  Synonyms: jovial, happy, upbeat, elated, exuberant, euphoric, exuberant, effervescent
  Antonyms: cranky, gloomy, lament, lugubrious

- **Judicious (adj.):** making good decisions
  Other forms: judiciousness, judiciously
  Synonyms: wise, thoughtful, cautious, prudent
  Antonyms: imprudent, reckless, ill considered

- **Juncture (n.):** an important point in time
  Other form: junction
  Synonyms: joint, connection

- **Juxtapose (v.):** the place side by side as a comparison
  Other form: juxtaposition
  Synonyms: comparison, analogy, adjacent
  Antonyms: contrast, nonadjacent

K

- **Keen (adj.):** paying attention to and holding onto information very quickly
  Other forms: keenly, keenness
  Synonyms: sharp, quick, smart, astute, tenacious, acute (smart), perspicacity, perspective, cognizant
  Antonyms: dull, slow, unintelligent, unintelligent, obtuse

L

- **Languish (v.):** to lose energy or motivation
  Other forms: languor, languorous
  Synonyms: weak, depressed, despondent, desolate
  Antonyms: motivated, determined, assiduous, diligent

- **Laud (v.):** to praise
  Other forms: laudable, laudly, laudatory
  Synonyms: extol, worship, acclaim, accolade, adulation, eulogize, exalt
  Antonyms: castigate, reprimand

- **Lethargic (v.):** tired and sluggish
  Other forms: lethargy, lethargically
  Synonyms: drowsy, sluggish, inactive, listless, inert, ponderous
  Antonyms: quick, energetic, active, invigorate, expedite (quicken)

- **Loath (adj.):** unwilling
  Synonyms: reluctant
  Antonyms: willing

- **Loathe (v.):** to hate
  Other forms: loathsomeness, loathsomely, loathsome, loathing
  Synonyms: dislike, contempt, abhor, detest, despise
  Antonyms: love, not scornful, like, penchant (strong liking)

- **Lofty (adj.):** placed very high or ambitious
  Other form: loftiness
  Synonyms: elevated, noble, sublime (Noble), pretentious, high
  Antonyms: lowly, meager, poor, low

- **Lucid (adj.):** easy to understand
  Other forms: lucidly, lucidity
  Synonyms: transparent, clear, rational, understandable, pellucid
  Antonyms: unclear, muddled, confused, ambiguous

VOCABULARY

- Ingenuous (ad.): unintelligent
  Other forms: ingenuousness, ingenuously
  Synonyms: unsophisticated, naive, inexperienced
  Antonyms: ingenious, disingenuous, shrewd, incisive

- Inherent (adj.): built-in and having a quality that rises from within
  Other forms: inheritance, inherently, inherentness
  Synonyms: innately, natural, within, intrinsic
  Antonyms: acquired, unnatural, learned, extrinsic

- Innocuous (adj.): harmless
  Other forms: innocuously, innocuousness
  Synonyms: inoffensive, mild
  Antonyms: offensive, shocking, wild

- Inscrutable (adj.): mysterious
  Other forms: inscrutability, inscrutable
  Synonyms: arcane, enigmatic, cryptic, mystic, ineffable, indeterminate, abstruse, arcane, conundrum, obscure, elusive, confounding
  Antonyms: unambiguous, clear, accessible

- Insolvent (adj.): unable to pay bills
  Other form: insolvency
  Synonyms: bankruptcy, liability
  Antonyms: restitution, remuneration

- Interminable (adj.): seemingly endless
  Synonyms: continuous, lasting, durable, longevity
  Antonyms: transitory, transient contemporary, ephemeral, evanscent

- Intractable (adj.): stubborn and immovable
  Other forms: intractability, intractably
  Synonyms: haughty (proud stubborn), snotty narcissistic (ego), arrogant, insular, adamant (refusing to change), obdurate, obstinate
  Antonyms: humble, polite, self-effacing

- Irate (adj.): very angry
  Other forms: irateness, irately
  Synonyms: irascible, infuriated, ballistic, indignant, livid, choler
  Antonyms: delighted, pleased

J

- Jargon (n.): specialized language used by a particular group
  Synonyms: sectarian (religiously limited), esoteric (does not have to be language), endemic (native to particular country)

- Jaundice (n.): yellow in color or envy and resentment
  Other form: jaundice

- Jeopardize (v.): to create a threat or possibility of danger
  Other form: jeopardy
  Synonyms: peril, menace, hazard, endanger, threaten
  Antonyms: safety, harbor, protect, support

- Jettison (v.): to throw overboard
  Synonyms: discard, slough, cast off
  Antonyms: keep, hold on to

- Jocular (adj.): joking and playful
  Other form: jocularity
  Synonyms: witty, jesting, levity, frivolity
  Antonyms: boring, unlively

VOCABULARY

- Ludicrous (adj.): absurd
  Other forms: ludicrousness, ludicrously
  Synonyms: ridiculous, preposterous, derisive
  Antonyms: lame, dull, unamusing

M

- Magnate (n.): a person with great power
  Synonyms: tycoon, monarch, lord

  Malefactor (n.): a person who tries to hurt others
  Synonyms: criminal, felon, miscreant, culprit, malice (v.)
  Antonyms: lawful, legal, legitimate

- Malleable (adj.): able to be reshaped by force
  Other form: malleability
  Synonyms: flexible, pliable, impressionable, elastic, plastic
  Antonyms: inflexible, immutable, inelastic

- Misconstrue (v.): interpret incorrectly
  Synonyms: misunderstand, err
  Antonyms: understand, rectify

- Monologue (n.): a long uninterrupted speech by one person

N

- Negligent (adj.): careless in a situation that could result in harm
  Other form: negligence
  Synonyms: neglectful, apathy, precarious (risky)
  Antonyms: care, cautious

- Nocturnal (adj.): active at night
  Other form: nocturnal
  Antonyms: diurnal

- Nostalgic (adj.): wishing to return to the way things were or longing for the past
  Other forms: nostalgically, nostalgia
  Synonyms: homesickness, wistful

- Nuance (adj.): shades of differences
  Synonyms: discrepancy

- Nullify (v.): remove or cancel all value or force
  Other forms: null, nullification
  Synonyms: negate, cancel
  Antonyms: approve, allow

O

- Obviate (adj.): eliminate the need for something
  Other form: obviation
  Synonyms: unnecessary, unimportant
  Antonyms: vital, essential, significant, important

- Onerous (v.): burdensome
  Other forms: onerousness, onerously
  Synonym: oppressive
  Antonym: unburdening

- Opportunist (adj.): one who takes advantage of the situation
  Other form: opportunistic, opportunistically

VOCABULARY

P

- Pacifist (adj.): person who refuses to fight
  Other form: pacify, pacifier
  Synonyms: peaceful, calmness, equanimity
  Antonyms: terror, belligerent, bellicose

- Paragon (n.): model of excellence
  Synonyms: best, exemplar, prototype
  Antonym: worst

- Pecuniary (adj.): having to do with money
  Synonyms: financial, economical

- Perfunctory (adj.): without enthusiasm
  Other forms: perfunctorily, perfunctoriness
  Synonym: routine
  Antonym: extemporaneous

- Pious (adj.): exhibiting religious devotion

- Preclude (v.): make impossible
  Other forms: preclusion, preclusive
  Synonym: prevent
  Antonym: allow

- Precocious (adj.): mature at a young age
  Other forms: precociously, precocity
  Antonyms: immature, childish, puerile

Q

- Quarantine (n.): forced isolation to prevent the spread of disease
  Other forms: quarantine the verb, quarantined

- Quell (v.): to alleviate or to suppress
  Synonyms: crush, defeat, conquer, suppress, relieve,
  Antonyms: incite, provoke, inflame, encourage, catalytic

- Querulous (adj.): argumentative
  Synonyms: difficult, irritable, cantankerous, quarrelsome, grouchy, cranky, petulance, carping
  Antonyms: amiable, friendly, affable, kind, genial

R

- Rancorous (adj.): expressing bitter hostility
  Other forms: rancor
  Synonyms: belligerent, truculent, pugnacious
  Antonyms: friendly, benign, genial, amicable, amiable, affable,

- Raze (v.): to completely destroy
  Other forms: razer
  Synonyms: demolish, erase, pulverize, rupture
  Antonyms: build, construct, erect, salvage

- Rampant (adj.): widespread or unrestrained
  Synonyms: unrestrained, wanton, inundate, expand, pervade, diffuse, dissipate, permeate. dissolution (spread)
  Antonyms: constrained, contract, duress (restrain), abstain (to hold back)

- Rebuttal (n.): the act of refuting
  Other forms: rebut
  Synonyms: refute, deny, disprove, invalidate, argue, contend
  Antonyms: agree, accept, recognize, believe, support

VOCABULARY

- Reciprocate (.v): to give and take mutually
  Other forms: reciprocity, reciprocator
  Synonyms: repay, recompense
  Antonym: enmity, mutual hatred

- Recant (v.): withdraw from a statement or a belief previously held
  Synonyms: abjure, unsay, retract, rescind, qualify (verb)
  Antonyms: adhere

- Recede(v.): to shorten, draw back, or diminish
  Synonyms: retreat, withdraw, decrease, wane,
  Antonyms: increase, lengthen, wax

- Reclusive (adj.): withdrawn from society
  Other forms: recluse, reclusion
  Synonyms: isolation, solitary, introverted, reticent, taciturn, tacit, aloof
  Antonyms: extrovert, social, friendly

- Recrimination (n.): a retaliatory accusation
  Other forms: recriminate, recriminatory

- Redolent (adj.): strongly scented or fragrant
  Other forms: redolence
  Synonyms: aromatic, odorous, sweet
  Antonyms: foul, noisome, putrid

- Remorse (n.): a feeling of guilt or regret
  Other forms: remorseful, remorsefully
  Synonyms: sorry, guilty, apologetic, gloomy, lugubrious, desolate (empty)
  Antonyms: shameless, indifference, pride

- Renovate (v.): to renew by repairing
  Other forms: renovation
  Synonyms: refurbish, fix, remedy, cure, refresh, repair, recuperate, enhance
  Antonyms: demolish, destroy, weaken (enervate), deterioration

- Repudiate(v.): disown, reject, scold, criticize or to disapprove of, belittle
  Other forms: repudiation
  Synonyms: reprove, reproval, reprimand, renounce, upbraid, berate, censure, castigate, chasten, chastise, denounce, deplore, deprecate, disparage, decry, denigrate, detract
  Antonyms: rhapsodize, rhapsodic, revere, venerate, validate

S

- Sagacious (adj.): perceptive and wise
  Other forms: sagacity, sagaciousness
  Synonyms: wise, shrewd, clever, learned, astute, discerning, prudent
  Antonyms: foolish, thoughtless, irrational

- Sanctimonious(v.): showing false piety
  Other forms: sanctimony

- Salubrious (adj.): promoting health
  Other forms: salubrity
  Synonyms: salutary, curative, healthful
  Antonyms: disadvantage, unhelpful, damaging

- Saturate (v.): to completely fill with or fill with maximum capacity; fill with water
  Other forms: saturation, saturated
  Synonyms: flood, inundate, overwhelm, replete, soak, imbue (color or feeling)
  Antonyms: unsaturated, dehydrated (parched), desiccated, dry, arid, wither

VOCABULARY

- Sanction (v.): to approve or give consent
  Other forms: sanction as a noun means the complete opposite
  Synonyms: ratify, confirm, concur
  Antonyms: rebuff

- Sanguine (adj.): optimistic or cheerful
  Other forms: sanguineness, sanguinity, sanguinely
  Synonyms: happiness, glad, vivacious, jaunty,
  Antonyms: somber, solemn, sullen, languid, lethargic, melancholy, doleful, morose

- Scanty (adj.): small in quantity or insufficient
  Other forms: scantily, scantiness, scant
  Synonyms: sparse, limited, inadequate
  Antonyms: adequate, abundant, plentiful, profuse, myriad

- Scrutinize (v.): examine or inspect very closely
  Other form: scrutiny
  Synonyms: analyze, scrupulous, peruse, meticulous
  Antonyms: disregard, overlook, ignore, condone

- Servile (adj.): like a slave or servant
  Other form: servility
  Synonyms: submissive, obedient, slavish, subjugate (enslave)
  Antonyms: disobedient, dominant

- Specious (adj.): having false or misleading appearance
  Other forms: speciously, speciousness
  Synonyms: deceptive, misleading, false, fallacious, spurious, facade, affected, belie (v.)
  Antonyms: straightforward, true, forthright

- Sporadic (adj.): occurring in frequently and without predictability
  Other forms: sporadically
  Synonyms: spontaneous, random, unsteady, irregular, erratic, volatile, fickle
  Antonyms: habitual, constant, continuous

- Stagnant (adj.): motionless and unchanging
  Other forms: stagnate, stagnation
  Synonyms: soporific, dull, boring, static, sedentary, torpid, latent, pallid
  Antonyms: stimulating, exciting, lively, dynamic, kinetic

- Stoic (n.): a person who shows no response to pleasure or pain; someone who is impassive
  Other forms: stoical, stoically
  Synonyms: emotionless, apathetic, forbearing, impassive, indifference, phlegmatic
  Antonyms: complaining, impatient, protesting

- Subtle (adj.): hard to see or understand
  Other forms: subtly, subtlety
  Synonyms: elusive, indirect, intricate (also to make more difficult), recondite, implicit, convoluted
  Antonyms: extricate, direct, innocent, guileless, explicit, extricate (also to disentangle)

- Succinct (adj.): short and to the point
  Other forms: succinctly, succinctness
  Synonyms: terse, concise, sententious, laconic, brevity, pithy, elliptical
  Antonyms: windy, wordy, verbose, lengthy

VOCABULARY

- Succour (n.): assistance or relief
  Other forms: succor the verb
  Synonyms: solace, support, relief, aid, harbor, mollify, alleviate, ameliorate, mitigate, appeasement, assuage, placate, consolation
  Antonyms: hurt, harm, impair

- Superfluous (adj.): more than necessary
  Other forms: superfluously, superfluity
  Synonyms: extraneous, surfeit, surplus, redundant, gratuitous
  Antonyms: indispensable, necessary, vital, essential

- Surreptitious (adj.): secret
  Other forms: surreptitiously
  Synonyms: covert, stealthy, sneaky, clandestine, furtive
  Antonyms: open, honest, direct, disclose (reveal), divulge

- Sustain (v.): to support or nurture
  Other forms: sustainable, sustaining, sustenance
  Synonyms: keep going, maintain, foster (propogate), bolster, reinforce, buttress (structural support)
  Antonyms: abandon, stop, quit, give in

T

- Tactile (adj.): relating to the sense of touch
  Other forms: tactility
  Synonyms: tangible
  Antonyms: intangible, abstract

- Tangential (adj.): slightly connected or touching lightly
  Other forms: tangent
  Synonyms: aside, digression, irrelevant, deviate
  Antonyms: relevant, pertinent, germane

- Tantamount (adj.): equal or comparable
  Synonyms: equivalent, analogous, parity (balance)
  Antonyms: unequal, incomparable, incongruous (out of place)

- Temperate (adj.): moderate or at normal levels
  Other forms: temperance, temper, tempered
  Synonyms: balance, restraint, pleasant, mild, healthy
  Antonyms: abnormal, imbalance, extreme, severe, intense

- Temperamental (adj.): unpredictable in behavior
  Synonyms: volatile, moody, erratic
  Antonyms: reliable, dependable, even-tempered

- Tenacious (adj.): determined to hold on
  Other forms: tenacity, tenaciously
  Synonyms: strong, persistent, robust, resilience, resolve, resolute, resolution, fortitude
  Antonyms: weak, yielding, undetermined, resign, give up, acquiesce, hesitant, flaccid (limp/lacking firmness)

VOCABULARY

- Tentative (adj.): not fully developed or definitely planned
  Other forms: tentatively, tentativeness
  Synonyms: extemporaneous, uncertain, hesitant, desultory
  Antonyms: planned, prepared, definite, sure

- Tenuous (adj.): thin and flimsy
  Other forms: tenuousness, tenuously
  Synonyms: weak, fragile
  Antonyms: robust, sound, strong

- Terrestrial (adj.): of Earth or land
  Other forms: territory, terrain

- Thrifty (adj.): careful about managing money
  Other forms: thriftiness, thriftily
  Synonyms: frugal, economical, sparing, parsimony (extreme stinginess)
  Antonyms: squander, wasteful, prodigal, spendthrift, wastrel

- Timid (adj.): afraid and shy
  Other forms: timorously, timorousness, timorous
  Synonyms: trepidation, fear, anxiety, apprehension, demure (modestly shy)
  Antonyms: composure, equanimity, intrepid (fearless)

- Toady (n.): someone who flatters is superior in hopes of gaining a favor
  Other forms: toadyism
  Synonyms: sycophant, servile, obsequious

- Tirade (n.): a long bitter speech
  Synonyms: diatribe, harangue

- Transgression (v.): a violation
  Other forms: transgress
  Synonyms: wrongdoing, disobedience, offense
  Antonyms: favor, good deed

- Translucent (adj.): allowing light to pass through
  Other forms: translucent, translucently
  Synonyms: clear, transparent
  Antonyms: opaque, dense, thick

- Treacherous (adj.): untrustworthy or disloyal; dangerous or unreliable
  Other forms: treachery
  Synonyms: unsafe, dangerous, hazardous, perilous, reprehensible, heinous, wicked, devious (tricky), perfidy
  Antonyms: harmless, safe, gentle, mild, benign, benevolent

- Trite (adj.): common and overused
  Other forms: triteness, tritely
  Synonyms: cliche, stale, boring, hackneyed, vapid, dull, lackluster, tedium, insipid, banal, plain, austere, mundane, platitude (dull statement), mediocre, prosaic
  Antonyms: new, innovative, brilliant, captivating, interesting

- Turbulent (adj.): violent
  Other forms: turbulence
  Synonyms: chaotic, tumultuous, confused, cacophony, virulent, fractious, dissonance (disagreement), discord (disagreement)
  Antonyms: harmony, orderly, calm, phlegmatic, equanimity, tranquility, consonance

VOCABULARY

U

- Ubiquitous (adj.): existing everywhere at the same time
  Other forms: ubiquity, ubiquitousness, ubiquitously
  Synonyms: common, usual, routine
  Antonyms: unfamiliar, uncommon, unique, isolated, cloister

- Unanimous (adj.): in total agreement
  Other forms: unanimously, unanimity
  Synonyms: agreeable, congenial, amicable, consensus, unison, conciliatory
  Antonyms: disagreement, conflict, dissensus,

- Undermine (v.): to weaken by wearing away the foundation usually through secrets or false rumors
  Synonyms: sabotage, slander, vilify, defame, malign
  Antonyms: praise, revere, venerate

- Undulate (v.): to move in a wavy manner
  Other forms: undulation, undulated
  Synonyms: serpentine, coiled, twisted, winding, meander (walk aimlessly), indirect, circuitous
  Antonyms: straight, linear, direct

- Unerring (adj.): without making a mistake
  Other forms: unerringly
  Synonyms: faultless, infallible, impeccable
  Antonyms: fallible, err, error, incorrigible

- Unheralded (adj.): little known and unexpected
  Synonyms: unpredicted, unannounced,
  Antonyms: foretold, expected, forecasted, foresight, portend, divination

- Uniform (adj.): consistent throughout
  Other forms: uniformity, uniformly
  Synonyms: homogeneous, standardized, unchanging
  Antonyms: heterogeneous, different, dissimilar, diverse

- Unkempt (adj.): messy and sloppy
  Synonyms: unclean, sully, stain, soil, defile
  Antonyms: clean, tidy

- Usurper (n.): someone who takes possession without the right to do so
  Other forms: usurp, usurpation
  Synonyms: seize, take over, expropriate, embezzle
  Antonyms: give up, resign, surrender, capitulate

- Utopian (adj.): perfect example of
  Other forms: utopia
  Synonyms: perfect, ideal
  Antonyms: problematic, flawed, dystopia

V

- Vacillate (adj.): unable to decide or to move back and forth between choices
  Other forms: vacillation
  Synonyms: oscillate, fluctuate, hesitate, ambivalent, waver, indecision, capricious, unpredictable, erratic, mercurial
  Antonyms: stabilize, determined, stubborn, invariable

VOCABULARY

- Vacuous (adj.): empty, stupid, or purposeless
  Other forms: vacuity, vacuously, vacuousness, trivial,
  Synonyms: blank, void
  Antonyms: saturated, full, practical or utilitarian

- Vagrant (n.): someone who is poor
  Other forms: vagrantly, vagrancy, vagrant
  Synonyms: indigent, homelessness, destitute, poverty, penury
  Antonyms: rich, sumptuous, opulent, affluent, wealthy, lavish, munificent (generously rich)

- Variegated (adj.): spotted with different assortments
  Other forms: variegation, variegate
  Synonyms: varied, diverse, multiplicity
  Antonyms: singular, uniform, homogeneous

- Veracity (n.): the truth
  Other forms: veracious, verify
  Synonyms: factual, sooth
  Antonyms: false, inaccurate, mendacity

- Verbose (adj.): very talkative
  Other forms: verboseness, verbosity
  Synonyms: loquacious, chatty, garrulous, wordy, circumlocution
  Antonyms: taciturn, reserved, laconic, reticent, shy, diffident, hesitant

- Verdant (adj.): associated with the color green or with plants
  Other form: verdancy
  Synonym: florid(flowery); florid can sometimes mean reddish

- Versatile (adj.): having many talents or uses
  Other form: versatility
  Synonyms: adaptable, resourceful, multi-talented, virtuoso
  Antonyms: limited, narrow, restricted

- Vestige (n.): a trace of something left behind
  Other form: vestigial
  Synonyms: remainder, remnant, linger

- Vex (v.): to trouble or annoy
  Other forms: vexation, vexing
  Synonyms: bothersome, pester, annoying, exasperate, frustrate, irritate, exasperate, discomfit
  Antonyms: please, satisfy, calm

- Vicarious (adj.): experience through someone else's actions by the way of the imagination
  Other forms: vicariously, vicariousness
  Antonym: empirical (experience through personal observation)

- Vindicate (v.): to confirm with evidence or defend
  Other forms: vindication, vindicating
  Synonyms: substantiate, corroborate, warranted
  Antonyms: disprove, untenable

- Virtuoso (n.): someone was very skilled
  Other form: virtuosity
  Synonyms: skilled, expert, master, whiz, ace, dexterity, adroit, expertise, proficient, adept,
  Antonyms: amateur, beginner, hobbyist, inept (not skilled)

VOCABULARY

- Viscosity (n.): the ability to resist flow or a quality stickiness
  Other form: viscous
  Synonyms: sick, gluey
  Antonyms: thin, runny, mellifluous (sweetly flowing)

- Voluble (adj.): comfortable with speech
  Other forms: volubility, volubly
  Synonyms: fluent, talkative, loquacious, eloquent, articulate
  Antonyms: inarticulate, unvocal

W

- Whimsical (adj.): based on sudden carefree ideas that are usually playful
  Other form: whim
  Synonyms: fanciful, quickly, eccentric, unique, frivolity
  Antonyms: normal, regular, ordinary

X

- Xenophobia (adj.): the fear of something that is foreign for the fear of someone foreign
  Other forms: xenophobe, xenophobic

Y

- Yield (v.): to produce, to give in, or to give up
  Synonyms: gain, profit, income, surrender, capitulate, submit, relinquish, deference (yield out of respect)
  Antonyms: resistance

- Yoke (v.): to link or to tie together
  Other forms: yoke (n.)
  Synonyms: marriage, join, clamp, connect
  Antonyms: separate, unyoke, disconnect

Z

- Zealot (n.): a person who has extreme passion and enthusiasm for an activity or belief
  Other forms: zeal, zealotry, zealousness, zealous, zealously
  Synonyms: fanatic, excited, enthusiasm, passionate, fervent, ardor
  Antonyms: lethargic, listless, bored, apathy, carelessness, uninterested

- Zenith (n.): the highest point
  Other forms: zenithal
  Synonyms: apex, top, summit
  Antonyms: bottom, ground

THANK YOU FOR YOUR PURCHASE OF THIS BOOK. YOU ARE ENTITLED TO A

FREE CONSULTATION + 50% DISCOUNT

ON YOUR FIRST HOUR OF IN-PERSON PRIVATE TUTORING.

WE ALSO OFFER TUTORING IN

TESTING	MATHEMATICS	READING	SCIENCE
SHSAT	ALGEBRA 1 & 2	ENGLISH	EARTH SCIENCE
SAT	TRIGONOMETRY	TOEFL	CHEMISTRY
ACT	PRE-CALCULUS	IELTS	BIOLOGY
SSAT	AP CALCULUS		PHYSICS
LSAT	STATISTICS		
MCAT	GEOMETRY		

CONTACT US
info@einstein-academy.com
(347) 927 2711

ARGO BROTHERS

Made in the USA
Lexington, KY
07 May 2016